which have
surgeons.
Hill Sports Book of the Year, with *Dark Trade* and *In Black & White*. He is a three-time Interviewer of the Year winner and has also won Sports Feature Writer of the Year for his work in the *Guardian*.

Praise for *A Man's World*:

'One of the most absorbing books of recent years, a riveting read' *Observer*

A Man's World is more than a boxing book, more than a sports book. t is a story of very human endeavour, about death and not a little reconciliation in the end. Wonderful' *Guardian*

'An astonishing story, simply told through a mix of sensitive interviews and deep reading' *Financial Times*

'Delving deep into the worlds of sexuality and violence in 1960s America, McRae produces a triumph' *Sunday Times*

'A deeply moving story ... and always absolutely gripping' *Sport*

'A colossal, emotional tale – someone make it into a film already' *Shortlist*

Also by Donald McRae from Simon & Schuster:

Dark Trade: Lost in Boxing

Winter Colours: The Changing Seasons of Rugby

In Black & White: The Untold Story of Joe Louis & Jesse Owens

Every Second Counts: The Extraordinary Race
to Transplant the First Human Heart

The Old Devil: Clarence Darrow – The World's
Greatest Trial Lawyer

Under Our Skin: A White Family's Journey through
South Africa's Darkest Years

A MAN'S WORLD

THE DOUBLE LIFE OF
EMILE GRIFFITH

Donald McRae

SIMON &
SCHUSTER

London · New York · Sydney · Toronto · New Delhi

A CBS COMPANY

First published in Great Britain by Simon & Schuster UK Ltd, 2015
This paperback edition published by Simon & Schuster UK Ltd, 2016
A CBS COMPANY

1 3 5 7 9 10 8 6 4 2

Simon & Schuster UK Ltd
1st Floor
222 Gray's Inn Road
London WC1X 8HB

www.simonandschuster.co.uk

Simon & Schuster Australia Sydney
Simon & Schuster India New Delhi

The author and publishers have made all reasonable efforts
to contact copyright-holders for permission, and apologise for
any omissions or errors in the form of credits given.
Corrections may be made to future printings.

A CIP catalogue record for this book
is available from the British Library.

ISBN: 978-1-4711-3236-0
Ebook ISBN: 978-1-4711-3237-7

Typeset in the UK by M Rules
Printed and bound by CPI Group (UK) Ltd, Croydon, CR0 4YY

Simon & Schuster UK Ltd are committed to sourcing paper
that is made from wood grown in sustainable forests and support the Forest
Stewardship Council, the leading international forest certification organisation.
Our books displaying the FSC logo are printed on FSC certified paper.

For Alison

920GR1
ANF

B53	107 445 4		
	11/18		
GiFT	£9.99		

CONTENTS

Talking to Ghosts

Nassau Extended Care Facility, Hempstead, Long Island,
8 December 2012

Emile Griffith's hands were so small it was hard to believe they had once killed a man. They were curled into tiny black fists, resting against the white sheets, but they did not look like the weapons that had helped him become a five-time world champion during an era when boxing still carried profound meaning. It was easier to believe that these were the delicate, almost girlish hands with which he had held different men. Emile, showing as much courage as he did inside the ring, had remained true to his real self at a time when homosexuality was derided as a disease, condemned as a sin and classified as a crime.

Fifty years since his life had changed forever at Madison Square Garden, on the night he and Benny Paret fought for the third and final time on 24 March 1962, Emile gazed unseeingly into the distance on a snowy winter afternoon in Hempstead. The metal frame of his bed had been raised so that, even though the great old fighter remained on his back, he was propped up in a hopeful attempt to help him engage with a world that moved ahead without him. Emile's last lover and closest friend, Luis Rodrigo, who also called himself the dying man's adopted son, embraced the former champion.

'Hey, Junior,' he said, 'look who's come to see you.'

Luis glanced encouragingly at me. He then turned back to Emile, his round face creased with love. 'C'mon, champ,' he said to the nursing home patient he visited every day, in between working Monday to Friday in the post room of a Manhattan film production company and as a Domino's Pizza delivery man in Hempstead at night. 'Give us a smile.'

Emile did not smile, blink or emit any other sign of life as he stared at me. It was hard to reconcile that empty shell with the brave and vibrant man who had straddled opposing worlds of brutality and frivolity, fame and secrecy.

No other boxer had fought as many as the 337 world championship rounds that Emile had racked up in a career spanning nineteen years – from 1958 to 1977. He had fought fifty-one more world title rounds than Sugar Ray Robinson, and sixty-nine more than Muhammad Ali. Emile had won his first world title in 1961, defeating Paret in the opening bout of their savage trilogy, when there were only eight divisions and one champion of each weight category. To most respected fight historians, he was one of the finest welterweights in history.

Yet his place in the pantheon was darkened by the death of Paret, the Cuban fighter who had taunted him as a '*maricón*' (a faggot) at the weigh-in before their deadly battle in the Garden. The fight had happened before my first birthday but the ghosts of our past swarmed around us.

Luis understood. Four hours earlier, in his and Emile's cramped apartment down the road in Hempstead, surrounded by old photographs, world championship belts and their little dog, Princess, I had explained the black fighter's impact on my life as a white South African. 'Take Emile's hand,' Luis suggested on that hushed Saturday afternoon, 'and tell him what you told me.'

It felt strange at first, my hand curled around Emile's, my words sounding stilted in our one-way conversation. Luis leaned down to tilt the champ's head on his pillow, so that his eyes once more locked onto me. It became more natural to talk about the days when I was fourteen and, in August 1975, Emile visited South Africa. He stood up to apartheid and helped change the way I thought about black people. Emile stripped bare the power of boxing, even near his ravaged end as a fighter, and I was never quite the same again. I learned to think more clearly for myself after Emile left Johannesburg.

I wanted to write about Emile as an extraordinary fighter and as an ordinary man, an aspiring hat designer turned world champion boxer. I wanted to explore his relationship with the two white men, Howie Albert and Gil Clancy, who had discovered him as a boxer and remained with him long after the last of his 112 bouts. I wanted to write about him and Luis, and his years of friendship with Calvin Thomas and Freddie Wright, a go-go boy at Stonewall Inn in June 1969 when gay America caught fire amid the riots. Those three black musketeers had danced together in the gritty chain of bars and clubs around Times Square where Emile felt most at home, surrounded by the gay men and drag queens who revered him.

Panama Al Brown, the former world bantamweight champion, had supposedly engaged in a homosexual affair in the 1930s with Jean Cocteau, the French writer and experimental film-maker; and there had been whispers about other boxers. Emile had visited gay establishments all his adult life – yet he still found it impossible to come out with a public statement about his sexual preference. Such complexity always shadowed him.

I told Emile about Orlando Cruz, who had just become boxing's first openly gay fighter. He would once have been impressed that a gay Puerto Rican, who had boxed professionally for twelve years, had found the resolve to declare his sexuality publicly.

Six weeks earlier, at home in San Juan in October 2012, in his first newspaper interview as a gay boxer, Orlando Cruz told me how he had 'decided to be free'. We had spoken about Emile, and the tragedy he shared with Benny Paret. Orlando had looked as if he was close to crying when I read to him a quote from Emile: 'I kill a man and most people forgive me. However, I love a man and many say this makes me an evil person.'

A strange expression flitted across Orlando's face. 'It shows the hypocrisy of the world,' he said in Spanish. 'But, fifty years ago, Emile was not living in the moment we are now. He was not as lucky as me.'

Luis told Emile that, on my next visit to Long Island, Orlando Cruz would join us. Orlando would also fight for a world title in 2013, and he promised to dedicate that history-making night to Emile. I recalled Orlando's words: 'I have been living with this thorn inside me. I wanted to take it out of me so I could have peace within myself.'

The Puerto Rican had glanced down as if in search of an invisible wound. 'You can't see it,' he said of his hurt at the age of thirty-one, 'but it was here. Now it's different. They can call me *maricón* or faggot and I don't care. Let them say it because they can't hurt me now.'

Benny Paret had sneered '*maricón*' with such wounding intent that he had paid for that insult with his life. Emile had struggled to forgive himself for the next half-century, and had suffered from nightmarish visions of Benny, but I was moved by the way in which he had lived both in and outside the ring. I knew how one man, in particular, had helped him.

Willie Toweel had also been hounded as a 'killer' by an unforgiving press and public. His name echoed through my own past; and I decided to write this book when I read the letter Willie had written to Emile in 1962. They had fought at Madison Square Garden, in October 1960, and the white South African of Lebanese descent and the black American from the Caribbean had forged a bond as former opponents. Willie helped Emile in the bleakest days of his life.

I was not gay. I had never been a boxer or killed anyone. But the entwined fate of Emile Griffith and Willie Toweel, both suffering from severe dementia pugilistica, transfixed me. Their darkest memories had been beaten out of them and they had slipped away, almost in mute relief. But they had told us enough in the past. They had been through life and death and, approaching the end, they remained deeply human.

Emile's skin looked very black against the white bed linen and his mustard-yellow T-shirt. I still held his small hand. Luis leaned over and stroked Emile's blank face.

'Hey, champ,' he said. 'Don read Willie's letter. You remember the letter, Junior?'

Luis paused. 'Did you see that?' he asked as he looked up in surprise. 'Did you see Emile smile? It's gone now but I saw it. He heard us. He heard us ...'

CHAPTER ONE

Facing a Killer

Emile Griffith, at the blissful age of twenty-two, was happy and beautiful. He had the body of a fighting machine, with fast and lethal fists, but his fluting voice and sashaying walk belonged to a gentler man. Emile carried that tangled contradiction with the same panache he wore his tight white trousers and red silk shirt to a meeting with New York's fight press. He was about to step back into the ring at Madison Square Garden on 22 October 1960.

Willie Toweel, his opponent, was different. He came from South Africa and, in his grey flannel suit, he seemed as conservative as Emile was flamboyant. They met for the first time at the Round Table, a restaurant on East 53rd Street, where mobsters like 'Fat Tony' Salerno and 'Trigger Mike' Coppola devoured plates of pasta and steaks so thick and juicy they needed piles of freshly baked bread to mop up the oozing pools of blood. Fat Tony had put up most of the cash to finance the previous year's world heavyweight title fight between Ingemar Johansson and Floyd Patterson.

There were no mobsters to be seen when Griffith and Toweel were surrounded by a crew of cigar-chomping and trilby-wearing sportswriters at the Round Table. Boxing was attempting to shake off the gangster-led corruption of the 1950s – while Fat Tony and Trigger Mike were far too busy to waste an afternoon with some fast-talking scribblers and soft-spoken fighters.

Toweel was offered a contrasting reception to his American debut at the Garden. In November 1959 he had been dismissed by the New York press as 'a limey' and 'a palooka' before his bout against Len Matthews, a grim-faced black fighter from Philadelphia. The fact that Toweel had fought extensively in London was at the root of the ridicule. It was thought that, as an often British-based boxer, he would surrender quickly to a big-hitting 'Negro'.

Matthews knocked Toweel down with a left hook early in round eight and, after the South African rose to his feet, bombarded him with heavy combinations. Toweel refused to succumb. He returned to the slick counter-punching that had built up an early lead over Matthews. But in the tenth and last round Matthews unleashed another brutal attack.

In front of a rapturous crowd, swept away by Toweel's sweet punching and the ferocious contest, they went to the judges' score-cards. Unusually, the overseas fighter won the split decision. The crowd chanted Toweel's name and the *Long Island Daily Press* led the plaudits: 'Willie wowed 'em. There hasn't been a boxer as good as this South African smoothie since Willie Pep was dazzling the fans and his opponents. Toweel moved like Sugar Ray Robinson in his prime.'

Willie looked down at the Round Table. Tragedy had marked him and, before a fight, darkness shrouded his heart.

His brother, Alan, was also his trainer. Alan liked to do all Willie's talking when the press swarmed around him. 'I'll answer that,' Alan said whenever a question was put to Willie. The trainer used the word 'we' as if he would also be throwing punches in the ring.

Willie was relieved he had Alan at his side as the reporters tried to press-gang him into responding to questions about his past. They had started cleverly, asking Emile how he felt about facing 'a killer' in the ring.

'I don't worry about nothing like that,' Emile said innocently. 'Willie and me will put on a great show. Don't forget – it's Date Night at the Garden.'

Willie smiled at Emile's quip. Teddy Brenner, the urbane but tough matchmaker, had explained that they would headline the second Madison Square Garden 'Date Night' in a new programme of Saturday fights where women were allowed into the arena free of charge if accompanied by a male escort.

'Do you like to dance, Willie?' Emile asked, his voice carrying a lilting echo of the Caribbean, and the Virgin Islands where he had spent the first twelve years of his life.

'I'll answer that,' Alan Toweel said snappily. 'Willie's a brilliant dancer. But, Emile, you won't be in the mood for dancing at the end of this date.'

Emile laughed. No one in boxing danced better than him – especially when he was away from prying eyes and with his closest friends around Times Square. Emile said he was sure Willie would be a far better dancer than his talkative brother.

Before Alan could answer, Willie jumped in with a cheerful confirmation. 'I am. I love to dance . . .'

'Me too, champ,' Emile said.

'This is too friendly for my taste,' Brenner growled. 'These boys are coming to the Garden to fight.'

The reporters needed little encouragement to return to murkier terrain. They asked Willie how it felt to have killed a man – for he had fought Hubert Essakow at the Johannesburg City Hall and beaten him into a coma and then death in March 1956.

'We don't want to talk about the Essakow fight,' Alan protested. 'That was four years ago . . .'

It was too late for Willie. He was back in the sombre place he had never really left. 'I think of Hubert every day,' he murmured. 'I said mass for him again this morning. I will do the same tomorrow.'

Alan moved the reporters onto a different subject but Willie was stuck. He couldn't get Essakow out of his head. His eyes glazed as

Alan spoke at length about the way victory over Len Matthews had proved they could mix it with the best American fighters.

'Hey, champ,' Emile said quietly as he glanced at his disconsolate opponent. 'We're nearly done.'

Emile Griffith left the Round Table at three that afternoon in a tight-knit group of four. He was led by his managers, Howie Albert, a 39-year-old, red-haired, bespectacled Jewish New Yorker in the hat-making business, and Gil Clancy, who was a year younger and an Irish Catholic schoolteacher turned boxing trainer from Rockaway Beach in Queens. The days when gangsters like Frankie Carbo would seize control of boxers like Emile had gone. Carbo was banged up in Alcatraz and humane men like Gil and Howie could act more compassionately in boxing. They did not value a fighter just on his money-making potential. Emile was thankful. He felt cared for by his two white father-figures.

The boxer and his friend Calvin Thomas were young and black. Emile called Calvin 'my running buddy', but they did not pound the road together during training. Calvin and Emile, instead, secretly cruised around Times Square, along 42nd Street and outside the Port Authority Bus Terminal. They knew that some men yelled 'Faggot!' or 'Fucking fairy!' at anyone wandering into the dingy joints they loved to visit. And so they had to be fanatically careful. Sometimes their secret was rumbled and they were spotted; but few men would ever insult Emile because his broad shoulders carried a rippling power. Calvin, being short and squat with a portly belly, seemed an easier target. He was still tougher than Emile. It went against his jovial character, because he was full of laughter, but Calvin carried a lead pipe in his bag. Emile had once seen him reach for the pipe when a stray fairy-basher tried to taunt him.

'You wanna fight?' Calvin snarled at the guy, who backed down fast.

Calvin, Emile's best friend and protector, loved boxing. He knew the game intimately and hung out at the city's best boxing gyms, especially Gleason's, where Benny 'Kid' Paret trained. No one at Gleason's ever said a word to Calvin about his sexual preference and he was allowed sometimes to man the front door and collect the monthly dues. But, most of the time, Calvin just ran with Emile. They were set for one hell of a ride – as long they could keep their love lives hidden.

It was imperative to bury the truth because sport and homosexuality could not mix. A gay boxer was an unimaginable phrase. In 1960 the subject was not only taboo – it was impossible to even believe that any sporting hero, a man's man, could be a homosexual. Emile didn't like thinking about it much. He was just happy belonging to two contrasting groups of men, whether he was fighting them or loving them.

He also had a girlfriend. Esther Taylor was a sweet and pretty girl from his old neighbourhood in Harlem. She and Emile had met in church five years earlier, when he was seventeen and she was fifteen. Esther was smitten with Emile and he cared for her. Their families knew each other and, almost naturally, they had started going out together. Emile was a wondrous dancer, and fun to be around, but in his more serious moments he realised that Esther harboured deeper hopes for their relationship.

Yet she had no idea how much he needed men, and wanted to be with them. Emile reckoned it was better that way. Esther only knew that her boyfriend was, as she always said, 'a real busy person'. She understood that part of his life. He was on his way to becoming famous and so Esther, who could see how hard he trained, gave Emile the space he craved. She believed that, eventually, they would be together forever.

For Emile, the occasional presence of Esther in his life served a dual purpose. He liked being around her, and enjoyed her company. Yet, in a more complicated way, Esther provided him with a cover so that, more furtively, he could be his real self. She was a lovely buffer against all the doubts that whirred in an unspoken hum around him.

People in the fight business maintained a public silence around

Emile and Calvin's sexuality. Fighters, trainers and reporters voiced private suspicions, but nothing was said out loud in public. It was almost as if they could not bear the burden of the truth. And, anyway, didn't he have a girlfriend – an apparently foxy young sweetheart from Harlem?

Gil Clancy liked it that way. He was an essentially conservative and religious man, a husband and a father of six. The only nancy he wanted to think about was his beloved wife, whom he had met at a basketball dance in Rockaway Beach. They were ribbed mercilessly for the rhyming simplicity of her married name: Nancy Clancy. Gil could put up with wisecracking. But he ignored the gossipy rumours curling around Emile like wisps of smoke. He disliked words like 'nancy' and 'fairy' – and hated 'queer' and 'faggot'.

Clancy thought of Emile as a potential world champion fighter and a sensitive young man, who was like another son to him. He had no quibble with Calvin either. The roly-poly kid had boxing in his blood. Gil didn't care what he or Emile did in their spare time. As long as it didn't get in the way of Emile's training and fighting, Gil avoided details of a world he had no wish to understand.

Howie Albert was different. He worked in the fashion trade, having taken over his father's hat factory, and always felt able to ask Emile about his latest friend, usually a slinky young Hispanic boy who turned up to watch sparring. Howie knew about the police raiding the bars Emile and Calvin frequented because it was illegal for two men to dance together. He shook his head at the hypocrisy of society but, apart from the odd quiet warning that they should be careful, he did not question his fighter's sexuality.

The kid's nominal girlfriend, the demure and quiet Esther whom Howie had met a few times, helped them present a straight story to the outside world. Howie was smart and sophisticated enough to realise the essential nature of Emile. It was his role as manager to try to help his gifted but complex fighter negotiate a way between two such different and difficult worlds. Emile had also changed Howie's life by making him famous at ringside. Their first meeting four years earlier had already entered boxing folklore.

On a sweltering afternoon in New York's garment district, on West 37th Street in the summer of 1956, the factory at Howard Albert Millinery had turned into a hotbox. Even the walls of the plant had begun to glow with condensation as, in the stockroom, eighteen-year-old Emile Griffith asked his cousin, Edigo Lambert, if he could peel off his shirt. It felt like he would expire from the heat if he did not strip off.

Edigo, who had helped Emile get his $40-a-week job almost a year earlier, nodded. He couldn't see any harm in the kid, who worked so hard, becoming comfortable in the stifling conditions. But the female hatmakers and packers looked as if they could do with a few fans to cool off once they saw Emile's shirtless torso as he walked in and out of the stockroom. His shimmering skin stretched across a 26-inch waist, which fanned out to the extraordinary sight of a muscled 44-inch chest. When he reached up for another box, so that he could pack a pretty bonnet fresh from the Howard Albert production line of fashionable hats, there was a gasp as they stared at his massive shoulders. Emile's sinewy muscles flexed beneath his taut skin, but he did not recognise the reaction of the flushed women around him.

He only paused in his work when the boss came over, wearing a double-breasted suit and a look of wonder on his face. Mr Albert had never noticed Emile before, but he had different thoughts in mind from those of his female employees as he began to quiz the young Adonis. Howie Albert, a mediocre former amateur boxer without a meaningful bout to his name, loved old-time fighters like Benny Leonard and Gene Tunney, as well as a modern master in Ray Robinson. He was convinced Emile's magnificent physique must have been honed in a gym. Howie asked if he had done any boxing.

Sure, Emile said, smiling at the question. He had been boxing for almost a year. 'Where?' Howie asked, expecting to hear the names of the city's most venerable gyms – Stillman's or Gleason's.

Emile spread his arms wide and, with a matching grin, said, 'Right here, boss.'

He explained that Catherine and Mabel on the factory floor brought the new hats to him so that he could fit them into a box, which he would then store on the right shelf. Edigo would have labelled them correctly, so Emile made it easy for the delivery guy to find the next box that needed to be whisked away. Emile loved boxing-up more than anything else because it allowed him to hold the most beautiful and stylish hats for a while. He secretly wished that he might get a chance to design ladies' hats himself one day. Emile did not want to be a storeroom boy forever.

Howie took off his steamed-up glasses and wiped them clean. He still shook his head in foggy disbelief. How could the kid be so naive? Howie shoved his specs back on, rubbed his red hair and held up his fists in a fighting pose to demonstrate a more manly kind of boxing.

'Oh,' Emile said, in disappointment. '*That* boxing . . .'

Howie convinced him to give it a try. At first they did a few casual workouts in the stockroom, but it soon became plain that the kid shadow-boxed with a graceful symmetry while real force lurked inside his imposing body. Howie, drunk on a wild idea, decided to enter Emile into the 1957 Golden Gloves – the prestigious amateur boxing tournament held at Madison Square Garden and sponsored by the *New York Daily News*. He did not reveal his plan to Emile, who was alarmed when summoned one day, by letter, to the *Daily News* office for a medical examination.

'Mommy,' Emile said with a quivering voice to his mother, Emelda, 'I think I'm being drafted.'

When he turned up for his physical he was startled to discover that the medical was for a boxing tournament. He had never heard of the Golden Gloves and, while boxing was better than the army, Emile felt disgruntled. His suspicions that Howie was behind everything were confirmed the next day when, returning to the storeroom, he was met by his boss, who presented him with a new pair of boxing trunks.

Emile responded angrily. He didn't want to be a fighter. Instead, he was more interested in flowery bonnets and elegant pillbox hats.

Howie considered him calmly before explaining that all the factory girls had clubbed together to buy his satiny white trunks. Maybe, given time, the girls would understand Emile was too frightened to fight in the Golden Gloves.

Emile glowered a little longer. Howie seemed a good boss most of the time – but he was sneaky and tough. What could Emile do but hold the trunks up against his waist to check their fit before finally saying, okay, he would give it a try, for the sake of the girls.

Howie had already picked out Gil Clancy as the best possible tutor in the few months they had left before the Golden Gloves. Clancy worked at the 28th Street Parks Department gym; but he was dubious about the scheme. He didn't like the answer when he asked Emile why he wanted to be a boxer.

It did not sound like burning ambition when Emile said his boss wanted him to box. The trainer scrunched up his face. He did not have time to waste on anyone who didn't want to fight.

Clancy was a teacher, who had obtained his BA and then his MA at NYU. He could not believe he agreed to take on Howie Albert's curious project to turn a reluctant novice into a Golden Gloves fighter in a matter of months. But there was something about the hatmaker and his young factory worker that snared his attention. Clancy soon liked them both. It also helped that, every afternoon just after five, Emile was waiting for him, dressed in boxing gear and ready for work.

After a couple of weeks even Clancy began to imagine that something special might unfold. At first, Emile had been beaten up in sparring by a pro called Roger Harvey. But he was determined and, listening closely to Clancy, he was soon battling Harvey on an equal footing. The improvement was startling in an amateur who had never boxed before. Clancy took him to Madison Square Garden for the Golden Gloves Novice Finals on the freezing Monday night of 18 February 1957. Calvin and their friend Bobby Miles, whose cousin was Ezzard Charles, the former world heavyweight champion, watched Emile reach the final – where he lost narrowly on points to Charles Wormley.

A year later, Calvin and Bobby whooped as Emile became the national Golden Gloves welterweight champion. He then made his professional debut on 2 June 1958, winning a four-round fight against Joe Parham. Emile was on his way, with his two white mentors guiding him through every twist and turn.

Two years, four months and three weeks down the line, Emile had only a few days left before he ducked back into the ring at the Garden. Clancy expected Toweel to be fiercely determined.

As the gang of four left the Round Table, with Howie heading back to the hat factory and Calvin going home to New Jersey for a few days, the trainer looked at his fighter. They would visit the gym for one last session. Nothing could be left to chance against a man whose punches had proved deadly in the past.

Willie Toweel wanted a voice. He wanted to be heard. At home in little old Benoni, where he had grown up on the stark East Rand, twenty miles outside Johannesburg, Willie kicked up a racket. As the fifth kid in a family of eight – with six boys outnumbering the two girls – he was boisterous and funny, generous and incorrigible. But Willie wanted to make a difference beyond his family. He was tired of the insults.

The Toweels were always fighting. They had no choice when they were young because, almost every day, they were called 'white Kaffirs' and 'dirty Syrians'. It riled Willie because they were just as South African as the Afrikaners and English-speakers who got stuck into them. They weren't from Syria, either, for they were of proud Lebanese descent.

They were ridiculed for being poor and sallow-skinned, but Willie just wanted to be treated as an ordinary person. He'd had enough pain as a small boy. When he was just six, in 1940, Willie had lost his mother. He witnessed the harrowing sight of his dad, Papa Mike, sobbing over her coffin as it was lowered into the red earth. Papa Mike changed that day. He gave up drinking and smoking and fighting in hotel bars. Instead, he stayed home and looked after his children, with the help of his sister-in-law, Mary, whom he married three years later, on 6 April 1943, Willie's ninth birthday.

They had, by then, discovered boxing. Papa Mike built a gym made out of corrugated iron at the bottom of the garden. The tin shanty was cold and unforgiving on winter mornings, and a steaming hellhole on summer afternoons. They called it the 'Sock Exchange', as fighters from all over the Transvaal were drawn to Benoni to train with the fighting Toweels.

In the backyard at 12 Balfour Street they broke the laws of apartheid by allowing a few hard-hitting natives to join them for illicit sparring. Native boys and girls, meaning black men and women, were not supposed to enter any white neighbourhood unless they were domestic servants or gardeners. The idea that they should be encouraged to punch white men in the face would have shocked almost everyone in South Africa. But the Toweels would do anything to make it in boxing.

Vic Toweel, Willie's second-eldest brother, was not only the best fighter in the family – he became the greatest boxer in South African history and the first to win a world title when, in May 1950, in only his fourteenth professional bout, he defeated Manuel Ortiz in Johannesburg. Ortiz had fought 118 times but he could not hold off Vic, who became world bantamweight champion. Vic was nicknamed 'Dynamite', the 'Benoni Buzzsaw' and the 'White Henry Armstrong' because he fought with relentless ferocity.

In a secret only really known to his family, Vic loathed boxing. He hated the torturous battle he endured every fight to make weight, as well as the violence of the ring. Vic would have been happier leading an ordinary life; but his extraordinary boxing talent was a curse.

The scales, in the end, got him. Before he lost his world title, after two-and-a-half years, Vic furtively arranged for blood to be drained from his starving body to help him make the bantamweight limit of 118 pounds. He was so depleted that he could not stop the Australian Jimmy Carruthers from overwhelming him in the first round. Vic was knocked out again by Carruthers in their Johannesburg rematch and it was a relief when, after three more fights, he retired in November 1953.

Willie was determined to regain the world bantamweight title for the family. He got his chance in September 1955 when, trained by Alan and managed from a wheelchair by his polio-ridden brother Maurice, Willie fought Robert Cohen in Johannesburg. Cohen was regarded as the best French fighter since Marcel Cerdan and he dropped Willie twice in the opening round. Willie survived and boxed beautifully over the next fourteen rounds. He seemed to have won the title – only for a draw to be ruled.

Tears ran down his face at dinner late that night. 'If only they were fair,' Willie cried.

Three months later, he suffered his first defeat when forced to retire against Jannie van Rensburg in a Commonwealth lightweight title fight. It was two weight divisions up from bantamweight because, like Vic, Willie was dying on the scales. He knocked van Rensburg down in the first few minutes and was clearly in front when he tore his ankle ligaments. Willie was tagged a 'quitter'.

He had to move down to defend his South African featherweight title against Hubert Essakow. Willie was Lebanese and Hubert was Jewish but, despite the conflict between their communities, the fighters were friends.

There was tension, however, as they prepared for battle at the Johannesburg City Hall on 19 March 1956. Willie felt unsettled at the prospect of facing Hubert and he was stricken with weight problems again. The Monday morning of the weigh-in, on the day of the fight, was disastrous. Willie woke from a fitful sleep and, stepping on the scales at home, found he was six pounds over the limit. His metabolism seemed to have gone awry and he paced agitatedly around the house in Benoni. The contest was to be broadcast live on national radio and Willie was contractually obligated to fight.

There was bedlam when they stood on the scales. Gasps and boos greeted the confirmation that Willie's weight was a few ounces under 132 pounds. Essakow looked pensive as he watched from a distance. He had his own small problem for, a few minutes later, Essakow was twelve ounces over the stipulated 126-pound mark. His team protested that he could easily run it off; but they were not prepared to make him do so when Toweel was six pounds heavier than he should have been.

A compromise was struck. Willie would be stripped of his championship, but he had to get down to 129 pounds so that he and Hubert could meet in a non-title bout. He spent the morning sweating and starving in an effort to shift a few more pounds. At lunchtime, Willie weighed 129½ pounds. The fight was on.

At the City Hall all the old animosity towards the Toweels resurfaced. Their Lebanese ancestry and domination of South African boxing sparked a snobbish jealousy. It was time they were put in their place – and who better to beat up 'a bloody Leb' than a Jewish kid like Hubert Essakow?

A chant for the unbeaten challenger, robbed of his shot at the title, rose up with rhythmic urgency: *'Eh-sah-kov! Eh-sah-kov!'*

Willie felt better in the ring. All his distressing problems melted away and serenity descended. From the opening minute of round one it seemed as if he could not miss Essakow with thudding jabs and spiteful combinations. Toweel boxed with measured force, calibrating the heavy torque of his punches far more effectively than he had managed his weight.

Essakow refused to be discouraged. He poured forward no matter how hard he was hit. His features were swollen and he had barely won a round when, in the eighth, it looked as if Toweel was starting to wilt from the exhausting routine of bouncing punches off the head of his opponent. Essakow landed a withering body shot in the ninth and Toweel would say later that it felt as if he had been cut in half.

The tenth round saw a return to the previous pattern as Toweel jabbed and hooked with crisp authority and, for the first time, Essakow sagged. He slumped on his stool before round eleven with a dazed expression. His corner pushed him out when the bell sounded and Toweel picked Essakow apart even more easily. It was still surprising when a routine right to the chin sent Essakow toppling backwards.

Essakow's head snapped back against the third and lowest rope and he lay in a stupor – staring blindly at Toweel. His bloodied mouth hung open.

Slowly, like a drowning man sinking beneath dark waters, he slid down from the bottom rope to the canvas. The referee counted to ten, and spread his arms to signal the end.

Willie's smile eventually faded into incomprehension. Hubert lay very still on the canvas. Willie walked towards him, pushing his way through the crowd of officials who had filled the ring.

'Hubert, Hubert,' Willie said urgently. 'Wake up, man. It's me – Willie ...'

Hubert Essakow remained silent and still.

There was trauma in Willie Toweel's dressing room. He knelt on his bony knees on the red cement floor. His robe was still draped around his shoulders as he crossed himself with bandaged hands.

'Please pray with me,' he said to Papa Mike and his brothers Alan, Maurice, Jimmy, Vic and Fraser.

They gathered around Willie and bowed their heads as he repeated the same words again and again. 'Please God, don't let him die ... please God, don't let him die ...'

Willie allowed his brothers to help him out of his fight gear. The robe, his hand wraps, trunks, socks and boots were peeled away so that he could be led to the shower. Then, with water hammering down on him, Willie closed his eyes and tried to imagine it was just a nightmare.

It did him little good and, soon, he scrambled into his street clothes. His damp hair stood askew on his head as he and his brothers ran to the car.

At first, Willie's entrance to Hubert's room at the Johannesburg

General was blocked. The doctors were reluctant for anyone to see the fighter while they monitored his deteriorating condition.

The Essakow family huddled together in the corridor. They said little as Willie approached them with his mumbled apologies. He turned back to the doctor. 'Please, doc,' he said quietly. 'I did this to Hubert. I've got to see him.'

'Take it easy, son,' the doctor said. He would allow Willie to enter Hubert's room for a few minutes as long as the Essakow family did not object.

Paul Essakow, Hubert's brother, nodded his consent. They all knew that Willie had not meant it to end this way. Hubert's trainer, Johnny Mansour, leaned over and squeezed the fighter's shoulder.

Willie entered the room hesitantly. He did not know what he expected but he almost gagged. Hubert's face was covered by a criss-crossing mesh of tubes, which had been fed into his mouth and nose. His breathing made a rasping sound. It did not look as if Hubert would win this last fight of his life.

After he had left the room, Willie covered his face and cried.

Alan drove him around the deserted streets of Johannesburg late into the night. Willie stared out of the window, refusing to go home. They drove through the dark until Alan, who was exhausted, finally turned the car round and headed back to Benoni at three in the morning.

Their Sock Exchange glinted in the moonlight. Willie felt like tearing the garden gym apart, sheet by tinny sheet, but Alan steered him towards bed. In his pyjamas and propped up in a wheelchair, Maurice sat at Willie's bedside for three hours as they waited for the night to end. Maurice tried to persuade his brother to rest, but Willie persisted in talking and staring at the hands that had ruined his friend.

Vic called them soon after daybreak. He phoned from a public telephone at the Princess Nursing Home where, after Hubert had been transferred from the general hospital, an emergency operation had been carried out shortly after one in the morning. The surgeons established that there was nothing they could do to ease the swelling of Hubert's brain.

The morning newspapers were dominated by the tragedy. Willie was fixated by the front page of the *Rand Daily Mail*, which featured two photographs from the night before. A panoramic view of the ring stretched across the top third of the page. Willie could see himself looking down at the fallen figure of Hubert Essakow. The bottom rope was trapped by Hubert's back, while his right arm waved helplessly. Below that wide-angled shot a far more terrible photograph captured a side-on view of Hubert's face as, with that hanging jaw, he gazed at Willie. He looked as frightening as the headline:

ESSAKOW RUSHED TO HOSPITAL AFTER TOWEEL FIGHT – "Condition Critical" Say Doctors

It needed all the powers of Papa Mike and his brothers to persuade Willie to take a sleeping draught, prescribed by their family doctor, soon after eight o'clock that rainy morning. He slept for four hours – returning to the nightmare at lunchtime when he arrived at the Princess Nursing Home and was immediately surrounded by reporters shouting questions at him and by photographers flashing their cameras in his face. Willie bowed his head in the rain and hurried towards the entrance.

Hubert had been attached to an iron lung, as they called the ventilator that helped him breathe. But the sinister oedema, the fluid on his brain, had increased.

He remained unconscious for fifty-two hours. Finally, at 2 a.m. on 22 March 1956, Hubert Essakow died from the injuries he had sustained against Willie Toweel. He was twenty-one years old.

Willie released a short statement later: 'There is nothing I can say which is good enough about such a great man and courageous fighter as Hubert Essakow. I shall always remember the times we spent together. We were great friends and we travelled together to fights. I knew him well – but when I met Hubert in the ring at the City Hall I also found out what a brave heart he had. I shall never forget him.'

His torment was deepened by the inquest and repeated calls to ban boxing in South Africa. There was further pain as he was hounded by newspapers – stretching from Johannesburg to London. They were willing to pay him serious money for an exclusive but Willie refused. He could not escape the crank callers as easily. As soon as he answered, they would ask to speak to 'Hubert Essakow' or wonder how it felt to be a killer. They seemed intent on driving him out of his mind.

Alan reminded him that many great fighters, from Ezzard Charles to Sugar Ray Robinson, had endured the same ordeal. Sam Baroudi, in the case of Charles, and Jimmy Doyle after he fought Robinson, had also died.

Reluctantly, Willie Toweel went back to boxing. He remained unbeaten for his next eight fights but only stopped two of his opponents, for he worried about hurting them. Willie considered retiring before Alan and Maurice convinced him to start again in London. From the moment he won the Commonwealth lightweight title in Earls Court against Dave Charnley in August 1957, Willie was rejuvenated.

He was feted by British fight fans, who appreciated his skills, and he fought eleven times in the UK before setting up his contest against Len Matthews at Madison Square Garden. He earned only two technical knockouts in Britain, preferring to outbox his opponents and win on points. In contrast, before the Essakow fight, he had scored fifteen stoppages in his first twenty-one bouts.

Willie seemed happier when he returned to South Africa after his rousing defeat of Matthews. But on 17 September 1960 he went back to the Johannesburg City Hall, the scene of the Essakow tragedy, and faced Jannie Botes in a South African welterweight title contest. Willie built a classy lead over Botes, but they were in the same ring where Hubert had spent his last conscious moments.

He was convinced that, as they moved into the ninth of a ten-round fight, he could see Hubert in front of him. Botes disappeared and the spectre of Hubert Essakow took over. Willie could not stand it. He had to get out of the ring and so, in desperation, he hit Botes with a deliberately low blow. The crowd howled in disbelief as Toweel was disqualified. It was the only way he could escape the haunting vision.

Boxing was under pressure. After 600 episodes of *Friday Night Fights*, famously sponsored by Gillette, NBC had abandoned the sport in June 1960. They had presented live boxing on Friday night television for nearly sixteen years – starting with Willie Pep's defeat of Chalky White in September 1944. An average seventeen million people watched *Friday Night Fights* every week for the first dozen years, with the high point being a televised battle between Cuba's Kid Galivan and Chuck Davey in 1953 when 67.9 per cent of the national audience tuned into the bout. But ratings began to slip with mismatches and the suspicion of fixed fights as the mob wielded its grimy influence.

Benny Paret, the world champion whom Emile Griffith hoped to challenge, had headlined the Garden's first non-televised main event in over a decade when he knocked out Garnet 'Sugar' Hart in July 1960. It was a non-title bout but, also, confirmation that boxing could no longer command an automatic television audience. The fight game had, forty years before, been the most popular sport in America. But the world was changing. Boxing seemed too crooked and violent for a respectable new age.

A vision of wholesome decency shaped America's view of itself. As the economy recovered from its wartime slump, middle-class families took to the suburbs and embraced conformity and consumerism. New cars and television made life seem more attractive – even if the conservatism of the early 1950s prevailed.

Boxing no longer fitted as neatly into America's narrative as it had done in the 1920s and 1930s. Where it had once given struggling communities a way out of poverty – including waves of Irish, Italian and Jewish fighters – there were cleaner opportunities in a changing America. Boxing was hard and dirty and, while there were still many white fighters, more black and Hispanic men made their living from a dangerous trade at the start of the 1960s.

ABC still believed that boxing could attract millions of viewers every week and so they decided to produce a show called *Saturday Night Fight of the Week*. It remained a risk because, as a reporter for the *Television Magazine* suggested, 'Friday at 10 p.m. had become accepted as the man's hour in front of the TV set. But Saturday night belongs to the ladies.'

Madison Square Garden would supply the overwhelming bulk of the promotions. Teddy Brenner had been the Garden's match-maker for just a year, but he had won himself the prestigious position by producing some viciously competitive bouts at smaller New York arenas like St Nicholas and Eastern Parkway. Emile Griffith had become Brenner's favourite young fighter after his first twelve professional contests took place at St Nick's on West 66th Street. The matchmaker knew he could depend on Griffith's technical excellence, stamina and punch resistance to keep the fans hooked.

Griffith's next fight would be only the third week of ABC's new partnership with the Garden – and he and his opponent needed to produce a compelling contest to seal the idea that Saturday was America's new fight night. And so Brenner had sent a telegram to Maurice Toweel in Johannesburg. They had worked together on the Willie Toweel–Len Matthews fight, one of Brenner's earliest cards at the Garden, and the memory of that fierce contest shone brightly. He offered Toweel significantly more money than he had made against Matthews and promised him a crack at Paret's welterweight title if he beat Griffith.

Alan Toweel did not want the fight. He knew that Griffith, a natural welterweight, was far too big and strong for Willie. But Maurice argued that this was their brother's final chance and his biggest payday. After the fiasco of his Johannesburg City Hall disqualification, this could be Willie's last fight.

*

Larger battles consumed the United States. The colour lines divid-
ing black and white America ran deep. Emile Griffith walked down
them every day, with the racial discrimination he sometimes suffered
being accentuated by the unchallenged prejudice against his sexuality. In the late summer of 1960, John Steinbeck campaigned against
inequity in a simple way.

'I am constantly amazed at the qualities we expect in Negroes,'
Steinbeck wrote in a passionate article reprinted in the *New York
Amsterdam News*, the city's only black newspaper. 'We expect Negroes
to be wiser than we are, more tolerant than we are, braver, more dignified than we are, more self-controlled, and self-disciplined. We even
demand more talent from them than from ourselves.

'A Negro must be ten times as gifted as a white to receive equal
recognition. We expect Negroes to have more endurance than we in
athletics, more courage in defeat, more versatility in music and dancing, more controlled emotion in theatre. We expect them to be more
courteous, more gallant, more proud, more steadfast. While main-
taining that Negroes are inferior to us, we prove our conviction that
they are superior in many fields.

'In the Alabama bus boycott we knew there would be no Negro
violence – and there wasn't. The only violence was white violence.
In the streets we expect courtesy from Negroes even when we are
ugly and overbearing. In the prize ring we know a Negro will be
game and will not complain against a decision ... When Martin
Luther King was stabbed by a hysterical woman, he might have
felt some anger or hurt or despair. But his first words on coming
out of the anesthetic were: "Don't let them hurt her. She needs
help."'

Two years before, on 20 September 1958, King had been stabbed
in Harlem, where Emile lived. A woman called Izola Carr had
plunged a knife deep in his chest, reaching his sternum. King, who
had led the successful bus boycott of the segregated public transit
system in Montgomery, Alabama, from December 1955 to December
1956, survived the attack. But in the week of the Griffith–Toweel

fight, on Wednesday 19 October 1960, he was jailed in Atlanta. King had joined around a thousand students, who staged a sit-in protest against lunch-counter segregation at Atlanta University. He was the most prominent of the 280 people who had been imprisoned.

Emile did not understand how a man who spoke so much about peace and reconciliation could be subjected to assassination attempts and arrest. The world could seem confusing and mean.

In October 1960, amid the deep conservatism and racism, America also teemed with the promise of change. Vice President Richard Nixon and the Democratic Party's John F. Kennedy, striving to become the first Catholic president of the United States, were embroiled in a 'jet-age election'. For the first time in history the presidential candidates engaged in live television debate – with four contests between Nixon and Kennedy. The opening debate had been held on 26 September and seventy million viewers watched JFK face the far more famous figure of Nixon in a television studio.

The vice president had campaigned hard all day and, beneath the unblinking glare of the television lights, he looked pale, sweaty, stubble-faced and tired. Kennedy had prepared for television and, on a black-and-white screen, where every blemish of age and appearance was accentuated on Nixon's face, the younger man looked charismatic. He spoke directly to the camera and wore a blue suit and shirt, which stood out more brightly – while Nixon opted for a grey suit, which blurred with the monochrome setting. Kennedy was hailed as the overwhelming winner.

On Friday 21 October, the night before ABC turned its attention to boxing and Griffith v Toweel, the final debate was screened. Nixon fought back hard, but it was clear that the momentum of the election had been transformed by the power of television and JFK's emergence from relative obscurity.

Kennedy had also contacted Correta Scott King, Martin Luther's wife, to pledge support and help release him from prison. In return, he was confident that he would have the widespread backing of black voters in America. It seemed as if a different country might soon emerge.

Willie Toweel paused in surprise. Killing time before the weigh-in at the New York State Athletic Commission office, his gaze was caught by a half-page newspaper advertisement for a 'Thrilling new SOUTH AFRICAN star . . .'

He liked the way they had written 'SOUTH AFRICAN' in capital letters but, above the words, he saw the darker image of a young native. Willie knew that many white people in Benoni would have called her a 'Kaffir girl'. Miriam Makeba was a young singer who had escaped apartheid for political exile. She had been discovered by Harry Belafonte and the advert for Makeba's first LP suggested that her music was a 'striking blend of the highly sophisticated and the primitive'.

Emile swanned into the office and, with a chuckle, peered over Willie's shoulder. 'She's pretty, champ,' he said of Makeba. 'Do you like her?'

Willie looked up in surprise. Did this boy not know you could be locked up for even talking about a white man and a black girl?

'Relax, champ,' Emile said with a smile.

The weigh-in took place at noon and the joint was packed. Before stepping onto the scales, Willie was subjected to a rigorous medical examination. The doctor checked almost every part of his body – except his mind. At least he was fighting in the grand old Garden, rather than the Jo'burg City Hall, and Willie cracked a smile as the doctor declared him 'fighting fit'.

He was less sure how to react when, after he had stripped down to his underpants, he felt a hand pat his right buttock cheek.

'You're in shape, champ,' Emile said as Willie wheeled round to see who had touched him.

Emile wished his opponent good luck. '*Ja*, you too,' Willie replied. For such a dangerous boxer, Emile Griffith was a curiously friendly fellow.

Willie Toweel stood on the weighing machine and felt relieved that, for once, he would not have to worry about the numbers they would shout out. He made the welterweight limit easily, scaling three pounds under at a precise 144, and he raised a fist in acknowledgement.

Emile followed him and, just in his trunks, he cut a magnificent figure. There was not an ounce of wasted flesh on his hard and muscled frame, which weighed 147 pounds.

'Gentlemen,' Teddy Brenner said with a wolfish grin, 'we've got a date in the Garden tonight . . .'

CHAPTER TWO

Date Night

Madison Square Garden, New York, Saturday 22 October 1960

Esther Taylor did not bloom in the Garden. She avoided the hot glare of the ring and moved back towards the darker and smokier reaches of the arena. The atmosphere was clogged and choking, but she felt safer at a distance from the brutality of boxing. Emile had offered Esther and her sister, Carol, seats near ringside, in a place of honour as his girlfriend, but she had declined.

'I don't want to be too close,' she told Emile.

As a sensitive man, and a fighter too, he understood. Emile did not love the raw sounds and bloody sights of the fight game. He just happened to be a ring natural, a boxer who did everything he needed to do between the ropes with easy accomplishment. But he had no desire to watch another man being hurt. There was something deadly about the breath being taken from a fighter by a venomous body punch. It was grim, too, when a boxer's face was split open by a hook or his nose was broken by an uppercut.

The knockouts were far worse. They resembled a kind of dying, as the fallen fighter was swallowed up by oblivion. His eyes rolled back in his head, which often hit the canvas or one of the surrounding ropes. Emile didn't like to see a fellow stretched out on his back for twenty seconds or more. He was much happier when the beaten opponent got up, just a little drunkenly after the count of ten, and smiled a woozy smile of acceptance. He had lost but he was fine. He had been buzzed but his head had already started to clear.

Emile knew the feeling. He had taken some heavy punches in his short career but they seemed to have done him no harm. He still appreciated why Esther did not like seeing him being hit – or watching him show savagery himself as he pummelled a decent man like Willie Toweel. So he made sure Howie Albert arranged discreet seats for the Taylor sisters.

Esther still had trouble even thinking of Emile as a boxer. Five years earlier, when they had first exchanged shy but intrigued looks at each other in church, he had appeared to Esther as a dreamy-looking older boy with a huge smile and a gentle face. Emile was easy to fall for because he was as charming as he was handsome. At fifteen, she liked his good manners and soft voice. His body was already incredible, but she needed the innocent reassurance of his kindness most of all. When he finally asked her out she learned a touch more about him. Esther liked the fact that he was good at sports – especially baseball – and that he was a hard worker who loved his family. Emile was different from all the rough and wild boys in Harlem whom Esther avoided. He valued her; and she fell in love with him.

She was still in high school when, out of nowhere, like some ominous roll of thunder, he suddenly became a boxer. Esther was not quite eighteen when Emile won the Golden Gloves after just a year of boxing. She understood it was a sizeable feat because of the clamour it unleashed around their close-knit community in Harlem. Emile, her boyfriend, had become a champion. She didn't need him to win some glittering title to spell out that truth to her but, of course, she shared in the pride and giddy excitement. Emile, a black kid from their neighbourhood, was on his way to becoming a star of world boxing.

It was not easy being young and black in America. The stain of prejudice spread whenever they took the subway into the unsettling white world of Manhattan. You had to battle hard, and bite your lip sometimes to stop crying out at the injustice of it all, but she and Emile were used to hardship. They skirted around the trouble and inequality that framed their lives – just because the colour of their skin was different from the white folk with power and money.

Once she was out of school Esther worked in all kinds of jobs. She was like Emile in being ready to graft as a way of building something clean and good. Emile knew that Esther was much cleverer than him and so she was always going to end up in an office. She was intelligent and resourceful and, by October 1960, she was a book-keeper in Manhattan. It was solid and respectable work, and a real achievement for a twenty-year-old black woman, and Emile liked to boast about her. His girlfriend worked in Manhattan, in an office, crunching numbers much more prettily than he crunched punches into the swollen faces of his opponents.

Emile, however, was in the limelight. He was heading for fame and glory and, maybe, even riches. Esther didn't care about the money he was making. She just wanted Emile to emerge from every fight safe and well and with his familiar smile intact. If she had been given a choice, Esther would have preferred it if Emile had been more ordinary and working in a normal job rather than being an acclaimed fighter. She would have even liked it more if he was in baseball, as she knew how much Emile had loved to play ball, as a catcher, but Esther was wise enough to let him live his life. He was on a path to somewhere strange and new, and she accepted the need to step back and allow him to fulfil everything that made him so distinct.

Esther would have loved to have been courted properly by Emile. It was a thrill going out with him, to dance and have dinner, but their dates were sporadic. Emile had such little time, amid the training and fighting and everything else he needed to do, that she accepted the limitations. When she sometimes found it difficult to stop the disappointment creasing her face, Emile could be especially attentive. He murmured sweet words to her then, and he mentioned the possibility of marriage one day. It helped her to know that he was thinking ahead of their life together. And so she could endure the sacrifice while she waited for him.

Emile wanted to have a good time with Esther. He just wanted to dance and laugh and lose himself, and her, in fun. Esther called him 'a fabulous dancer', but she kept up and glowed when she was with him. Emile dressed more beautifully than any man she knew and he liked talking to her about clothes and hats and the kind of stuff that usually remained between her and her girlfriends.

There were plenty of women at the fight that Saturday night. It was Date Night and, gaining free entry alongside their boyfriends and husbands, many of them would have wished to swap places with Esther, had they known her role in his life. Yet she did not think of the prestige and the status. Emile was her boy. He was her guy. She just wanted him back unharmed.

As the lights dimmed in the Garden, and the crowd's drone turned into a roar, Esther felt a tightening in her stomach. She was nervous, and anxious for Emile, but she was proud too. Esther looked around the crammed arena and saw that people were ablaze with fervour. They were all talking about her boyfriend, hollering out his name as he and his opponent prepared to walk to the ring. Esther felt amazed again at the power and charisma of Emile. She felt lucky to be in love with him; but she just wanted the fight to be over so that she might see him smiling and laughing and teasing her again about their next date.

Esther bowed her head and said a silent prayer amid the bedlam.

Draped in a black robe, and wearing white trunks, Emile Griffith moved in a solemn dance in his corner of the ring. Gil Clancy and Howie Albert stood next to him. Willie Toweel wore black trunks so that he and Griffith stood out even more clearly on monochrome television screens across America. On the back of his gown, his name and 'South Africa' had been stitched into the fabric. His brother Alan was dressed all in white, with 'Willie Toweel' emblazoned across his shoulders. Jimmy August, the American trainer who looked after the Nigerian middleweight world title contender Dick Tiger, was also in their corner.

Don Dunphy, at ringside, had established himself as one of the most famous voices in America after calling the Gillette *Friday Night Fights* on radio for nineteen years. Having moved to ABC, he was commentating on just his third television boxing programme. His nasal-voiced familiarity rang out as he advised millions of viewers that, 'Both boys feature superb boxing ability, so we're looking for a fast fight from gong to gong. We invite you to look for darting left hooks mingled with sharp right-hand counter-punching. And now let's move to our ring announcer, Johnny Addie ...'

Dressed in his customary tuxedo, Addie nodded to the fighters while the gleaming microphone was lowered from the rafters and down towards the centre of the ring. It would not be long before he called them together. But Addie had a special guest to hail first at the Garden. 'Ladies and gentlemen,' he yelled, 'in the audience tonight, retired, undefeated heavyweight champion of the world ... *Rocky Marciano!*'

Marciano waved as he skipped across the ring to greet Toweel. He then turned back to touch Griffith's arm before taking his leave. After the fighters had been introduced by Addie, the referee took charge. 'Now,' Al Berl told Toweel and Griffith, 'you've boxed here before. You know the rules. I want you boys to give us a good, clean fight.'

The two boxers brought their gloves together for the start of Toweel's fifty-fourth bout and Griffith's twenty-third.

Bouncing on his feet, like a dancer, Toweel moved away from Griffith at the opening bell. The pattern of the fight was set as Griffith, much the bigger man, slipped naturally into his role as the aggressor. He stalked the nimble mover with his own flatter feet as if wanting to maximise the power of his punches.

The first three rounds were evenly matched, with Griffith's combinations being countered by Toweel's slick jab and occasional right hand. A decent body shot from Toweel encouraged a loud 'Attaboy, Willie, attaboy!' from Jimmy August.

The two fighters nodded at each other at the conclusion of round three as Dunphy, in his commentary, confirmed that, 'this is a very close fight'.

Fifteen seconds into the fourth, however, Griffith followed up a sweet combination with a peach of a right hand. The South African went down in a heap, the force of the blow making his black hair fly up on his head as he landed on the canvas with a thump. But Toweel was tough and he rose quickly, at the count of three. The referee kept counting, adding a finger to accompany every spoken digit, '... *four ... five ... six ... seven ... eight ...*', while Toweel wiped his gloves on his trunks as if wanting to rub away the stain of being knocked down.

Toweel looked ragged and he was reduced to holding as Griffith tried to end it with a big shot. 'Toweel has plenty of courage – as he showed in the Matthews fight,' Dunphy said.

Griffith was hasty and most of his punches flew wildly over Toweel's head. As they clinched in the centre of the ring, Dunphy noted that, 'Toweel is using all his ring cunning to stay in there.'

Toweel still needed his brother to spray his face with cold water in the corner. Alan wiped him down and Jimmy August went to work, waving smelling salts under Willie's nose.

A small cut had opened up over Toweel's right eye and, as the fight wore on, he struggled to keep Griffith at a distance with his jab. Toweel was under severe pressure and, in the break before the seventh, Clancy urged Griffith to 'get him out of there'. Those stark words worked because Griffith came out firing. Toweel buckled and Griffith connected with a fizzing left and a fierce right to score a second knockdown.

Toweel got to his feet slowly. He was soon hurt again by a Griffith uppercut and two more right hands. Toweel wobbled but held on until the bell.

'Are you okay, Willie?' Alan asked above the bedlam of the Garden.

'*Ja*,' Toweel said, as his brother pulled his trunks clear of his gut so that he could suck in as much oxygen as possible. They both knew he had been badly hurt.

'You've got to keep him off you,' Alan said. 'Jab and move, Willie.'

The outcome was still predictable as Griffith hunted him down in round eight. Toweel was pinned against the ropes when a right cross and a left hook to the body dropped him. Toweel clutched the bottom rope as, on one knee, he listened to the count. He was up before eight but Griffith was already moving in to finish him. The South African went down again just as the bell rang.

Toweel made it back to his corner, but his brother was so concerned that they forgot to bring out the stool. August scrambled for the small wooden seat and they were soon joined by the ringside doctor. He did not linger for long before gesturing to the referee. It was over.

Emile Griffith visited his opponent's locker room. 'I'm sorry, champ,' he said. So much hurt was etched into the beaten man's face that Emile recognised the truth. Willie Toweel, at the age of twenty-six, was done as a fighter. He would never box again.

They had little in common, apart from the fact that they had spent twenty-four minutes that night trying to knock each other out cold. But Emile liked Willie. He sensed a kindness in the South African, which overcame everything he had heard about white people in that country.

Emile knew Willie was a good man. And so, even after they had run out of words to say to each other, he hung around the locker room a little longer. Emile patiently answered Alan's questions about the best gyms in New York and listened to the trainer's stories about his encounters with great cornermen like Ray Arcel, Charley Goldman and Cus D'Amato.

It helped when Rocky Marciano arrived to offer condolences because the Toweels were awed to meet him. Emile could say goodbye. He embraced Willie, kissing him on the cheek.

'Thank you, champ,' Willie said as his smiling conqueror wheeled round one last time to give him a big thumbs-up. It looked as if Emile, his skin shiny with victory, had never seen a ghost in his life.

An hour later Emile and Calvin Thomas rolled out of the artists' entrance at Madison Square Garden and climbed into a yellow checker cab on 8th Avenue. Just off 50th Street they had to cross eight blocks of Saturday night traffic to get to Times Square. Emile always felt most alive in that cold and glittering heart of New York City. There was a sense of danger and excitement along the neon-lit streets, which made him feel like he had reached home – and the crossroads of the world.

Esther Taylor was his girlfriend but he had to be with Calvin. He couldn't say the words out loud to anyone, not even to Calvin and never to Esther, but he needed to be with men in a dark and sweaty place. He felt the urge most strongly after a fight. It was as if the perils of the ring needed to be followed by the thrill of a more seductive night of risk.

Calvin and Emile lost themselves among all the boys and men who made their heads spin. They weren't partners, but they shared that same urge to dance and kiss and touch men more than women. Esther was a good girl, and Emile loved her in his own way. But, above all, he valued the freedom she gave him. She made few demands and so, instead of insisting that he see her after a fight, Esther allowed him to disappear. She knew he was 'busy', that he had people to see, and Emile felt it best that her innocence was not ruined. He would keep his different worlds separate from each other. It was the only way he had of salvaging his happiness, and sanity.

Howie Albert had followed Emile and Calvin up the stairs. 'Be careful,' he'd shouted, for he knew how risky New York had become amid the crackdown. Emile nodded. He understood how much he needed to guard his mostly secret life.

It would have been safer if they had headed down to Greenwich Village because, in the fall of 1960, only Bon Soir, Café de Lys and

Julius' had been allowed to remain open as the rest of gay New York crumbled. Among their many haunts across town, Lenny's Hideaway, Mais Oui, the 415, Tic-Toc, 316, Big Dollar and even Floradora in Jackson Heights, Queens, had been raided and closed by the police over the previous six months. Each of them had created their own atmosphere. The Big Dollar regulars wore leather jackets, while the 415, a dance club for mostly young Hispanic men, was more to Emile's taste. But the bars Emile loved most had all been around Times Square. Their dusky interiors contrasted with the flickering strip joints lining a grid of gaudy streets.

They were all gone. The New York City Police Department had shut down over forty gay bars in less than a year. Only the Village trio had been spared because each claimed to be a legitimate business. An eighteen-year-old Barbra Streisand sang at Bon Soir during a residency that ran from 9 September to 20 November 1960, as the venue continued to promote musical events to offset any allegations that they simply catered for a homosexual clientele. Meanwhile, Café de Lys was connected to a theatre and Julius' operated as a restaurant in the Village.

Celebrated writers like Tennessee Williams and Truman Capote, who had published *Breakfast at Tiffany's* in 1958, dined at Julius'. But it was too theatrical and stuck-up for Emile, and he hated the way the management at Julius' harassed less renowned visitors. They were terrified of losing their licence because the New York State Liquor Authority implemented a law that prohibited the serving of alcohol to homosexuals. The bar staff were under instruction either to evict young gay men or to force them to avoid eye contact with famous diners.

Emile preferred the grittiness of 42nd Street and the way in which, even after they were shut down, bars found a way of opening in a new place under a fresh name. He could not keep up with all the name changes, but he and Calvin knew that a small bar had just sprung up in the basement of a club called The Joint, which had been closed a month earlier. Emile and Calvin would be likelier to find their favourite friends there – rather than in the Village.

It was still risky with so much police entrapment. There was a simple ruse whereby a vice officer, out of uniform, propositioned a lonely soul at the bar or in the restroom. The fact that the entrapped man was often married or working in a respectable job added to his shame. Emile could never work out why, if someone was friendly and apparently attracted to you, it was a crime to respond in kind. It seemed rude to shun a fellow coldly – but acting more naturally could lead to arrest.

Sexual relations between people of the same gender were still a criminal act in every state of America. The Sodomy Law covered all forms of homosexual sex and carried potential jail terms for those found guilty of between two and twenty years, with accompanying fines of up to $2,000. Even consensual sex between two adult men in the privacy of their home could result in imprisonment.

Emile and Calvin had usually escaped before a bar was raided. Such collusion was typical of the way the police and the mob worked together. Before a raid, the bar about to be invaded would be tipped off by a cash-hungry cop who was paid for his information. The lights on the dancefloor would suddenly blaze into life and everyone ran for the exit. One or two stragglers might be snared, but most people got away without being thrown into a cop car. And then, for a few months at least, the place would be closed.

The clampdown of 1960 was much harsher. There were fewer warnings and the closures seemed permanent. The authorities were out to shut down every aspect of homosexuality. Policemen and federal agents planted microphones in the backs of park benches to record illegal homosexual advances, and used two-way mirrors and peepholes to monitor gay activity in public toilets. Even if two men were caught lingering together over a cigarette they would be given a nudge in the back with a truncheon and a police officer's blunt order: 'Move on, faggots!'

Robert Wagner, the mayor of New York, had instigated the purge in late 1959 after latching onto a campaign driven by Lee Mortimer –

a syndicated gossip columnist and crime reporter, who was obsessed with the Mafia using illicit homosexual venues to launder their money. Mortimer took particular relish in calling the bars 'daffodil dens' for 'the dainty hand-on-hippers'. He argued that mobsters, rather than homosexuals, were his primary target.

'They're the ones I'm gunning for,' Mortimer wrote, 'not the deviates who excuse their aberrations on the grounds of sickness.'

Mortimer still spent hours in the 'lavender holes' – and he wrote reams of outraged but titillated copy about the 'diseased debauchery' he witnessed. Popular magazines like *Coronet* made even more hysterical claims: 'Some male sex deviants do not stop with infecting their often-innocent partners. They descend through perversions to other forms of depravity, such as drug addiction, burglary, sadism and even murder. Once a man assumes the role of a homosexual, he often throws off all moral restraints.'

Mayor Wagner endorsed 'weeding out the daffodil dens' as hard evidence that his administration, with an election looming, was tough on crime. Homosexuals were an easy target. Regarded as criminals and perverts, homosexuals were also diagnosed as being sick by the medical profession. In 1952, the American Psychiatric Association had declared homosexuality to be a 'sociopathic personality disturbance' – a clinical diagnosis that would not be challenged for another twenty years.

Such prejudice ran all the way to the White House. Soon after his inauguration in 1953, President Dwight Eisenhower had signed an executive order that listed 'sexual perversion' (meaning homosexuality) as a reason for a federal employee to be sacked from his position. Six hundred and forty homosexuals lost their government posts over the next sixteen months during the Lavender Scare – which matched national Red Scare paranoia about communism and the atomic bomb.

In 1953, four years before he wrote *West Side Story*, Leonard Bernstein lamented that, 'We are not living in experimental times.' Bernstein was a married gay man, a great composer and conductor boxed in by convention. 'We are not producing real tragedy, or real satire. All the caution and fear prevents it and we are left with art that is whiling away the time until the world gets better or blows up.'

Gore Vidal, another gay American writer, would complain later that, 'The fifties was the bad decade.'

Deep into 1960, it seemed as if the old decade had never ended – and just got worse. Emile hunkered down in the back of the old yellow cab, willing the driver to weave faster through the traffic so that he and Calvin could shake off the shackles in Times Square. He was in the mood to dance.

Emile had travelled a long way from the sunlit Caribbean to the seamy neon of New York. He had been shaped in Charlotte Amalie, the largest city on St Thomas, part of the United States Virgin Islands, where he had lost his father and, for a while, his mother too. Emile had also found his true self on the island.

He was happy during his earliest years. Emile went to school, did his household chores, swam in the sea, played baseball and stole fruit with his friends for fun. It was only when his father, Emile Senior, left them, that Junior shrivelled on the inside. His mother told them that their daddy had gone for good, or bad, to New York City. Junior wondered if his father might have looked in and kissed him goodbye while he slept. He did not dare ask his mother in case she answered with a blunt 'no'.

Emile Sr was a bull of a man and his rippling physique, if not his crude character, would eventually be inherited by his eldest son. When he was still young, Junior kept dreaming of his daddy, seeing him return home in his sleep. But every morning he woke to an empty feeling as his father was still missing. In the evenings, before bed, hoping he might have the same dream that night, he would sit alone in front of their small house. Emile would throw a baseball in the sultry air, catching it and liking the comforting thud as it landed smack in the middle of his battered old glove. When his eyes were not following the white ball spinning slowly up into the sky, he would turn his gaze towards the mountain road. Emile wished that, one day, he might see his father walking home in the fading light.

His mother had always been a wonderful cook. But, once Emile Sr left, all the joy went out of her cooking. Money and pleasure were rationed – and worry consumed Emelda. She had to find work and, when the break came, their lives were never the same again. Emelda was offered the chance to become the official cook for the governor of Puerto Rico. Only eighty miles separated Charlotte Amalie from the exotic world of San Juan but, to a boy of ten, it felt as if he had lost his mother. Emelda was also distressed, and it was only when her own mother and sisters insisted that they would look after her five children that she agreed to leave. She would sail home for a visit every three or four months.

At first, living with his grandmother, Emile remained hopeful. Life only darkened when she fell ill and Emile moved in with his cousin Blanche. She lived in a cottage with her two children and his arrival threw her into a fury. Blanche made him work as if he was a man twice his age. Emile's day started at dawn, when he carried a metal drum down the mountain so that he could fill it with fresh water, which he would then haul back up the steep climb. He was also responsible for the yard and getting the kids to and from school. Whenever he made a mistake, or he did not clean the house or polish the floors until they were beautifully shiny, Blanche punished him. If it was not the belt being used to a point where bloodied weals were raised on his flesh, it was the torture of being made to hold two cinder blocks above his head.

He stayed away from Blanche as much as possible and it was on an afternoon when he hid in the woods that more complicated trouble seized him. Emile jumped when he felt a hand grip his shoulder. A large stranger beamed down at him. The man had an eerie smile and a gold tooth gleamed inside his dark mouth. It made him look like a pirate. But the man insisted he was Emile's uncle. Emile thought it strange that, aged twelve, he had never met his mysterious uncle before.

His new uncle laughed a lot as he enticed Emile back to the shack where he lived. They were on their own, and Emile's curiosity turned to fear.

The shack was cramped and smelly and his uncle made it even smaller by towering over him. Emile tried to make his excuses. Blanche would be angry if he did not return home to complete his chores. The uncle shook his head and flashed another gold-toothed smile. It would be best if they both had a little rest first.

There was only one bed and Emile's uncle cackled. He joked that, without an aunty to keep him warm, he slept alone. But the bed was big enough for the two of them.

Emile tried to wriggle away when his uncle steered him towards the bed. But the man was too strong. He held Emile tight and lay down with him. Emile closed his eyes, pretending to sleep, but his uncle was wide awake. His hands crawled across Emile's body like giant scuttling spiders. They scared Emile and he attempted to break free. There was no chance of escape and, with the man whispering hoarsely, Emile lay very still. The big rough hands kept moving, dipping down from beneath his shirt to places that Emile knew they did not belong. He felt dirty and wanted to cry when the man touched him inside his shorts.

The jokes and smiles had stopped. Emile was overpowered and made to do things he did not really understand. He thought he might die in that stinking shack, for he was helpless until it was over. It was only then that, as the man rolled away from him, he could slip off the bed. Emile pulled on his clothes, biting his lip to stop the tears from falling. He turned quickly when, as if waking from madness, the man pressed some coins into his hand and told him to buy himself some sweets.

As he ran from the shack, Emile hurled the coins deep into the bushes. They made him feel so sick that he threw up on the side of the dirt road.

That ordeal made him yearn for his mother and a refuge from sadness. Emile could not put his feelings into words and so, quietly, he retreated into himself. He stayed clear of the woods and spent his free hours wandering along the fringes of Charlotte Amalie. For some strange reason he was drawn towards Mandal, an imposing building on the edge of town. He had always been told that Mandal, a reformatory, would be his worst fate if he hung around with bad kids.

Outside the high walls, he heard the boys playing in the courtyard. All the warnings that you would be locked up forever seemed less sinister when the kids inside sounded happy and free. Emile found a way to talk to some of the boys. They peered at him through the iron railings of the main gate, their curious faces pinned flat against the bars, alive with chatter and questions. Beyond telling them his name, Emile could not really explain what had brought him to the juvenile prison gates. He had his own questions.

Did they get beaten in Mandal? Nah, not much.

Did they get fed? Yeah.

Did they have lots of friends? Of course.

So the place was okay? Yeah, sometimes.

Those short answers were enough to convince Emile that the kids in Mandal had a better life than he did.

A few days later he ran away from Blanche and turned up at the front gate. He asked to see the supervisor with a simple request. Could he live at Mandal? The supervisor looked confused. Had he committed a crime? Emile shook his head. He just wanted to move into Mandal. The supervisor chuckled and said he would arrange for him to be driven back home.

He liked riding in the jeep, feeling the wind in his face, as they drove up the winding mountain road to Blanche's cottage. But he wept when, after she had listened to the driver and thanked him slyly for his trouble, she beat Emile with the belt and made him hold the cinder blocks above his head for longer than usual.

Emile tried again the following week. There was something so raw in his face that the Mandal man listened sympathetically to his plea. He still insisted that the reformatory was no place for good kids who already had a home. With a gesture of kindness, he gave him a bowl of chowder. Once Emile had devoured it, he was driven back again in the jeep.

The beating this time was even worse – and the cinder blocks felt heavier than before. Emile seemed to have lost all hope.

Fate intervened in bloody fashion when his little sister Joyce, living once more with their grandmother, stood on a large garden fork. One of the tines ran deep inside Joyce's foot and Emile reacted quickest to her screams. He managed to hoist Joyce onto his back and ran all the way down the mountain to Mandal. It was the only place which he thought might help.

Emile was exhausted by the time he reached the reformatory. The nurse at Mandal began to work immediately on Joyce and, after she had cleaned the wound, she stitched it shut. As Joyce recovered in a bed in the sick bay, the nurse and the supervisor turned to Emile. His bloodied shirt was stuck to his back and, carefully, they removed it. They saw vivid tracks consistent with the marks made by a strap. Emile had not been lying about his cousin. He really did need a new place to live.

Blanche wrote to Emelda to complain that her son had gone crazy and moved away from the family to the devil. Emelda returned home in a rush. It was true. Junior had left Blanche's cottage for Mandal. And yet, as the supervisor confirmed to Emelda, he had not been caught doing anything wrong. If he could not stay with his mother he simply preferred to live at Mandal.

Emelda agreed that Junior would remain in the reformatory as long as she worked in Puerto Rico. She returned to San Juan, promising Junior and all her children that they would be reunited one day, and life settled into a more stable routine. Emile thrived amid the discipline and structure of Mandal while, outside of school and work time, he made new friends. An intimate bond between him and some of the boys developed easily.

There were some, sensing the truth about Emile, who sought to take advantage. Flashbacks of his dangerous uncle recurred when

Emile was propositioned by a much older boy in the showers. They were alone, standing beneath the cascading water, when the bigger kid backed him into a corner. He moved towards Emile with a swagger that suggested he was used to getting his way with any boy who took his fancy. Emile told him he was no fairy; but the bruiser grabbed Emile. They began to wrestle. The older boy laughed, as if this was how his kind of fun always started, but Emile stopped him with a hard punch.

There was anger, then, and the boy clawed at him. But Emile kept hitting his attacker until the big kid began to cry. He never came near Emile again.

Emile relaxed with a couple of the good kids. He didn't need to lash out at them because they made their moves in warmer ways. These boys offered Emile comfort and tenderness – and a whole heap of fun. He explored his sexuality with them while hiding it as much as he could from everyone else. Emile knew that, on the outside, it was best to stay discreet and quiet. But he felt as if he had found something that belonged to him. On the inside, tucked away in Mandal and his deepest self, Emile had discovered a new way of living. There was worry and guilt, but a secret happiness too.

Whenever his mother returned home for a visit, he would stay with her and his grandmother. As soon as she went back to Puerto Rico, he returned to Mandal. There were fewer surprises there than with his own family. On a trip to San Juan, to see Emelda, he had been startled when he discovered she had a new husband, Antonio Castillo, and three stepchildren. Emile was more intrigued, as a teenager, in slipping out at night. His interest in Hispanic boys was sealed on summer nights in San Juan.

Time passed quickly and Emile was stunned when, eventually, he realised that he had spent almost four years at Mandal. Turbulence and bewildering change still stalked the Griffith family. Emile never understood what went wrong between Emelda and her second husband; but he accepted it as a hopeful sign that his mother might get back with his father when she suddenly announced that she was leaving Puerto Rico, and Antonio, for New York. She would send for each of them in turn.

Junior, being the eldest, was the first she summoned and he was shocked by the sight of his father waiting for him at LaGuardia airport. He had not seen his dad for six years and he felt like bursting into tears. Emile Sr was not the sort of man who believed his teenage son should ever cry and so Junior blinked in disbelief. Mommy and Daddy were back together – well, for a while, until Emile Sr ducked out of sight again.

His dad always went missing just before the landlord arrived at their tiny apartment in Harlem to collect the rent. Eventually, Emile Sr moved out permanently and the old pattern of their lives resumed. Junior went to see his dad at the garage where Emile Sr worked as a mechanic, but his visits did not last long. His father also never showed up to watch him play baseball or box at the Golden Gloves. When Emile Sr died from a heart attack, as he left the garage one Friday evening, the news tore up Junior.

'He never saw me do nothing,' he said softly to his mother.

Emile found refuge among his closest new friends – who felt just the same as him. They had picked him out as quickly in Harlem as others had done in Mandal and San Juan.

The morning after he had defeated Willie Toweel, Emile was slow in leaving his bed. Howie Albert and Calvin Thomas were, as always, waiting for him. So was his entire family, led by Emelda, who had screamed '*Junior! Junior! Get him, Junior!*' throughout the fight. Emelda's high-pitched shrieks terrorised even menacing mobsters and grizzled sportswriters who thought they'd heard it all before. But they had heard nothing like the piercing arias of Emelda Griffith. She could break up a crowd, as the unfortunate souls nearest her took refuge on the other side of the ring when she hit a penetrating decibel count. Emelda screamed all night at the Garden, and even Willie Toweel had asked Emile about his mother.

'Mommy can't help it,' Emile had said through a gurgling laugh.

He told Willie that he called her Chubby Checker. She sure got in a twist whenever he fought. Willie, despite his sadness, chuckled.

After every fight, Emile spent another chunk of cash bringing the next family member over to New York from Charlotte Amalie. The rest of his purse looked after them. Emile had three younger sisters and a brother and he was responsible for all of them, except Gloria, the second-eldest. He also had his two stepbrothers and a stepsister.

Gloria was married and, being smart, she tried to persuade Junior not to give away everything to their mother and the others. Emile shrugged. He loved them and there would always be another fight, and another big payday. He knew Howie, as his manager, also worried about him and his money. Emile regarded Howie and Gil Clancy as two new fathers to replace the bad old original. They would always care for him and Emile, in turn, would look after his family.

Emelda was not smiling at the kitchen table in Queens. 'Where you been, Junior?' she asked as Emile rubbed his eyes.

Emile told his mother the truth. He and Calvin had been out dancing.

His younger brother Franklin rolled his eyes and made his usual disapproving noises. More than anyone, Franklin expressed dissatisfaction with Emile's way of life. He was happy enough for Emile to pay for his education and clothing, but he disliked all the fairy stuff in his brother's world. Franklin told Emile exactly what he thought. He should straighten himself out and live like a real man. Why didn't he settle down with Esther or another woman?

Gloria accepted him, and even teased Emile playfully about his boyfriends, but their mother chose a more tangled response. Emile did not hide the truth from her, and Emelda even met some of his friends who were far daintier than Calvin, but she never mentioned his sexuality. Emelda also knew Esther well and she liked the fact that she was a good Christian girl. She was a decent enough girlfriend for her special boy. But Emelda was certain that Emile needed her more than he needed Esther. As long as that fact remained unchanged and Junior looked after the family, and kept winning, she would yell out her support for him.

'You need to talk to Howie,' she said. 'He's got our money.'

Howie was the conciliator and he kept everyone happy. With a simple flourish of the cheque that he had picked up late the previous night from Teddy Brenner at the Garden, he said they should all rejoice in another great victory. In another six months, he predicted, Emile would be one of just eight men entitled to call himself a world champion boxer. The words thrilled everyone.

Six months, however, seemed a long way away. Emile suddenly remembered who stood in his path before he reached the champion Benny Paret. The thought suddenly scared him in a way that no other fight had ever done before. No ordinary opponent loomed over him.

Emile could not bring himself to say the name of '*El Feo*' – the Ugly One – out loud.

Howie patted Emile on the arm. 'Let's go see Gil,' he said. 'Gil will know what we gotta do . . .'

Emile Griffith had fought seven times in the first eight months of 1960. Teddy Brenner, his matchmaker, loved him because the kid would fight anyone and he brought in a noisy crowd. Griffith had already beaten Gaspar Ortega, who had racked up seventy previous bouts, when Brenner gave Gil Clancy a chilling message in the sultry summer of 1960: 'I wanna make Griffith with Florentino Fernandez . . .'

'Fernandez?' Clancy had replied in his Irish New York drawl. 'Are ya kidding?'

Clancy's left eye was almost completely blind. His vision had been impaired after a sliver of steel from a pneumatic drill flew into his face when he was just three years old. But you only needed one good eye to see that Fernandez's punching was vicious. According to Ortega, who lost twice to Fernandez in 1959, 'His eyes said: "I'm gonna kill you."' In his home town of Havana, Fernandez was revered as '*El Barbaro del Knockout*', for his left hook resembled a small incendiary device.

Brenner was canny. He promised Clancy that if Griffith beat Fernandez he could avoid an even more ominous Cuban fighter. The undefeated Luis Rodriguez, another cruel hard-hitter, was far more skilful than Fernandez.

Clancy left Brenner's office at Madison Square Garden to study film footage of Fernandez. After a while, the prospect of Griffith facing a pure puncher in *El Barbaro del Knockout* didn't seem quite so unsettling. Out of his good right eye, and the corner of his nearly blind left eye, Clancy saw a way to neuter Fernandez. He was a huge hitter but his blows came winging in from out wide. Griffith just needed to step inside with a jab and some swift combinations. His speed and dexterity would allow him to avoid Fernandez's biggest punches while he carved up the Cuban on the inside.

'Okay, Clancy,' Griffith had replied in his lilting Caribbean falsetto, 'you're the boss.'

When they stepped into the ring at the Garden on 25 August 1960, Griffith was so well prepared that Fernandez barely landed a punch. Griffith busted up *El Barbaro* so comprehensively that the winning margin on points was as wide as his huge smile.

Brenner could hardly contain himself. 'Now you gotta fight Rodriguez,' he'd urged Clancy.

'*Whaddya mean?*' Clancy yelled.

Brenner agreed that he had said they would have one more easy fight before getting a crack at Paret's title. But Emile had looked so good that he had no reason to fear Rodriguez. Who else but Emile – a young, beautiful and brilliant boxer – could take care of the Ugly One?

Two months later, Willie Toweel was meant to be a tune-up before Griffith faced *El Feo* in a final eliminator. Brenner had lingered over that word 'final' with relish as his white teeth gleamed.

Griffith versus Rodriguez, the gorgeous hatmaker against the Ugly One, would sell out the Garden. The ABC television executives would love the contrast in character, as well as another loaded clash between the United States and Cuba, while high up in the bleachers a more basic thirst for blood might be sated.

It would be a Saturday night treat for every fight fan in the week before Christmas. There was no escaping the savage truth. On 17 December 1960, Emile Griffith would face the Ugly One.

Emile and Esther sounded like a sweet fit. Even their names made a kind of match. Esther felt hope for the future surging inside her, despite knowing her boyfriend had a dangerous man on his mind. She was still oblivious to his nocturnal adventures with Calvin and simply believed he was immersed in the fight business. The closer he came to a difficult bout, the more he saw her. Emile was disciplined, especially in preparing for Rodriguez, and so he curtailed his trips to Times Square. He knew it was better for him to stay at home and rest in Queens. Esther came over regularly to visit him, as a distraction from the Ugly One, and he was always happy to see her.

Esther's visits, however, could be troubling for her. She could not be certain if boxing alone prevented Emile from committing himself more to their relationship. He seemed happy to allow everything between them to reside on a light and airy level. Emile did not talk in any depth to her. He told her nothing about his past on St Thomas, about being abused by the man who claimed to have been his uncle or the fact that he had ended up in a reformatory as a safe house. He kept her apart from Calvin, whom she had never met, and only introduced her to Gil and Howie as a way of proving to his managers that he also liked girls. She thought the two white men were 'pleasant enough', but Esther did not understand boxing. It was hard to know if they were as good for Emile as he always claimed. She concentrated less on boxing, anyway, than Emile's complicated relationship with his mother.

The more she saw Emile in the build-up to the forbidding fight with Rodriguez, the more Esther realised that the unspoken problem she sensed was rooted in his relationship with his mother. She tried to avoid judging people, but it finally became impossible for Esther to regard Emelda as a benign presence. Emile had always admitted that he was 'a momma's boy', and at first Esther had laughed along with him. She found it almost endearing. Esther did not know many other men who were confident enough to talk openly about how much they loved and even revered their mother.

Yet the bond between Emelda and Emile, between Mommy and Junior, became unsettling. Esther might have been innocent and even naive; but she was intelligent. She could no longer remain blind to the fact that Emelda was a controlling force. It was crucial that she kept a tight hold on her son. He always needed to be reminded that she was the most important person in his life – the woman who had given birth to him, cared for him and loved him more than anyone else. Emelda believed her maternal role gave her the unending right to reside at the very heart of her son's life. She made it plain that a mother would always be more important than a girlfriend. Esther began to wonder if Emelda would allow anyone, even a girl as mild and thoughtful as her, to become Emile's wife. It was as if she wanted Emile all to herself.

Emelda and Emile began to sound more of a match than Emile and Esther. The strangeness of it all confused the fighter's young girlfriend.

There was jealousy and resentment, too, whenever Emile tried to spoil Esther. He would buy her a gift but, even before he could give it to his girl, it would be annexed by his mother. And when he spoke about taking Esther away after the fight, Emelda moved in quickly. She needed a holiday. He should take her away first.

'Okay, Mommy,' Emile grinned, unaware of his mother's manipulation and its impact on the girl who loved him.

Esther tried to curb her dejection. She knew that he had more difficult and perilous battles ahead. But how could a 'momma's boy' withstand the power and the fury of *El Feo*?

*

On 8 November 1960, five weeks before he stepped back into the ring, Emile watched a fierce fight end in an outpouring of relief. The election of the thirty-fifth president of the United States of America had become a desperate battle for votes. Dwight Eisenhower, the immensely popular outgoing president, had campaigned hard on behalf of Richard Nixon and the Republican Party to close the gap on John F. Kennedy. Pollsters seemed unable to split the candidates, as the surge in JFK's popularity after the television debates was curbed by the experience of Eisenhower and Nixon.

The result was the closest in American political history – with 49.7 per cent of votes cast for the winner compared to 49.5 per cent for the defeated campaigner. Emile didn't care much for politics, but he liked the fact that Kennedy, at forty-three, would be the youngest man ever to become president. JFK was good-looking, a snappy dresser and married to a beautiful woman, Jackie, who wore hats with style. Emile was sure he could have a fine conversation with Jackie Kennedy about fashion, while her husband supported the Civil Rights movement and Martin Luther King.

JFK offered a new kind of hope. He made it possible, in a conservative and forbidding world, to believe in change and a fresh start.

'What a *mensch*,' Howie Albert said of JFK, while teaching Emile another Yiddish word.

Clancy, an Irish Catholic, could hardly believe it. The United States had just elected its first Catholic president. He told Emile, who shared his faith, that fear and prejudice had retreated a little during a momentous vote. Anything felt possible now.

Emile, crossing himself, was bolstered as he turned towards the frightening figure of *El Feo*.

CHAPTER THREE

The Ugly One, the Kid & His Girl

Luis Rodriguez had the legs of a dancer, the jab of a magician and the nose of a clown. Angelo Dundee, his trainer, didn't care about the huge nose. The Ugly One was the best boxer he had ever seen. Who cared what Vincent van Gogh looked like, ear or no ear, or that some pug-ugly writer could string together achingly beautiful words on paper? It was about the art, and the craft, for Dundee. *El Feo* had the gift. He was an artist of the ring, a Cuban master with an instinctive sense of balance, space, timing and power.

The smart-ass American sportswriters, who had followed Rodriguez for over a year, compared him to Cyrano de Bergerac. He had a nose almost as big as Cyrano but Luis didn't mind. 'Cyrano and I,' the exiled Cuban boxer said of the French writer, 'have more in common than our noses. We are both poets.'

Dundee had never seen a fighter with hands as quick as Rodriguez. He would say the same words fifty years later, long after he had trained Muhammad Ali and Sugar Ray Leonard throughout their astonishing careers. The Ugly One's hands moved with blurring symmetry – and, increasingly, with the devastating force of heavy weaponry. Ever since Rodriguez had settled in Miami in October 1959, and begun working at the 5th Street Gym, Dundee taught him to plant his feet and hit with hurtful solidity.

El Feo had been smart enough to read the language of the revolution. Fidel Castro, his brother Raul and the Argentine Marxist revolutionary, Che Guevara, had led the 26th of July Movement which, after six long years, had finally ended the dictatorship of Fulgencio Batista on 1 January 1959. Batista had fled Cuba for Spain the night before, on New Year's Eve, and the revolutionaries took charge.

Castro, who recognised the power of sport, especially boxing and baseball, suggested that, 'Our athletes are an example to the revolution.' But the charismatic, cigar-smoking, fatigue-wearing, fist-pumping bearded wonder also warned: 'We are in one of the most difficult periods in our history. Why? Because we're alone, confronting the empire. Only a weak, cowardly people surrenders and goes back to slavery.'

Rodriguez loved Cuba, and he could understand the idealism and guerrilla warfare of Castro and Guevara, but he felt uneasy whenever his new leaders denounced the evil of America. As an artist and a fighter, he preferred subtlety to crudity and Rodriguez feared that professional boxing would soon be banned in Cuba. Castro had begun to make fiery denunciations of the 'Americanisation', 'gangsterism' and 'capitalistic exploitation' of the fight game.

Kid Chocolate, the greatest Cuban fighter in history, who had since become the chief supervisor of boxing on the island, warned *El Feo* in private that the end loomed for the professional. He recognised Rodriguez's extraordinary talent and urged him to continue his career in the United States. It was non-revolutionary advice from one phenomenon of the ring to another, and Rodriguez took the plunge before Castro brought down the shutters of repression. He left Cuba for America with a 24-0 record.

You did not need to be especially sage to read the runes of Cuba. Two more Americans, found guilty of 'counter-revolutionary activities', had been executed by a Cuban firing squad in Havana, on 17 October 1960. Just before the final presidential debate between

Nixon and Kennedy, Castro declared that America's leading politicians were 'perfect imbeciles' and that 'our army is ready for battle'. The world had become a much more dangerous place.

It had once been very different. Kid Chocolate, the Cuban Bon Bon, had arrived in America in 1928 and established himself as the most delicious presence in world boxing and a hero in his homeland. His real name was Eligio Sardinias Montalvo but, at the age of eighteen, Kid Chocolate was a perfect alias. For a decade he dazzled the world with his brilliant flashiness and a big dipper of a right hand. Kid Chocolate enjoyed smiling so that he could show off his gold teeth, which shone in the middle of his round, luminous face. He only became angry if anyone dared touch his inky black hair, which was plastered down with an immaculate sheen that matched his dark chocolate-coloured skin.

Kid Chocolate engaged in two epic battles against Jack 'Kid' Berg, the Jewish Londoner who called himself the 'Whitechapel Windmill'. Berg fought like a man trying to smash his way out of a burning building and his intensity made a compelling contrast with the silky sweetness of the Cuban Bon Bon. Kid Chocolate lost both bouts on a split decision – but he became Cuba's first ever world champion in 1931. Chocolate fought all across America, as well as in Barcelona, Madrid and Paris.

Kid Chocolate was followed by Kid Gavilan who, in 1943, began another exuberant Cuban career. Gavilan, named Gerardo Gonzales at birth, was almost as flashy as Kid Chocolate. He wore white boxing shoes and his hair was shaped into an ostentatious pompadour – a rippling high sweep of hair which Madame de Pompadour, the mistress of King Louis XV, had originated in Paris in the eighteenth century. Gavilan's hairstyle complemented his outrageous bolo punch – a half-hook, half-uppercut, which he said was honed by all the years spent cutting sugar cane with a machete in Cuba.

Gavilan, also nicknamed the 'Cuban Hawk', first fought in America in November 1946 and, over a dozen years, he shared a ring with renowned fighters like Sugar Ray Robinson, Ike Williams, Rocky Castellani, Carmen Basilio, Bobo Olson and Gaspar Ortega. Robinson said Gavilan was the toughest man he ever faced – and the Hawk became Cuba's second world champion when he won the welterweight title in 1951.

A decade later Benny Paret, Luis Rodriguez and Florentino Fernandez ensured that Cuba claimed three of boxing's top ten welterweights in a fiercely competitive division. Rodriguez was regarded by fight connoisseurs as the best of the trio, for he had already beaten Paret twice in Havana. Many Cubans believed he would surpass even Kid Chocolate and Kid Gavilan. Rodriguez was also the most avoided welterweight in the business, which explained why Paret had been given a world title chance before him.

A young heavyweight called Cassius Clay would learn much from working in the same Miami gym as Rodriguez. Dundee had already told Clay: 'Watch Luis – he's the kind of fighter you want to be.'

Clay had pursued Dundee for months in the hope of convincing the trainer to run his corner. Bill Faversham, the head of the syndicate backing Clay, travelled to Miami in early December 1960. Dundee was preparing Rodriguez for Griffith but he struck a deal. He agreed to train Clay with one proviso. They could only start working together on Monday 19 December 1960, two days after Rodriguez would have surely given Griffith a beating at Madison Square Garden.

Cassius Clay liked to call himself pretty – but the Ugly One came first.

Madison Square Garden, New York, Saturday 17 December 1960

Eight weeks had passed since Emile Griffith stopped Willie Toweel in the Garden. His mood that night had been serious but supremely confident. He felt very different as Gil Clancy wrapped his hands in white gauze, bandaging them tenderly before the hurt began, as he waited for the moment he would face Luis Rodriguez. His hands trembled and Gil looked carefully at him out of his one working eye.

'You okay, Emile?' he asked quietly.

Emile nodded. He could not trust himself to talk. His mouth felt dry and he tried to lick his lips. Rodriguez held a flawless 35-0 fight record.

Clancy looked down and continued his work. He had never known Emile look and act scared before. Clancy didn't like it when the wiseguys joked about Emile being a fairy behind his back. There was nothing fairy-like about him in the ring. He was a brave and accomplished fighter. And so, eventually, he said those words out loud to Emile.

'One more thing,' Clancy murmured just before the knock came on the locker-room door. 'He's not that ugly either. It's only a nick-name. Rodriguez is just a man – like you.'

Emile Griffith still shook a little as he walked to the ring. The noise of the crowd flattened into a low din that echoed a long way outside his body. He felt lost to the world in a strange, brightly lit tunnel.

There was the usual commotion between the ropes and, in his satiny gown, he pumped his arms back and forth. In Rodriguez's corner, the Cuban jogged on the spot while Angelo Dundee watched impassively. He had weighed in at 148 pounds that afternoon, while Griffith scaled 147¾. They were that close.

The bellowing roar for each of them, when introduced by Johnny Addie, was marginally in favour of Griffith, the adopted New Yorker. He wore black trunks while *El Feo* chose pristine white. Griffith avoided looking into Rodriguez's stony face as the referee, Mark Conn, gave them their instructions. Clancy removed Griffith's gown only when they returned to the corner. And it was there, in the small and still place which would be his fleeting refuge at the end of every round, that Griffith knelt on one knee and crossed himself three times. It lasted mere seconds, but that silent request for help soothed him.

As he turned back to confront Rodriguez a clear thought entered his mind. He would later describe it in these words: '*I calmed down and when I saw that chunky Cuban coming at me, I thought: "Well, this is it, Emile, you got to stand up and be counted or get wiped off the face of the earth."*'

Griffith was the first to throw a jab as, at ringside, the ABC television commentator Don Dunphy said chattily, 'Both boys have darting left hands – and Rodriguez's is probably a little better.'

They settled into an early pattern, swapping jabs and body punches, only to smother each other's assault by clinching. A stinging left hand from Griffith was the first meaningful punch of the fight and it pushed Rodriguez back. Griffith swarmed towards him, driving the Cuban into a corner and pinning him against the ropes. He used his right arm, jammed tight against the throat, to push Rodriguez's head back. It was a dirty sign that Griffith, the sensitive milliner, might not be intimidated by *El Feo*. As they returned to the centre of the ring, Griffith landed a hard left hook which Rodriguez swallowed without blinking. They traded and held each other and Griffith, so much more muscled than the Cuban, looked the stronger man. But when Griffith connected, Rodriguez usually managed to counter with his own punch.

'Your round, Emile,' Clancy said emphatically when Griffith sat down on his stool at the end of the first. He felt more like his old self after just three minutes of fighting.

In the second, Griffith's combinations were wild and Rodriguez glided smoothly under them and kept on throwing his peppery jab. Griffith was more effective when fighting on the inside and he managed to hit the Ugly One to the body. But Rodriguez, settling into a malevolent rhythm, had won the round.

Griffith was more purposeful in the third and he rocked Rodriguez with a spiteful combination that sent the Cuban tottering backwards. Emelda Griffith screamed even more loudly – '*Junior! Junior! Get him, Junior!*' – as her apprehension turned to shrieking. She wore a new floral dress and hat, and waved her umbrella in the air. Emelda always carried an umbrella because, unlike back home in St Thomas, she thought it might start raining at any moment in New York. Rodriguez withstood the storm and they finished the round, which had gone to Griffith, by brawling in the middle of the ring.

Rounds four to six showed how they cancelled out each other's best attributes with their fast movement and solid defence. It was a bruising, prickly contest, which was devilishly difficult to score. Emelda Griffith was the only person who sounded certain she was backing a winner.

'Neither boy seems any the worse for wear,' Dunphy said in the middle of round seven. 'They're both in fine shape.' Griffith and Rodriguez still moved with a light bounce in their step, snapping out smooth jabs, but they were just as quick to tie each other up and blunt most attacks. It was almost as if they had too much respect for the excellence of each other's skills.

Griffith showed more intent at the start of the eighth, but Rodriguez again resorted to pinning his opponent's hands with his arms. Referee Conn had to break them apart repeatedly as the action became increasingly scrappy. It was not, as many had predicted, a beautiful fight between two purists of the ring. Instead, as they entered the final two rounds, it was a fractious contest.

'The issue is in the balance,' Dunphy growled into his microphone.

'C'mon, Emile,' Clancy yelled above the racket created by Emelda Griffith. But they slipped back into the same routine – forcing the ref to bark, 'Get outta the clinch. Let's keep this clean!'

Griffith poured forward but *El Feo* was determined to put a lock on him by holding him tight and preventing the left hand doing any damage to his unforgettable nose. A few boos and catcalls echoed around the Garden. With a minute left in the ninth, Griffith forced Rodriguez against the ropes and let his hands fly before he was pinned again by the Cuban's relentless arms.

'Get him, Junior!' Emelda Griffith implored.

At the start of the tenth and last round her beloved son climbed off the wooden stool. Clancy had already urged him to win the round as the fight was so close, but Griffith felt proud that he had found the courage to stand toe to toe with the Ugly One. He knew that some people mocked him as a faggot, but he had shown the Garden, again, that he was a fighter. Griffith no longer feared *El Feo* and they went at it one last time.

'There've been no knockdowns and no one's been hurt,' Dunphy confirmed. 'But it's been a dandy, a swell boxing exhibition all the way.'

At last Griffith found enough space to throw some combinations which landed. Rodriguez fired back and the uncertainty of the outcome deepened the tension. A familiar roaring returned to the Garden. They ended in a clinch and, at the bell, tapped each other's upper arm before turning away to their corners with the expectant air of winners.

They looked more nervous a few minutes later as, both dressed in their gowns, they waited for the decision. Johnny Addie finally walked to the centre of the ring.

'Referee Mark Conn has it 5-4 with one even,' he shouted before turning and pointing in the direction of the first favoured fighter. 'To Griffith!'

Addie held up his right hand for quiet and continued hollering into the microphone. 'Judge Bill Recht has it 6-4 ...' It looked as if Addie was about to point to Rodriguez but, suddenly, his hand gestured dramatically in the other direction. '*For Griffith!*'

An exuberant Griffith jumped straight into Clancy's arms while Addie, having ended the drama, shouted out that, 'The other judge, Tony Castellano, has it 5-4, one even, for Rodriguez.'

Griffith was back on his feet again, planting a big kiss on Clancy's forehead, as Addie completed the announcement. 'The winner by majority vote – *Griffith!*'

He raised his arms and walked quickly across the ring to meet Rodriguez. Griffith squeezed him tight and then turned to kiss Addie next. And, soon, Clancy and Howie Albert hoisted Griffith up on their shoulders in celebration as Rodriguez left the ring in dejection.

The Ugly One from Havana had lost for the first time; the beautiful boy from Charlotte Amalie had earned a crack at the world title. Emile Griffith was ready to become a champion.

Benny 'Kid' Paret lit another Camel and pressed the icepack against his swollen face. He sucked smoke deep into his lungs and nodded wearily as his wife, Lucy, offered him a couple of aspirin for his headache. She mixed his usual drink, a stiff slug of Hennessy and pineapple juice. Benny had fought the previous night in Los Angeles, on 25 February 1961, and lost on points against Gaspar Ortega – the vastly experienced Mexican.

Lucy loathed the vicious business of boxing. She feared what it might do to Benny if he kept on fighting. Lucy knew it had brought them together, for she would never have met Benny had he not left the sugar-cane fields of Cuba for the boxing rings of New York. She also knew that their new apartment in Miami, where they lived with their baby son, Benny Jr, could not have been bought but for the fact he was a world champion boxer. But nothing could soften her dislike of the ring.

The fight had been screened live on ABC and she had struggled to watch the small black-and-white television in the corner of the same room where she tended to her battered husband. Lucy didn't care that he had lost to Ortega at the Olympic Auditorium in LA – and Benny said it didn't matter much because it was a non-title contest. Ortega won the fight, but Benny remained world welterweight champion. As long as he was all right, and his head didn't throb too much, she was happy. He was home.

Lucy had been born in Puerto Rico and grew up in New York. She was still getting used to the idea that Miami had become their home. It was different for Benny. Only ninety miles of ocean separated Miami from Havana and he enjoyed pretending, on clear days, that he could see the island if he squinted hard enough in the shimmering sunshine.

Fifty thousand Cuban refugees had fled to Miami since the revolution – and still more arrived every day, either on Pan American flight 422 from Havana or across the sea by boat. The *Herald* reported that 900 new Cubans fled every week and that Miami would soon be declared a 'distressed area' by the Department of Labor. Unemployment was rising and there was increasing resentment among both white and black locals of Cubans seeking jobs. At least Benny did not need to stand in a job or welfare line. He had his fists and hard head to keep them going.

Lucy spoke a little Spanish and Benny had just a smattering of English. He kept promising he would try to learn English, but he was always too busy fighting, or recovering, to concentrate on anything as boring as a new language. When he did have time to himself, the Kid preferred dancing to talking.

Benny's family lived in Santa Clara in the central region of Cuba. They were so poor that Benny, one of eight children, had to leave school and work in the same sugar-cane fields as his father. By the time he started fighting professionally, when he was just seventeen in 1954, he earned $2 a day as a cane cutter. Boxing promised a much better way of making money.

Between the plantation and the ring, Benny had never learned to read or write. Lucy felt a tug of sadness whenever she saw how, closing in on his twenty-fourth birthday, he struggled to sign his name on yet another boxing contract he could not understand. Yet Benny would have been condemned to the plantation his whole life had it not been for boxing. It was the reason, he tried to tell her, she should love boxing rather than hate it. His fast hands and incredible punch resistance had changed their lives forever. Benny Paret had become a world champion boxer in America rather than a cane cutter in Cuba.

Fidel Castro had followed his career closely. Shortly before Benny fought for the world title, against Don Jordan in Las Vegas on 27 May 1960, Castro had sent him a telegram. Benny could not read it, but his manager, Manuel Alfaro, who had brought him from Santa Clara to New York, smiled his curious smile as he told Benny what Castro had said:

'*I won my revolution. Now it's up to you to win your battle.*'

Castro and the revolutionaries felt an affinity with Santa Clara. Che Guevara and his men had hidden in the hills above the city, secluded near the top of Loma del Capiro, while they planned their final assault in late December 1959. The rebels had expected it would take months to defeat the government forces, but, inspired by Che, the Battle of Santa Clara was over in a few days. It was the decisive conflict of the revolution and, twelve hours after Santa Clara fell, the Batista regime had crumbled.

Benny Paret was a son of Santa Clara and so Castro placed special emphasis on his world title fight against an American. Castro's television interviews usually lasted for four hours but, on the night of the fight, he cut his appearance to forty minutes because, as he told reporters, 'I want to let Cubans see Kid Paret win the world's welterweight boxing championship.' He had promised viewers that America's threat to take economic and political action against Cuba is 'of no importance whatsoever to us. The Cuban revolution is invincible and we cannot be intimidated.'

The Kid felt far less invincible – even though he was in better shape than Don Jordan. A combination of managerial and marital problems, complicated by his drinking habits, had turned Jordan into a shambling version of a world champion. Three months before he fought Paret, Jordan was found guilty of driving while drunk and the judge, who fined him heavily, warned, 'You are on a one-way ticket to skid row.'

Jordan was guaranteed $85,000 for his title defence, but he agreed to sign over all the money to his former managers, to escape his existing contract, and his ex-wife, who was also suing him. Sly old Don, however, refused at the last minute to walk to the ring at the Convention Center unless he was given $2,000 in 'expenses'. Jordan boxed listlessly, like a man fighting for peanuts, and Paret won a wide verdict.

The new champion displayed his extremely limited English in the locker room as, beaming in delight, he spoke a few of the phrases he had learned since arriving in America: 'Money – I love you' and 'I slippy'. The newspapermen translated the last word, correctly, as 'sleepy' and decided that Paret, even as a dozy and illiterate Cuban, was a more deserving world champion than a bad egg like Jordan. Paret came to fight and he was willing to take plenty of hard punches to land a big one of his own.

His first title defence had been another of Teddy Brenner's 'Date Night' specials at the Garden, a week before Griffith and Rodriguez squared off. It was a gruesome date between Paret and his old adversary Frederico Thompson. The Cuban and the Argentine had fought a violent draw at Madison Square Garden nine months earlier – but even that crude slugfest could not prepare anyone for their rematch.

In the third round, a slashing right hand from Paret split Thompson's top lip with such force that blood spurted in a way which suggested that either an artery or a bottle of heavy claret had been opened. The red stuff covered both fighters and the referee. At the end of each three-minute burst of bleeding and hitting, Thompson's corner managed to slow the gory flow to a trickle. It did not help much because Paret soon opened up Thompson's gash again, as well as a cut across the dented bridge of his nose, while absorbing some terrible punishment of his own on the way to a unanimous decision in his favour.

Afterwards, in another locker-room encounter with the press, the reigning champion spoke in Spanish. His words were translated by his manager. 'Benny says,' Alfaro explained, 'he never feels a punch. He says Thompson hits hard but Benny never felt the punches.'

'Then how does he know that Thompson hits hard?' a wiseguy cackled.

Alfaro, a short, thick-set man who saw dollar signs whenever he looked at Paret, shrugged. It was hot in the basement and his fighter looked exhausted. 'He can feel,' he said of Paret, 'but it don't hurt him.'

The pain was bearable when Paret's pay packet was the biggest of his career – $28,000 compared to the $5,000 he had picked up for winning the title.

It was part of Alfaro's money-making plan that Paret would fight regular non-title bouts – and, besides his defeat to Ortega, he had lost a split decision to Denny Moyer and beaten Garnet Hart. The serious stuff would begin again on 1 April 1961, when he met Griffith. His title would be on the line, but they were five weeks away from the bout. The champ could afford one more Camel and another shot of Hennessy.

Lucy had just settled little Benny Jr and she smiled at her husband as, seeing him relax and push the icepack to one side, she made him another drink. She was only twenty and had not expected life to end up this way. When she first met Benny in 1958, all Lucy really wanted to do was dance – rather than fall pregnant and get married.

At sixteen, Lucy Hernandez had lost her mother. An unexpected death was followed by the suicide of Lucy's sister. Her father remarried and his second wife, wanting a clean break from his turbulent past, told Lucy she needed to move out and start a new life. Broke and bereft, but able to dance, she found work at various Latin clubs in the Bronx and Harlem. Lucy was happiest at the Tropicana, which had been opened as a nightclub and restaurant in the Bronx by Manuel Alfaro and his brother Tony, in 1945. Life as a Tropicana showgirl helped Lucy buy food and clothes, and pay the weekly $5 rent for the room she shared with an elderly woman two blocks from the club.

The showgirls at the Tropicana were known as '*Las Diosas de Carne*' (the Flesh Goddesses) and they had danced behind Josephine Baker, Carmen Miranda and Nat King Cole. For a teenage girl from the Bronx, the Tropicana was a world like no other. It stretched across 36,000 square metres and, lined with palm trees and two stages and dance-floors, attracted stars like Edith Piaf, Ernest Hemingway, Marlon Brando, Jimmy Durante, Sammy Davis Jr and Benny Paret as customers.

Lucy was just one of fifty showgirls employed by the Alfaro brothers at the Tropicana. When Manuel Alfaro decided to form a Benny Paret Fan Club, consisting entirely of Tropicana showgirls, Lucy was happy to join the gang and scream for the Cuban boxer at the St Nicholas Arena. Benny had knocked out Andy Figaro in the first round. He also noticed Lucy that night, in November 1958. She was the only one of the showgirls in his impromptu fan club who, the very next morning, received a beautiful bouquet. No one had ever sent Lucy flowers and she was smitten. She understood that Benny was famous in the Bronx; and she loved to watch him dance at the Tropicana.

When Benny took to the dance-floor, everyone moved to one side to give the Kid space to move. He danced the rumba, the cha-cha and a mean mambo. The salsa surged through him, turning his body liquid while lighting up his face with happiness. Benny, usually, looked pensive and even sad when he was not dancing. He carried the grind of the cane cutter, and the seriousness of the ring, in his expression when he was away from the music and bourbon. But as soon as the rhythmic heat of the salsa exploded across a dance-floor, Benny stripped off his fighter's mask. He lost himself in joyful delirium.

Benny had been much quieter when, a day after she had received his flowers, he turned up at the club to ask her out on a date. It was hard for Lucy to understand him. His Spanish was too quick for her, and even her simplest form of English did not really register with Benny. He just grinned at her, looking away when she smiled back. Eventually, he spoke again in Spanish. Could he take her out one night?

Yes, you can, the showgirl eventually said to the boxer. '*Sí, se puede.*'

Benny took Lucy and the old lady who shared her rented room out on their first date. Lucy knew she would look cheap if she did not have a chaperone. It helped Benny behave like a gentleman even if, when the elderly woman was distracted, he gazed at Lucy with an expression which told her silently that he really, really liked her. He wanted her too. Even without a shared language, they understood each other as well as any young couple going out for their first night together.

Lucy soon cast aside her chaperone. She loved being with Benny – especially when they danced and laughed. He was lithe and graceful, with a much harder and slimmer body than her own, but she sensed his past troubles. Benny did not seem much like a hard man to Lucy. He looked more like a boy who had felt a lot of pain.

Lucy had heard men around the Tropicana swear in wonder when they discussed how the Kid could take a punch without even blinking, let alone wincing. She thought differently. Benny was more vulnerable than anyone imagined – it made her care for him even more deeply.

She was seventeen when she moved into Benny's apartment on the Southern Boulevard in the heart of the Bronx. And Lucy was eighteen when she gave birth to their son – Benny Jr. They married a month later and, three months after that, Benny Paret became world welterweight champion when he beat Don Jordan.

He returned home to the Bronx from Vegas in ecstasy – convinced they were on their way to becoming millionaires. Lucy was less sure, and she always felt uncomfortable when Manuel Alfaro was around. It looked as if Alfaro thought he actually owned Benny. He had brought the Kid from Cuba and turned him into a television fighter in America – but Benny took all the punches and suffered the bruises and headaches. Lucy wondered if more money went to the manager than to his fighter.

Benny did not want to discuss contracts and deals. He just wanted to let go of boxing when he was with her and Benny Jr – saying, 'My son, my son . . .', while he held the baby. Lucy was happy when he promised her that he would never let little Benny become a fighter. He had far grander plans in mind for his son. Benny Jr would be a doctor or a lawyer one day.

On such nights, over a couple of cigarettes and some Hennessy,

Benny would confess his deepest secret. He did not want to be a fighter for too much longer. It was too hard. His head hurt so bad that he knew he would not be able to lie again on his side when they finally went to bed. He would have to stretch out flat on his back and wait for sleep.

Benny had a dream. It was a simple but lovely dream. He would live with Lucy and Benny Jr and however many other children they had in the years to come. They would stay in Miami and he would no longer be a boxer. He would have enough money to run a business of his own. And he knew the exact kind of business that would suit him best. Benny 'Kid' Paret dreamed of, one day, becoming a butcher.

They called Miami the 'Magic City'. At Paret's gym, a steaming hot-house rather than an icy abattoir, they made the most of that snappy nickname. The Magic City Gym was run by Lou Black, a crusty old trainer who insisted on lending his name to the joint where they studied pugilism. He had even painted the home-made sign outside, which welcomed everyone to Lou Black's Magic City Gym.

Benny Paret had decided he better get used to calling Magic City his fighting home. He would never box in Cuba again. On 23 February 1961, two days before he'd fought Ortega in Los Angeles, Fidel Castro had banned professional boxing in Cuba. Castro insisted that the professional fight business was 'a parasite' of America, which would suck the blood from Cuba's finest athletes. Only amateur boxing would be allowed in Cuba. Any Cuban who defied the law would be imprisoned or condemned to exile.

There was little surprise in Castro's announcement. Paret, Luis Rodriguez, Florentino Fernandez, Isaac Logart, Sugar Ramos and the other US-based Cuban professionals had discussed the situation among themselves for months. Castro might have made much of Paret becoming world champion but, since then, he had ensured that Cuba aligned itself openly with the Soviet Union. He had also nationalised the last remaining American companies in Cuba and threatened further retaliation in response to US imperialism. In

January 1960, the United States had terminated all diplomatic relations with Cuba. It was becoming increasingly difficult to travel between the countries and so, at the start of 1961, Paret had returned home for a brief visit to his mother. He did not know if he would ever see her or Cuba again.

The Miami boxing writers were mystified while watching Paret prepare for his defence against Griffith. It was as if all hope had been drained out of him by Castro's decision to outlaw professional boxing. Paret allowed himself to be hit so hard and so often that the reporters grimaced as they observed the champ being beaten up by his sparring partners Bobby Shaw, Glen Holloway and Ike Vaughn.

Those hard-bitten gym rats looked like typical journeymen, with bent noses and ridged scar tissue that had replaced much of their eyebrows. They tore into the seemingly helpless figure of the Cuban as if each one of them was a champion. Vaughn suggested that, 'Benny will let you hit him several times if he thinks he can hit you back.'

The dubious Manuel Alfaro, described by Edwin Pope in the *Miami Herald* as 'Paret's courtly manager', reiterated that, 'Benny does not seem to feel punches. He lets his sparring partners abuse him as much as they like. I can sit him down in a corner and walk away and he will sit there for three hours without saying a word. He might just listen to music and if you speak he does not hear. You have to pinch him several times before he looks at you.'

Alfaro shrugged when asked if he was concerned about the damage being done to Paret. 'We don't like him to do it that way, but he says it helps him get ready for a fight. He trains one way and fights another. When we were in New York some bookies came around to see him train for Federico Thompson. They ran out very fast and bet on Thompson. You know how that one came out? Paret in fifteen.'

Pope suggested that Paret only ever said one word. He replied, '*Bien, bien*' whether Pope asked how he felt, how sparring had gone or to describe his mood before meeting Griffith.

'But just why he is saying "good, good" this close to Saturday's title fight remains a mystery,' Pope wrote on 26 March 1961. 'Paret seems to enjoy being bashed up. It is as though he is bound by some special Benny Paret Rule that compels him to accept four punches for every one he throws.'

The boxing writers feared for him when, at the end of another seemingly disastrous sparring session, the expressionless Cuban sat on a chair away from the ring. Sweat poured down his face, like tears, and he looked lost to the world. At least he would earn $45,000 for fighting Griffith.

'I hope he saves it,' Pope wrote of Paret's fight purse. 'No matter the result against Griffith on Saturday, Benny Paret looks good for about one more year in the big leagues. No man can go on indefinitely absorbing as much as Benny Paret and still be as much of a man.'

CHAPTER FOUR

Glory in Miami

Emile Griffith liked the 5th Street Gym from the moment he stepped inside its crumbling interior. On the corner of Fifth and Washington in Miami Beach, you could hear the rats scurrying and bugs scuttling whenever there was a rare break in the reassuring beat of the heavy bag being hit or the speed ball going *whappity-whappity-whap* as another fighter went to work. It was a stinky down-at-heel place, in a seedy neighbourhood, and it made Emile feel as if he was back on Times Square.

The gym had been opened in 1950 by Chris and Angelo Dundee, two Italian brothers drawn to boxing's shadowy business. Luis Rodriguez was their star and Chris, promoting the Paret–Griffith title fight on 1 April, worked the phones at his desk in a corner of the gym while Angelo took charge of training.

Cassius Clay, the beautiful young black heavyweight, amused Emile when he got involved in the build-up to the world heavyweight title fight between Floyd Patterson and Sweden's Ingemar Johansson. It was the third time they would meet in less than nine months and each man had won one bout. There were no decent sparring partners for the Swede in Miami and Harold Conrad, who helped promote the deciding fight, asked Angelo Dundee if anyone could help.

'Yeah,' Dundee said before shouting out to Clay: 'Hey, Cash, c'mon over.'

Clay ambled across the gym floor as Dundee popped the question: 'You wanna work with Johansson?'

'Johansson?' Clay said as his eyes opened wide. He was too cute to offer a simple 'yes'. Instead, he started to shimmy and holler: '*I'll go dancin' with Johansson . . . I'll go dancin' with Johansson!*'

'What the hell is this?' Conrad asked.

Dundee smiled the smile of a man who had worked with Clay for almost seven weeks. 'You ain't seen nothing yet with this crazy bastard.'

Clay taunted Johansson and outboxed him. 'C'mon, sucker, what'ssa matter?' he mocked the former world champion with all the cheek a five-fight novice could muster. 'Can't ya catch me? I'm the one who should be fighting Patterson – not you!'

His jab snaked out and hit Johansson again and again. The Swede's trainer, the venerable Whitey Bimstein, ended their sparring session after two humiliating rounds.

'I took the palooka to school,' Clay told Griffith.

Emile could not quite believe how Clay spoke to the reporters who were there to watch him prepare for Paret. Clay held court on subjects ranging from his own brilliance to Angelo Dundee's suitability as a trainer. 'I like Angelo, 'cause he's half-coloured,' Clay joked. 'He's Italian and passes for white, but he sure got a lot of nigger in him. Everybody likes Angelo. He's got the connection and the complexion to get me the right protection, which leads to good affection.'

The place rocked with laughter. But Emile noticed how silent Clay fell whenever Rodriguez stepped into the ring. Clay watched the Cuban with eerie seriousness. He loved studying Rodriguez's sweet boxing skills and fluid movement, and it made Emile feel proud that he had beaten the Cuban three months earlier. Pat Putnam, in the *Miami Herald*, called Emile the 'Cuban-Killer', because he had already conquered Kid Fichique, Florentino Fernandez and Luis Rodriguez. Benny Paret was next.

Clay encouraged him. 'If you can beat the Ugly One, who is so damn fine, you can beat anyone.'

'Thanks, champ,' Emile said.

'Champ?' Clay replied. 'Now ya talkin' . . .'

Easter arrived in Miami. The Paret–Griffith fight was scheduled for Saturday night, and Cuba dominated the news. There were fears that a plot to kidnap Caroline Kennedy, the president's three-year-old daughter, had been instigated by Castro's supporters. The story was splashed across the front pages as Pierre Salinger, the White House's press secretary, admitted the secret service had doubled its forces as they guarded the president and his family on vacation in Palm Springs.

The previous day, on Good Friday, the Cuban government had arrested fifty Catholics who were part of a procession of 70,000 people that had marched through Havana chanting in favour of Christianity rather than communism: 'Cuba, *sí*, Russia, *no!*' and 'Long live Christ the King!' Thirty miles south of Havana, in Guines, police had rounded up the entire cast re-enacting the Passion Play and fired submachine guns over the heads of the crowd.

Paret, Cuba's only world champion, was the betting favourite against Griffith – but the *Herald* suggested that, with gamblers swaying towards the American against a tense backdrop, 'there is a chance it could be an even-money contest by fight-time tonight.'

Miami Beach Convention Hall, Miami, Saturday 1 April 1961

Benny 'Kid' Paret was plastered across the front of the official programme. In the black-and-white photograph he pummelled a speed ball with bandaged hands. It was obvious he was the world champion, for the challenger only featured on pages four and five. In an article for the programme called 'This One Figures to Be a Real Scrap', the boxing writer Herb Lowe began with a pertinent question for Griffith:

'Can a 23-year-old boy, with only two years of professional boxing experience, become the champion of his division?'

In his hushed locker room, Emile said little. Boxing was hard, and it could be scary. He still would have preferred making ladies' hats to punching dangerous men in the face. Howie Albert had liked the last hat Emile had designed for him with his small, deft hands. It was a pretty floral bonnet, featuring a dainty lace veil, and Emile had placed it on his manager's desk with bashful pride. Howie knew instantly that the design would sell. It told him again that Emile really could become a hatmaker. But Howie was certain Emile would be a better, and richer, fighter. A world title fight proved him right.

Lowe made no mention of Emile's bonnet-making expertise – or the more shocking fact that he was a homosexual. His copy was bound to the rigours and conundrums of the ring. However, he did allude to the fact that Benny and Emile were acquaintances, if not quite friends.

Benny and Emile had known each other a while, and sometimes they'd even played a couple of pick-up basketball games together. Emile often went up to Gleason's, then based in the Bronx, to see Calvin. His friend worked on the front desk at the gym, while Benny sparred or skipped. They got along fine and, occasionally, they joined another bunch of guys on the local court. Benny never let on if he knew anything about Calvin and Emile's private life. He just grinned and tried to beat them at basketball.

In terms of age, height and weight, little separated Benny and Emile. They were both twenty-three and 5 feet 7½ inches tall. Emile had weighed in that afternoon at 145½ pounds. Benny had scaled 146½ pounds. Emile might have been fractionally lighter but he looked more imposing. His chest expanded to 43 inches, while Benny's reached just 38. Emile's reach was also longer – 72 inches compared to 69 – and his thighs were a couple of inches thicker. He was happy to be slimmer around the waist – 27 inches to Paret's 29½. The tale of the tape would reveal less than the size of their hearts.

Emile seemed calm as Clancy laid out his eight-ounce gloves, the colour of dried blood, and then wrapped his hands.

One of Paret's cornermen stood quietly over them, ensuring that nothing illegal was done during the wrapping. In the champion's locker room, Syd Martin, Clancy's assistant trainer, observed the same protocol as Paret's hands were prepared by his trainer.

Outside, in a distant section of the arena, a Cuban salsa band became increasingly loud in anticipation of the fight. But Paret looked in the mood to fight rather than dance.

It was different at ringside. Emile's mother and his cousin, Bernard Forbes, were ready to drown out the band with their screaming for Junior. Emelda wore a shimmering white beaded dress and a fluffy Easter bonnet, while Bernard was dressed in a yellow shirt, white trousers and blue suspenders.

The boxers were draped in traditional gear as they made their long walk to the ring. Griffith was clad in black, Paret in white.

Griffith bowed politely when he was announced as the challenger, while Paret raised his arms and did a skittering mambo after being hailed as the world welterweight champion. They were brought together by the referee, Jimmy Peerless, who said, conversationally, into the booming microphone, 'Fellers, you received your instructions this afternoon and I'm here to enforce them rules. When I tell ya to break, I want ya to break clean and watch yourself at all times. Shake hands now and come out fighting.'

They had been here before, with forty-seven professional fights for Paret and twenty-seven for Griffith. Peerless encouraged them by saying, more softly, 'Good fight.' They wheeled away to their corners for the final prelude.

Clancy removed the gown and then Griffith, as always, went down on one knee and crossed himself. Slowly, he turned to face Paret in a twenty-foot ring for the championship of the world.

Paret was the busier and more aggressive fighter in the opening two rounds, shading the scorecards thanks to his quick feet and slick body-punching. His ability to absorb a hard blow was also obvious in between a cautiously probing opening and occasional clinching.

'The referee, Jimmy Peerless, is saying "break" in both English and Spanish,' Don Dunphy told millions of television viewers. 'He's a linguist.'

Before the third round, Griffith spat into the bucket that had been placed between his feet. Martin, a cornerman with thirty-two years of professional boxing behind him, methodically smeared Vaseline over his fighter's eyes. As head trainer, Clancy put on a small display of vicious body-punching to encourage Griffith to switch the focus of his attack. Howie Albert just made sure the iron bucket was still positioned correctly in a business less sophisticated than the millinery trade.

Paret leaned back in his own corner, as if relaxing in an armchair with a Camel and a shot of Hennessy and pineapple. Instead, it was also Vaseline, a spit bucket and a slug of water supplied by his cornermen – Joe Di Maria, Luis Gonzales and Manuel Alfaro.

In a timely reminder to the champion that he was in a place thick with hurt, Griffith shook Paret with a couple of sharp crosses. They unleashed a roaring to drown out the band's bongo drums and saxophones.

'They're starting to hit harder,' Dunphy suggested into his microphone. Two shuddering left hooks by Griffith, and a short right uppercut, split Paret's left eyebrow. It had been a big round for the challenger.

The fourth was even but the fifth went to Griffith, as two scything right crosses again hurt Paret. He also pushed the champion back onto the ropes and outworked him on the inside, ending with a flourish as he landed lefts and rights to Paret's defiant jaw.

Griffith seemed to take a rest from the sixth to the ninth as, drawing breath, he allowed Paret back into the fight and the champion stole the rounds on work rate. 'There's a lot of science in this fight if you watch them in close,' Dunphy told his audience. 'I'd say it's a pretty close fight right now – even if the champion has definitely taken charge at this point. Both boys are pacing themselves to go the full fifteen.'

Warned by Clancy that he was losing narrowly, Griffith edged the tenth round despite being belted by a jolting left. He finished strongly and three right hands, thrown in blurring tandem, sent Paret reeling back to the ropes. Paret was hurt and Griffith tagged him with a left just before the bell. Griffith was back in the fight as the hall seethed with noise.

'Listen to the crowd,' Dunphy yelped, knowing such a primal sound said more than any elegant commentary. But he tried to temper the fervour: 'I've got a problem for young Emile Griffith – he's never gone fifteen rounds. Paret has gone fifteen rounds twice. We're looking in on Paret's corner, where there is a little bit of con-sternation. Paret has gone the fifteen-round distance against Frederico Thompson and Don Jordan – winning both of them. But Emile Griffith has never gone beyond ten rounds.'

The television cameras swung towards the challenger's corner. 'There's Gil Clancy,' Dunphy explained as the trainer hunched over Griffith, punching the air with deadly combinations. 'He's giving Griffith the merry-what-not over there. Coming up to round eleven of a fifteen-rounder and it's very, very close.'

Paret looked tired and listless as Griffith sank right uppercuts to the head and heart and left hands to the gut. As usual, Paret fired back when hurt. Griffith had still won the round on two of the score-cards, with the third making it an even 10-10. After eleven rounds, referee Peerless and judge Stu Winston both had Paret winning by a point. Judge Bunnie Lovett scored the fight by the same margin in favour of Griffith.

Paret appeared rejuvenated when they came out for the twelfth and he out-hustled Griffith. Even when swallowing a couple of body shots and a right cross, Paret powered forward. 'He's a game little fighter, that Benny Paret,' Dunphy enthused.

Clancy had had enough. He ducked between the ropes with real intent. A cotton swab was tucked behind his left ear and he lowered his head to be at eye level with Griffith. To Clancy, it was so obvious what needed to be done that his voice rose angrily above the crowd. He told Griffith how easy it was for him to get under Paret's right hand and nail him with a left hook, which would win him the fight.

As the cameras caught the masterclass in Griffith's corner, Dunphy enthused that, 'Clancy is a fine teacher of battling.'

Clancy might have been an erudite schoolteacher, with his various degrees, but he knew that talking was not enough. As his fighter looked down meekly, Clancy slapped Griffith across the cheek. It was a stinging rebuke that got Griffith's attention more clearly than any of Paret's previous punches. The young fighter looked up, his eyes opened wide, and he stared at the man he considered a second father.

'Wake up, Emile!' Clancy exhorted, his eyes blazing as he urged Griffith again to start throwing his hook. 'Don't you know you're fighting for the championship of the world? Get out there and start fighting!'

Griffith came out for the thirteenth with more bounce in his step and steel in his gaze. Paret kept him at bay for a minute and then, as if Clancy was still chattering inside his head, Griffith took a short step forward and threw a withering left hook. It caught Paret square on the jaw. The Cuban tottered backwards and Griffith moved fast, nailing Paret with another hook and following it with a right. Paret collapsed in a heap on his back. As Peerless picked up the count, the fallen champion managed to roll over. He propped himself on his left side as he gazed vacantly into the darkened crowd.

The referee shouted out the numbers – '... *three ... four ... five ...*' – and flashed his arm in front of Paret's dazed face as if he wanted to give the champion every chance to recognise the severity of his count.

In the second row from ringside, a white woman bounced up and down in crazy excitement, using her left arm in a scything motion, chopping up and down, as she echoed the Peerless count with glee.

'... *six ... seven ... eight ...*'

Paret did not even try to move. He just lay on his side, like a man staring at his early morning alarm clock but feeling too befuddled to even know how he might find the energy to shut it off.

After he had yelled '... *nine!*' into Paret's empty face, Peerless brought both hands down in a decisive scissoring motion. '*Ten!*'

The referee turned away, only to be shocked as a figure hurtled towards him like a missile.

Griffith had not been able to stop himself. He leaped straight at the referee, his legs flying high above the canvas. The new champion realised his mistake just as he was about to land with a thud inside the startled embrace of Jimmy Peerless. He twisted his body and Peerless dropped him. Griffith turned his roll into a somersault.

Clancy, his intended target, was in the ring and as soon as Griffith got back to his feet he jumped at his trainer. This time he got his man. Clancy caught him and they danced around the ring. Howie Albert and Syd Martin had to hold Emile up to stop him falling again.

Emile flung his head back in disbelief. Howie jumped up and down and waved his hands in the air.

Hysterical shrieking broke out as a plump figure in white careered towards them, aiming for Emile with one hand holding onto her hat as she screamed: '*My baby ... my baby!*'

Emelda Griffith hugged her son and then, overcome with emotion, promptly fainted. It was left to the redoubtable pair of Clancy and Albert to catch her. She was much heavier than her son and, with great effort, the co-managers hauled her prostrate body to the corner. They managed to prop Emelda up on the fighter's stool, which looked tiny beneath her limp frame, while Howie fanned her with a towel.

Amid the chaos, her beautiful 23-year-old baby walked around the ring. He held his arms aloft and allowed the joy to pour out of him. Emile Griffith was a world champion.

He was also a Saturday night television fighter and so he and Clancy were soon cornered by Don Dunphy, wearing a tuxedo. An

ABC microphone was waved at them and, after he had been con-
gratulated, Griffith looked suddenly shy. 'Thank you,' he said. 'It
was a very great fight.'

'What do you think about Benny "Kid" Paret?' Dunphy asked.

'He's a good boy,' Griffith said simply.

Paret approached them quietly and Griffith kissed him on the
cheek. 'Good luck to you, Benny, you're a fine champion,' Dunphy
said before turning back to the new hero.

'Emile . . .' he began, trying to regain his attention.

'Yes, sir?' Griffith replied politely as, at the same time, Syd Martin
cut the gloves from his hands.

'Any plans?' Dunphy asked. 'Have you got a return match in your
contract?'

Clancy leaned across to confirm, in his New York drawl, that,
'We'll give Benny a return match. We think he's a good, tough
fighter. He was a good champion and we'll be glad to give him a
return.'

Griffith looked across the ring at the lonely sight of Paret leaving
the ring. His head was bowed and covered by a white towel. The
former champion looked a broken man.

Emile and his team celebrated until the early hours of Sunday morning at Jimmy Grippo's nightclub, 21, on Miami Beach. Grippo was a
magician and former fight manager. He wore thick-rimmed glasses
and resembled a nervous used-car salesman who, somehow, had a
knack of attracting famous movie stars and sportsmen to his club.
The fight press also packed Grippo's joint in the hope of discover-
ing more about the new champion with the fluting voice, prancing
walk and deadly left hook.

They soon uncovered a story that intrigued them. Switching back
and forth between a shyly smiling Griffith and his genial managers,
they learned a little about his character. Leading writers like the
grizzled Jimmy Cannon, who had coined the famous line about Joe
Louis being 'A credit to his race – the human race', had never met

a boxer who openly admitted he wished he could have become a ladies' hat designer.

Cannon rattled off his copy the next day, telling the extraordinary story of Emile Griffith, beneath a headline which said: 'No Frills On The Mighty Milliner's Crown'. 'Griffith, an elegantly mannered kid, held a handkerchief to his bruised ear and explained that he was a reluctant fighter forced into becoming a champion,' Cannon wrote in a column syndicated across the country. 'Born in the Virgin Islands, Griffith went to work for Howard Albert, Inc., makers of ladies' hats, in Manhattan's garment district as a stockroom boy. Eventually, he would design some bonnets and picked up side money by posing for artists.

'The apprentice milliner, a slender boy, pinch-waisted and broad-shouldered, sat in leg-clutching pants and, although only a champion for a couple of hours, was being asked for autographs. A fat man came up to Griffith and scrutinized him with awed inquisitiveness. The stranger held out his hand and Griffith shook it. "I just wanted to shake your hand, champ," he said.'

Tommy Devine, the sports editor of the *Miami News*, exalted in the surreal fact that 'a hat trimmer in a New York millinery factory, who didn't want to be a prize fighter, is the new world welterweight champion'. The *Miami Herald*, meanwhile, hailed 'a twenty-three-year-old hat designer from Manhattan who whacked the world welterweight crown from the aching dome of Benny (Kid) Paret... hats off to a very different kind of champion'.

Emile Griffith was a king and a queen rolled into one. Wherever he went in New York, he was hailed as royalty. 'Hey, champ!' he would be greeted. A small crowd formed around him and people cried out: 'Champ, champ! Great work!' In 1961, boxing still had the power to make a new world champion, one of just eight men on earth, immensely popular. These were undisputed giants of the land, who were loved and revered. Emile was mobbed in the street and whisked off to television studios and fancy restaurants.

Esther Taylor, his occasional girlfriend, was proud of him, if a little sad on the inside that becoming a world champion would move Emile still further away from her. She knew he would be even more in demand. It looked as if he was going one way, and she was being left behind on a different road from the past. Esther was a honey and she was good to Emile. She gave him space and love, which was a difficult and subtle combination for a young woman of twenty-one. Esther had always let Emile run free, without pursuing him in search of details he knew would upset her. It was becoming more difficult and yet Emile did not want to lose her entirely. He cared deeply for Esther; and she helped to curb the rumours surrounding him.

Emile's veiled suggestions of a possible marriage no longer excited or even soothed Esther. She doubted that they would ever be together. It had begun to feel to Esther that, amid boxing and up against his mother, she would never get Emile to herself. Slowly, they began to drift apart.

Esther did not know it then but a simple truth ticked away at the heart of him. He was a gay man who also liked women. 'Bisexual', however, was not a word Emile would ever use. And the idea of calling himself a 'homosexual' seemed even more impossible once he became such a public figure. He rarely said the word to Calvin, his closest friend and a gay man. The mystery of Emile Griffith was buried tight inside him. He felt no shame or guilt in holding a man, in kissing him and doing much more. Emile was rarely tormented the following morning. He did not tell himself that he needed to change and stick to a straight and narrow life. Emile loved to be with the friends and lovers who mattered most to him. He and Calvin accepted their illicit sexuality – but they knew that life was safer if they refused to name it out loud.

And so, even as a new world champion, he was back in Times Square, laughing and dancing with the hustlers and strippers, the young Hispanic gay crowd and the old drag queens. Emile still insisted on walking through the front door of his favourite bars and yet, in a secret pain, it felt forbidden to give voice to his true self.

Homosexual acts were illegal even if, to Emile, pleasure and joy rather than any sense of criminality shaped his love of men. The repression of America, the conservatism of his Caribbean family roots and the brutal nature of boxing denied him the liberty to talk about his feelings. But his happiness with his real nature allowed him to revel privately in the embrace of New York's gay community.

'Queen of the game!' the female impersonators and transvestites yelped whenever Emile joined them on the dance-floor. They could hardly believe that such a powerful man, a world champion who had bludgeoned his way to the title, could be so gentle and joyful. They covered him with kisses and compliments, running their big hands and painted fingernails across his wonder of a body as he danced with them. Emile felt as if he belonged with men who loved men – and with men who wished they looked like women but were almost amused that they didn't.

In 1961, there were more laws in America against homosexual men and lesbians than in the Soviet Union, East Germany and Cuba – the three countries most criticised by the White House for their oppressive ideologies. And so the press left Emile alone as soon as he stepped into his illegal realm. They knew the world would not be able to bear the truth. A fairy of a knockout artist? Who would believe them?

The smears and scandals that would engulf a secretly gay sports-man in later years were held in check by a puritanical morality. Newspaper editors were careful not to alienate their readers with gossip that many would consider shocking and even distressing. Such strictures instilled a curious and often unhelpful ambivalence within Emile himself. He was allowed to lead a private life free from the malevolent prying and hounding that would eventually come to characterise the mass media, especially in a different century. Yet he knew that his sexual inclinations were regarded as being so 'per-verse' they were deemed to be 'unspeakable' in ordinary society. A schism of hurt opened up still wider inside him.

His mother knew the truth, but she did not want to be confronted with the disturbing intimacy of facts. Emelda was happier looking away, feigning ignorance of her son's sexuality, and concentrated instead on Emile's assertion to the press that he was going to look after her in grand style. 'I can give Chubby Checker what my father couldn't give her,' he said, and Emelda didn't mind him using her old nickname as long as he kept more serious truths to himself. It also helped her mood that Esther was fading from their lives. It felt to Emelda as if she had most of Emile to herself again.

Emile's championship purse had helped him buy a new house for them all. It was his mother's castle, as much as his own, a huge ten-bedroomed home on the corner of Colfax and 110th Street in Hollis in the New York borough of Queens. He didn't mind that his whole family moved in with him – his Chubby Checker mom, Gloria, Franklin, his two other sisters Eleanor and Joyce, his step-brother Guillermo and step-sister Karen, as well as Gloria's five children. Her husband, Wilfred, a friend of Emile's, had been shot dead in a street in Harlem.

He was lucky that he had Gil and Howie to keep him busy both in and out of the ring. Gil took care of the boxing while Howie worked the press and cut him plenty of deals outside the fight game. Howie loved hanging out with Emile, taking him to the most stylish places in town, where the glamorous worlds of fashion and movies and music fascinated them. They enjoyed being feted by beautiful people.

Howie and Gil had been amazed by the newspaper boys running with the jaunty hat-making angle of Emile's story. Rather than muzzling it, Howie decided to make a feature of his fighter's difference. It was one way they could control and steer the unwritten narrative of Emile's sexuality. He would continue to design the odd hat – not that he had much time to spend on millinery – and they told the press he turned up at the factory every day to cast his eye lovingly over each stitch and twirl in their bonnets and fascinators.

The story was rooted in a semblance of truth because Emile and Calvin scooted over to West 37th Street a few days every week.

Before training they would slip into the hotel next door, where they saw their friend Bobby Miles, who loved boxing. They would then drift over to the factory to say hello to the girls and Howie. Emile loved picking up the hats and running his fingers across their delicate patterns; they were so different from the heavy headgear he wore in sparring. It helped him keep up with the styles and trends so that, whenever he met the press, he could talk as much about hat-making as fisticuffs.

He had been a sensation in the build-up to his first title defence, a rematch against the hardened Gaspar Ortega. Emile said the Mexican was the toughest man he had ever fought after their first bout in February 1960. They met again at the Olympic Auditorium in Los Angeles on 3 June 1961, exactly two months and two days after he had knocked out Paret to become world champion. Before the fight, rather than discuss the prospect of another gruelling battle, Emile held court on pillbox hats and the bouffant coiffure. The press lapped it up as they polished Emile's hat-making quotes until he sounded like a master milliner:

'*The Jackie Kennedy pillbox will remain in vogue; she's done a great job selling it for the millinery world. But hats will come in a greater variety of shape and materials than ever this year. We're featuring carabou, ostrich, novelty braids, feathers and velours. With the bouffant coiffure still in vogue, look for higher pillboxes.*'

It made a change from traditional fight talk where ugly bruisers like Two-Ton Tony Galento seethed: 'I'll moider da bum!'

Emile was far more interested in chitchatting about Jackie Kennedy's high-end pillbox than real life. He had only a vague inkling of her husband's role in the disastrous Bay of Pigs invasion, which had unfolded just weeks after he beat Paret. President Kennedy had claimed full responsibility for the utter failure of the CIA-backed attempt to overthrow Fidel Castro on 17 April 1961. Rather than inspiring a rabble of Cuban exiles in their attempt to bring down the revolutionary government, the US plot resulted in acute embarrassment for Kennedy's administration. The exiled forces were routed at Bahia de Cochinos (the Bay of Pigs). Castro unsettled the White House further by declaring that, in the face of flagrant US aggression, he would seek closer ties with the Soviet Union. The Cold War had turned dangerously icy.

Flamboyance and fun, while the world turned uneasily, was much more enticing to Emile. He and Howie were thrilled to learn that news of his unique straddling of two such divergent trades, fighting and hat-making, had crossed the Atlantic. They had rocked delightedly when, reading a two-week-old copy of the *Daily Mirror*, they realised that Emile was becoming famous in Britain. His fights on ABC were shown the following Saturday afternoon on the BBC's new flagship sports programme, *Grandstand*. Griffith was already known to the British sporting public, but the *Mirror* uncovered another side of the world welterweight champion to their millions of readers.

Echoing the tenor of reporting in America, the *Mirror* exclusive began in striking fashion. 'The big, but so gentle hands of a twenty-three-year-old man fashion smart hats for smart women. Deftly he stitches lace to mink, the obedient servant of fashion's whim. But he's very much a man's man. All ten stone of him. For hatmaker Emile Griffith is also the world's welterweight champion.

'In the boxing ring those not-so-gentle hands pack the sort of punch that brings him $45,000 a fight. His working life away from the ring is spent in a first floor hatmaker's shop near New York's bustling Fifth Avenue. There, his employer, Mr Howard Albert, spotted a future champion in the young hatmaker.'

The accompanying photograph, of Emile thoughtfully holding a lacy ladies' hat, revealed that his hands were smaller than suggested. But the tale of Emile's unexpected entry into the fight game was repeated in *Boxing News*, the famous old British weekly magazine. Under a headline of, 'He Preferred Hat-Making To The Noble Art', Eddie Baxter also wrote that, 'As paradoxical as it may seem, those same fists of Griffith that have brought destruction to opponents in the prize ring turn to the delicate work of designing ladies' hats.

Welterweight champion and hat designer – in and out of the ring Emile Griffith is an artist.'

He proved himself a brutally effective artist against Ortega. Relentless and vicious as he retained his title against the courageous Mexican, he dropped Ortega twice in the seventh round. The challenger had never been stopped in eighty-one previous fights against men as formidable as Kid Gavilan, Carmen Basilio, Florentino Fernandez, Luis Rodriguez and Benny Paret. But Ortega, who had worn a sombrero and a robe to ringside which Don Dunphy described as being 'a composite of every Mexican sunset', was no match for the hatmaker. In the twelfth round, the beating was so merciless the referee stopped the fight.

Griffith cupped his opponent's bowed head tenderly with his glove; and Ortega wept bitterly in his locker room. He knew he would never be a world champion. He would never be as great a fighter as Griffith.

Benny Paret watched from a distance. He could afford to wait for revenge. The hatmaker, the man Paret secretly called a *maricón*, had hurt him badly. Paret thought Griffith was as limp-wristed outside the ring as he was iron-fisted between the ropes. He had not cried in public like Ortega after he lost – but his world had been ripped apart. All his hopes of becoming impossibly rich were out of reach without the title. He needed it back. The only way he'd ever become a butcher would be if he made enough money as champion to buy a store in Miami.

There had been a rematch clause in Paret's contract against Griffith – but Manuel Alfaro persuaded him to surrender it. In exchange, Paret and Alfaro were paid $20,000 to step aside for Ortega by the fight promoter George Parnassus, who had been convinced that the Mexican, backed by a fervent Latino crowd in LA, would upset Griffith. Parnassus was wrong. Paret and his manager were twenty grand richer and Alfaro had a cast-iron guarantee that they would get the next crack at Griffith.

Paret had fought so often, and his head hurt so much, that he needed a break. He kicked back at home with Lucy and little Benny. The rematch was already set – for the last night of September 1961.

Benny Paret was bent on vengeance in the Garden.

Gil Clancy had first worked with boxers when he was a full-time teacher in a troubled neighbourhood – Bedford-Stuyvesant in Brooklyn. Outside of school hours, he moved across the boroughs and took kids on the pads and heavy bags at a Police Athletic League gym in South Jamaica, Queens. It was a rough, black area, but Clancy, who came from a blue-collar part of Rockaway Beach they called Irishtown, took the gig, which earned him an extra $1,000 a year. He had not expected it would spark a lifelong addiction.

Clancy was eventually offered a safer boxing job – at the gym on 28th Street where he met Emile. He taught at school from eight until just before three every day, and then raced over to the gym. Clancy would train fighters from three-thirty until eight every night. His twelve-hour days were steeped in discipline and sacrifice.

Griffith, his first world champion, matched his dedication. From the day they began working together, they had not missed a beat. As the money rolled in for both of them, it became possible for the trainer to turn the gym into his permanent schoolhouse. Griffith and Clancy forged an unbreakable partnership.

Clancy could not imagine any other boxer winning a world title just over two years after he first laced up a pair of gloves. Griffith had a startling ability to absorb technical information, and translate it into an effective fighting style. He did not have one astonishing skill – for there were fighters who hit harder than him and moved more fluidly – but he was accomplished in everything he did.

The only boxing attribute that Emile lacked consistently was, in Clancy's old phrase, 'the killer instinct'. He had knocked out opponents, stopping nine men in twenty-five pro fights, but it seemed as if Teddy Brenner only matched him with tough guys who hardly ever went down. Clancy was satisfied with the progress even if the difficulty remained that Emile, unlike most great fighters, took no pleasure in hurting an opponent. Griffith wanted to win, always, but he was often just as content boxing his way to victory. Clancy knew it would be best if they could settle for some savagely quick nights.

There were encouraging signs that Griffith was slowly turning himself into a puncher. Neither Paret nor Ortega had ever been kayoed before, but they were both stopped by Griffith. Two straight knockouts, in title fights, gave the new champion belief in his power. In the gym, working hard for the Paret rematch, Griffith intimidated his sparring partners and impressed the boxing scribes.

The *New York Times* reported in mid-September 1961 that Griffith 'has become unpopular with sparmates because of his vicious handling of them. Walter Daniels and Frank Sallee have walked out on him – vowing never to return. Daniels caught a Griffith left hook, padded by a sixteen-ounce glove and softened by a foam rubber headguard. It still took twenty minutes to bring him round. "Who needs that kind of work?" said Daniels as he packed away his training gear.'

Sallee, described as a Paret-style mauler, was equally quick to dismiss any notion that he might keep his short-term gig. 'Griffith hits too hard for gym money.'

Clancy was convincing when asked by Jerry Izenberg, a future great boxing writer who was then still a young reporter on the *Newark Star-Ledger*, to identify the reasons for Griffith's newly venomous hitting. 'Maturity and confidence,' Clancy said. 'He had the punch before but he couldn't bring himself to use it.'

Griffith nodded in agreement. 'I'm more relaxed and not as anxious anymore. And I listen more closely to Clancy. He told me I could knock out Paret. He told me during the fight that when I hit him solid with a hook, he would go. When he went down and stayed down I was really surprised. But I wasn't as surprised when I stopped Ortega in my next fight. Clancy told me I could do it.'

The champion cackled in delight and he threw a playful punch at his trainer's gut. Clancy almost smiled as he held up a warning finger. He was still the boss.

'Will I knock out Paret again?' Griffith wondered. 'If the opportunity comes I will try. I know one thing for sure – Paret will be after me very early. He wants his title back. You just need to look at his face to know what he's thinking. He will throw everything at me.'

Griffith paused, as he anticipated that reality. And then, reassuringly for Clancy, he said: 'I hope he does because I'll be ready to meet him from the opening bell.'

The 28th Street gym erupted with whoops; and Clancy noticed the latest addition to Emile's crew. There was something unsettling in the hunger with which this new Latino boy stared at Emile. It was obvious he was not studying any boxing moves or power punching. He had something different in mind. Clancy didn't like it much, but he was not going to start asking Emile about his private life. He knew that Esther, the demure girlfriend, was no longer much on the scene, and so Clancy gave the boy a stony Rockaway Beach glare – as if to warn him Emile was busy. The kid gazed at him coolly. He did not look likely to back down from getting anything he wanted.

His name was Matthew. He arrived one day on 28th Street in the hot, late summer of 1961. The kid turned up at the gym with his uncle, who knew much more about boxing than he did. Matthew still understood enough to lock his attention on the world champion. It was difficult not to focus on Emile. He was the famous one. Emile also cut a magnificent figure as, sweat flying from him, he worked in the draining heat. Matthew's gaze followed Emile everywhere, never allowing the boxer to escape his attention. Emile did nothing to discourage the boy. He looked over at Matthew during his breaks and smiled and waved at him. It did not seem as if Emile was thinking much of his problems with Esther during such moments.

Emile was a sucker for the waif and the stray – especially if he was a young, slim, Latino male. He sauntered over cheerfully to Matthew, not bothering to towel himself down, and stretched out his hand. Emile said he wanted to hear all about Matthew and discover why he had come down to West 28th Street.

'You,' Matthew said simply. 'I came to meet you ...'

Emile cackled and clapped his hands, as if he could not quite imagine anyone travelling across town to meet him. He welcomed Matthew and said he hoped they'd see much more of each other.

Matthew did not need the invitation but it spurred on his adoration. Every day he arrived early for training. His uncle no longer accompanied him but Matthew was always there, watching ravenously as Emile prepared for a dangerous fight. As the weeks slid past, and Emile kept on chatting flirtatiously with him, Matthew became increasingly bold. He not only waited until long after training had ended each day, but he took it upon himself to scoop up Emile's bag and saunter out of the gym with him.

'You don't have to do that, champ,' Emile would chide gently, but Matthew insisted. It was almost as if he regarded it as his new role in life to look after Emile. He liked to go all the way to the champ's home in Hollis. Emile was so polite and friendly that he always invited Matthew in for a juice. Emelda, Gloria, Franklin and everyone else soon got used to his new friend. They didn't like Matthew as much as they cared for Calvin or any of the drag queens they knew so well. But apart from Franklin, who grumbled more than normal, they got on with ordinary life on Colfax Street.

Inevitably, Matthew's visits to Hollis stretched out longer and longer. An hour one night became two the next until, eventually, it felt too late for Matthew to catch the subway home. He was only a teeanger – and Emile thought it was sensible for Matthew to stay over. They made up a bed for him on the couch and Emile checked he was comfortable. There was nothing more between them because, just weeks from the fight, Emile needed to sleep. Anyway, the kid was not quite eighteen yet. They would wait until after the business with Benny Paret, a very different kind of 'Kid', was done.

CHAPTER FIVE

Taunts & Beatings

Boxing was no wonderland. Even Emile Griffith, the Mad Hatter from Manhattan as the press called him, could not shake the ominous spell that settled over him in the last days before a fight. Apprehension gripped him as he waited for the hours to pass before he stepped back inside the ring.

The day of the fight was always the worst. A lunchtime weigh-in made the morning drag for a starving boxer. Emile usually handled his weight easily, as he was in supreme condition and rarely out of the gym. But a week before the Paret rematch he was six pounds over the 147 welterweight limit. Emile ate little from then on and he was only a pound over early on the morning of the bout. A fast fifteen-minute run brought him down to his exact fighting weight. But he could not eat anything before the weigh-in and Clancy only allowed him to suck on ice cubes all morning.

At least their ping pong ritual occupied Emile. They set up the table and the fighter took on his trainer in a seriously competitive match – as they did most mornings of a fight. Any kind of battle between Gil and Emile helped pass the time. They could not see a basketball court without Clancy challenging Griffith to a one-on-one game, or have Emile issue an invitation to see who might shoot the most hoops out of twenty free throws.

Clancy v Griffith was a noisy scrap no matter the setting. A few weeks before, they had even tested each other down 9th Avenue. They were sauntering along with Howie when the usual jokey chitchat about identifying the better athlete resulted in a flat-out sprint down a busy New York street on a midweek morning. Howie kept walking, pretending he did not know the racing demons hurtling ahead of him, as the white trainer and black fighter darted through the honking cars and past bewildered people.

On the Saturday morning of the Paret fight, the table tennis was fierce. The little white ball flew back and forth across the net. Neither man minded smashing it down hard at his opponent when the chance came.

'Kill or be killed,' Clancy growled when he smacked a vicious winner past Emile's nose.

Emile roared back at him, threatening murder or a cross-table smash of his own, and the game zipped from one point to the next. It was a healthy diversion on a morning when, otherwise, the gaunt face of Benny Paret filled his head.

Clancy won the ping pong in a tense five-setter, and there was just time for a quick shower and a change of clothes before they headed for the weigh-in. The usual quartet of Emile, Gil, Howie and Calvin was expanded by the old assistant trainer Syd Martin, Griffith's cousin Bernard Forbes and, surprisingly, Matthew. It was the first time the kid had accompanied Emile to a public engagement and Gil pulled a disapproving face at Howie. Howie shrugged and made a conciliatory gesture. The kid was quiet and Emile was already in fight mode.

Griffith and Paret had faced each other earlier that week at a midtown gym near Madison Square Garden. They had met the press and taken part in a joint photoshoot staged by John Condon, the arena's publicity director. It was all part of the Garden and ABC's determination to promote the fight as hard as they could, and Griffith entered into the spirit as a genial champion. Paret was much surlier as he endured Condon's photo drills, which required him to strip down to his boxing trunks and boots and lie face up on a rubdown table. A medicine ball was placed between his feet and he had to lift it up with straight legs in an exercise that showed off his rippling stomach muscles. It was Griffith's task to scratch his head as if bewildered by the challenger's training regime.

Behind Griffith, a handwritten sign made a request: Please Do Not Smoke While Boxers Are Training.

Paret looked as if he wished he could light up a Camel while he put up with the charade. He was ready to fight Griffith in a burning warehouse in the Bronx if he could win back his world title.

On the hard wooden floor of the gym, he did as the snapper gestured and moved into a traditional boxing pose. Paret stared straight down the barrel of the lens, holding up his fists, refusing to smile as the light fell across the scars lining his upper cheeks. Everlast – the name of the boxing equipment company – stretched across the white band of his black shorts.

Three days later, at the weigh-in, when Griffith appeared in his own Everlast trunks, Paret insisted on changing into a stark black pair devoid of lettering. Paret kept the same brooding expression as he and Griffith were asked to walk over to the steel weighing scales in the packed offices of the New York State Athletic Commission. Most of the fight press was there, as were boisterous groups backing the two fighters. It was a chaotic affair and Griffith just wanted to make the weight and get out so that he could devour a thick and juicy steak at McGinnis' restaurant. He had been dreaming of that steak all week.

Paret, the barefoot challenger, stepped on the square metal stand first. He and Griffith, surrounded by officials, watched the red needle move along the numbers on top of the thin weighing pole that nearly reached Paret's chin. The line eventually stopped quivering and the lead official double-checked the digit.

'Benny "Kid" Paret,' he shouted out, 'weighs in at 146 pounds . . .'

The Cuban's sombre face suddenly broke into a glorious smile. He held his right fist aloft – not only to celebrate being a pound under the welterweight mark, but in anticipation of regaining his title that night.

Griffith followed him and the pattern was repeated. 'Emile Griffith,' the official yelled in confirmation, 'weighs in at 147 pounds ...'

They slipped on their boots again. Griffith also slid a gold chain around his neck as they prepared for the final pre-fight photos. The mood was quiet and tense as the photographer asked Griffith to climb back on the scales, while Paret was instructed to point at the 147-pound marker. There were no calls for smiles this time. Neither man looked in the mood for jollity or small talk.

Once the cameras had finished popping, with the flashes lighting the room in an eerie glow, Griffith stretched out his hand to Paret. The Cuban hesitated and then, without looking at the man who held his title, he shook Griffith's hand disdainfully.

They would meet again in the Garden just after ten that night. There was no need to waste any words when, with empty stomachs and dry mouths, they needed sustenance as quickly as possible.

Emile took his shirt from Matthew and pulled it over his head. He then accepted a large glass of water from the kid and began to drink greedily. The glass had just begun to tilt upwards, as he emptied it, when cackling broke out from the opposite side of the room. Emile looked over the rim in the direction of the crude laughter. He swallowed hard when he saw the cause of the mirth.

Paret minced up and down, flapping his wrist. He put his hand on a hip and puckered his lips towards his manager and friends. Manuel Alfaro was laughing so hard it looked as if he might snap the suspenders holding up his trousers. The rest of Paret's corner roared in amusement.

A couple of fight reporters asked Paret, in Spanish, about the commotion. Paret replied in a high and fluting voice. He added a soft singsong calypso lilt to his quip and it was obvious that he was trying to imitate the world champion.

It was then that Emile heard the echoing word: '*Maricón* ... *maricón* ...'

Emile's head was in a whirl. Could he have misheard? Could Paret have said some other word?

The hacks smiled uneasily, knowing that they could not include such words in their newspaper copy. But, as if he wanted to make sure that Emile had heard correctly, Paret turned and looked straight at the world champion. His hand was still on his hip and the expression on Paret's face was cruel and mocking. It was a look which said, clearly, '*maricón*'.

Emile felt small and dirty. He sensed none of the warmth that once filled him when he and Benny played basketball in the Bronx. Emile could not believe he was being humiliated.

Paret held the look for a few more seconds before smiling scornfully. With an exaggerated flounce of his hips and a wave of his wrist, he tottered over to his Cuban gang. They yelped their approval as Emile turned away. Apart from his brother, Franklin, no one had ever dared ridicule him openly before.

Emile was nobody's *maricón*. Esther had been his girl for years. He also had a string of boyfriends and, suddenly, he had Matthew as a special friend too. But nobody, until now, had cared whom he held in the dark. Nobody, until now, had made him feel ashamed of his sexuality. Nobody, until now, had mocked him as a faggot in public.

He didn't mind that Benny tried so hard to hurt him in the ring. He was trying to do the exact same thing back to Benny. It was plain and honest. No one else really understood what they endured in the ring. They experienced different outcomes, victory and defeat, triumph and despair, but they shared the pain, exhaustion and sheer strangeness of being exposed before a large crowd. Why else did fighters embrace and kiss just moments after attempting to damage each other? They were bound together by a twine of respect. After it was over, they were closer than brothers.

Benny had broken that bond of brotherhood. It was even worse than being taunted as a nigger. If a white fighter had sneered at the colour of his skin, Emile would have shrugged it off. But the onslaught against homosexuality ran deep and wide, all the way from the White House when Eisenhower was in power just before Kennedy. The state and the church and the courts, the police and the doctors, the newspapers and the magazines, the rich and the powerful, the poor and the illiterate, were united in their condemnation of men like Emile Griffith. A homosexual, to them, was sick and cowardly. He was depraved and absurd.

What else could you feel, as a gay man in 1961, but the hot shame that coursed through Emile Griffith?

Benny Paret seemed to speak for the whole world as he ridiculed the champion. Emile pulled on his street clothes and told Gil and Howie that he needed to eat. He needed to get away.

'Okay, Emile,' Clancy said quietly. 'Let's get outta here . . .'

At the end, just after eleven o'clock on the night of Saturday 30 September 1961, their grudge looked even more bruising in the Garden. They were both marked up. Griffith's right eye was underscored by a small mouse of a swelling. The Kid's face looked far worse. Paret was puffy around both eyes. Blood wept slowly from just below his left eye. The inside of his mouth had also bled steadily from the fourth round.

The fight writers at ringside agreed. Eighteen out of twenty-two newspapermen gave the verdict to Griffith. It had been an unremitting contest, similar to their first fight, and Griffith had come closest to repeating the stunning knockout that settled the Miami stalemate. In two rounds, the fourth and the eleventh, Griffith punished Paret. The Cuban looked close to going down, especially in the fourth when he was backed against the ropes and pummelled to the point where his white mouthguard protruded helplessly from his mouth. Thirty seconds were left in the round as Griffith ripped punches into him. But Paret hung on and, just before the bell, he fired back.

Griffith looked the stronger fighter as, gleaming with sweat, he bullied Paret and snapped his head back and forth as if playing a brutal game of ping pong. But he sometimes eased off. Paret out-worked him and the Cuban was much more effective on the inside, with his percussive body-punching. It was close. There was also a strange intimacy as they sometimes rested their heads against each other while grappling.

At the start of the last round, which marked the first time Griffith would complete the championship distance, Paret gave him a per-functory slap on the gloves as referee Al Berl brought them together. The spite was even more obvious at the end as, just before the bell, they stood toe to toe and landed vicious punches on each other.

Paret's trainer, Joe Di Maria, was the first to join them after the fif-teenth round ended. He charged across to Paret to signal his certainty that they had won. Griffith simply raised his right arm before he turned back and tapped the Kid kindly on his head. He had fought with dignity and discipline, apparently having forgiven Paret's behaviour at the weigh-in. The Cuban, in turn, remembered his manners. He stretched out his arm to Clancy and Albert in acknowledgement of a hard fight.

Johnny Addie soon knew that, surprisingly, he had a split decision to announce. 'Judge Tony Castellano ... 8-6 ... one even ...', Addie shouted before he used his left hand to point to the winner on the first card. '*Paret!*'

Griffith began to pace, walking backwards in disbelief, down the length of the ring while boos cascaded around him. He then walked forward again towards Clancy while he waited for the next score.

'Judge Arthur Aidala ... 9-6 ... to *Paret!*'

Benny Paret jumped up in the centre of the ring. By the time he had landed, Griffith had arrived to embrace him briefly. But they had already parted before Addie made his last announcement.

'Referee Al Berl ... 8-6 ... one even ... *Griffith!*'

Di Maria and Alfaro raised Paret on their shoulders as Addie made it official: 'The winner by majority vote and once again the welter-weight champion of the world ... *Benny "Kid" Paret!*'

Griffith, swallowing his hurt, returned to congratulate the new champion again. They were still brothers in boxing. Paret nodded and grinned – but he was less gracious in the post-fight interview.

When Don Dunphy brought Paret and his manager in front of the ABC cameras, with millions watching, Alfaro indicated that he would translate. 'Tell me,' Alfaro was asked, 'did Griffith hurt him on the inside when he held him on the ropes early in the fight?'

Paret shook his head contemptuously as Alfaro spoke in Spanish. The Kid answered quickly. 'Nothing,' Alfaro then said in English. 'He says Griffith don't have any kind of punch at all to hurt him.'

'Now, Manny,' Dunphy said more reasonably, 'is there a return bout in the contract?'

Alafro shook his head. 'No, there is no return-bout contract. We can fight anybody we want.'

'Will you fight Griffith?'

'I do not have to fight him,' Alfaro replied, as if he was the lean welterweight world champion rather than a portly manager. 'But if they pay me well I will fight anyone.'

Griffith, in his corner, looked stricken. Disappointment crumpled his face and even Howie Albert could not console him. They all remembered how Griffith and Clancy had praised Paret after the Cuban had been knocked out in the first fight. They had both insisted that they would happily give Paret a rematch.

Alfaro and Paret were even more bullish when they got out of the ring. They heard Gil Clancy talking angrily: 'We were robbed without a gun.'

As the press gang swarmed around them, telling Alfaro and Paret that the overwhelming majority believed that Griffith had won the fight, the Cubans laughed.

'Any chance you'll give Griffith the rematch he deserves?' someone asked.

Paret grinned while Alfaro spelt out his bleak message to the *maricón*: 'Nowhere, no how, no place.'

Emile curled up inside himself throughout the next week. He rarely left the house on Colfax Street. The defeated fighter hardly even stepped outside of his bedroom, as he struggled to overcome his invisible wounds. The only people allowed to visit him were Calvin and Esther. They no longer called each other by those innocent words of 'boyfriend' and 'girlfriend'; but Emile felt in need of Esther's tenderness. There was something about her compassion and gentleness, as a woman, that consoled him a little in his bleakest moments. And Esther, devoid of bitterness and anger, was happy to try to help. They were still friends; and she hated to see Emile hurting.

He was in no mood to party or flirt with any of his boyfriends. Matthew was smart enough to know that he should stay away – for no one could cheer up the lost champion. Yet Emile felt just as wretched when he was alone. Years later, he remembered that miserable week and said, simply, 'I couldn't get along with myself.'

Emelda, his beloved mommy, cooked all his favourite meals, but Emile pushed his food around the plate. He didn't eat much and he smiled even less.

'Go see Clancy,' Emelda urged him in the second week of October, just as the trees changed colour from yellowy-green to red and a darker brown. The cold also began to spread and bite. A long winter loomed.

Emile shrugged but Emelda insisted. 'Go on, Junior,' she said. 'Clancy will tell you what to do . . .'

Clancy and Howie Albert, of course, had it all mapped out. They knew that there was no shifting Alfaro and Paret, and so it was best they helped Emile back into the usual routine. He should fight often and rack up the wins. Eventually, Paret would have no choice but to give him a rematch. The fans would demand a decider – particularly as most people thought Emile should still be champion.

Emile only brightened when Howie said they had lined up a bout for him in Bermuda on 4 November, against a journeyman called Stanford Bulla. After so many hard fights he deserved a gift of a win. Bulla had won just three out of his twelve fights. He had lost the other nine. Emile could soak up some sun in Bermuda and then turn the heat on poor old Bulla. After that, they had earmarked a contest just before Christmas in New York and then he would celebrate his birthday with a homecoming fight in Charlotte Amalie on St Thomas in early February 1962. It would be the first time Emile had returned to the Virgin Islands since he left for Harlem more than eight years earlier.

The prospect of seeing Charlotte Amalie again made Emile smile. 'Okay,' he said, 'let's do it.'

Less than four weeks later, in a ring set up on a windswept tennis court, in Hamilton, Bermuda, he blew away Bulla. Emile knocked him out in four rounds and then went dancing in a Bermuda night-club.

'Benny "Kid" Paret had better watch out,' he warned with a grin.

Manuel Alfaro plotted a different path for his boy. He was the boss; the Kid was just a fighter. Paret had been promised $25,000 for his rematch with Griffith in the Garden. That figure represented 30 per cent of the combined net gate and the money from a Gillette-sponsored television fight. ABC had paid the Garden $60,000 for the fight and, with a crowd of almost 7,000, he seemed to have earned a decent purse. But all the digits made Benny's head hurt and, some-how, he ended up with around half of the expected amount. Alfaro had a long list of expenses that needed to be covered. But he told the Kid not to worry. He had a scheme in mind that would add another zero to the $25,000 they had nearly shared.

Gene Fullmer was a savage puncher and the world middleweight champion. He was no fancy dan or slick mover. Instead, he was a much bigger and harder-hitting version of Paret. The huge nose on Fullmer's ugly mug was so squashed it was obvious he believed in the Cuban's mantra, which suggested it was worth taking five punches to land a big one. Fullmer loved nothing more than a bat-tering brawl.

The Kid was not so sure he wanted the fight. He didn't think he could beat the big old white bruiser – and he knew the champion hit with terrible force. Fullmer came from West Jordan in Utah and he was thirty years old. He was nearing the end of a long and violent career after sixty professional fights. But Fullmer was on a roll. He had stopped Carmen Basilio to win the middleweight title in August 1959 and had held onto it for over two years, including six title defences. Fullmer had lost just one fight, to Sugar Ray Robinson, in six years. He had also drawn with Robinson, and beaten him twice, most recently in December 1960 at the Convention Center in Las Vegas – the venue for his battle against the Kid.

Paret only agreed to the fight when he heard the terms Alfaro had apparently negotiated. There was talk of $250,000 in an offer made by Fullmer's manager Marv Jenson. Paret realised that any quoted number would shrink by more than half before it reached him – but it was such a huge sum he could not refuse. It was sweetened further by the fact that he and Fullmer would only fight for the middle-weight title – as the Utah slugger was too big to make the welter limit. Paret would remain the world welterweight champion no matter how hard Fullmer hit him in Vegas.

Fullmer weighed in at 159¾, while Paret struggled to bulk up to 156¾ before they stepped into the ring on 9 December 1961. It seemed as if the extra ten pounds he piled on as security against a heavy hitter was down to a diet of pancakes and syrup rather than a changed training regime. He might have been lighter than Fullmer but Paret, sacrificing some of his speed, looked fleshy.

The additional weight did not help him. Fullmer rumbled from his corner with flat-footed intent. He backed up Paret, giving him little room to use anything flashy, and immediately started hitting the smaller man with heavy artillery. The blows were many in number and ominous in impact. They were like the pounding of an axe against the soft bark of a tree. Fullmer chopped down on Paret, again and again, and the tough little Cuban snapped back at him like a thin and whippity branch. Paret had some success, as the middle-weight champ was easy to hit despite his cross-armed defence – but the Cuban's punches were a light drizzle compared to the rolling thunder of Fullmer's barrage.

Later, reflecting mournfully on a massacre of a fight, Fullmer said, 'I never hit a guy so many times before he went out ... I never beat anyone worse in my life than Kid Paret ...'

Fullmer wore down Paret and pummelled him into oblivion. It should have been stopped long before it ended, but, whenever he rocked under the deluge, Paret threw a flurry back at Fullmer. He even opened up a small cut above Fullmer's scowling forehead. It was a nick in contrast to the chasm of pain visited upon Paret.

At the start of the tenth round, Fullmer had begun to hit Paret so hard that the sound of his gloved fist smashing into the flesh and bones made a doleful thud. Paret sank back against the ropes and Fullmer went to work with even more menace. He landed a concussive combination that made Paret reel towards his own corner. It was akin to the moment that a tree finally creaks and begins to fall beneath the sustained assault of a swinging axe.

Fullmer piled into him and Paret crouched down woozily. Each time he bent, Fullmer straightened him with a savage uppercut. Paret could not stay upright for long and he would crumple again – only to fall into another uppercut which snapped him awake. The poor Cuban sugar-cane cutter slid down onto his haunches, almost as if begging for refuge.

The count began and Paret got up. He spread his hands and shook his head. What was the point of it all?

Fullmer had turned into the butcher Paret wished he would himself become one day – working in his own store in Miami rather than being flayed in an abattoir of a ring by an expressionless hulk.

Paret was strung up again near the ropes, in Fullmer's favourite corner, and the beating resumed.

Suddenly, like a dying beast kicking out in desperation, Paret fought back. He threw a series of fast punches that made Fullmer pause in his butchering.

'Those rallies take something out of a fighter,' Don Dunphy warned Paret's supporters on television, 'and so let's see what happens.'

Fullmer clubbed Paret even more ferociously, as Dunphy was hushed into silence.

Eighteen unanswered punches smashed into Paret, with Fullmer breaking up his deadly routine by switching from the head to the body and back again. He couldn't miss because Paret just stood there, pawing helplessly at Fullmer as if asking for mercy.

Eventually, with a gruesome slide, Paret collapsed onto the canvas after a left followed a succession of right hands. Fullmer turned away and headed for a neutral corner while the referee put his hand on the back of the Cuban's neck.

Paret forced himself to rise. His arms were down, his mouth was open and his eyes were glazed. He looked vacantly into the distance. The referee, Harry Krause, wiped Paret's gloves on his white shirt. It was a signal to Fullmer that the carnage was not yet over.

Krause waved him eagerly forward and clapped his hands as if to say, 'Let's get this done.' Fullmer did not need an invitation. He hit Paret with a right hand that landed just below the waistband. Fullmer followed it with a roundhouse left that landed flush on Paret's jaw. As the crumbling fighter imploded, like a building detonated from the inside, Fullmer hit him again with an explosive right hand.

Paret fell on his back. He supported himself on his right elbow and stretched out his left hand, holding onto the rope as if afraid that Fullmer might hit him again. Krause counted to ten without Paret even trying to move. After it was over, Paret got to his feet before falling again. The referee helped him up.

Fullmer was soon surrounded by a dozen grinning handlers and cornermen. His father wiped his face, which was strangely swollen despite the one-sided beating.

At first, in Paret's corner, they covered his bowed head with a white towel. It looked like a shroud. But then they lifted it and packed it around the upper part of his chest as they pulled his gown tightly around him. Paret smiled sadly as Fullmer walked towards him.

'There's Benny "Kid" Paret apparently none the worse for wear – managing a smile,' Don Dunphy suggested as he prowled around the ring with his microphone. 'Benny shouldn't feel too badly – he'll get well paid for tonight. There's Fullmer. They're talking to each other. They have a lot of respect for each other – even though they were trying to murder each other not too long ago.'

The idea that Paret was 'none the worse for wear' was not shared by everyone. Pete Hamill, the esteemed boxing writer who then, at the age of twenty-six, worked for the *New York Post*, had not been sent to Las Vegas for the mismatch. He watched the fight on television. Hamill understood boxing well enough to think Paret's hammering by Fullmer could be 'a career-ender'. Such a beating had to erode the will of even a man as brave as Paret.

Hamill looked at the Cuban and saw a car-wreck of a fighter. He knew they would take Benny Paret out into the cold desert night. They would patch him up and send him home to his young wife in Miami. Hamill said it would almost be like they were sending him to a bodyshop where, with time and work, he would have the dents smoothed out. His cuts and bruises would fade and normality would return to his features, just like a lick of paint could make a repaired car looked almost new again. But some cars, after a crash, are never the same.

It happened to boxers too. They could heal on the outside but, internally, they would be unhinged. Something deep inside was ruined forever. On that bleak December night, Benny Paret looked battered beyond repair.

Gil Clancy sat alone with his fighter in the locker room at Madison Square Garden. It seemed strange not to be with Emile Griffith. But, at the age of twenty, Cassius Clay was convinced he would become the greatest, and the prettiest, fighter in history.

They already loved him in the Garden office. Teddy Brenner had promoted his previous three fights, in a perfect 10-0 record, but they had all been held in Clay's home town of Louisville. It was a simple arrangement that worked well for the Garden. As Clay was too little-known to headline a bout in New York, they worked with a local promoter who put on three shows built around the Olympic gold medal winner. Brenner and the Garden were paid by ABC and they used the television money to settle the fighters' modest fees, while the Louisville promoter pocketed the live gate money. It was time, however, to discover whether Clay could really fight – in the Garden against Sonny Banks, on 10 February 1962.

Brenner hoped he could because he was smitten by the charisma and decency of the big-talking charmer. They had met before the 1960 Olympic Games, when Clay had turned up at Brenner's office to introduce himself. 'My name is Cassius Clay and I'm going to the Olympics,' he told Brenner. 'I'm gonna win a gold medal. I'm gonna be the next heavyweight champion of the world and I wanna borrow ten dollars.'

Clay was on his way up to Harlem, to see the foxes, those beautiful girls he loved, and he needed some money for a good time. Brenner gave him the cash without expecting it would ever be repaid. But not long after the Rome Olympics, the kid had returned to Brenner's office with $10. He was hard to resist – especially when he began his outrageous stunt of predicting the round in which he would knock out his next opponent.

Before his previous bout in Louisville, on 29 November 1961, Clay had mocked his experienced opponent Willi Besmanoff: 'I'm embarrassed to get into the ring with this unrated duck. I'm ready for top contenders like [Floyd] Patterson and Sonny Liston. Besmanoff must fall in seven.'

It was such a mismatch, with Clay outclassing the 78-fight journeyman, that Angelo Dundee berated the emerging genius. 'Quit playing,' Dundee grumbled as Clay toyed with Besmanoff. 'Get him outta there . . .' But Clay had his prophecy to protect and he only went to work with intent at the start of his chosen round. Besmanoff duly fell in seven.

All week long Clay had shaken up New York City. He wore a

smart suit and a bow tie wherever he went, and he and John Condon, the Garden publicist, had transfixed the press with a series of appearances to hype his fight against Banks. The prediction, of course, came early. Banks would be shut down in four.

Clancy was used to working with flamboyant young fighters – and he allowed Clay to get on with his incessant chatter, just as he ignored Emile's excursions in Times Square. Clancy concentrated on boxing. It was the reason Dundee had asked for his help in New York. Dundee and Clancy had first worked together in 1950 and they kept in close touch – even if, as when Luis Rodriguez fought Griffith, they were sometimes in opposing corners.

Clancy recognised the difference between Clay the showman and Cassius the boy just out of his teens. Whenever there were people around, Clay was a one-man riot – joking, shouting, smiling, whooping – but he was much more serious on his own with Clancy. Clay respected Clancy, for he had seen how the trainer had steered his best young fighter to a win over Rodriguez.

Twenty minutes before the opening bell, Clancy and Clay were alone in the locker room. 'Hey, Gil,' Clay asked softly, 'do you really think I can beat this guy?'

Clancy had heard the same tone in Emile's voice, and seen the same sheepish expression, before he fought Cuban monsters like Rodriguez and Florentino Fernandez. All boxers felt trepidation. It was the trainer's task to remind his fighter, without saying it out loud, that the other guy was also shaking with nerves. But no fighter liked to talk about being scared. The trick was to boost him in a fresh way.

A measure of truth always seemed the best option to Clancy. There was no point saying a strong opponent would be a pushover. It was more important to explain how the other fighter's best features could be blunted. Banks was a banger. Like Clay, he had ten victories to his name and nine were by knockout. But Clancy reminded Clay of a more salient truth. Banks had little of Clay's speed, skill, movement or intelligence. In fact, all Sonny Banks could really do was punch. There was a chance that Clay might be tagged, but he would almost certainly be too slick for Banks.

Clancy was always cautious around the big talkers and the pretty boys. They were often found out. You couldn't be completely sure of Clay until he showed whether or not he had the whiskers and the ticker to withstand a shellacking. It was one reason why Brenner had chosen Banks for Clay's first big New York fight. There was no point carrying a prospect. 'Swim or sink,' Brenner always said.

'You'll be fine, Cassius,' Clancy assured him.

Banks looked tough and fearless. At twenty-one, he was only a year older than Clay, and still hungry. Clay was much faster and landed early, but Banks came back at him hard. They were still midway through the first round when, in a corner, Banks threw a short left that landed flush on the jaw. Clay went down.

Clancy thought Dundee might faint with shock as he watched his great hope crash to the floor. Dundee said later that he saw Clay's eyes close as he tumbled to the canvas. But, more romantically, Dundee also claimed that the moment he fell in love with Clay as a fighter was in the instant the kid got back up on his feet to take a mandatory eight count from the referee, Ruby Goldstein. There was no quit in him.

The kid, moving and firing, controlled the rest of the round. By the third he was in such command that he picked off Banks with snap and verve. It looked as if Banks could go at any minute, but Clay had his prediction to protect – and he also took a few more hard licks. Clay did not even blink. In the fourth round, as he had forecast, the fight ended when Clay's fast jabs and clubbing blows landed.

'Hold it, hold it,' Goldstein barked as he jumped between the fighters. He wrapped his left arm around Banks' neck and held him tight around the waist.

Booing echoed around the Garden. Fight fans like a knockout and Banks was close to being stretched out on his back. But Goldstein wanted Banks to fight again another day.

'You did the right thing, Ruby,' Clancy told Goldstein once they were back in the lockers.

The press surrounded Clay. They were more interested in his recovery. 'That was my first knockdown as a professional,' Clay said as, sitting under a stark light, he wiped his face with a white towel. 'I had to get up and take care of things because it was rather embarrassing. As you know, I think I'm the greatest so I'm not supposed to be on the floor. I had to get up and put him out in four – as I predicted.'

Clay looked young and beautiful, and only a little chastened. The kid was obviously a star – and a real fighter. But Clancy was glad he had his own fighting star. He had Emile Griffith.

Exactly a week earlier, on Saturday 3 February 1962, Emile's twenty-fourth birthday, he and Clancy had been in a different ring, at the Lionel Roberts Stadium in Charlotte Amalie on St Thomas. It was his homecoming and, even though a journeyman called Johnny Torres ran like a thief all night, Emile won a shutout on the score-cards. His reception was far more riveting than the fight itself. The governor of St Thomas declared a national holiday and Emile was presented with the island's Medal of Honor. They also renamed a lovely green field after him – the Emile Griffith Park – and cele-brated his achievements with a ticker-tape parade. He had accomplished much since he had been abused in the woods as a boy and forced to find refuge in a reformatory.

Cassius and Emile were unusually distinctive names for two gifted young fighters – but Clancy was convinced they were both on the path to boxing greatness. Emile just needed to regain his world title from Benny Paret to complete his resurgence.

A guest had moved permanently into Emile's new house on Colfax Street in Queens. Matthew told his uncle, who had first taken him to the gym to watch a champion at work, that Emile had adopted him. The fighter was his 'new pop'. It was difficult for anyone to believe that Emile, at twenty-four, could be an adoptive father to a boy just six years younger than him. But some kind of explanation was needed to justify a teenager moving into the home of a young man who seemed far too playful for a paternal role.

Matthew was a street kid and he had learned to fight for what he wanted. He bristled whenever anyone came too close to Emile. It was his way of saying that Emile was his man. At a time when secrecy was needed to protect any gay relationship, Matthew pushed against social convention. Politeness and decency mattered little when he felt threatened. It was more important to head off any unwanted competitors.

Emile was strong enough to make it clear that his friendship with Calvin – and his partnership with Gil and Howie – could not be undermined. He would also still see Esther occasionally because they had known each other for so long. Matthew didn't mind. Esther, being a woman and no longer even a girlfriend, was no rival to him.

Matthew snapped at his more casual male acquaintances; and Emile was flattered the kid seemed ready to go to war over him. Others were less impressed by the changed dynamic. Clancy felt increasingly uneasy, while Emile's brother, Franklin, was much more strident. Franklin always carped about Emile's choice of friends, and his unmanly social life. Matthew moving into their house infuriated Franklin. He warned Emile that people were beginning to discuss his behaviour. Was he crazy? Did he want to shame the whole family?

Emile pretended to ignore his brother but the words stung. The ache Benny Paret had opened up in him the previous September had not healed. In his head he sometimes still heard the Cuban whispering 'maricón'. Each time Franklin complained about Matthew, it felt as if the scab was picked and hurt seeped out. He didn't like the way his brother tried to change him, but deep down Emile knew that Franklin was right. People would judge him. He resolved to be more careful in public – especially as the third fight with Paret had just been agreed. They would meet in a title decider at Madison Square Garden on 24 March 1962. Emile was consumed by the thought of winning back his championship.

At night, it was different. When the house was dark and heavy with sleep, Matthew walked quietly along the hallway to Emile's bedroom. A few months previously, Emile had always resisted and led Matthew back to the couch. The pattern had since changed. Matthew had turned eighteen. Emile liked the way Matthew slid into his bed and reached out for him.

Soon, before Franklin could quite believe it, Matthew had moved permanently into Emile's bedroom. Matthew even had a new name for himself. He was Emile Griffith's boyfriend. There was nothing anyone could do about it. Emile and Matthew were a couple like no other in the hard world of boxing.

CHAPTER SIX

Maricón

The hounding of Emile Griffith had begun. Even the rigid conservatism of America in 1962 could not curb the insidious spread of public rumour around his sexuality. The insulting machismo of Benny Paret at the weigh-in to their second world title fight had unshackled some of the restraints that made homosexuality such a taboo subject even in the more crass New York newspapers. Titillated gossip columnists began to make knowing reference to the fey 'difference' and 'outrageous flamboyance' of the former champion boxer. There was no direct use of the word 'homosexual' but the inference was obvious.

Homosexual activity was still illegal and subject to a prison term. Emile, and Howie Albert as his manager, could not easily shrug off the creeping allegations. Gil Clancy stayed out of the discussions – he had enough on his mind plotting victory over Paret in the decisive fight of a ferocious trilogy. Howie, however, knew that they had to do something in answer to the whispering hints of scandal.

He asked Emile if he had seen Esther recently. Emile shook his head. So much had been going on that a few months had passed since he and his old girlfriend had last met up.

Howie hesitated and then, finally, he asked Emile a plain if difficult question. Would Esther help them?

'Yeah,' Emile replied softly. 'I think so . . .'

It was not an easy call for him to make. Emile knew he had hurt Esther and that, in the end, he had disappointed her. Yet it was better for both of them that they were free to live their own lives. Esther had said it herself. He went down one path, and she stayed on a different road. But he could not forget how Esther had comforted him after he had lost to Paret. It was just hard to turn to her again.

Emile skirted the full details of the gossip when he explained to Esther that some of the papers were putting a nasty spin on their coverage of him. Would she consider doing some positive publicity with him? Would she mind playing the part of his girlfriend again – for some photoshoots?

Esther didn't care what the newspapers might be writing about her old boyfriend. And so she did not miss a beat.

'Emile,' she said, 'why would I mind?'

He was humbled by her generosity and did not quite know how to thank her. And so, in his habitual way, Emile tried to make her laugh. Maybe they could both get their dancing shoes on and knock 'em dead with their dazzling footwork.

'Sure,' Esther said. 'Let's have some fun . . .'

They did two publicity photoshoots, with Esther and Emile looking adoringly into each other's faces as girlfriend and boyfriend. And they did have some fun, even if she did not feel like a movie star or Emile's girl. Esther was under no illusions that this was anything other than a showbiz scam. A more serious truth bound them together.

Esther knew she was one of Emile's most trusted friends; and she would always want to help a friend she loved when he needed her most. She did not even look away when Emile suggested to the press that one of these days, sometime real soon, he and Esther would finally settle down and get married.

*

It rained often high up in the Catskill Mountains, a hundred miles northwest of New York City, where Emile Griffith buried himself in the seclusion of his training camp. He didn't like the rain when Gil and Jimmy Glenn, who looked after the sparring partners, woke him early for his morning run. Emile felt like staying in bed, curled up in the warmth at the plush Concord hotel in Monticello. There was no Matthew to distract him, and he would have loved to have slept in, but Gil and Jimmy were insistent. It never took them long to rouse him because an image of Benny Paret rose up in Emile's head.

Emile splashed water on his face. He pulled on his underpants, vest, sweater, training trousers, socks and running boots in the same order every morning. Emile then reached for a woolly hat to keep out the damp cold as he met Gil, Jimmy and three sparring partners in Gene Tapia, Felix Santiago and Ray Lacen.

They ran in the hills surrounding the Concord. Emile set a fierce pace. He thought often of Paret on those misty mornings in the Catskills. Emile was in the mood to punish the new champion. The loss of his title still hurt him, but Paret's words haunted him. He wanted to show Paret he was more than a '*maricón*'.

Sweat flew from him as they came back down and ran around the fringes of Kiamesha Lake. It was a long grind but, by the time they reached the Concord, an exclusive holiday resort for the pampered, Emile and the other fighters were grinning and chatting. The sanctuary of the showers, breakfast and then resting again in bed lifted their mood.

They made a curious group at the Concord, standing out among extremely wealthy guests who gawped at them with surprise tinged by awe. Once, when they were joined for the day in mid-March by a group of reporters including Howard M. Tuckner of the *New York Times*, the contrast between the fighters and the hotel's clientele provided reams of copy. Tuckner was intrigued by the way in which Emile was 'surrounded by turtleneck sweaters, seal coats and Ottoman club chairs ... Today, however, when Griffith walked into the dining room after lunch had begun, the Lake Erie smelts and the scrambled eggs with lox and onions lost the decision. Emile, who only eats steaks, was all business. He is serious about his work.'

The fight writers watched intently as, on press days, he sparred ten rounds in a ring that the hotel had set up for him on a floor above an ice-skating rink. Tuckner reported that 'Griffith took apart his sparring partners' with sleek and vicious technique. The open secret of his sexuality had been discussed more regularly since Matthew had appeared at his side in New York, and the Paret insult had been followed by the gossip columns whirring into gear. But Tuckner, Red Smith, A. J. Liebling, Jim Murray, Jerry Izenberg and other leading sportswriters deliberately chose not to explore Griffith's private life. They knew that their readership in 1962 was simply not ready for the truth – that a former world boxing champion, challenging again for the title, had a boyfriend.

It was difficult for them to express empathy for a homosexual man in a parochial society, but, recognising Griffith as one of the world's great young fighters, they supported him by concentrating on his boxing prowess. For the New York popular press, however, a taboo subject was deliciously thrilling. They kept on skirting Griffith's sexuality with their constant allusions to his hat-making panache.

Howie Albert fed them millinery stories to keep them satisfied. He told them that Emile had recently created one of the company's biggest-selling hats – covered in a pattern of pretty roses. But he made sure to remind everyone that Emile was inspired by his longtime girlfriend, Esther Taylor. Had they not seen the beautiful photos of the young couple together? Did they not know that marriage was looking likely?

It was not enough to stifle the curiosity of the *New York Post*'s Milton Gross. During an in-depth interview at the Concord with Emile, Howie by his side, Gross went further than any other writer as he probed the 'difference' in 'a fighter who talks in a soft and gentle singsong calypso'.

Gross persuaded the boxer and his manager to discuss the rumours around his 'difference'. Howie admitted that, 'Emile is what people think he shouldn't be.' But neither he nor Gross, on the scent of a truly radical disclosure, could utter the word 'homosexual'. They danced around the issue, knowing that Emile's conundrum remained. He could act on his impulses; but he could never discuss them.

As Gross asked him again about the whispers rustling through his life, Emile spoke bluntly: 'People see me with queers, and they get the wrong idea. Of course, I deny it.'

He had no choice. Just over a week before he fought, for the third time, the man who had derided him as a *maricón*, what else could he say? Raw honesty, in 1962, was impossible for a gay boxer.

Gross persisted and asked if Emile had seen the latest Broadway gossip column, which had hinted at all the talk about his 'difference' a week earlier? 'Yes,' Emile said, as distress poured out of him in a garbled jumble of words. 'Well, actually, I heard about it. My mother saw it and it upset her so, and she has a bad heart too. Then my girlfriend Esther saw it – or somebody showed it to her. And she said, "Emile, I didn't know about you being that way." So I hit her.'

One lie to cover a bigger lie unsettled Emile. Of course, he had not hit Esther. Instead, she had helped provide him with a cover. It was an act of friendship and love that had touched him deeply. He would never raise his fist to a woman, let alone a woman he respected like Esther. Yet the more entangled he became in confusion, the worse he felt.

Emile thought he might sound manly, and less like a queer, if he pretended to Gross that he had hit his girlfriend. The double deceit ate away at him. It was even more bizarre that the *New York Post* made no comment about his claimed assault. It was as if violence against a woman was more permissible than love between two men. The madness of it all would break Emile's heart if he kept thinking so deeply about it.

Howie was worried. The innuendos had begun to gather sinister momentum. It was one of the reasons why Gil had insisted that Matthew stay away from the Concord. Emile could not afford to be distracted as Paret closed in on him. After the Gross interview, Howie suggested a fresh tack. Instead of dragging Esther back into the mess, they would look elsewhere.

A beautiful young black woman singer, Ce'Vara Livsey, had arrived at the Concord. She snared everyone's gaze and Howie conjured up his latest plan. Ce'Vara was still a relative unknown, but she was ambitious and gorgeous and Emile had heard her sing once before at the Copa Lounge in New York. He liked her and Howie persuaded Ce'Vara that it would boost her rising career if she did a photo session with Emile. She was easily convinced. And what harm could it do if, with a knowing wink, Howie let it slip to the UPI agency snapper that something might be cooking between Ce'Vara and Emile. They did not have to consider much how Esther might feel – when she and Emile were friends rather than lovers.

The fighter and the singer liked the look of each other even more, up close, and the photoshoot was a breeze. Emile was persuaded to strip off his top and Ce'Vara opened her big eyes a little wider in admiration of his rippling stomach and huge shoulders. They smiled at each other as she was instructed to bunch her small fist and rest it against the boxer's washboard stomach. Ce'Vara was very pretty and rather voluptuous and Emile enjoyed being close to her. Girls could sometimes get to him too.

As his camera popped and flared, the UPI man cooed in delight. Emile and Ce'Vara felt a little more shy then.

The photograph appeared the next morning in newspapers across America. Howie was especially thrilled that it had even made the sober pages of the *Washington Post*, where the caption read: 'A REAL PUNCH – Welterweight challenger Emile Griffith has his solar plexus tested by curvaceous chanteuse Ce'Vara, with whom he has been romantically linked as he works out in Monticello, N.Y.'

'Yeah, yeah,' Gil Clancy muttered when Howie told him the news. The trainer glanced across at Emile, who stared out the window of his large suite at the Concord. It was still raining steadily in the Catskills and, judging from his clouded expression, inside the fighter's head as well.

Gil walked over while Howie flicked through the rest of the morning papers. 'Hey, Emile,' Gil said softly. Emile looked up as his trainer told him to forget everything else. None of it mattered. And then Gil murmured seven words that would become eerily prophetic. 'It's all about you and Benny now ...'

Down on River Road, on the border of Summit, a town in the northwestern corridor of New Jersey's Union County, Benny Paret trained at a much grittier camp. There was none of the lush opulence of the Concord at Ehsan's, a wooden farmhouse located on a hilly stretch of land. It had been a fighters' hideaway for over forty years. World champions like Battling Siki, Gene Tunney, Mickey Walker, Ike Williams and Jake LaMotta had all trained at the complex once run by the formidable Madame Bey. But she had died twenty years before and the camp was crumbling.

Benny still relished the fact that Kid Chocolate and Kid Gavilan, his Cuban heroes, had trained there, at a time when the camp was named Madame Bey's. She had loved the flashy Cuban champions. Benny would have liked to have been a bit more like Kid Chocolate himself. Since regaining his world title from Griffith he had bought a new gold 1962 Eldorado Cadillac. And once he had got over his beating from Gene Fullmer, he used his far larger pay packet to buy another new car – a red 1962 Thunderbird.

He had also bought a new house in Miami six weeks earlier. Lucy worried that he was spending all their money, but Benny reassured her. He would receive $50,000 for fighting Griffith, while the challenger got just $17,000. Benny was still the top dog in the welterweight division and, while he was convalescing after Fullmer, he also bought Lucy some pretty dresses and a necklace to go with the house. He added to his own jewellery collection with a gold neck chain. Benny wanted to look like a rich world champion rather than a poor Cuban kid who had once cut sugar cane in the plantations around Santa Clara.

The news from Cuba was depressing. Fidel Castro had introduced a rationing scheme to cope with dire food shortages on the island. Milk, butter, eggs and beef were virtually unobtainable and, if you were Cuban, according to the *New York Herald Tribune* on 18 March 1962, 'you live on a diet of black bean soup, rice – imported from Red China – and low-quality bread. Food-buying has become a weary day-long battle for Cuba's housewives. In Havana the food lines start forming between 3am and 5am and by mid-morning stretch eight blocks long and three persons deep. Taunting the hapless women, with an endless repertory of trite Communist political and economic clichés blared from roaming loudspeaker vans, has become a popular sport among the militia and secret police.'

Manuel Alfaro, his manager, paraphrased the worst stories to convince Benny how lucky he was to be fighting instead for big money in America. There was no mention of the fact that, since the revolution, Cuba was on the path to radically improving the rate of literacy on the island. It was of little use to Benny. He still could not read or write. So he just listened quietly while Alfaro told him that the American papers were full of bad news. Cuba was a police state. Cuba was a Red puppet under the control of the Soviet Union. Cuba was starving. Cuba was ruined. Benny was lucky to have got out just in time.

There was wild talk that Castro was planning to launch a Cuban attack on the US naval base at Guantanamo Bay – but President Kennedy insisted there was no evidence to cause alarm. Kennedy also downplayed fears in mid-March 1962 that the Soviet development of an 'invulnerable global rocket' could lead to nuclear weapons being launched against the United States. It seemed as if the Red menace was everywhere – but Benny concentrated on his next pay packet.

In the early mornings, he ran along River Road and then up and down the agonising climb of Snake Hill. Fullmer had hit him so hard that his head throbbed for weeks afterwards. Alfaro waved away suggestions that Benny should see a doctor or have his brain x-rayed. Benny just needed a break, Alfaro insisted, and three-and-a-half months outside the ring would help.

He didn't mind the different kind of pain when his lungs burned and his legs ached up on Snake Road. It was a clean kind of pain which, once his dawn run was over, left him with fresh hope for a decisive battle in the Garden. Benny knew he would not easily recover from another defeat to Griffith. The loss of his world title, again, would put a terrible dent in his future earnings. When he left Miami for New York, Benny had promised Lucy he would talk to Alfaro about getting out of boxing. He just needed to hold onto his title and get one more big-money title fight to secure their future. Benny had begun to dream even harder of buying that butchery, which would help him escape the boxing slaughterhouse.

Griffith didn't hit nearly as hard as Fullmer, or move like Luis Rodriguez. But Benny had still found him a nightmare to fight. Griffith was as strong and accomplished in the ring as he was a wilting pansy on the outside. It was going to be another long, hard night and, sometimes, the thought depressed Benny. He was about to fight for the fiftieth time as a pro and it was difficult to dredge up the will to sustain himself.

Alfaro thought he could supply the edge – and undermine Griffith at the same time. Benny listened when Alfaro warned him that he could not lose again to a fucking *maricón*. Once was embarrassing; twice would be unforgivable. Benny would never live it down if he was defeated again by a faggot. It was obvious that Benny had distressed Griffith at their last weigh-in. Alfaro was convinced they should repeat the stunt.

Benny didn't like faggots. He had never done but, in regard to Griffith, his early suspicions had been deflected by his respect for a fellow boxer. When they had played basketball together in the Bronx, the sheer athleticism and power of Griffith on the court had overshadowed his soft voice and hip-swaying walk off it. And in the build-up to their first fight, before Griffith beat him, Benny had ignored the backdrop of gossip to concentrate on the threat his challenger posed in the ring. It had not helped him much and his title was ripped away on a stoppage. The bitterness Benny felt, in terms of his lost prestige and the amount of money Griffith had taken from him, hardened his attitude.

Alfaro was right. They had got to Griffith at the last weigh-in. They would get to the fucking *maricón* again at the next one. Benny was ready to do whatever he needed to hold onto his world title.

The press, having visited Griffith at the Concord, descended on Ehsan's in the week of the fight. They missed the sumptuous feast spread out before them at lunch in the Catskills – but Benny Paret fed them riveting copy. He complained about Griffith's sexuality with harsh mockery. Alfaro acted as his translator and gave the words a vicious spin as the reporters jotted down his quotes with gusto.

'I hate this kind of guy,' Alfaro said in an emotive translation after Paret had expressed doubts about Griffith. 'A fighter's got to look and talk and act like a man. What kind of fighter wears the kind of clothes Griffith does? What kind of fighter talks like that? What kind of fighter hangs around with the people he does?'

Alfaro flopped a limp wrist at the reporters. He made them laugh and spelt out his meaning without saying the words – homosexual, faggot, *maricón* – they could not print in 1962.

Paret continued talking in Spanish, prompted by his manager. 'Where I come from,' Alfaro said on behalf of Paret in English, 'it's important to be a proper man and a proper fighter. When I was a kid, I wanted to be like Kid Gavilan. He was a real fighter. And, more than anything else, he was a real man. He knocked out men and loved women.'

Alfaro pointed to the tattoo on Paret's left arm. The blue ink had faded, but the writers could make out the faint imprint of flowers and hearts cut into the fighter's dark skin.

Two words had been written above the swirling pattern. 'Do you know what that says?' Alfaro asked the press pack and then, before anyone could reply, he gave them the answer. 'True love.'

Alfaro allowed his words to settle in the soft evening air. 'Benny had those words tattooed for a woman,' he eventually said. 'That is true love – between a man and a woman.'

The manager kept talking in English – explaining that Paret's 'sense of machismo had been hurt and offended by Griffith'.

Alfaro was asked what he meant. '"Macho" is the word in Spanish,' he said. 'Benny Paret is macho. It means he is a man. A strong and brave man. A real man. Griffith is the opposite.'

Paret rocked himself in silence and the *New York Daily Post* described his mood that late Thursday afternoon of 22 March 1962. 'Paret is a gruff man. He finished the equivalent of kindergarten in Santa Clara, Cuba, before graduating to sugar cane. In the tiny, airless cubicle at Ehsan's Training Camp, near Summit, N.J., his hatred of Griffith was direct. But it wasn't simple ... before this reporter left, the fighter said to be sure to be at the weigh-in Saturday morning. "It should be fun," Paret said, almost grimly.'

Emile Griffith and Benny Paret had been examined and declared fit by Dr Alexander Schiff of the New York State Athletic Commission. Schiff had travelled to their respective training camps and checked their blood pressure, pulse rate and reflexes. He shone a small light into their eyes and asked some rudimentary questions to ascertain their mental wellbeing. There were no problems. They were ready to fight.

The last training drills had been done and they headed back to New York on Friday 23 March. Benny went alone to his old apartment in the Bronx, while Emile was meant to be based for the night at the Belvedere hotel. But, on his way into the city, he took a diversion out to Queens so he could see Matthew. They had been apart for weeks and Emile wanted to reassure him that the stories about Ce'Vara, the 'curvaceous chanteuse', were just a ruse dreamed up by Howie Albert.

Howie and Gil Clancy were already ensconced in the office of the New York State Athletic Commission where, with Manuel Alfaro, they had whittled down a shortlist of six officials to two judges and the referee. They were certain that Ruby Goldstein should take charge of the fight. He was the finest referee in the world and this was boxing's fight of the year.

Alfaro grumbled about Goldstein's tendency to opt for a cautious early stoppage and reminded everyone that, in Paret, he had a fighter with extraordinary punch resistance. He did not want Goldstein stepping in too soon, as he had done when stopping Cassius Clay's fight with Sonny Banks.

Clancy spoke up for Goldstein, reminding them that the New Yorker was steeped in boxing. Goldstein had been a fine welterweight in the 1920s and 1930s, nicknamed the 'Jewel of the Ghetto', and had won fifty-four of his sixty bouts. As a referee, he was sufficiently famous to have rescued Joe Louis in his last fight against Rocky Marciano in 1951 and to have appeared on *The Ed Sullivan Show* alongside Sugar Ray Robinson – where his compassion as the third man in the ring was praised.

Alfaro was more convinced that Al Berl should not be the referee – for in Paret's winning rematch he was the only official to agree with the ringside writers that Griffith had won the fight. So they settled on Goldstein. Clancy also got his way in rejecting Artie Aidala and Tony Castellano, the two officials who had given the nod to Paret six months before. Tony Rossi and Frank Forbes were elected as judges.

Emile was oblivious to the protracted negotiations. He took the raspberry-coloured 7 train to Queens. A cab would have been more private, and more suited to a man dreaming of becoming world champion, but Emile wanted the grimy feel of the subway after five weeks in the damp open air of the Catskills. He needed to see the underground colours and faces of New York again, and breathe in the hot fumes of home. Emile also liked seeing the posters and adverts in the paper for movies and concerts that weekend.

There was a huge image of Paul Newman, smouldering and barefoot, in a new movie version of *Sweet Bird of Youth*. Newman looked defiant and irresistible to women, and men like Emile, above a logo that promised: 'He used love like most men use money!'

Subtitled foreign films were the rage in New York and that weekend there were screenings of Ingmar Bergman's *Through a Glass*

Darkly, Alain Resnais' *Last Year at Marienbad*, Federico Fellini's *La Dolce Vita* and Roger Vadim's *Les Liaisons Dangereuses*. There were also more familiar names – like Rock Hudson and Doris Day in *Lover Come Back*.

On Broadway, Henry Fonda and Olivia de Havilland would soon star in a play called *A Gift of Time*, about a doting wife and her terminally ill husband, while Ibsen's *Ghosts*, Jean Genet's *The Blacks*, and *Brecht on Brecht* offered more challenging productions in the new Off-Broadway movement, which had emerged in the late 1950s. There were also significant gigs that weekend – with John Coltrane and Count Basie both playing in Greenwich Village.

The world would keep turning while Emile Griffith and Benny Paret settled into silence and starvation. They would talk and eat properly again once they had stepped off the scales at the official weigh-in. Only the fight, to the finish this time, would be left.

Emile and Matthew took the subway on Saturday morning back into Manhattan. His plan had been to travel alone, but Emile gave in when Matthew stood at the door to the Colfax Street house. Matthew held Emile's two bags in his hands and shook his head to stop any arguments. They agreed that Matthew would accompany him to the Belvedere and then, to avoid Paret's sneers, he would return to Queens.

The boxer and his boyfriend sat together on the swaying 7 train. Emile had pulled his hat down over his eyes. He was not in the mood to talk or make eye contact with anyone. They could have clattered through the subway all the way to the Garden, just around the corner from the New York State Athletic Commission offices, and a block away from the Belvedere. But Emile got off at 42nd Street. He wanted the solace of walking along the familiar streets of Times Square.

Just before 11 a.m. on a Saturday morning, and on the day of the biggest fight of his life, he was not about to duck into any of his haunts. Once he got Paret out of the way he would be able to savour everything he loved about Times Square, but, at that moment, he and Matthew just walked quietly through the area that defined his life. Men, women, drag queens, hookers, junkies and shop owners called out to him – wishing him good luck and giving him the name 'champ' he loved. Normally, he would stop and offer his hand, while yakking away to whoever wanted to talk to him. But, then, he just raised his fist to his people and walked on. He would be fighting for them too.

The Belvedere, where he would meet Howie and Gil, was on Broadway and 48th Street. When they reached the entrance, Emile took the bags from Matthew. He gave him the most fleeting of embraces and reminded him to head straight home. For once, Matthew did as he was told.

Gil and Howie were already waiting in a suite at the Belvedere. Emile had checked his weight at home but, to reassure his trainer, he stepped on the scales again. He was lighter than he had been for a long time – three pounds under the welterweight mark.

'Think of McGinnis's,' Howie murmured. 'Think of that steak . . .'

Emile had threatened to punch Paret if he tried to taunt him again. Gil had come down hard, warning that he would ruin five weeks of brutal work if he lashed out too early at Paret. The commission would fine him, and they could even ban him from the ring. He needed to control himself.

None of them felt in the mood for their usual fight-morning table tennis lark and so they mooched around the hotel until just before noon. The tension stifled them and they walked in silence to the weigh-in.

Benny 'Kid' Paret bounced around the room. He looked as cheery as Griffith was withdrawn. The Cuban seemed to be in a party mood. But Griffith looked like he was undressing for a funeral as he stripped off first for the scales. He knew he would make weight but, with the heaters turned up high to keep the fighters warm, he just wanted to get out of the sweltering room.

Griffith stood in his underwear and socks while he waited for the call. He kept his head down, deliberately evading Paret. He could hear cackling and jabbering, but, remembering what Gil had told him, he tried to block everything out.

When the nod came he slipped off his socks and stepped onto the giant weighing scales. Griffith stared straight at the red measuring marker as it leaped forward and flickered in front of him. Even his resolute gaze could not stop him noticing the shadow of Benny Paret at his side. Emile kept looking steadily ahead, but he could sense the leering grin of his opponent as Paret pointed at the marker and laughed. It was as if he could not believe Griffith had come in as light as a fairy – at 144 pounds.

Paret's face was wreathed in a mocking grin. His eyes were narrowed as he cocked his head to look up at Griffith. It was a provocative invitation but Griffith stayed strong. He resisted the temptation to turn towards Paret and waited instead for the official announcement of his weight.

The Cuban disappeared from view and Griffith nodded a thank you to the announcer. He was just about to step off the scales when he heard Clancy's voice: 'Hey, watch it!'

Griffith wheeled round and turned cold. Paret was feigning intercourse with him, smirking with spite, as his manager and trainers whooped hysterically. He then waggled a finger at Griffith and reached out to touch him.

Paret spoke in his own language – but it was basic enough for Griffith, who understood some Spanish. 'Hey, *maricón*,' Paret said in a cooing lisp, 'I'm gonna get you and your husband.'

The Cuban's corner roared. They had seen how the words hurt Griffith.

Paret had told the world that Emile and Matthew were *maricones*. They were faggots. Paret had effectively accused them of being criminals and deviants. Emile, in private, was proud that he could fall for a man. In public, aiming to become a world champion again, he felt ashamed and angry that his secret life was being highlighted and demeaned. How could Paret be so calculating and cruel? Did he not know how much danger such a slur could bring down on Emile?

In the sanctuary of Times Square, Emile could be himself even if he did not dare admit it out loud. He knew that in the strict terms of the law he could be locked up in jail or a madhouse for being a gay man. How could Paret hurl such a deadly insult at him in an atmosphere as fraught and macho as a world title weigh-in?

Emile was about to hit Paret harder than he had hit anyone before when Clancy dived between the fighters. He wrapped his wiry Rockaway Beach arms tightly around Emile.

'Save it for tonight, Emile,' he hissed.

The trainer needed all his strength to hold Emile, twitching with fury, as Paret leered at him.

Eventually, the rage ebbed. The sour taste of humiliation rose up in Emile's throat like bile. He allowed himself to turn limp in Clancy's grip, his way of telling his trainer that he had heard him. Emile was close to crying and Clancy, sensing the changed mood, patted him on the back. The fighter dressed hurriedly. He could not believe Paret had done it again.

They left the building in a tight huddle, Clancy and Albert flanking him, and walked quickly towards McGinnis's. It was a cold and blustery March day and Clancy urged Griffith to calm down. He needed to save his anger for the Garden.

'Breathe, Emile,' Clancy said softly, 'breathe . . .'

Benny Paret went back to the Bronx. All the mischief of the weigh-in had drained out of him. He felt empty and lonely. Benny wished that Lucy had come with him to New York. She would have helped him. He remembered how, just four days before he left for his training camp, Lucy had held him when he had cried. They had taken little Benny Jr to the zoo in Miami but, at the entrance, they had been turned away.

'You're coloured,' Benny and Lucy had been told bluntly.

It was hard to take and Lucy had been stunned when, as they left, her husband, rather than their small son, had shed tears. The injustice got to him because it reminded him that, rather than being a world champion boxer, he still looked like a poor cane cutter.

Benny had tried then to persuade her to leave Miami with him and little Benny, so that she could watch him hold onto his title. But Lucy hated boxing more than ever. For weeks, even though she had not told him, she had been haunted by nightmares. Lucy dreamed terrifying dreams of Benny being hurt. She had seen how badly battered he had been by Fullmer and could not shake the images from her head.

Lucy made her excuses. She was seven weeks pregnant with their second child. It would also be better for Benny Jr if she stayed in Miami and looked after him. They would be waiting for him on his return.

The night before he fought Griffith for the third and last time, Benny Paret called his young wife. He had lain down on his bed in the Bronx for an hour. His head had begun to hurt again and he felt lonely. Benny normally never said much – but, that night, the words spilled out of him like blood from a gash.

Benny told Lucy the truth. He felt bad. His head hurt and he did not want to fight.

Lucy pleaded with him to withdraw from the contest. He had turned twenty-five two weeks earlier, on 14 March 1962. Lucy had missed spending his birthday with him because Benny had been away training. She wanted him back – especially with another baby on the way.

Manuel Alfaro would never allow it. They were in too deep. There was too much money riding on him fighting Griffith. He had no choice. Benny Paret, just twenty-four hours after that anguished phone call, would step into the ring one last time.

He said goodbye softly, and put the heavy receiver down on the black cradle of the phone. It made a quiet click as the line went dead. Lucy Paret would never hear from her husband again.

Madison Square Garden, New York, Saturday 24 March 1962

At ringside, alongside the cigar-wielding gangsters and bent politicians who had snaffled the rest of the front-row seats, the fight writers were still absorbing the shocking weigh-in. They could hardly believe that Benny 'Kid' Paret had acted so graphically – or that Emile Griffith had reacted with such raw pain.

It had been hard for them to know how to write about the incident for their early evening editions, but Howard M. Tuckner, of the *New York Times*, tried his best. He had written sensitively about the weigh-in, aware that homosexuality spelt out forbidden territory on the sports pages. But it was plain to all the writers, especially Tuckner, Pete Hamill of the *New York Post* and Jerry Izenberg of the *Newark Star-Ledger*, that a previously unspoken boundary had been crossed. Tuckner, with the liberal and authoritative *Times*, needed to describe the awkward situation with a degree of honesty.

He filed his copy just after two that afternoon and wrote about the jibe Paret had aimed at Griffith's sexuality. Tuckner knew that *maricón* was the worst, and deadliest, insult, in Hispanic culture. He was also aware that they lived in a society where Liberace was still allowed to pretend that he was a firmly heterosexual man. Boxing was not a game. It held up a mirror to its fighters and revealed their real nature in the ring. Tuckner, like everyone else on the boxing beat, knew that Griffith was a homosexual. But that did not impinge on his decency as a man and his ferocity as a fighter.

Out of respect to Griffith, and a conservative world, Tuckner made no comment about the fighter's sexual preference. He just reported soberly that Griffith had been subjected by Paret to a slur about his sexuality. Tuckner would have liked to have explored the issue further, but he understood the restrictions.

Just before 9 p.m., while ringside at Madison Square Garden, he collared young Pete Hamill and proceeded to rage against the totalitarian idiots on the copy desk at the *New York Times*. Hamill worked for the *Post*, a tabloid, but Tuckner had made it to the peak of his profession and the supposedly magisterial sports desk of the *Times*. Tuckner was incandescent. At the *Post*, they had allowed Milton Gross to ask Griffith about his 'difference' – and had even allowed the fighter to deny that he was 'queer'. But the subeditors at the *Times* were too timid to print the word 'homosexual'. It frightened them, and so they reached for the blue pencil and ran a line through Tuckner's copy whenever he wrote 'homosexual'.

In their wisdom, the *New York Times* copy editors replaced the offensive word with the meaningless phrase, 'un-man'. Tuckner could not believe it when, on his way to the fight, he had picked up the paper and, under his by-line, read that Paret had accused Griffith of being an 'un-man'.

Tuckner shouted out his disbelief to Hamill. '*Un-man?*' he yelled. 'What the fuck is an un-man? A butterfly is an un-man. A rock is an un-man ...'

He did not need to say anything else. As writers, who watched fighters risk their lives, they respected the humanity of boxers above all else. Emile Griffith was more than just a challenger for the world welterweight title. He was a very real man, as brave as he was vulnerable.

Tuckner was still yelling, '... un-man ... what is an un-man? These lunatics ...', when the lights dimmed in the Garden.

A visceral roar echoed around the arena. The battle between the macho Cuban sugar-cane refugee and the hat-making 'un-man' was about to begin.

The champion was dressed in a beautiful white satin gown with the name Benny 'Kid' Paret stitched in black on the back. His challenger wore a gold robe with Emile Griffith printed in stark letters. Griffith, jogging parallel to the ropes, back-pedalled his way down the ring. Then, with a skittering series of small hops and jumps, he bounced back to his corner where Clancy readjusted the shiny robe.

'Let's get going up in the centre of the ring and have the festivities started,' Don Dunphy said at ringside, as his voice boomed across America. 'Here's our very good friend, Johnny Addie.'

After a stirring rendition of the national anthem and Addie's grand introduction of both Griffith and Paret, Ruby Goldstein called the two fighters towards him. While Goldstein spoke plainly, repeating his instructions for a good, clean fight, Griffith's gaze fixed on the canvas. He was unsure he could trust himself not to attack Paret if he heard the same word again.

Goldstein asked them to shake hands, but Griffith just backed away, evading any contact with the man who had called him *maricón*.

As always, Griffith wore black trunks. Paret was in white as, disrobed, they began round one of the fight that would change their lives.

They started cagily with thirty seconds of jabbing and feinting. Griffith then landed a sharp combination, a rat-a-tat-tat left jab and overhand right. Paret tucked in, crowding his opponent, and tried to slow him with some early body shots. Griffith pushed him back and landed a solid right that rocked the Kid's head. His jab then snaked repeatedly into Paret's face. Griffith was much sharper and more accurate. He looked deadly serious as he backed up the champion and shook him with another right hand.

Griffith bullied and pummelled Paret again in the second, with the Cuban relying on counters to stem the aggression. Don Dunphy sensed there was something different about Griffith at the end of the round. 'It looks as if Griffith is trying for the knockout, while Paret is hoping to win on a decision – as he did last time.'

Returning to his corner, Paret pushed the white gumshield out of his mouth and sat down heavily on the stool. Joe Di Maria, his trainer, tried to reduce the swelling on the right side of Paret's face by pressing an iced compress against his eye and cheek.

The third was worse for Paret. A small cut began to weep beneath his puffy eye and, as he absorbed more punishment, Dunphy wondered if the damaging effects of the Fullmer fight could be seen in Paret. Griffith's punches looked vicious as he brought new malice to his work.

Paret was more effective after a minute's rest and the fourth round was an intense affair, as they swapped hard combinations. For the first time in the fight, the champion snapped back the head of his old rival with an uppercut. The Cuban was soon backed up again and he began to bleed above the cheekbone. 'Paret's a good, game fighter and sometimes he appears hurt when he really isn't,' Dunphy suggested. 'He has great recuperative powers. Paret seems to be in trouble, but he's one of those fighters who fights better when he is hurt.'

The champion began the fifth more solidly, even brightly, but midway through the round he walked into a short left which seemed to unhinge him. Griffith followed with another distressing combination that set the Cuban reeling backwards. 'Paret is hurt,' Dunphy yelped.

He was a fighter, though, and Paret dug deep into his darkest instincts and fought back. Griffith's surge was stemmed as Paret hooked to the body. They finished the round by trading blows, with Paret having, seemingly, recovered.

The new pattern continued in the sixth as Paret landed a few piston-like blows to Griffith's stomach and flanks. His sudden success galvanised him. Paret's jab was suddenly tersely belligerent and Griffith began to box much more cautiously, as if he could sense the changed mood. He scored a few crisp punches and Paret was returned to his familiar place on the ropes. But Paret was landing the cleaner blows and, with twenty seconds left in the round, he set Griffith up with a right uppercut and then nailed him with a brute of a left hook.

Griffith collapsed in the corner – ending up on the canvas for only the second time in his career. His left hand hung over the ropes and he used his right glove to cross himself as if, blearily, he was asking for help before he tried to rise. It was a bad knockdown and, even though Griffith was up at the count of six, he looked disorientated.

'The round is almost over but I don't think he knows where he is,' Dunphy yelled as he watched Griffith hold onto the top rope for support.

As Goldstein gestured them to fight on, Griffith staggered towards Paret. His arms flailed in drunken imitations of punches as the bell sounded – rescuing him from a likely knockout.

Gil Clancy and Syd Martin went to work in the corner while Howie

Albert watched anxiously. They doused Griffith with cold water, and then Clancy staunched the bleeding from his fighter's nose and began to talk calmly. A wave of smelling salts, which Martin sneaked in from the side, made Emile snort and shake his head. He drew in a deep breath and Clancy, having offered him a drink of water, reminded him that he had to keep punching. It was crucial that he did not stop throwing punches until Paret fell.

Griffith threw back his head and then, almost as if he was about to vomit, hunched over the steel bucket between his feet. He opened his mouth and bloody water gushed out. Clancy wiped him down and shoved the gumshield back in place. 'Keep hitting him, Emile,' he said. 'Don't stop hitting him.'

'Here comes round seven,' Dunphy said excitedly as the bell tolled. 'Boy, that changed things in a hurry . . .'

Griffith held and grappled and pushed Paret away early in the seventh as he waited for his head to clear. Paret, searching for the knockout, missed with some huge swings and, gradually, Griffith recovered. There was a minute left in the round when Griffith returned to the attack. He hurt Paret – but was then wobbled by the Cuban's left hook. They swapped blows at the bell – and Griffith, feeling the animosity of the weigh-in returning, pushed Paret angrily as they parted.

Griffith edged the eighth and ninth rounds, as they both took a little breather between punches, but each time they brawled and wrestled after the bell. It was a spiteful but compelling battle.

Paret landed a low blow to start the tenth, but, after being rebuked by Goldstein, he raised both arms above his head in apology. It was a reminder of the darker trouble between them. Griffith stalked Paret with increasing malevolence as he began to hit the man who had wounded him so badly eleven hours earlier. The punches rained down on Paret in percussive flurries. His mouth opened, involuntarily, and his head sagged. One blow after another connected with shuddering force. Griffith was picking his punches carefully, ensuring their destructive accuracy. Paret survived and Griffith eased off for the rest of the round and much of the eleventh. Darkness would soon fall.

Before the start of the twelfth round, Paret, as usual, was up first. He danced lightly while waiting for the bell. Griffith remained on his stool until the bell rang.

Their heads rested against each other as they both went to the body. Paret held more often and the referee had to instruct them to break, like they were two teenage lovers caught canoodling on a park bench.

'They seem to be pacing themselves for what might be a furious finish,' Dunphy said innocently. 'Two minutes left in this round.'

Griffith forced Paret into a corner, but the Cuban, still looking slippery, slithered away. His escape did not last. He was backed up against the same wooden post but he managed to hold Griffith off a little longer.

'This has probably been the tamest round of the entire fight,' Dunphy complained mildly.

It started then – with two short and brutal right hands from Griffith. They arrived in close-up, one straight after the other. Paret teetered backwards. Griffith saw the damage before anyone. He leaped forward ferociously, like a big cat bringing down his prey, and threw another right.

A left and right, followed by the exact same combination, opened Paret up. He buckled sadly, already slipping away into oblivion.

In that moment, Griffith might have stepped back and allowed the champion to fall. But he was a fighter fuelled by bitter rage. All the hurt of the weigh-in poured out of him. All the years of secrecy and shame coursed through him. He was about to punish Paret, and the world, in a way that no one watching would ever forget.

An uppercut made Paret sag a little more, and Griffith used the right hand to hit him again. Paret tried to hold his guard up but his arms were too weak. They fell limply to his sides. Paret turned side-on, away from Griffith, so that he was propped up by the ropes.

Griffith now had a clear and open target of Paret's lolling head. He had also turned his body so that he could gain maximum torque and power with every punch he threw. Each one of them landed with deadening force. Griffith threw the right hand again and again and again and again, making Paret's head rock back and forth on a neck that looked like a broken plinth. He used his left arm to pin Paret against the ropes while his right, a sawing uppercut that he pumped back and forth, did its worst.

One punch followed another, echoing the insult from the weigh-in, in a swift and shocking cortège. It was as if each blow was in answer to the taunt.

Maricón? A right uppercut whipped in and snapped back Paret's helpless head.
Maricón? Another right uppercut.
Maricón? A right uppercut.
Maricón? Another uppercut.
Maricón? A fifth right uppercut.
Maricón? Again.
Maricón? And again.
Maricón? Another right uppercut.
Maricón? The same punch again.
Maricón? A tenth right uppercut.
Maricón? The eleventh right uppercut.
Maricón? A twelfth right uppercut.

The blows were so savage that Ruby Goldstein, boxing's most compassionate referee, seemed helpless, as if the ferocity had turned him blind. He stood dumbly, as if the sound of a fist smashing into a cracked jawbone had deafened him. At ringside they could hear the sound of every punch, encased in a thin six-ounce leather glove, as if it was the distant echo of a heavy spade digging a grave.

Paret did not cry out. He just lay there, his head being snapped back and forth in a brutal nod of recognition by each uppercut.

Griffith seemed lost in the thicket of his fury. But, after his dozen uppercuts, he suddenly threw the left hand as well. The sight of two fists, drilling like pistons into Paret's defenceless head, finally snapped Goldstein out of his stunned reverie. He leaped between the fighters at last.

The only way he could stop Griffith hitting Paret was by wrapping his arms around a man who had been deformed into a punching machine. As Goldstein and Griffith staggered away in a drunken embrace, Benny Paret slid down. His eyes began to close as he started to die.

Paret's right arm was trapped against the ropes, while his left spread out in a surreal crucifixion.

'Paret sags to the canvas,' Dunphy screamed. 'Paret goes down from sheer exhaustion.'

His trainers scrambled around him. Di Maria reached into the gaping hollow of Paret's mouth and pulled out the bloodied gumshield. He was obviously unconscious.

'Dr Schiff is coming to look at him,' Dunphy said desperately. 'Paret has collapsed from exhaustion after that beating on the ropes. Dr Schiff is trying to get at him. The fight has been stopped and the winner and new champion is Emile Griffith. But we're more concerned about the condition of Benny "Kid" Paret than we are about the title at the moment.'

They laid out Benny Paret as if he was already a corpse.

'The time, at two minutes and nine seconds, of the twelfth round,' Johnny Addie cried out from the centre of the ring, 'and the winner by a knockout … and once again welterweight champion of the world … *Emile Griffith!*'

The new champion raised his arms and smiled happily, with Gil Clancy at his side. Then, as if noticing the ghostly vision in the opposite corner for the first time, his face changed. Griffith walked over to check on Paret. But they would not allow him near the man he had battered. He was led away and, in confusion, raised his arms again.

Griffith, however, was no longer smiling. He had seen the body of Benny 'Kid' Paret.

At ringside, Gaspar Ortega, who had fought both Paret and Griffith, was distraught at the sight of twenty-three unanswered blows smashing into Paret. The way in which Paret had slipped away, as if he had already left his limp body, frightened Ortega. He began to cry as, reaching for his wife's hand, he pulled her away. They needed to escape the Garden.

In the middle of the ring, Don Dunphy had not understood the outcome as completely. 'Here is Emile Griffith, the young man who has regained the world welterweight championship in an exciting fight with Benny "Kid" Paret, whom he dethroned,' Dunphy said as he pulled the winner towards him. 'I want to congratulate you, Emile, but we're all holding our breath to see how Benny "Kid" Paret is.'

'Thank you very much, Don,' Emile said politely, wrapped in his robe, 'I'm very proud to be welterweight champion again and I hope Paret is feeling very good. But they won't tell me how he feels.'

'Benny,' Dunphy said, before correcting himself. 'Emile ... I want you to take a look at our screen here. We're going to replay the knock-out in slow-motion videotape. And I'd like you to describe what happened – if you can remember. It was very exciting.'

'Well, I was moving away from him,' Emile said, in a daze, as he watched himself and Benny on the small black-and-white monitor. 'I was trying to jab him away. I hurt him in the last few rounds.'

Clancy spoke up. 'Describe what you see there, Emile,' he said, pointing at the monitor. 'That's what you gotta do. Describe what you see right in front of you – what you're doing right there.'

Emile hesitated, as he saw himself beating the life out of Benny Paret.

'Was it any one punch, do you remember?' Dunphy asked.

'No,' Emile said, with a sad shake of his head, 'it was a series of punches in the corner. After I hurt him, he went through the ropes. I kept on punching.'

'Now there it is!' Dunphy exclaimed, as the first big right hand crashed into Paret again on the screen. 'That did it, that did it!'

'Yeah, it's over now,' Clancy said bleakly.

'He's hurt now, see,' Dunphy said, encouraging Emile to look more closely.

'I hurt him there,' Emile agreed, 'and then I was punching inside.'

'That beautiful camerawork there,' Dunphy enthused.

'Yeah, terrific,' another voice confirmed as, on the monitor, the deadly procession of uppercuts was counted out. It was the first time in television history that a slow-motion replay had been used.

They fell silent as they watched. But Dunphy, knowing that dead-air on television was a crime, eventually chipped in: 'There it is,' he said.

'Yes sir, no sir,' a colleague exclaimed.

'And that's just about it, Emile,' Dunphy suggested.

'I just kept punching,' Emile said, horror thickening his voice as he watched himself helplessly. 'I just kept punching . . .'

CHAPTER SEVEN

The Letter

Lucy Paret had covered her head in a scarf, as if it were a shroud, and slipped a large gold crucifix around her neck. She was a tiny woman, less than five feet tall, and she looked as if she was drowning in the big black coat she had wrapped around herself. Her usually pretty face resembled a waxy mask. All her distress had been stunned and sealed as, outside the Roosevelt hospital on 10th Avenue in New York, she scuttled through a corridor of yelling photographers who wanted her to stare into their cameras. Lucy clutched her two-year-old son, Benny Jr, closer to her chest and tried to escape.

The chaos and noise faded inside the hospital. They had been expecting her arrival from Miami on that cold Sunday afternoon. She was taken to the second floor and led down a long and echoing passage. The doctors would talk to her but, first, she could see her husband.

There were eight beds in the room. Six of them were empty. The two occupied beds faced each other. Lucy did not know it then but they both supported brain-damaged fighters. Her gaze fixed on the sombre sight of the man she loved.

Benny Paret had tubes sticking out of his nose and throat. They made a hushed gurgle. A nurse told Lucy that the curved piece of plastic that filled Benny's mouth helped him to breathe. His head was bandaged because, in the early hours of that morning, they had operated on his brain. Benny's eyes were closed and, as she leaned down to kiss him, Lucy saw the iced bags surrounding his body. The nurse told her not to worry. They were cooling him down because his temperature had risen to 104 degrees. Everything was under control again.

It was then that Lucy noticed, for the first time, a young woman sitting at the bedside of the other patient. She stood up, held out her hand and offered her sympathy to Lucy. Her name was Marie Ryff and her husband, Frankie, was also a boxer. Marie tried to help Lucy by distracting Benny Jr. She picked him up and took him to the window, so that she could point to the clouds changing shape and colour in the sky.

When Dr John Crisp arrived, he spoke calmly to Lucy. Benny was in a serious condition, but Crisp, one of the hospital's three chief surgical residents, reassured her that they had done everything they could to assist him. Benny had arrived at the hospital from Madison Square Garden at 11.32 the previous night. Surgery had begun at 12.20 a.m. and they had worked on him for three hours. Dr Robert Schick, a neurosurgeon, performed the operation, and he had drilled four holes, each the size of a quarter, into Benny's skull.

Two acute subdural haematomas, or blood clots, were found. The first was on the left side of the brain, the second on the right. Each of the four openings revealed discolouring on the surface of the brain and clear evidence of bleeding. Both clots were drained of eight cubic centimetres of fluid. They had also found evidence of oedema, or swelling of the brain, but Crisp said that this was common in boxing injuries and less concerning than the damage done by the haematomas.

Lucy asked the question that mattered most to her. She needed to know whether her husband would live.

Crisp said they would not give up on him. But he hesitated and then decided to tell her the truth. There was only a very small chance that Benny would recover. When he had arrived from Madison Square Garden in an ambulance, his body twitching on a stretcher, he had been bleeding from the mouth and nose. At least they had eased the pressure on his brain and stabilised him. But he was in a coma and the situation was critical. They could only hope and pray that he would improve in the wake of the operation.

Lucy began to cry after Crisp left. Marie called for help and a nurse took Benny Jr by the hand and led him away to a room set aside for small children. Lucy wept for a long time, her head buried against the increasingly damp blouse of Marie, the kind stranger she had just met. Eventually, they parted and the two women sat down again next to their respective husbands. Lucy found the words to ask Marie about Frankie. What had happened to him?

Frankie Ryff was also a professional boxer. He had only decided to quit in 1959 when he lost three fights in a row. But Frankie had still won thirty bouts and his losses had come against skilled boxers like Ralph Dupas, who was mentioned regularly as a potential challenger to either Benny or Emile Griffith in a world title contest. Marie was relieved when Frankie got out of boxing, but she knew he wasn't happy. He still missed it and dreamed of fighting again. Frankie had even spoken to Gil Clancy and the trainer had agreed that they might work together as long as he got back into shape first.

Frankie was on the way back when, on 19 January, he had been working on a construction site in midtown. He had slipped and fallen eight storeys down an elevator shaft. Frankie had suffered similar brain damage to Benny and had been in a coma for ten weeks. But Marie had hope now – and she urged Lucy not to give up either. Frankie was paralysed but he was out of his coma and, twice a day, she was allowed to feed him. Marie was also encouraged to help him learn how to talk again. She would say simple words over and over and, sometimes, Frankie would thrill her by managing to repeat a mangled version of the same sound. A long road stretched out in front of them, but she could believe again that Frankie would survive and, maybe, return to some kind of ordinary life.

Lucy nodded. She was pleased for Marie but her face crumpled again as she turned to look at Benny. 'I just want him to open his eyes,' she said.

Later that afternoon, when Manuel Alfaro arrived, Lucy went for a walk. She did not like being in the same room as Benny's manager, and her former boss at the Tropicana, and so she told Alfaro and Marie that she needed a coffee.

Alfaro dealt in blunt specifics and he knew Kid Paret had fought his last fight. He had already met with the press and revealed that, according to Dr Howard Dunbar, a neurosurgeon at the hospital, Benny's chances of recovery were 'one in 10,000'. Alfaro blamed Ruby Goldstein for the tragedy. 'I lost a champion because of negligence on the part of the referee,' he said, claiming that in the last round he had jumped on the apron of the ring and screamed: 'Stop it! Stop it!' Goldstein had ignored him and they now had to face the worst. 'It's up to God,' Alfaro said with a shrug.

Lucy made it down to the ground floor and stood at the end of a corridor looking frazzled and distraught. She was lost in her tangled thoughts when a young man approached. Pete Hamill worked for the *New York Post*. Lucy wasn't sure if she wanted to talk to a reporter but this guy seemed different. He told her how much he liked Benny and how he hoped her husband would pull through. Hamill then asked Lucy how she was coping amid the shock and the hurt.

'I got no more tears left,' Lucy told Hamill. 'I'm dry.'

But the words soon flowed from her and she opened up to Hamill. Lucy admitted that even the thought of Benny fighting Griffith for a third time had unsettled her for weeks. 'I dreamed he was going to get knocked out,' she said, as Hamill copied down her words in his notebook. 'I dreamed it. I couldn't eat for two days before the fight. When he lost to Griffith a year ago I asked him to quit. I told him, "Benny, don't do it no more." I thought he would get hurt. I never liked boxing. But it was his life and I didn't want to interfere."

Why did Benny keep fighting? Lucy shook her head. 'He didn't know how to do anything else. He wanted to take the money from this fight and open a butcher shop in Miami. He loved that stuff – working with his hands. He loved the idea of becoming a butcher.'

A large black woman walked down the green-walled corridor carrying her exhausted son. Benny Jr, wearing a plaid jacket, was crying. Lucy knew it was time she took him back to her sister's home as his sleep had been disturbed the night before. Woken by her screams, Benny Jr had waddled into the living room. He had stared at the television, and pointed at his father. He kept saying, 'Papa ... Papa ...'

As Lucy left the hospital she was engulfed by voracious reporters. They all wanted to hear her speak. The questions became harder and Lucy's pain spilled out. She told the newspapermen that Benny was still in a coma. Lucy could not help herself. She admitted that she was pregnant and that she had been worried about Benny for a long time.

Everything seemed to have gone wrong since he fought Emile Griffith. Lucy said that she knew there was 'bad blood' between her husband and Griffith. Pressed for the reasons, she said she had heard it was because Benny had called Griffith 'a woman' at the weigh-in. But it was not Benny's fault.

So who did she blame for the terrible outcome? 'The referee should have stopped the fight,' Lucy said, 'but I blame Griffith. He knew my husband was knocked out but he kept hitting him. He was very mean. I know that Griffith wanted to win but he shouldn't have tried to kill my husband.'

On the twentieth floor of the New Yorker hotel, with a panoramic view of the city spread out below him, Emile Griffith gazed instead at the walls in anguish. He was dressed smartly – in a crisp white buttoned-down shirt, black silk trousers and black Italian boots – but the words fell from him in a broken mess.

The writers who had gathered around him, just thirty-six hours after his fists had battered Paret into a coma, struggled to keep up as

Emile spoke in blurring chunks that Monday morning. 'The last two nights I just sleep and wake, sleep and wake, all the time,' Emile said, as if talking to himself. 'I don't know if I even want to be champ now. It seems like it just means trouble. I wanted to win the title back, but not like this. It's turned into a nightmare. I'm sorry about Paret. God knows, I'm sorry about Paret.'

His words would appear in all the New York newspapers, and across the entire country in the syndicated UPI and AP reports, but Emile didn't care. It seemed important he try to explain what happened – even if he was not entirely sure how they had ended up in such a crisis. He could not quite keep the anger out of his voice when he remembered how it all started. 'We've been feuding since our second fight. Paret was trying to needle me. But I've never hung around with queers. What am I going to hang around with queers for when I'm in the public eye? Or even if I wasn't in the public eye ...'

Emile looked down. It was hard to smudge the truth when he felt so bad. 'The first time we fought in Miami and we were perfect gentlemen. I went to Paret's camp to take pictures – no bad remarks were made. He came to my camp to take pictures. No remarks. But we came up to New York and that was it. He set about trying to needle me. It wasn't right.'

The reporters crowded in closer. They were so used to unfettered access to Emile that, even at his lowest and most vulnerable, they were not about to step back. So what had he been thinking in those last fatal seconds of pummelling Paret with one deadly, unanswered blow after another? Emile scratched his head, as if trying to recall exactly how he felt in the ring, and then sadness crunched up his face. 'My mind kept saying, "You're looking good now, just punch, punch, punch ..." I didn't know what I was doing.'

Emile looked as if he was about to cry as, in desperation, he turned to his trainer and shouted: 'No, no, Clancy! The whole thing sounds so bad. The Kid's lying up there and I'm talking about how I felt ...'

Gil Clancy stood up and steered Emile towards the sanctuary of the adjoining room. Once Emile had disappeared, and Clancy had closed the connecting doors, the trainer gathered the writers around him. He wanted to knock some sense into them.

'They talk about his clothes,' he said of Emile. 'Why? We buy our clothes at the same tailor – Gabe Piro's on Central Park West – and nobody makes cracks about me. It's just that Emile's got that damn 26-inch waist and 44-inch chest. Emile's just a sweet and innocent kid – and a great world champion. He's caught between two worlds, but it ain't what Paret or anyone else suggests. They all got it wrong.'

His friend Buddy Garaventi, who was Frank Sinatra's cousin, chipped in to support Gil. 'It just takes one malicious guy to spread false rumours. But this stuff about Emile is so far from the truth. He's just gentle and he has manners – not like other fighters. I can show you any of these showbiz guys – Paul Anka, Tommy Sands – they wear the same clothes Emile does. So what if other fighters don't? Emile's not a typical fighter.'

Syd Martin, Clancy's assistant trainer, spoke even more forcefully. 'This boy is a normal boy,' he said fiercely. 'There's nothing wrong with him. And all those stories about him being a milliner – that's just a lot of publicity too. He came into that place looking for a job as a handyman and when he started fighting it was good publicity for Howie Albert. If they had any real evidence that Emile isn't normal, it would have come out by now. But they don't. It's just names and hints – and talk. People ought to know better.'

If there was blame to be apportioned, Martin was convinced it should be directed towards Paret's manager and his trainer. Martin did not like either Alfaro or Joe Di Maria. 'In the ring before the fight,' Martin recalled, 'Di Maria kept patting Paret on the back and calling him *maricón*. I asked him why he was doing that. He said, "I'm just trying to get my fighter ready." I said, "You're a man. You should know better than that." Paret's an illiterate, but I honestly think he has more reason in his head than either Di Maria or Alfaro. Paret's all right. I don't think there's really any venom in him. He was just incensed by what these guys were telling him.'

In a *Sports Illustrated* feature headlined 'The Deadly Insult', Gilbert Rogin was unsparing in detailing the cause of the bitter blows that had driven Paret to the point of death. He returned to the weigh-in, and told his readers that, 'As before, Paret called Griffith *maricón*, gutter Spanish for homosexual. It is the most vulgar epitaph in that violent idiom and is particularly galling to Griffith, who has a piping voice, wears extravagantly tight clothes, has designed women's hats and is, ordinarily, a charming, affectionate kid. Paret laid a gratuitous, slighting hand on Emile's back. "Keep your hands off me," snarled Griffith.'

If it was clear that some writers were becoming braver in their willingness to confront the way in which Paret and Griffith had voiced the previously unspeakable ties between sport and homosexuality, it was even plainer that boxing was in crisis. The governor of New York, Nelson Rockefeller, sent a telegram to Melvin L. Krulewitch, the chairman of New York State Athletic Commission, to order an investigation into boxing – which would start with the submission of 'full and specific reports on the fight' within twenty-four hours. Rockefeller promised that if negligence had caused a homicide, he would refer the case to a grand jury.

The chief of police at West 47th Street station had also instigated his own investigation, and his officers interviewed ringside officials and made further inquiries at Roosevelt hospital. It was suggested that, if or when Paret died, they would take further statements to decide whether a homicide had been committed. Emile Griffith could, possibly, be charged with murder.

An editorial in the *New York Times* argued that, 'The question everybody is asking is whether this fight was allowed to go on too long. A better question might be whether it, or any other professional prizefight, should be allowed to start.'

The poison-pen writers and the crank callers took their cue. Vitriolic letters, addressed to Emile, were delivered to Howie Albert's office. Some even reached him at the New Yorker hotel and

Emile broke down when he read the words that accused him of being a heartless killer or a murderous faggot. Until he learned not to answer the phone in his hotel suite, he also had to endure abusive calls from unknown people who asked him how it felt to have killed a man.

Benny Paret was not even dead and they had him down for homicide. Hispanic fight fans had gathered outside the hotel to shout out their tirade against the devastated world champion.

Emile was still torn up by the reaction of Paret's cornermen when he'd tried to visit Benny at the Roosevelt on the night of the fight. Rather than explain that Benny was about to undergo surgery, they had taunted Emile – asking if he had come to the hospital to whip up 'publicity'. They turned him away and said he would never be welcome to visit Benny.

Only two moments could comfort him. The first was when Howie suggested that, with the Albert and Clancy families, they should all retreat to his training camp at the Concord hotel in Monticello. Emile could escape most of the crazies by going to upstate New York. He nodded and then shivered in relief when Gil read to him the response of Willie Toweel in Johannesburg.

'I hope Paret makes it – for his family's sake but mainly for the sake of Emile Griffith,' Toweel was quoted in the *New York Herald Tribune*. He also knew what it meant to kill a man, and the memory of Hubert Essakow would never leave him.

Emile looked up at Gil. He could remember how haunted Willie had seemed before their fight, when the New York writers had asked him how it felt to be a killer. Willie Toweel understood. Emile was consoled by the truth when his old opponent's words were read to him. 'I had a feeling of fear,' Willie Toweel said. 'I know it was the will of God, but I felt like I was the guilty one. It's enough to drive anyone mad.'

Hugging himself closely, Emile looked up at Clancy. 'Only Willie knows how it feels,' he said.

*

The days passed slowly on the second floor of the Roosevelt hospital, where Benny Paret lay in ghostly silence. Marie Ryff pinned a small crucifix to his white gown. Lucy said Benny would like the way it glittered beneath the unblinking lights. Marie also gave Lucy some St Jude oil – and she explained the significance. St Jude was the patron saint of the impossible. He was the saviour of lost causes.

Benny Paret needed a miracle and his wife prayed for one. 'To me, he's just sleeping,' she told the press four days into their vigil. 'I'm praying that any minute he will wake up.'

Manuel Alfaro, who might have traded in vats of St Jude oil if he had thought there was big money to be made, peddled false hope too. He told the waiting reporters that, at nine o'clock the previous night, on 27 March, Benny had opened his eyes when he was turned and moved. 'Positive movements were made,' Alfaro insisted. 'Paret was helped to a sitting position and he opened his eyes – although it was a glassy stare. His eyes closed when he was placed in a horizontal position again.'

There was much more of an eye-opening racket in the corridor outside Benny's ward. Beyond the pressmen, a large group of Benny's friends gathered each day. They all wanted to donate blood because they had heard that, on his first day in hospital, Benny had needed four transfusions. Alfaro stayed away from most of them, preferring to ingratiate himself with Tito Puente, the band leader, known as the 'King of Latin Music', who often came to visit Benny. Puente was from Puerto Rico, where Lucy had been born, and Benny had danced to his music at the Tropicana. Another Puerto Rican, Jose Torres, who had drawn his bout against Paret in San Juan in September 1959, joined Puente and Alfaro in the hospital room.

On 29 March, Benny's 56-year-old mother, Maxima Crespo, arrived from Cuba. She had flown to Miami and then New York after a ticket had been bought for her by the National Catholic Relief Service. Maxima was also given $10 and an accompanying note written in English, which said – on her behalf, because she only spoke Spanish – 'Take me to Roosevelt hospital where my son is. He is Kid Paret.'

She was interviewed on her arrival at Miami International by a Spanish-speaking writer for the *Herald*. 'My son is a good boy,' Maxima said. 'He would always send me money.' Asked if she had seen Benny's fight against Griffith, and pressed for Castro's reaction to the calamity, she replied: 'I had no desire to watch. Boxing is brutal. And I'm not interested in Cuban politics. Only in my son.'

Maxima had heard the news on state radio in Cuba; and Alfaro had only called her two days after the fight. 'The least he could have done was to let me know what happened to my son,' Maxima said.

On 1 April, the hospital released a statement: 'Benny Paret is fighting hard. But his condition has not changed for the past few days. He's still in a critical condition.'

A day later, however, there was a notable difference. It was revealed that Paret had caught pneumonia and his coma had 'deepened slightly'.

The depth of that coma soon reached its final point. In the early hours of 3 April 1962, at 1.55 a.m., Benny 'Kid' Paret died.

His wife, 21-year-old Lucy, was called at her sister's home, for she had been persuaded late the previous evening to head back to the Bronx for some rest and to see her son. She was back at the hospital within an hour. She was joined by Alfaro, as well as Benny's mother and one of his brothers, Antonio.

Alfaro slipped out of the room to talk to the reporters who, woken at the dead of night, had arrived soon afterwards. He told them that Benny's family was 'weeping uncontrollably and hysterically' and that Lucy had clutched her husband and cried out: 'Please, I want to go with you. Take me along.'

A hospital security guard ushered the press pack away from the room of death – only to return a few minutes later with a dry update amid the hysteria. 'The mother is screaming now,' he told the reporters. 'They're all crying. They don't want to see anyone. You know how it is.'

A black Cadillac took the body of Benny Paret from the Bellevue hospital morgue, where an autopsy had been carried out, to the Ortiz funeral home in the Bronx. He lay in an open casket and over the next day 17,000 people filed past to pay their respects to the fallen fighter. A less stately battle was waged in the back office of the funeral parlour, as arguments raged over where Benny would be buried. Maxima wanted her son returned in his coffin to Cuba, but Lucy was determined he would be buried in Miami.

'Castro would want Benny buried in Cuba,' Lucy told the journalists who had followed her across town. 'It would be a propaganda victory for him. But Benny's body will never go back as long as Cuba is ruled by that man. My husband will be buried in Miami or New York, where I can visit his grave.'

Those who had pitied Lucy as being too young and too fragile to survive as a pregnant widow and mother of a toddler were surprised. She refused to be derailed. New York and Miami had defined her years with Benny. A tombstone of remembrance would be erected at St Raymond's cemetery in the Bronx. Lucy completed all the other arrangements and flew to Miami seven hours before the coffin carrying her husband was lifted aboard National Airlines Flight 7 from Idlewild airport. They placed it in the front baggage compartment of the jet's underbelly.

Eventually, after the plane landed, more than 20,000 people arrived at the 'negro' Albert funeral home in Miami and slowly walked past the reopened coffin. It was Lucy's choice. 'I want it this way,' she said. 'I want people to see Benny one last time. I know he would have wanted it this way too.' She had arranged for Benny to be dressed in his best dark blue suit. A tiny Cuban flag was pinned to the lapel and a rosary was draped around his neck. The blue beret that he loved to wear outside the ring covered his head. He looked small and shrunken inside his coffin.

The pine box with bronze handles was sealed shut for the last time early that Saturday morning. Lucy placed a funeral memento on top of the casket. It was a white wreath she had bought in New York and, in gilt-edged letters, it spelt out one word: '*Champ*'.

Benny Paret was buried at Our Lady of Mercy cemetery on the remote western fringes of Miami at noon on Saturday 7 April 1962. Exactly two weeks earlier, almost to the minute, he and Emile Griffith had weighed in for the final act of their tragic trilogy. Everything had changed since then. Emile sat alone in his hotel room in upstate New York. His request to attend the funeral had been declined.

'I don't want him there,' Lucy Paret said of the man who had killed her husband. 'I never want to see him again ...'

On the morning of Benny Paret's burial, the consequences of another catastrophe for boxing were already evident. Tunney Hunsaker, the heavyweight best known for being the defeated opponent in Cassius Clay's first professional contest, lay in a coma in a hospital in Bluefield, West Virginia. He had undergone emergency brain surgery the previous night, after he was knocked out in the tenth round by another journeyman, Joe 'Shotgun' Sheldon, in the nearby town of Beckley. Dr E. L. Gage had operated in an attempt to relieve the pressure on Hunsaker's brain caused by an acute subdural haematoma – similar in size and scope to one of the two clots that had ruined Paret.

Doctors at the Bluefield Sanitarium said Hunsaker was in a critical state – with hopes for his survival 'no better than 50-50'. Hunsaker had not been beaten as badly as Paret and, after the fight was stopped, he had even spoken briefly to the referee before slipping into unconsciousness. But the surgeons worked on him for two hours late that Friday night.

Apart from being a professional boxer, the thirty-year-old Hunsaker was also the police chief of Fayetteville in West Virginia. He had since become friendly with Clay, who expressed his concern. But Clay, who had just turned twenty, took a simplistic view of boxing's plight. 'The idea is to fight,' he said. 'I don't like the fact that a guy, Paret, got killed or that Tunney Hunsaker is poorly. But this happens every ten years or so in boxing.'

The fact that two critical boxing injuries had occurred in less than a fortnight did not deter Clay. 'We should be more worried about people dying up in the sky. What about all these airplane crashes? They kill a hundred people every time. I cry like the devil getting on an airplane. But I ain't afraid of the ring no matter what's just happened. I'm the next champ.'

There were more serious concerns in Bluefield as Hunsaker deteriorated. A second operation was carried out on the night of Sunday 8 April – forty-eight hours after the first procedure. This time it seemed as if there was more success because, after surgery, Hunsaker showed some flickers of life.

'We're not out of the woods by a long shot,' Dr Gage said, suggesting that, 'it remains 50-50. I still feel like a tightrope walker.'

Eight days after the funeral of Benny Paret, tragedy struck again. Tunney Hunsaker was spared but Howie Albert felt cursed.

The good news came first for the Hunsaker family when the fighter emerged from his coma. He lay in an oxygen tent. His eyes were open and through the flap he could squeeze the hand of his wife, Phyllis. When Dr Gage asked him to stick out his tongue, Hunsaker complied. An ecstatic Phyllis ducked down into the tent and hugged her husband.

'Kiss me,' she asked, and he did.

'Kiss me again,' Phyllis cried, and Tunney Hunsaker managed to press his lips once more against his wife's cheek.

There was, in contrast, devastation for the Albert family. They had returned from their break with Emile at the Concord hotel because their children, Barbara and Eddie, were ill with chicken pox. Soon after they got home to New York, Howie's wife, Irene, who had been feeling feverish for days, was also diagnosed with chicken pox.

Irene's fever climbed drastically high that night and fluid filled her lungs. Even before Howie could call for an ambulance his beloved wife was dead at the age of thirty-nine – on 15 April 1962.

*

The champion of the world decided to quit. Emile Griffith, who had held the undisputed welterweight title for less than three weeks, was desolate. Irene Albert was gone. Her husband Howie, and Emile's close friend, was distraught. Amid such trauma Emile could not bear the thought of fighting again, of hitting another man in the head so hard that he might take his life. Gil Clancy understood his reasons and listened to his decision in silence. It was impossible to argue when death surrounded them.

Emile had also seen yet more of the letters which poured in each day. He was branded in ink as 'a murderer', 'a killer', 'a cruel nigger' and 'an animal that belongs in a cage'. Gil took the more threatening letters seriously enough to call in the police – who tried to reassure Emile that crank letter-writers were generally harmless even if they suggested that a tiny and cramped scrawl, and use of green or red ink, was proof of a psychologically disturbed person. Emile didn't care. He would be better off dead. Emile wanted to get out of boxing forever.

At first, he started drinking heavily. He went into a gay bar near the Port Authority terminus on 42nd Street and 8th Avenue and ordered some Manischewitz wine. It was a sweet kosher wine which he drank in honour of his Jewish friends, Howie and Irene. Emile knocked back his glass and ordered another. He got very drunk that night.

For the next few weeks he shuttled helplessly between his house on Colfax Street and his hideaways near Times Square, between Matthew and Esther, between drunken delusion and despair. Emile even mentioned to Esther that maybe they should get married after all, so that he could give up all his old ways, boxing most of all, and retreat to a secluded part of the country. They could raise chickens and have children. Esther had learned enough about Emile over the past year to know that, sometimes, it was best just to let him ramble and pretend that he could do without his real life in the ring and elsewhere. She understood that she would never have him to herself, but she still loved Emile and tried to protect him.

Emile needed refuge. He was always fretful and restless. Only boxing, when he was concentrated on training or a fight, offered him a quiet focus. But boxing had become impossible. The days drifted past in a jittery blur or plain old sadness. Glaring images of the last round, or of Benny's mournful face, filled his head during the most unexpected moments and he would be pulled down into the blank reality of what he had done. He had killed Benny Paret.

The story still filled the back and even the front pages as the consequences spread like a stain and the investigation into boxing continued. It was the first time in history that the killing of a man had been screened on live television. John F. Kennedy had yet to be assassinated, and Malcolm X and Martin Luther King were still alive, and so the death of Benny Paret on a Saturday night, replayed again and again in slow motion on network television, lingered. The purity of sport, and society, had been assaulted and the columnists and commentators examined the wounds each new day.

A grieving Howie tended to his children, while Gil took care of the letters which kept coming. They were all addressed to Emile, but, to spare him, Gil separated the deranged from the merely poisonous while searching for messages of compassion and sympathy. They also arrived with unerring regularity, for many people recognised the truth in Jim Murray's words when he wrote, in the *Los Angeles Times*, that, 'The tragedy of Benny Paret is the tragedy of Emile Griffith too.'

Gil read him the most moving letters of support. Howie always said that, for a supposed hard man, Gil had the softness of the Irish about him. The trainer had taken the death of Paret badly, but the letters touched and helped him and, he hoped, Emile too. A surgeon who was also a member of the Oregon Boxing Commission wrote passionately to Emile, urging him not to give up. 'I felt this many times when I had a patient die on the operating table,' the surgeon admitted. 'I, too, felt all was lost – and that I should quit. Then I thought things over. Life must go on. What would I accomplish if I did quit? Forfeit all the gifts I had been given to practice my profession? Look at all the good I could still do – which would be lost to the world should I throw in the sponge. You owe yourself and your family too much to quit because of an accident. You did not will this thing. Like life, it must be faced – and conquered.'

Emile said bitterly that a doctor was in the business of saving lives. A fighter was in the business of hurting people. If he gave up boxing he would never batter another man to death.

Gil read him next a letter from an ordinary working man – a truck driver who had knocked down and killed a child. 'I was inconsolable for weeks,' the driver told Emile. 'The guys I worked with – men who had been involved in serious accidents – came running to my side. They told me to consider my obligations to my family. What would happen to them if I continued to brood, to drink or to run away from my responsibilities? It took a little time but they were right. I had to accept it. You will, too, champ.'

How could he? A truck driver might not save lives but he did useful work. He delivered food or heavy materials needed to build houses or schools. Even the guys who drove the garbage trucks removed the stinking trash from ordinary life. What good could he do when he closed his hands into fists and smashed them into the face and head of another man?

It seemed as if no one could help Emile until, one day, Gil held up an envelope for closer inspection. The strange stamps and the air-mail sticker had made him pause. He studied the postmark because it was a letter from Africa. Gil sliced it open. He looked at the address, written in block capitals on the right-hand side of the page, and wondered who lived at 12 Balfour Avenue, Benoni, Transvaal, South Africa. It did not take him long to work out because the name at the bottom of the letter was also clear. Willie Toweel.

An hour later, after he read the letter and drove over to Queens, Gil handed the envelope to Emile. He did not say anything and Emile thought it was odd that Gil did not read him the latest letter out loud.

The fighter sat down at the kitchen table and, slowly, he spread the blue-lined page in front of him. His eyes snagged on the opening word of 'Champ'. And then he gathered himself. His head bent a little lower and his finger traced the words as he read carefully and silently.

Champ, I wanted to write to you for a few days now. Ever since I heard the news about Benny Paret you are on my mind. I can't think of anything else. I know how you feel. It happened to me as well. I accidently [sic] killed a man in the ring one night. Six years ago now. Hubert Essakow was a friend of mine. To do what I did to anyone, never mind a friend, felt the worst thing. It almost ruined me until I realised it could have happened to me. I could have been the one that went. It was just bad luck it was Hubert. It's the same with Paret and you.

It was a big honour for me to fight you in Madison Square Garden. I know you beat me in the ring but you were good to me before and afterwards. I always remember that and I want to say thank you.

Accidents happen, champ. They're not always our fault. This is not your fault. I want you to understand that. It took me a long time but I got to work out, in the end, that it wasn't my fault either – that Hubert died. It just happened.

I learned how to forgive myself Emile, and you must do the same. You and me have to learn to roll with the punches in this life. They are often harder to deal with than the ones we got in the ring. But we can do it. I think I did it and I know you will do it too. Good luck, champ.

Your friend

Willie Toweel

Emile looked up at Gil, his eyes swimming, and then he gazed again at the letter, absorbing its meaning.

'Oh, Willie,' Emile murmured, closing his eyes and rocking to himself, as if praying that his old opponent might hear him across the seas and the thousands of miles and different worlds that separated them. 'Thank you ... thank you.'

Forgiveness was a balm, and a curse. Emile could not shake Willie's letter from his head. The words helped him in a way that his former opponent would never appreciate. Willie had written so simply, and movingly, that Emile could finally believe others were also genuine in forgiving him for the fate of Benny Paret.

A deep regret still lurked. He had a tangled and battered idea of what Willie, and any other fighter, might say if confronted by his secret self. Emile knew how much the world at large hated and feared homosexuality. Even to the mildest and most pleasant of people it was still an unforgivable sin, a criminal outrage.

What might Willie Toweel think of the Times Square bars where Emile felt most at home? Would he be as understanding of gay love as he was of death in the ring? Would he be as forgiving if he saw Emile holding and kissing another man? Emile would never know the truth. And so all the usual denunciations of men loving each other as being 'depraved' and 'perverted', 'sick' and 'evil', rose up as a seemingly unstoppable force. Enshrined in law, bolstered by the church and supported by America's medical and psychiatric associations, the hurtful allegations could not be stemmed.

In the summer of 1962 words and feelings surged inside him in silent pain. Emile could only say them out loud forty-two years later, in 2008, to his friend Ron Ross, a writer and a deeply compassionate man: '*I keep thinking how strange it is. I kill a man and most people understand and forgive me. However, I love a man and many say this makes me an evil person. To so many people this is an unforgivable sin.*'

CHAPTER EIGHT

The Ghost of Benny Paret

On 1 May 1962, thirty-eight days since he and Paret had left the ring at Madison Square Garden, Emile Griffith went back to his old life. In the small, dimly lit room where Gil Clancy trained his fighters in the Park Department building, on West 28th Street, Emile arrived quietly. There was none of his usual laughter or shouting out to Gil. He headed instead for the adjoining locker room and, once he had changed out of his street clothes, he settled down on a chair at the back of the gym.

Everyone gave him space but, eventually, Gil ambled over. It had been Gil who, the previous afternoon, had met with Emile to pass on a simple message. 'It's time,' the trainer had said. There was no need to add any more words. Even Howie had returned to the hat factory. It was time to try to claw back some normality.

Gil asked Emile if he could help – for the fighter had taken out the adhesive tape from his bag and started to wrap his hands.

Emile shook his head. 'I'm okay, Clancy.'

They both realised that it would take Emile much longer to bandage his hands on his own than if Gil did the wrapping. It was the last way in which he could stretch out his delayed return to boxing.

Forty-five minutes later, flexing his hands so that his fingers moved freely above the wrapped knuckles, Emile nodded to Gil. The trainer brought over a pair of boxing gloves and a headguard and suggested that Emile start with a light workout on the heavy bag, which dangled from a gleaming chain attached to one of the metal girders.

Emile glanced down at the gloves and shook his head. He was not quite ready to hit anything.

Instead, he picked up a rope and retreated to another corner of the room where sunlight streamed in through a high window. The light left dappled patterns on the floor and Emile began to skip among the shadows and sunshine, eased by the familiar whirr of the rope and the sound of his feet moving up and down in a comforting rhythm. After fifteen minutes, with sweat glistening on his skin and breath falling from him in a steady rasp as the rope spun round and round in a blurring and beautifully mindless exercise, Emile was pulled back into the real world by Gil.

The trainer stood next to Jackie Kelly, an old fighter who had campaigned as an obscure featherweight on the undercards at St Nicholas Arena. Kelly had not fought professionally for four years but he still hung around Gil Clancy's gym. He would pose no threat to Emile and he was also wily enough to stay out of trouble himself. Kelly was just the kind of experienced sparring partner Emile needed.

Gil called Emile over and, silently, he towelled down his fighter. He then fitted the black gloves and headguard and tied the laces to keep them intact. Gil stood inside the ring while Emile remained on the safe side of the ropes. They could not put it off forever and at last, with Gil using a foot to push down the lower rope while he lifted the middle strand with his hand, Emile ducked down into the ring.

'Nice and easy,' Gil said.

The gym buzzer sounded, to mark the start of a three-minute round of sparring, and Griffith moved away from Kelly. No punches were thrown for the first twenty seconds as the two men circled each other. Kelly, finally, snapped out a couple of lefts, which Griffith easily avoided. The little man, who was now more a pudgy lightweight than a featherweight, moved in close and tried to land a few body shots.

'C'mon, Emile,' Clancy urged, 'let 'em go . . .'

The only punch that Griffith seemed prepared to use was his jab. In answer to Clancy's instruction, he threw a gentle series of left leads aimed at Kelly's chest. His jab was still accurate and, urged on by Clancy, he peppered Kelly and backed him up against the ropes. It was the perfect opening, and he just needed to step inside and follow up with a right cross and then an uppercut or a left hook. But he suddenly saw Paret instead of Kelly in front of him. Griffith let his hands fall to his sides and turned away.

Kelly did not go after him for he realised what had happened. The retired journeyman glanced across at Clancy.

'Okay, Jackie,' Clancy grunted. 'That's enough for today . . .'

Gil removed Emile's gloves and headguard. He knew Emile would listen to him when, after they parted at the gym door, he'd say: 'See you tomorrow, champ.'

They allowed one of Gil's favourite writers back into the gym on 7 May, when Howard Tuckner of the *New York Times* was invited to watch Emile at work. Tuckner had also needed a few weeks to get over the Paret fight and the ramifications of everything he had described. He was sensitive to Griffith's position and he began his feature with gentle restraint.

'The fighter sat in a wooden chair and stared at his hands,' he wrote of Emile in the *Times* on 8 May. 'How many times he has done this since the night of March 24, 1962 he cannot say. But the fear is always the same. There will come another night when a man will knock on his dressing-room door and shout, "You're on, champ." He will walk down the aisle to the ring in his silk bathrobe, and pray that nobody yells: "That's Griffith, the killer."'

When Tuckner said those words out loud to Emile, the fighter flinched. 'If it happens, I'll just try not to hear it. I did not mean to kill him. God knows this.'

He admitted to Tuckner that he dreamed of Paret, and that he sometimes saw Benny standing at the end of his bed. 'He was all dressed up,' Emile said of the ghost of Benny Paret. 'I said to him,

"Hi, how ya doing? What are you doing here?" He didn't answer me.'

Gil got them back onto firmer ground. He told Tuckner that, 'Boxing has been good to Emile. It enabled him to bring his family together and to take care of them. His life must go on – for his sake and theirs.'

The trainer said that, in a few months, Emile would fight again. Emile hoped for a warm-up bout but Tuckner noted that, 'Clancy apparently feels that a title fight will be best.' A real test would force Emile to 'go all out' and stop him thinking too much about Paret.

There was speculation that Emile might face Ralph Dupas next. No one seemed to remember that Dupas had fought and beaten Frankie Ryff – who still lay in the room where Benny Paret had died on the second floor of the Roosevelt hospital. Dupas was a tough and experienced campaigner, who would not fear the grieving world champion.

'Clancy looked for a sign of approval from the fighter,' Tuckner wrote. 'There was none. Griffith just stared at his hands and said: "It isn't possible. These hands are so small. How can they hurt someone like that?"'

Esther Taylor held those small hands in a warm grasp. She comforted Emile again, and urged him to stay strong. Before he left for Las Vegas they had gone out together, as one friend consoling another in a time of darkness and doubt, and Esther had seen Emile shout for the first time in her life. He was such a gentle soul, a man who avoided argument and confrontation, that she had been shocked when he stood up and yelped in fury and despair. A beer-guzzling wiseguy had taunted him about Kid Paret. How could Emile be out on the town enjoying himself with a girl when he had killed someone with his fists?

Emile had screamed at the man. The tormented words fell from his mouth in such a garbled rush that Esther could barely understand what he was saying. But she could see the meaning in his desperate face. He looked so wretched that she dragged him away from the joint and took him home.

The death of Benny 'Kid' Paret almost broke her heart too. Esther had watched the fight on television and she knew that it had turned bad even before they carried him out of the ring. She sensed the worst and it just made her want to weep for the Kid and for Emile.

Emile told her that Benny had left a pregnant wife; he had left his son without a father.

'I did that,' Emile said hoarsely to his old girlfriend. 'I did that to the Kid's family ...'

She could no longer remember what she said to Emile. All that stayed in her head was the heavy feel of his anguished body as she held him close. Her silent embrace, she knew, meant more to him than words.

You were meant to forget everything in Las Vegas. Your troubled love life, your job, your money problems and every last sliver of regret or concern were meant to disappear for a while in the glittering desert. Emile believed it might have been possible if he was just fretting over a boy or girl, his latest huge pile of bills or the future of the world amid fears of a nuclear bomb being launched by the Soviet Union. He would have been able, then, to set aside the woes and worries of ordinary life in an outrageous fantasy world. But not even Las Vegas could help him forget he had killed a man.

Emile carried the burden as, in the brutal heat and shimmering neon, he prepared to defend his world title against Ralph Dupas at the Las Vegas Convention Center on 13 July 1962. Friday the thirteenth seemed an ominous date in a city that traded on the bad luck of its deluded visitors. In a world where day and night merged into a 24-hour blur of jangling slot machines, whirring roulette wheels and rolling dice on the craps tables, reality seemed far away. But the ghost of Benny Paret held him close.

It was Emile's first time in Vegas and its excesses diverted him for a while. He stayed at the Thunderbird, on the Strip, and the nightly stage extravaganzas depicted almost as much nudity as you would see in a Times Square peepshow. But Emile was surprised that the topless girls displayed their wares with toothy smiles, rather than bored New York insolence, in front of smartly dressed couples wearing tuxedos and ball gowns. This was sex as sanitised and expensive entertainment rather than the cheap and grimy thrills he was more accustomed to seeing in the flesh-pits around 42nd Street.

Vegas peddled a different kind of decadence. Along the Strip, not far from the Thunderbird, they blew up a small dam every night on stage at the Stardust. It was part of a show called *Lido de Paris*, which was meant to bring French sensuality to Vegas, and they just threw in a nightly demolition for the hell of it.

They opted for another form of surrealism at the Thunderbird, where a 'Red Indian' theme provided the backdrop throughout the hotel and casino. Images of tomahawks and wigwams, war paint and wild horses adorned the walls, while casino waitresses and cigarette girls dressed as buxom squaws. Emile might once have slipped into the mindless swing of it all – but, ever since his deadly night in the Garden, life had become sombre.

There had been little chance to forget. On 22 May, Emile had been compelled to testify under oath at an official investigation into boxing. It was a public hearing, in front of a state legislative committee in New York, and Emile followed Ruby Goldstein and Manuel Alfaro onto the stand. But, first, he had been made to watch the entire fight in a screening at the investigation, which included the commercial breaks and slow-motion replays of the final torrent of blows. Emile, dressed in a conservative suit and tie, kept trying to look away but he was instructed to pay attention.

He had repeated his stock answer when eventually asked to describe his aims in the ring. 'I just kept punching,' Emile said in a quivering voice. 'My manager said to me, "When you hurt Paret, keep punching. You hurt him before – but you let him get away and then he hurt you."'

Asked how he felt about punishing another man in the ring, Emile had sounded heartbroken. 'As a fighter that's what I'm meant to do,' he said. 'I don't like doing it, but that's the job of a fighter.'

He had only looked briefly defiant when, after explaining that Paret had insulted him at the weigh-in, Emile resisted the accusation that his rage meant he had wished to harm his opponent permanently. 'You cannot be angry at a guy in the ring,' he protested. 'You have to fight with a cool head.'

The battle over boxing's future had yet to be resolved, with calls to ban the sport still echoing in the aftermath of Paret's death. Emile had signed to fight Dupas and, on the eve of his departure for Vegas on 28 June, he met the press. He was asked whether he would be able to set aside his memories of Paret and concentrate on his next challenger. 'I hope so,' Emile said, 'but I guess I won't know until I get in there. I know in my heart that Benny's death was an accident. But I'm still a little uncomfortable in the ring. In training I know what I want to do, and sometimes I can do everything and sometimes I can't.'

Gil Clancy was also uncertain. 'Emile has worked hard and he is in excellent condition. But how he will react against Dupas is anyone's guess. I don't know. Emile doesn't know. We'll only find out on July 13.'

The trainer paused and then changed tack. 'There's one thing everybody has overlooked,' he said. 'They're all asking about how Emile will feel – but what about the other feller? How's Dupas going to feel?'

Clancy did not add the distressing phrase – 'when facing a killer' – but the implication was clear. Dupas, who was no puncher, had to be anxious at the thought of the danger he would confront.

Pat Putnam of the *Miami Herald* called up Dupas, who had already set up camp at the Dunes resort in Vegas. He wrote that, 'Dupas' answer was a harsh, mirthless laugh that grated down the telephone line. "Paret was a dead man before he ever climbed into the ring with Griffith," the 26-year-old said. "Gene Fullmer beat him so bad that Griffith fought a dead man. If he thinks he's fighting another Paret he's got an awful surprise coming."'

Dupas dismissed the jibe that he ran more than he fought. 'Run?'

Dupas snorted. 'I don't run. I move. Only a sucker stands there and gets hit. I circle and I weave and I bob. And I'm always throwing punches. That's the only way to handle hitters like Griffith. Stay on top of them, keep them busy.'

Trained by Angelo Dundee, Dupas was a slippery veteran who, incredibly, had made his professional debut in his hometown of New Orleans at the age of fourteen. Twelve years later he had racked up 115 fights while still not making much money. Dupas had just declared himself bankrupt and admitted to debts of $12,000.

Whenever he arrived to train at Dundee's 5th Street Gym in Miami, alongside Luis Rodriguez and Cassius Clay, Dupas carried his kit in a brown paper bag. He remained one of boxing's definitive Cinderella Men. 'I took this fight for a lousy $10,000,' Dupas told Putnam, aggrieved that the champion would be paid four times that amount. 'If I lose I'm through. But I'm going to prove that the champion isn't always the best man.'

Dupas wished he could be fighting Griffith in New Orleans, but even his home city had given him rough treatment. He was one of eleven children fathered by a local fisherman, and the family had been so poor he claimed never to have owned a pair of shoes until he turned pro. There was no disputing the harsh racial bias of New Orleans. In 1957, soon after Dupas had lost his previous crack at a world title, when stopped by Joe Brown in the eighth round of their lightweight contest, an elderly white woman lodged a complaint against the 'swarthy' boxer. She claimed that Dupas was 'a Negro' living illegally as a white man. The case against Dupas was taken up by a zealous officer in the Louisiana state department.

He fought the charge and, at some cost and over many months, Dupas was finally able to prove he was a fourth-generation Louisiana citizen of French and Italian extraction. His privileged status as a white man, even a dirt-poor white man, was upheld. But there was a twist to the racial saga in the early summer of 1962. As negotiations opened for a contest between Griffith and Dupas, there was a plea for the bout to be held in the challenger's hometown. State law intervened again and the promoters were reminded that it was illegal for a white man to fight a black man in Louisiana. Ironically, if Dupas had lost his case five years earlier the bout could have been staged between two 'Negroes' in New Orleans.

Las Vegas, instead, won the right to stage the contest, with Joe Louis acting as matchmaker for United World Enterprises. There was nationwide interest, of a ghoulish kind, because so many people were intrigued to see if Dupas would become another victim of Griffith.

Emile struggled with his haunting memories and he tried to seclude himself as much as possible in Vegas. The promoters demanded that he carry out a certain number of public workouts, but, with Clancy keeping the reporters away from him, he avoided talking. A blanket ban on all newspaper interviews had been implemented after he had been upset by Sid Ziff of the *Los Angeles Times*.

Ziff had arranged a telephone interview in early June and he called Emile at his suite on the top floor of the Thunderbird. He began with a routine opening question as he asked Emile what he thought of Dupas. 'He's very good,' Emile said. 'He's the number one challenger and he's also an American. I didn't want to fight any Latino for obvious reasons.'

That immediate allusion to Paret gave Ziff his chance to follow up with a much more distressing question. 'Do you feel responsible in any way for Paret's death?' Ziff asked.

'Griffith reacted as though he had been touched by a live wire,' Ziff wrote. '"No, no, no, I don't," he cried, the words coming fast. Then he asked, almost hysterically, "Please don't talk about it. I'm training for a fight. I don't want to hear any more about it." I tried to soothe him and, at the same time, get him to talk. Suddenly I found I was talking to no one at all. He dropped the receiver and walked away.'

Clancy continued the conversation with a weary sigh. 'It's been real tough on him,' he told Ziff. 'He's been asked about the Paret fight and how he feels about what happened so many times that, naturally, it bothers him. We're trying to keep him busy. We try not to give him time to brood.'

The easiest way to stop Emile brooding was for Clancy and Howie Albert to refuse all interviews. Ziff's feature was called 'Emile's Ordeal' and the hacks were not happy that it resulted in a barrier being erected between them and the world champion. They were so used to Griffith being available that his sudden isolation seemed strange. At least his opponent was such a quotable character.

'I'm a very sensitive kid, too,' Dupas said, drawing parallels between him and Griffith. 'People ask me, "Are you scared of Griffith?" I just tell them, "I'm not a coward. I'm valiant."'

The challenger then attempted to quote Shakespeare, which surprised everyone. '"A valiant tastes of death but once. Of all the wonders I have heard, it seems most strange. Fear and death, a necessary end will come when it will come." *Julius Caesar.*'

It was a mild misquote, but the lowly fighter spoke with such Shakespearean passion that the reporters applauded him. 'I am a completely new person,' Dupas promised when comparing himself with the struggling journeyman he had once been. 'It may be esoteric but I feel so much stronger. I've punched the sandbag, chopped trees, rowed a skiff. Of course, I'll move the same way and Griffith – what a beautiful body he has to hit – will be so confused.'

Dupas also spoke out against the public anguish that had been spilled since the fall of Paret. 'People are blaming the referee and the manager for not stopping that fight,' he said, 'but you didn't hear anybody at ringside yelling to stop it. They kept yelling for more. That's what they want to see. It's the people watching who I blame – the public. Griffith's intention wasn't to kill anyone. I respect him but I'm not scared. When I die it will be of old age not because Griffith has hit me. I'll not only outbox him, I might even knock him out if he gets careless.'

The fight press crowded around Dupas after his last sparring session at the Dunes. They were looking for a couple of provocative quotes to dredge up some of the drama that had framed the animosity between Griffith and Paret. Dupas was asked by Ray Harwood of the *Oakland Tribune* if he respected the champion 'as a man'. A long silence followed as the ambiguous undertow simmered beneath the surface. Everyone could remember Dupas acknowledging Griffith's 'beautiful body' earlier in the week.

'You know what,' Dupas eventually drawled, 'Griffith might be a milliner. But he is all man.'

Emile felt all too human when he read Dupas' tribute to him. The simplest words could sometimes make him want to cry. If only Paret had showed him the same basic respect he might still be alive. Gil and Howie tried to stop him opening up the old wound, but they were helpless. Emile went over the fatal night again and again. He even admitted he feared hitting Dupas in case he caused another fatality.

The hotel room seemed suffocating and they suggested that Emile spend a few hours down in the casino on the Tuesday night before the fight. It was Howie's idea that they allow Jim Murray of the *Los Angeles Times* to accompany them. Emile's problem with the same paper had peppered much of the build-up and Howie decided it was best to offer Murray an opportunity to spend time with Emile. He was one of America's great sportswriters and he understood the trauma Emile had endured for eleven long weeks.

They met Murray at the illuminated pool in the grounds of the Thunderbird just as darkness settled over the Sierra Nevada mountains. Vegas looked brighter than ever beneath a black sky and, as they marvelled at the giant gleaming sign of the Sahara resort blinking across the street, Emile relaxed. 'I get up at five in the morning to go running,' he told Murray, 'and this place is still jumping. It's some town.'

He stressed, however, that 'the nudie shows do not interest me', and he told Murray that the previous night he had gone to a horror movie. It was the kind of scary film he could have watched in a midtown bughouse on a rainy afternoon back in New York. But the attractions of Vegas would have to wait for a happier time.

Murray persuaded him to amble down to the casino so they might have a little fun on the tables. Emile's striking figure snared attention and a gawping crowd gathered around him. 'Shouldn't you be in bed, champ?' the croupier quipped.

'I've done all my training,' Emile snapped back. 'Quit bugging me.'

The escapism of the tables had ended after just fifteen minutes. Emile retreated to his room where he was free from prying stares. Murray sat on the edge of the bed as the fighter propped up his head with a couple of pillows.

'Emile grew thoughtful,' Murray wrote. 'He talked of poor Paret for the first time. "I have not yet come to terms with it. I am not a saint but I have a lot. I have prayed a lot. I have eight people to support and I have no other profession. So I gotta go on. I know I'll be fighting myself as well as Dupas in that ring. But I've talked to Sugar Ray [Robinson] and other fighters who caused tragedies. They've explained that it's not like I was driving drunk and killed someone. Sugar Ray says it's not as if I was a killer or a murderer."'

On the sweltering morning of Friday the thirteenth, a solemn champion and a smiling challenger arrived at the Convention Center for the weigh-in. Dupas was in a jocular mood, wisecracking and grinning as if all his numbers were about to come up in a sudden shift of fate. Griffith said little. It was hard for him to set aside the memory of everything that had happened at his last weigh-in.

Dupas concentrated on flexing his muscles and blowing kisses to his wife and young daughter as he stood on the scales. His weight was confirmed at 145¾ pounds. Dupas raised his arms and whooped.

Griffith was half a pound lighter. He showed no emotion as, without a word, he dressed quickly. Clancy and Albert matched his silence as they watched anxiously over him.

It was left to Angelo Dundee to hold court. 'Ralph is the fastest welterweight in the world,' Dundee said of his fighter. 'He's quick of hand, quick of foot. He'll anticipate Griffith's moves and he's a sure thing to win. Emile is made to order for my guy. Emile won't be able to find him with a bloodhound.'

Ten hours later it looked as if the canny trainer could be right. Griffith dominated the centre of the ring and tried hard to pressure Dupas. But his resolve to land the same right hand that had ruined Paret could not be tested. Dupas ducked and weaved out of trouble, sliding away from Griffith at every opportunity. He snaked out a few jabs that were so mild Griffith hardly seemed to notice them. Dupas sneaked a few rounds, mainly by unleashing a fifteen-second flurry of light-hitting action before the bell, but Griffith was the aggressor as they entered the second half of the contest.

The television cameras had stayed away, out of respect for Paret and public opinion, and the 5,100 crowd was filled with polite observers who seemed willing to forgive both men for the lack of savagery. Dupas was determined to avoid being tagged, but Griffith kept after him. Their heads clashed a couple of times and the champion was cut – two small slits above his right eye and a nick across the bridge of his nose.

Yet any question over the outcome was settled in the last five rounds, with Griffith winning every one on each of the three scorecards. It was only in the final couple of minutes that Dupas was hurt. Griffith finally connected with a hard right that landed flush on his beaten opponent's jaw. Dupas wobbled and looked as if he might go down but Emile hesitated. Normally, he would have stepped in to finish the job, letting his fists seal the concussive ending. But, this time, he backed off for a few seconds, his head swimming with an image of Benny Paret.

The moment of a likely knockout disappeared and Dupas knew enough to cling and hold onto the champion. They had both survived the night without any lasting damage.

Emile was gripped by a complicated swirl of feeling after the fight. A few writers were allowed into his locker room, led by Gilbert Rogin of *Sports Illustrated*, and they noticed how Emile's right hand trembled helplessly. Aware of it twitching so obviously, he grabbed it with his left hand in an effort to regain control. 'But the hand vibrated in his grasp and he looked fearfully at it,' Rogin wrote. 'Once he struck it violently against the rubbing table and, overwhelmed with the mystery, ran bewildered into the lavatory.'

Later, when only Clancy, Albert, Syd Martin, a doctor and Rogin were left in the locker room, the writer noticed that, 'Emile doubled up from the tension. They laid him out on the dressing table and one held his fluttery hand. Then Clancy began to patch two eye cuts. "Hey Doc," he said, "I don't know how to sew up this kind of cut. Give me that needle with the hook in it. I've got to learn sometime." Emile cried out in feigned terror and then laughed for the first time, unburdened.'

Emile looked up at Rogin after he mentioned the 'great, resonant welcome' the champion had received. 'When I got such a reception from the crowd,' Emile said, 'I felt like crying. But I wouldn't let myself even if I just felt like letting all the water come out. I thought about Benny in there. In the fifteenth when I had Dupas in the corner I stopped and looked at him and I stepped away. But instinct took over most of the time. Time, they tell me, is a great healer. The more fights I have I pray and hope that I will forget.'

'Okay, Griffith,' Clancy said, after he had cleaned up his fighter, 'on your feet. Let's go out and get drunk.'

Emile held up his hand and, as Rogin described it, 'in his high, peremptory voice, he said, "Now, will you all keep quiet a moment."'

Dressed only in his underpants and a pair of rubber sandals, Emile walked to the far corner of the locker room. He knelt down and rested his forehead against the peach-coloured seat of a folding chair. Emile prayed silently for over a minute.

'All right,' he said as he got up off his knees and looked at everyone. 'You can all start screaming again.'

At a cocktail party held for him back at the Thunderbird, Emile sipped champagne but his celebrations were muted. 'This fight got me over the hump,' he told reporters who gate-crashed the party. 'There were times when I was fighting myself in there, times I doubted myself. But I got a lot of things off my mind.'

Did that include Paret? 'I don't know,' Emile said. 'I still think about him. He comes into my head all the time. I can be training in the gym and I suddenly think of what happened. I don't know if I can ever be free of it.'

There was no respite in New York. On drowsy mornings or sluggish weekday afternoons, Emile could be walking around midtown, drifting along, when a face in the crowd devastated him. He would reel back, as if struck, because he was convinced briefly that he had seen Benny again. Staring helplessly he would not call out Benny's name because he knew he had to be wrong. The unknown person would gaze back at him and, eventually, the different features came into sharper focus and he realised the resemblance was merely fleeting.

Sometimes the stranger looked so like Benny that Emile actually followed him – before he looked down in embarrassment or shame when the man wheeled round and said, in sudden recognition, 'Wow, hey champ!' Once, someone yelled at him as if he was just another New York crazy.

Even in sleep, especially in feverish and unsettled sleep, Benny Paret returned in much clearer form. He called out to Emile, and the haunted boxer would dream that he opened his eyes and saw Benny at the end of his bed. Benny spoke softly, urging Emile to get up and join him with a ghostly wave of his hand.

Occasionally, Emile would have a nightmare in which Benny stood at the side of his bed and cackled. Emile would murmur, 'Hello, Kid,' and try to say sorry again, but he could never get Benny to hear him.

The dreams that recurred most involved an empty seat. Emile would see himself entering a packed movie theatre. He would walk down a dimly lit aisle, searching for a place where he might sit before the movie started. Eventually, he would spot an unoccupied place. A shrouded figure would call out his name and push down the empty seat for him. Emile would walk quickly in his dream, relief seeping through him. He would settle down and, just before the theatre went black, he looked at the man in the adjoining seat to thank him. The figure nodded and stretched out a hand to clutch his arm. Emile felt the coldness of the clasp. It was Benny Paret, smiling knowingly at him. Emile always woke up then, drenched in sweat.

Even worse was the darker variation of that same dream where, back at Madison Square Garden, and late for a Saturday night fight, he rushed into the arena. Emile knew he was a spectator rather than a fighter and it seemed as if the whole venue was waiting for him to be seated. He scuttled up and down the aisles, moving between the hot-dog sellers and programme vendors, who seemed so vivid in the dream. His face stared back at him from the programmes they waved. Emile scoured the arena for his seat. Finally, it was illuminated by a single spotlight. He almost cried out, knowing he was safe at last. He could disappear from view.

Everything changed as soon as he sat down. The man next to him smiled a ghoulish welcome. It was the ghost of Benny Paret. Emile was trapped in his seat, alongside Benny, as the bell sounded. On the screen, the two fighters rose from their stools. Emile saw himself in one corner with Benny opposite him. He looked at the ghost in the adjoining seat and the spectre grinned at him. Emile and Benny were back together, watching their fatal last fight as a doomed pair of spectators.

The crowd sounded like distant waves crashing on the shore of a beach at night. Again and again the roar came, wave after wave, and Benny held Emile's hand tightly as their fight in the ring became more brutal. Benny was laughing, glancing slyly at him, as they entered the fury of the twelfth round. It was then that Emile would wake, screaming, as if it was the only sound that could stop the nightmare. He lay in his bed, shivering, sometimes crying, as he waited for a new day to start.

Gil and Howie aimed to keep him busy in the ring. Five weeks after he had beaten Dupas, Emile outpointed Denny Moyer in a non-title fight in Tacoma, Washington. Moyer was skilful and the action consisted once more of light skirmishes rather heavy punching. Neither man was hurt and there was less attention on Emile than there had been in Las Vegas.

Yet Madison Square Garden and the television cameras were

waiting. As a world champion, Emile could not avoid the home of big-time boxing or the unblinking TV screens, which ABC were ready to fill again with fighters. There had been serious debate within the ABC boardroom about abandoning boxing after another disastrous night when, on 21 September 1962, the Argentine heavyweight Alejandro Lavorante had sustained terrible injuries against John Riggins at the Olympic Auditorium in Los Angeles. Lavorante had briefly risen to number three in the world heavyweight rankings, but, before he stepped into the ring against Riggins, he had suffered knockout defeats to Archie Moore and Cassius Clay. Riggins battered him into a coma – and Lavorante would die seventeen months later while still in hospital.

It drew another pall over boxing and Brenner knew that his business was struggling. 'Our major problem is the Saturday night schedule,' Brenner said. 'It's a poor fight night. It's the night a man takes his wife or girlfriend to dinner and the theatre. On Broadway, if they didn't have Saturday nights they would go broke. It's the women's night out and she doesn't want to go see a fight.'

ABC were contemplating switching their coverage back to Friday nights (in a move they completed in September 1963 before totally shutting down their live programme a year later) and Brenner knew that he needed a young champion like Griffith to maintain public interest. It was decided that ABC would screen a non-title fight at the Garden between Griffith and Don Fullmer – ranked sixth in the world in the middleweight division. There was speculation that Griffith was more comfortable fighting bigger men, for they would be better equipped to absorb his punches. He would also earn more money in the heavier division against the champion Gene Fullmer, Don's brother, who had so damaged Paret.

Emile was less concerned by either money or another title than the upsetting prospect of returning to Madison Square Garden. He insisted on a few points being written into his contract because he could not bear the thought that he might use Paret's locker room, or fight out of the same corner in which the Cuban had lost his life.

A few weeks before the Fullmer fight, while shaving in his bathroom, Emile had looked at his reflection. The sharp razor scraped the stubble off his right cheek when he suddenly saw a familiar figure appear in the mirror behind him. Emile could have sworn that the apparition was real – but the ghostly shape of Benny Paret disappeared as soon as Emile spun around.

He had since started shaving without a mirror and the shock of seeing Benny was replaced by a wince as he nicked himself in two places. Blood dripped into the warm and foamy water of his bathroom sink.

The cuts were obvious enough to disturb Gil Clancy who, at first, believed that Emile had been fighting outside the ring. When he heard the real reason, he took Emile to a quiet corner of the gym and gripped the fighter's shoulder. Emile needed to regain control. He could not allow his life to be ruined.

Gil and Howie had been working on another diversion, and it felt like the right time to let Emile know that they had negotiated a fight in Vienna. It would be on the same bill as his idol, Sugar Ray Robinson, and their Austrian adventure would take place less than two weeks after the Fullmer fight. He was due to face Fullmer on 6 October 1962 and, if he won, he would step into a Viennese ring eleven nights later, against Ted Wright.

Emile had often spoken of his longing to visit Europe and his managers decided that the easiest way to get him away from the Paret saga would be to travel across the Atlantic. He was filled with an excitement that Gil managed to contain by reminding Emile that the fight would be off if he lost to Fullmer – or shaved again without a mirror. One bad cut and the trip to Vienna would be jinxed.

'You're a mean man, Clancy,' Emile said with a hint of a smile.

CHAPTER NINE

Cuban Missiles

The ghost still stalked Emile Griffith. On the morning of his fight against Don Fullmer, he flicked through the sports pages at the Henry Hudson hotel on West 58th Street. There were reams of reports about him returning to the Garden – accompanied by confirmation of Alejandro Lavorante's deepening coma.

'Why do they keep writing about it?' Emile asked Jimmy Breslin, who was shadowing him for a feature the *Saturday Evening Post* head-lined 'The Champion Who Can't Beat A Memory'.

He also read that Lucy Paret, who had been pregnant when Benny died, had given birth that week to her second son. A baby was already fatherless; and Emile felt responsible.

An hour later, he wore a suitably grey suit to the weigh-in. 'Don Fullmer, the opponent, seemed wary of Griffith when they got to the scales,' Breslin wrote. 'Emile didn't notice. He was lost in his own thoughts.'

At one of his favourite restaurants on 14th Street, waiting for his customary post-weigh-in steak with Albert, Clancy and Breslin, Emile buried his face in his hands.

Silence stretched across the table. Clancy spoke up in desperation. 'Do you know a good joke?' he asked Breslin.

'I'll pay the cheque,' the reporter quipped.

Emile only lifted his head when his managers started talking about Vienna. There was hope for him in escaping to Europe.

After the meal, at Emile's request, they walked up 14th Street to St Bernard's – a Roman Catholic church where the fighter could pray for Paret, Fullmer and himself. Breslin, with his mordant eye, gazed across the street at Redden's funeral home. He chose not to mention to Emile that, two years before, a fighter called Tommy Pachecho had been buried by the undertakers at Redden's. Pachecho, a Puerto Rican welterweight, had lost his life while fighting Benny Gordon at the St Nicholas Arena – in the same week that Emile had fought at St Nick's.

'You hoped that Griffith wouldn't remember,' Breslin wrote.

Emile was in a sour and tetchy mood all afternoon. He complained about the constant chatter of Breslin and his managers, as well as the 'knotted' fight socks that had been laid out for him on his hotel bed.

'All right, Emile,' Clancy said quietly. 'We'll unknot them. Get yourself some sleep now.'

They left him in peace for a few hours, but nothing could help him. By the time they reached the Garden, and Emile was stretched out on the padded rubbing table, the fighter was even more agitated. Suddenly he rose up and, as if about to vomit from nerves, he ran to the toilet. Howie Albert followed him.

'I'm afraid,' Emile eventually admitted between heaving gulps of air.

'What are you afraid of?' Howie asked. 'A guy like Fullmer?'

'No,' Emile said softly. 'I'm afraid of Paret.'

Clancy had joined them. 'Well,' the trainer said, 'you're fighting Fullmer tonight ...'

He steered Emile back to the locker room. 'Griffith stretched out on the rubbing table and looked up again at the harsh light,' Breslin wrote. 'Albert stayed in the bathroom and tried to light a cigarette. His hand was shaking. At last somebody opened the door and said it was time to get into the ring. Clancy put his arm around Griffith and walked him out of the room. There was noise from the crowd but Emile didn't hear it.'

Inside his corner of the ring, wearing a white satin robe, Griffith turned his back on everyone and skipped blankly. He lowered his head and his feet twitched beneath him in a blur.

In the opposite corner, Fullmer's crewcut made him look much more boyish than his bull-necked brother, Gene. He was twenty-three, a year younger than Griffith, who had crammed so much more into a complex life. But Fullmer was a natural middleweight and he had weighed in at 159¾ pounds compared to Griffith's 151 – four pounds over the champion's usual welterweight limit.

The familiar voice of Dan Dunphy echoed at ringside. 'We're now all set to take the show on the road with Johnny Addie,' Dunphy said as he watched the black-suited announcer reach for the long silver microphone dangling from the rafters. The usual ritual unfolded as fighters from the past and present were introduced before Fullmer's name was greeted with boos, while the New York homeboy, Griffith, was cheered.

The referee, Arthur Mercante, called the boxers towards him and, talking politely into Addie's microphone, said, 'Good evening, Emile and Don. You both know the rules of the New York State Athletic Commission. In the event of a knockdown you must take an eight count. Three knockdowns in one round will automatically end the contest. On the command "break", step back. You will be penalised for holding and fouling. Shake hands now and come out boxing.'

As they wheeled away to their corners before the first bell, Griffith knelt down on his right knee and said a quick and fretful prayer. He crossed himself and went back to fighting in the Garden.

Fullmer looked very nervous, while Griffith seemed unsettled. The cautious pattern was set in the first round when, as Jimmy Breslin wrote, 'Fullmer gave ground as Griffith came to him in a crouch. When Fullmer stopped going back, he was in the Paret corner. He stood there, waiting for Griffith to charge. But Griffith did not come. "I did not see Fullmer there," Emile said after the fight. "I saw the late Benny, and I could not get myself to go in there."

'For the rest of the fight,' Breslin continued, 'it was the same. Every time Fullmer moved into the corner, Griffith stopped and wouldn't move until Fullmer got out of there. Fullmer did nothing but hold and run, and Griffith chased him on only three sides. The spectators were booing and walking out. Griffith won the decision by a big margin, but none of the fans cared.'

'I tried to make a better night of it,' Emile said, 'but I couldn't do a thing to make him fight.'

He did not sound too sorry. The booing of a few thousand fight fans mattered little when set against the unscathed life of another man. Emile still felt a heavy drag across his heart.

At one-thirty in the morning, with the persistent shadow of Breslin at his side, Emile walked into an all-night diner. He and the writer sat down next to a couple of bus drivers. Emile pushed away the grease-spattered menu. He had no desire to eat. 'I should be in a hot bathtub right now,' he said. 'But here I am. I can't rest and I won't go to bed at all tonight. Tomorrow, or maybe the next day, I'll try and sleep again.'

Emile fought much more bitterly with Matthew, his needy boyfriend, than he had done against Fullmer. Matthew was unhappy that he would not be accompanying Emile the following week to Vienna. But the champion did not wish to expose his true self to Sugar Ray Robinson, the greatest fighter in history. There was a poignant undertow to the European trip, too, for it marked the first time in twenty-two years that Robinson would fight on an undercard. Emile's bout against Teddy Wright was the main event. Robinson, at the age of forty-one, had just slipped out of the world's top ten middleweights after losing successive contests to Phil Moyer in Los Angeles and Terry Downes in London. His record stood at 148 wins with eleven losses and three draws. Emile wanted to be with Ray in

Vienna as he entered a complicated phase of his once-glorious career. Matthew stayed in New York. He was fuming.

A different kind of plan had hatched in Emile's tortured mind. He had convinced himself that all his despair was rooted in his sexuality. The same words kept echoing in head.

'*I kill a man and most people understand and forgive me. However, I love a man and many say this makes me an evil person.*'

The nightmare would have never happened had he kept to the straight and narrow path. If Emile had chased girls, Paret would still be alive. Marriage to Esther would have kept him straight and true. He loved her too much to use Esther again but, on his way to Vienna, Emile decided to change.

He resolved to be more like Sugar Ray, whose pink Cadillac he loved. Sugar Ray also wore sharp fur coats, gold chains and snazzy suits. He just liked women rather than men when it came to sex. Emile believed that he might be cured of his malady if he could live a life more like Sugar Ray.

Robinson had also killed a man in the ring. But no jibes of '*maricón*' had been aimed at him before Jimmy Doyle died in 1947. He could deal with the scrutiny much more stoically. At the inquest into the death, Sugar Ray had been asked a loaded question by a district attorney: 'Isn't it true that you deliberately tried to get Mr Doyle into trouble?'

Robinson looked back evenly at the DA as he answered with the purity of truth: 'Getting a man in trouble is my business. I'm in the hurt business.'

Emile wanted to deal in simple clarity. Matthew, as a consequence, stayed in Queens while Emile and Sugar Ray flew to Vienna for a week of fighting and partying.

They both won at the Stadthalle before a crowd of 10,000 – Robinson knocking out the Spaniard, Diego Infantes, in the first round, while Griffith outclassed Wright in an easy victory on points.

The next morning the Austrian papers were filled with pictures of the two black Americans grinning as they walked into a nightclub in

Vienna flanked by a pair of statuesque and bosomy blonde women. Emile and Sugar, living a straight life to the full, had no idea that the world was on the brink of ending.

Five nights later, back home with his extended family in Queens, a jetlagged Emile struggled to understand the full meaning of the words resounding from his black-and-white television. But the president looked sick. His skin was very grey on the monochrome set and his face was masked by gravity. John F. Kennedy made it sound as if the world might end soon.

At first, Emile kept hearing the name 'Cuba' more than any other word. Ever since the Paret fight he had flinched inwardly whenever that small and mysterious island was mentioned. 'Cuba' made him think of Benny; and Benny made him think of 'the accident', as he called it. Kennedy kept saying Cuba, and Emile kept thinking of Benny. He couldn't concentrate on the words, but the exclamations of Franklin and Gloria, his brother and sister, told him that terrible times were about to unfold.

Emile became child-like in such moments. He looked around his strange house – filled with family, his best friend Calvin Thomas, his tetchy on-off boyfriend Matthew and a few people whose names he barely knew – and asked beseechingly for help. What did it all mean?

'They nuke us,' Calvin said bleakly, 'and then we nuke 'em . . .'

Emile stared at the screen. Calvin had to be kidding. The confused boxer listened more closely to the sombre president.

It was only late on the evening of 22 October 1962, after all the networks had replayed the most worrying fragments of the presidential address, that Emile pieced everything together. The world really was on the verge of blowing itself up. He could hardly believe it, but he had heard the speech so many times that he couldn't escape the truth. Kennedy underlined the tangible threat of nuclear war. Cuba was at the heart of everything – just as Benny Paret, and the 'accident', was at the blackened heart of all Emile's troubles.

JFK had appeared on every major network television station at exactly 7 p.m., just as a beautiful fall day disappeared into a cool and suddenly dark Monday evening. The usual din of New York settled into a breathless pause, as the news turned the world cold and quiet.

Kennedy linked Cuba, the Russians and nuclear war in three chilling sentences: 'Within the past week, unmistakable evidence has established the fact that a series of offensive missile sites is now in preparation on that imprisoned island. The purpose of these bases can be none other than to provide a nuclear strike capability against the Western Hemisphere. It shall be the policy of this nation to regard any nuclear missile launched from Cuba against any nation in the Western Hemisphere as an attack by the Soviet Union on the United States, requiring a full retaliatory response upon the Soviet Union.'

The Cuban missile crisis was a thirteen-day brush with Armageddon that Arthur Schlesinger, the historian and a close associate of Kennedy, would describe as 'the most dangerous moment in human history'. Robert McNamara, the US Secretary of Defense, wondered whether anyone in America 'would live to see another Saturday night'.

The White House and the Kremlin were already a week into the meltdown, with Kennedy and Nikita Khrushchev having exchanged long and emotive threats in private communiqués, when the president addressed the nation and spelt out the menacing possibilities of nuclear war. For the next six days, it seemed as if the world teetered on the edge of annihilation.

Emile still thought about Benny when he heard the dreaded name of Cuba – but he was also diverted from his own torment by the looming apocalypse. A nationwide poll discovered that one in five Americans was convinced that a Third World War, and the destruction of the planet, was imminent. It was hard to resist the paranoia when radio stations across the country insisted on playing advertisements with handy tips on how to survive a nuclear holocaust by building a shelter and storing food. Predictions that there were enough Soviet nuclear weapons in Cuba to kill 145 million of the US's total population of 185 million people were broadcast.

Even in New York, that toughest of cities, the usual biting comeback gave way to shivering apprehension. It was difficult not to succumb when schoolchildren around the United States were made to do daily 'duck-and-cover' drills. At the sound of a fire alarm, in practice exercises, every child was expected to duck down beneath his or her school desk and cover their heads. Emile couldn't quite work out how much good it would do anyone to just duck and cover when an atomic bomb landed – but he figured the experts knew what they were talking about.

He staggered away from his newly straightened path and, with the world about to end, went to bed with Matthew most nights. If they were going to be blown up it hardly seemed wrong to die in someone else's arms. And on the Saturday night that might have been their last, at least according to the fears of the Secretary of Defense, Emile and Calvin went to a new club in midtown and had some fun with a gang of young Puerto Rican men who partied as if they did not have a care left in a doomed world.

As always, the roots of conflict were knotted and hidden away beneath the surface. When Khrushchev and Kennedy had met in Vienna in June 1961, the Soviet leader had cornered the president with warnings to end Western occupation rights in Berlin. Kennedy had taken a step back and done nothing to halt the building of the Berlin Wall. The president felt diminished and he resolved never again to act so timidly.

Kennedy knew that the US's nuclear capability outstripped the Soviet Union's. The Russians possessed fewer than thirty intercontinental missiles, of varying efficiency, and they had neither the money nor the manpower to build many more. Both administrations were aware that US missiles could wipe out fifteen times as many Soviet targets, and Kennedy began to stress the advantage by implying that he might resort to 'first use' of nuclear weapons as a way of dismantling a spreading Soviet threat.

To the delight of Fidel Castro, Khrushchev reacted boldly and they agreed to plant medium-range Soviet missiles in Cuba. Castro needed to protect the Cuban revolution from American invasion and he and Khrushchev took solace from making the powerful United States feel acutely vulnerable.

China backed Khrushchev and Castro, as the *People's Daily*, the official state newspaper, declared that '650,000,000 Chinese men and women stand by the Cuban people'. Pope John XXIII voiced world-wide concern and, on 24 October 1962, he said: 'We beg all governments not to remain deaf to the cry of humanity, that they do all that is in their power to save peace – and the world from the horrors of war.'

After a few days, the Kennedy blockade, backed by nuclear bombers in the air, worked. Khrushchev ordered his ships, sailing towards Cuba, to return to Soviet waters. Dean Rusk, the US Secretary of State, suggested that, 'We're eyeball to eyeball, and I think the other fellow just blinked.'

A crisis was far from over. B52 bombers remained on alert and in the air, with nuclear bombs 'on board and ready for use'. Major Don Clawson, one of the US pilots, said years later that, 'We were damned lucky we didn't blow up the world – and no thanks to the political or military leadership of this country.'

It just needed one rogue pilot to be spooked into pressing a button and firing. Robert McNamara also admitted that 'we lucked out' in avoiding nuclear war.

On the morning of 27 October an American U-2 reconnaissance plane flying over Cuba was shot down by a surface-to-air missile. The pilot, Rudolf Anderson, became the first, and only, fatality of the crisis. For a few hours, Kennedy was urged by his chiefs of staff to launch an attack on Cuba that would obliterate, at the very least, all Soviet-made missiles. The president, aware of the dire conse-quences, wavered and resisted. However, later that afternoon, US destroyers dropped depth charges against Soviet submarines.

Besieged Soviet commanders, underwater and under fire, con-sidered unleashing nuclear torpedoes containing 15 kilotonnes of explosives, which would have been similar to the Hiroshima bomb in their devastating impact. A Russian second captain, Vasili Arkhipov, averted disaster by calming the mood and persuading his superior, Valentin Savitsky, not to fire at US destroyers from their *B-59* submarine.

The next twenty-hours were the most unsettling of the conflict, as the administrations in Washington and Moscow engaged in fretful negotiations and desperate brinkmanship. Khrushchev initially offered to remove all Soviet missiles from Cuba if the US agreed not to invade the island. As the Pentagon prevaricated over a straightforward deal, the Kremlin sent a second wired demand that their withdrawal of weapons from Cuba was also dependent on the US removing their Jupiter rockets, equipped with nuclear warheads, from Turkey.

Washington agreed to the first offer, while JFK sent his brother, Robert, to meet the Soviet ambassador and make a secret pledge that the United States would also dismantle its missiles in Turkey – on the condition that the agreement was not made public. The Soviets agreed, bypassing Castro's protests, and the following day, at 10 a.m. on a sunlit Sunday in Washington, 5 p.m. in a freezing Moscow, the Kremlin's state radio confirmed that the missiles would be removed in exchange for a guarantee of Cuba's independence and safety from invasion.

It seemed almost a miracle that nuclear war had been avoided.

Emile Griffith returned to Las Vegas for his final fight of a tragic year. The world was safe again but Benny Paret was still dead. Emile was back on the righteous path he had discovered with Sugar Ray Robinson. He still resolved to go straight and become a real man. On 8 December 1962, at the same Convention Center where he had defeated Ralph Dupas, Emile stopped Jorge Jose Fernandez in the ninth round of their world welterweight title fight. He wondered if his new regime had begun to work its magic.

Bernard Forbes, his cousin, ensured a stream of young women

slipped into Emile's Vegas hotel room. They were happy to hold his magnificent body, and feel the warmth of his fame and glory, while Emile found it easy enough to succumb to a burst of bisexuality. They weren't going to be bombed to smithereens and it felt right to celebrate. An amused Gil Clancy removed the ladies from the champion's bed.

Decades later, talking to their mutual friend, Ron Ross, the New York writer who understood them so well, Emile stressed how much he loved Gil and Howie. He also lamented their limited communication. 'They meant more to me than any father,' Emile said of his managers. 'I could not hurt them. Maybe if I felt Clancy would smile the same way pulling a guy out of my bed the same way he did finding a girl there ... I might have acted in a different way. So many times I wanted to say, "Meet my boyfriend ... my partner." They saw Matthew clinging to me all the time. But Gil saw what he wanted to see. I don't think anyone, except maybe Mommy, meant more to me than Gil. I wasn't going to hurt him, no matter what. I also think to myself, wouldn't it be funny if, all along, Gil knew and couldn't talk to me about it. Maybe not funny ... sad. I know. I'm the one who made my life more difficult. I'm the one who was afraid to be honest. But I was so sure that the two people I cared about most wouldn't be able to deal with the truth.'

As long as the rest of the world, even men as compassionate or sophisticated as Clancy or Albert, were so uncomfortable when considering homosexuality, Emile remained nailed to his cross of silent denial. He still could not bear to voice the truth out loud.

Freddie Wright knew little about boxing. But he understood how much Emile Griffith meant in a secret world. There were still only eight world champion boxers and just one of that select breed, the glorious Emile, hung out in New York's raw and sleazy gay bars and clubs. Freddie, who was just twenty in 1963, joked that he was 'a slut'. He was a good-time boy, a young black gay man who loved to dance and to party. Freddie felt only admiration when he saw Emile.

He knew that some things in life were too serious to be reduced to sex or jive-talking. Emile Griffith belonged to that exalted realm.

The boxer was back on familiar territory after his failed attempt to become a heterosexual stud. Emile looked happy again in his illicit and secret gay underworld. Freddie didn't hit on many people – he had more than enough men chasing his lithe dancer's body – and so he made no attempt to seek out Emile. He could respect him from a distance without guessing how close they would become a few years later.

Freddie had heard about Emile's troubles. He shared some of that same hurt. Freddie liked to dance and laugh, but it wounded him to endure, in his words, 'the double trials and tribulations' of being black and gay. He was used to being dismissed as 'a Negro', 'a coloured' and 'a nigger'. When he was spotted sneaking in and out of a gay bar, he would get yelled at for being 'a fairy', 'a queer' or 'a faggot'. Most of the time the abuse was twinned and he was ridiculed as 'a nigger faggot'.

'Is that the best you got, baby?' Freddie would say with a soft cackle.

Freddie felt lucky. He had never been beaten up. Of course, because he lived dangerously, he had made some narrow escapes. But, from the night he went to his first gay bar at the Cherry Lane Theatre in Greenwich Village, he had lived on his wits and avoided the worst trouble. The verbal abuse, and the bile directed at his skin colour and his taste for men, wore him down.

He had been born and raised in Queens and, as soon as he was fifteen, he was out on the street most nights, with his boys. Most of his gay friends were white and they would often be asked a brutal question: '*What ya doin' with that nigger?*'

Freddie just rolled his eyes but the word still hurt him. He tried to find another way in the straight world. At eighteen, he got a job and a cheap apartment while working as a scaffolder in Jersey. Freddie didn't like it much because he was not really suited to rough work. One morning he told his scaffolding crew he was taking a coffee break and he never went back. He headed home to New York City, where he yearned to become a dancer. Freddie could move like no one else he knew – and he danced freely to his favourite records on the jukebox of every bar he visited.

Emile did not share that same freedom. Something more tangled lurked inside the great boxer. It was hard enough that he was a gay black man in 1963. To be famous at the same time meant Emile carried a heavy weight on his mighty shoulders. The hope and pride of a derided community were invested in him.

No one suggested you could be cured of blackness. But it still felt as if most of America believed that homosexuality was a disease-spreading curse that needed to be cut out like a cancer. At least Emile gave many gay men, especially gay black men, belief that the world might start to regard homosexuality in a different light. Every time news spread that the world champion had arrived at Bon Soir or Dr Feelgood or Telstar, or any of the other gay joints where Freddie Wright danced, a jolt of courage surged through the clubbers like electricity. Emile made everyone feel just a little stronger.

The dirty old fight business kept on turning, even if the same problems remained. There were concerted campaigns to have boxing abolished in New York State and Illinois, but Emile went back on the road. He followed up his first European excursion in Vienna with a jaunt in Copenhagen where, in February 1963, he boxed Chris Christensen. The Danish journeyman called himself 'Gentleman Chris' and, as had become his custom, Griffith went out of his way to avoid a knockout. Instead, he stepped back whenever his opponent buckled. Griffith only opened up when it seemed heartless to prolong the fight. He dropped Christensen three times in the ninth round and gestured pleadingly to the referee to stop it. The Danish corner rescued both men by throwing a white towel into the ring.

In his locker room, Emile stripped off hurriedly and headed for the showers. He stood under the hot jets and, closing his eyes, let the water cascade down on him. Emile kept his head bowed, offering thanks that another night in the ring was over, and then slowly lifted his face to the warm water. All the sweat and grime of the fight was washed away as he soaped himself. Emile began to sing, softly and exultantly, ignoring the Danish photographer who persisted in shooting a spool of film of him naked but relieved.

It felt as if, maybe, he would be able to find a way to move ahead in boxing. He had spared his opponent the worst kind of punishment. That outcome mattered more to Emile than his latest victory.

Such unusual compassion from a fighter was interpreted differently by Desmond Hackett, a London-based reporter for the *Daily Express*. There was speculation in Britain that Griffith would soon defend his title against a Welsh boxer called Brian Curvis. The press wanted to get in early with their murderous profiles.

'Emile Griffith, the fearsome-looking welterweight champion of the world, turned in a fighting show of brutality and indifferently clubbed thirty-six-year-old Dane Chris Christensen into a ninth-round defeat here yesterday,' Hackett wrote from Copenhagen. Describing the fight as a 'senseless, pitiless slaughter', Hackett asked: 'Should Curvis be kept away from this man who knows no pity and who will cripple or destroy those who seek to take his title. My opinion is that Griffith, who has the odd off-fight job of hat designer, revealed a frightening streak of sadism. He appeared to enjoy mauling the brave and ageing Dane. There were times when it looked as though the next coldly exploded hook would be the merciful end for Christensen. Instead Griffith danced away, only his eyes betraying his remorseless urge to inflict more punishment. He completely ignored the demands of his manager: "Don't fool around, get in and pin him."'

Recoiling from Griffith's 'dark, expressionless head', Hackett compared the 'dull thud' of his 'pain-packed punches to the ominous sound of a scaffold being erected'.

Emile was mortified, while Howie Albert was incensed. 'Here was a guy who even turned Emile's reluctance to hurt anyone into an act of sadism,' Albert told the writer Ron Ross. 'His distortion of the facts bordered on the libellous. All we could do was share some of Emile's pain. It wasn't enough.'

El Feo was still waiting. Luis Rodriguez, the Ugly One, had not recovered from losing a split decision to Griffith in December 1960. The indignity still burned. Rodriguez was twenty-six and the wiseguys in the boxing press said he did not look a day over thirty-six. He didn't care. Rodriguez was convinced he was the best welterweight in the world.

He had been affected badly by Benny Paret's death. They were Cuban compatriots and the calamity hurt Rodriguez personally and professionally. He and Benny had been friends as much as rivals, while the broader consequences in the welterweight division lingered. Rodriguez had been forced to accept six routine bouts, and easy victories, because Griffith could not contemplate fighting him for a long time. But, as the perennial number one contender, *El Feo* eventually had to be given another crack at the title.

They settled on 16 March 1963, in Los Angeles. Griffith and Rodriguez would be the headline bout in a triple-header bill called the Carnival of Champions, with attention also focused on Davey Moore's world featherweight defence against Ultiminio 'Sugar' Ramos. The third bout would pit Battling Torres against Roberto Cruz for the newly vacant junior welterweight world title. Promoted by George Parnassus, a local businessman known as 'the Greek', and a flame-haired, feisty woman called Aileen Eaton, the three fights were so intriguing that the Olympic Auditorium, the traditional home of boxing in LA with a seating capacity of 15,000, was clearly not large enough.

'This is so big we gotta go outside,' George the Greek boasted, 'to the Dodgers.'

Parnassus and Eaton managed to secure Dodger Stadium, which had been built at a cost of $23m the previous year. It was the new home of the LA Dodgers, the contentious baseball franchise. The original Dodgers, the real Dodgers to New Yorkers like Emile, belonged in Brooklyn, but in 1958 the ball club had been moved by its owner, the reviled real estate magnet Walter O'Malley, to Los Angeles. The motivation was financial, as the heart was torn out of a great baseball institution.

The Brooklyn Dodgers had given Jackie Robinson the chance to break the colour barrier when he became the first black man to play Major League Baseball, and to do so brilliantly, in 1947. The club was so steeped in Brooklyn that the Dodgers name was a weaving wink to the ancient trick of dodging the trolley cars thundering around the streets of Flatbush near Ebbets Field. Even though they were also called Da Bums, because of an inability to match the grand New York Yankees, the Dodgers belonged to Brooklyn.

When O'Malley shut down the gritty old Brooklyn base so that the Dodgers could begin again in the seemingly vacuous world of sun-kissed Los Angeles, the anger was deep and wide. The joke ran that if you gave a Brooklyn Dodgers fan a gun with two bullets and shut him away in a room with Hitler, Stalin and Walter O'Malley there would be no doubting the outcome. He would shoot O'Malley – twice.

There were no trolley-dodgers in LA; but the reinvented Dodgers won the World Series in 1959 and their crisp, shiny new stadium was opened in late 1962. It appeared the perfect venue for the Carnival of Champions and a crowd expected to exceed 25,000 – with George the Greek and Aileen Eaton predicting a gate of $300,000.

Sugar Ramos was an ally of Rodriguez, but he shared a darker fate with Griffith. The Cuban featherweight also knew what it meant to kill an opponent. In November 1958, in Havana, he had knocked out Jose Blanco in the eighth round. Blanco called himself '*Tigre*'; but the Tiger was culled that night. He died from a brain haemorrhage four hours after he had been carried from the ring.

As a semi-literate sixteen-year-old, who had lied about his age and started boxing professionally a year earlier, Ramos had no alternative but to keep fighting. He stopped five of his next six opponents and, even when he was extended to a points decision, the victories kept rolling his way. Ramos had lost just once in forty-two bouts by the time he signed to fight Moore. His only serious defeat had occurred at the hands of Fidel Castro, rather than Rafael Camacho, to whom he lost on a disqualification. The Cuban ban on professional boxing meant that, like Rodriguez and Paret, Ramos had been forced to leave his home forever. But rather than heading for Miami or New York, he opted for an original choice in Mexico City.

Ramos was twenty-one and he'd had five years to get over a ring death. He loved playing the bongos, listening to Látin music and flashing a dazzling smile whenever he arrived in America – where Angelo Dundee helped work his corner. He looked certain to become a world champion one day.

'He's the same kind of "Sugar" as Sugar Ray Robinson,' the trainer Howie Steindler said at his Main Street Gym in Los Angeles. 'Ramos is the best I've seen in this gym.'

Informed judges argued that even that potential would not be able to withstand the power and class of Moore – rated one of the world's best pound-for-pound fighters in 1963. Known as the 'Springfield Rifle', after his hometown in Ohio and his deadly fists, Moore was the son of a preacher. He was just five feet three inches tall, and Jim Murray called him 'a sunny little man' in the *Los Angeles Times*. That cheerful disposition had hampered Moore's progress during his earliest years as a pro, for, reluctant to train, he had lost five of his first twenty-seven fights.

Moore had been on the brink of quitting because it was hard to make decent money as a black featherweight. He was only persuaded not to retire by the veteran fight manager Willie Ketchum, who convinced him that, if he applied himself, he could still become a world champion.

Everything changed for Moore when, in December 1958, he faced Ricardo Moreno – the savage Mexican known as '*Pajarito*' (Baby Bird). Baby Bird had a butcher's cleaver of a hook and so, for the first time in his career, Moore was afraid. He had to get Baby Bird first. He knocked Moreno down twice before stopping him in the opening round. That sensational win served up his shot at a world title and Moore battered the champion, Hogan 'Kid' Bassey, in thirteen bloody rounds in March 1959.

He had lost only once in the intervening six years. At twenty-nine, he was at his peak as he prepared for Ramos. His boxing passion was such that the little man reacted angrily when asked, in the week of the fight, what he thought of critics of the sport following the death of Paret and Alejandro Lavorante's coma in a Los Angeles hospital.

'I think anyone who wants to abolish boxing is sick,' Moore exclaimed in a radio interview. 'People are dropping dead in the streets and you don't hear nothing about them. There are a lot of other sports that you get crippled and die in. A race driver can get killed. Why don't they stop the Indianapolis 500? I'm a fighter because I like the sport. It pays well and it's done me no harm. In fact, it's done me a great favour. It helped me out quite a bit. Once I wanted to be a football player but I just stopped growing.'

Moore was a foot too short, and a hundred pounds too light, to have made it in American football. But, playing football as a schoolboy, he remembered that, 'I was fast, man. Those cats were grabbin' air when I had the ball. But now I'm doing something even better. I know how to fight and I just love boxing.'

Griffith and Rodriguez were less cheerful. The press had begun to describe Griffith as the 'Moody Milliner' as they observed him snapping at Gil Clancy while training in Santa Monica. Griffith seemed edgier than at any time since the Paret fight. *El Feo*, meanwhile, had promised he would knock out the champion. Griffith's response was unusually curt: 'The last time we met all he did was run and run.'

The ongoing animosity between the United States and Cuba had escalated again throughout the week, lending an added charge to the build-up. Exiled anti-Castro militants had shelled a Soviet camp on Cuba's north shore on 18 March 1963. They had killed at least two Russian soldiers. Such aggression infuriated the Soviet high command because Nikita Khrushchev had just instigated the withdrawal of 1,600 Russian troops from Cuba. Khrushchev had also encouraged Castro to free two American women imprisoned in Havana since the revolution. There were suggestions that, for a $53m ransom fee, Cuba would release a further twenty American prisoners.

Just five months on from the Cuban missile crisis, the Kennedy administration remained deeply suspicious of communism. Two US fighter jets had chased a couple of Soviet reconnaissance aircraft over the southwestern corner of Alaska. On the night of 14 March, they had scrambled and tracked the intruders by radar and swept down on the Red planes from out of a cold black sky. It would have been easy for the American pilots to shoot them down, but they were under orders to simply harry the Soviets out of US airspace.

In Moscow, the US ambassador, Foy D. Kohler, made a formal protest. He demanded that the USSR should 'take all necessary measures to prevent any repetition of violations of US territory'.

John F. Kennedy also flew to Costa Rica on 18 March to join a Latin America summit against Cuba. In tandem with the leaders of Guatemala, El Salvador, Honduras, Nicaragua, Panama and Costa Rica, the US president denounced Cuba. He persuaded his Latin allies to join him in isolating Castro. 'We will build a wall around Cuba,' Kennedy promised. 'It will not be a wall of mortar or brick or barbed wire but a wall of dedicated men determined to protect their own freedom.'

Rodriguez was in exile, but he and Griffith still represented two very different countries amid the endless tension of the Cold War. And so it seemed a typically American touch that the promoters had built the ring on the pitcher's mound at Dodger Stadium.

Griffith's mood was not helped when, forty minutes before the first fight was due to start, and with 15,000 drenched spectators already in their seats, George the Greek postponed the Carnival of Champions. A huge storm had broken over Los Angeles and, since arriving at Dodger Stadium, both Clancy and Angelo Dundee had stressed their concern. Even though the ring was covered, rain would slant in and make the canvas slippery.

'Either guy could break his leg,' Clancy warned and, at last, sense prevailed. Even though it meant Parnassus and Eaton lost $100,000 of ABC's network television money, they would go back to their hotels for the night and await a safer time to fight.

Four days slipped away before they could step in the ring. Time slowed to a weary trudge, dragging past hour by hour, day after day, and the battle to make weight all over again seemed harder than ever. Emile felt drained and strained, and Clancy tried to bolster him with a reminder that it was just as difficult for Rodriguez. The sunken expressions on the faces of Moore, Ramos and every other boxer on the bill made it obvious that they also endured the same agonies of fasting and waiting.

On a strange day for a world title fight, a Thursday, Griffith and Rodriguez both made weight at the glitzy Alexandria hotel in down-town LA. Rodriguez was determined, but he was too dignified to replicate Paret's taunting. He said nothing mocking or contemptuous at the weigh-in. It would be enough to try to knock Griffith out on a night that would become clogged with tragic violence.

CHAPTER TEN

Who Killed Davey Moore?

Dodger Stadium, Los Angeles, Thursday 21 March 1963

Two nights before the first anniversary of Benny Paret's catastrophic fall at Madison Square Garden, Emile Griffith went back to work again. He had felt the opposite of a champion most of the 363 days and nights of his second reign as king of the welterweight division. But the old competitive zeal had returned. *El Feo* had an ability to concentrate a fighter's mind as he loomed dangerously.

The challenger ducked between the ropes first. Jimmy Lennon, the ring announcer, introduced the Cuban, extending his o's and z's and rolling his r's in a growly Latino-inflected style, as he hollered: '*Loooooooooo-is Rrrrrrrrodrrrrrriguezzzzzzz!*'

Lennon's voice turned syrupy as he gestured grandly to the American champion. 'And now ladies and gentlemen,' he cried, 'it's my pleasure to present to you, fighting out of the black corner, wearing black trunks, the hard-punching welterweight champion of all the world ... *Emile Griffithhhhhh!*'

The referee, Tommy Hart, called the corners together. Angelo Dundee accompanied Rodriguez, while Gil Clancy massaged his fighter's neck tenderly as if he might be able to release the stress in Griffith.

Back in his corner, Rodriguez extended both his arms and punched skywards as if calling down some mysterious power to enter his fists. Griffith simply jogged on the spot.

Rodriguez was a brilliant stylist, and from the first round he danced and feinted around Griffith in a subtle attempt to unbalance the titleholder. The Cuban was also an adroit counter-puncher and he picked off Griffith when under attack. But the American, in his flat-footed way, was the harder hitter and the more aggressive fighter. Thirty seconds before the end of round one, Griffith pummelled his rival in the kidney area as if to prove he was willing to fight rough again. Rodriguez responded with a good dig to the gut.

In the break, Dundee applied Vaseline to the flanks of his fighter so that Griffith's punches to the kidneys would slip and slide. He did not need to say much to Rodriguez because they knew the pattern of their preferred fight. It was vital that Rodriguez kept his distance and, to sustain himself against the supreme fitness of Griffith over fifteen rounds, fought in calculated bursts of action designed to make most impact on the scorecards.

Rodriguez popped off a jab to start the second as Griffith barrelled towards him. The champion looked unsettled, but then, with his fast hands, he cut through the slick defence and landed a huge right. Rodriguez held off Griffith for a while but a beautiful combination again opened up the Cuban. The Ugly One looked a less pretty boxer as he clinched.

'You're holding, Luis,' Hart yelled. It didn't matter, as Griffith had squared the rounds at one apiece.

Rounds three and four were even until, amid a frenetic flurry, Rodriguez landed an uppercut, which he followed with a right cross. The Cuban had the longer reach, and the fancier footwork, even if he was not as obviously strong or as belligerent as Griffith.

Rodriguez ensured that a cagey fight continued until, after the bell had rung for the end of the eighth, he hit Griffith twice illegally.

That spat ensured a spicier round nine, as they swapped meaty left hooks before a jarring right hand, and the best punch of the fight, rocked Griffith.

'His eyes aren't glassy,' the ringside commentator said of Griffith. 'He's plenty okay!'

They settled into the same old routine: Griffith landed the heavier single shots, while Rodriguez was flashier, with starbursts of punches in the closing half-minute of rounds nine to twelve.

For much of the thirteenth they were brawling up close, before Griffith reeled off a trio of blows that penetrated Rodriguez's tight guard. Dundee started counting down the seconds left in the round as a way of spurring his fighter on. Rodriguez let his hands fly and a sharp right caught Griffith just as the bell rang.

They covered the champion in his corner with a white towel, and Clancy instructed Griffith to fight with greater urgency in the last six minutes. A gruelling battle of skill and will boiled down to two final attritional rounds. The fight, made absorbing by the difficulty of separating two evenly matched technicians, gathered intensity – especially in the final round. Rodriguez and Griffith went to war in the centre of the ring, and it was the Cuban who looked the cooler and more effective marksman. He swayed out of the way, or deflected Griffith's rollicking punches, while landing precise combinations. It had been Rodriguez's round.

Soon after the bell, the UPI wire reporter phoned in his unofficial score – eight rounds to seven in favour of Griffith.

The champion raised his arms and walked around the ring, apparently confident that he had retained his title. Griffith's gesture was booed by most of the Latino-dominated crowd backing Rodriguez.

Griffith eventually removed his gloves and pulled on his gown as he danced in seeming anticipation of good news from the ring announcer.

Jimmy Lennon raised his hand for silence and a bell tolled in a clanging prelude to the scorecards. 'Your attention, ladies and gentlemen,' Lennon said in his warbling voice. 'We have a unanimous decision. Judge Lee Grossman at ringside scores it 8 to 5. John Thomas, judging at ringside, sees it as 8 to 6. Referee Tommy Hart scores it 9 to 5 to the new welterweight champion ... *El Feo* ... *Loooooooooo-is Rrrrrrrrodrrrrrriguezzzzzzz!*

Griffith, who had been walking up and down the ring in giddy anticipation, kicking alternate legs high at the confirmation of each scorecard, suddenly stopped. His head slumped just as Rodriguez was raised high on the shoulders of his seconds.

A local television man with a microphone reached the winner. Rodriguez was still being held up in the air when he was asked, 'Hey, champ, how do you feel?'

'I feel good, I feel great,' Rodriguez said in his heavily accented English.

'Now tell me, Luis,' the friendly interviewer said, nodding across to the forlorn figure of Griffith, 'will you give him a chance at your title?'

'I'll fight anybody,' the Ugly One grinned down from the smoky clouds, as his handlers began to bounce him up and down.

Griffith looked miserable; and Clancy and Albert were irate. 'This is the second time they took the title away from us without a gun,' Albert moaned, recalling the contentious loss to Paret in 1961, when Clancy had compared that decision to a mugging.

The trainer sounded incredulous. 'How can a man win a title when he runs away?' Clancy asked. 'Rodriguez is a safety-first fighter and he won the title running. Yeah, he fought hard the last ten seconds of every round. But what about the other two minutes, fifty seconds? The wrong guy got the decision. What can you do? It's boxing.'

Davey Moore recognised the bruising reality of the fight business when there was a sharp knock on his closed door – accompanied by a warning yell of, 'Fifteen minutes, champ ...'

Trepidation and fear were wrapped up in a dark bundle of emotion, which made it seem as if he was about to face the hangman.

Boxing's equivalent of death row became even more ominous when the man opposite, the apparent executioner, was roared on by a vociferous crowd. It always seemed as if little Davey Moore was alone. He fought anywhere and everywhere, in the other guy's backyard in Mexico, England, France, Spain, Italy, Finland and Japan. Moore lamented that, 'I don't have no rooters. I'd like to have someone out there say, "C'mon, Davey!" But they don't come out to cheer for poor old Davey.'

In July 1958, Moore had fought a Mexican, Kid Anahuac, in Tijuana. Moore won the decision and the crowd was so incensed that a live snake was thrown at him. Moore was asked later if the snake had been poisonous. 'I never stopped to inspect him,' Moore replied dryly.

Even as a respected world champion, on the biggest bill of his life nearly five years later, Moore felt outnumbered. The attendance had just been announced at 28,809 and it was estimated that at least 10,000 Mexican fight fans had descended on the Dodgers' gleaming new home carved into the hillside of Chavez Ravine. They would support their countryman, Battling Torres, as well as Ramos, an adopted Mexican. Around 5,000 exiled Cubans had also arrived to bolster Ramos. The Dodgers' 'Blue Heaven', at least to Moore, was a Latino vortex of colour and devilish noise.

Moore had not spoken much since the postponement five nights earlier. One of his cornermen, Eddie Foy, said that, 'Davey wouldn't talk to anybody. He was pensive, real quiet. He read the Bible.'

Griffith and Moore had both been assigned the office of Dodgers manager Walter 'Smokey' Alston to use as their locker room for the night. Alston was also known as the 'Quiet Man', and it seemed an appropriate place for the muted champion as he waited for the moment when all hell would break loose against Ramos. He pulled on his maroon-and-gold robe. On the back, a giant gold letter 'K' had been stitched in honour of Keifer Junior High – the school he'd attended back in Springfield, Ohio, which felt a million miles from Chavez Ravine.

In the ring, Ramos was introduced by Jimmy Lennon as 'the challenger on my left, in the black corner, fighting out of Mexico City, from [and here Lennon slipped into his Hispanic growl] Mantazas, Cuba, the outstanding, undefeated ... *Ultiminio 'Sugar' Rrrrramosssss!'*

The Cuban lifted his gloves and nodded politely to all four sides of the ring. The lucky horseshoe that had been embroidered into the back of his silky gown gleamed under the lights.

Moore looked very short, dwarfed by cornermen who were hardly giants. The boxer's head was shrouded by a white towel, which hid his expression as Lennon slipped into his intro: 'On my right, in the white corner, wearing black trunks, same weight, 125¼ pounds, from Springfield, Ohio, the world's featherweight boxing champion ... *Daaa-veyyy ... Mooooore!'*

Willie Ketchum, standing next to Moore, slid a gumshield into the fighter's mouth. Moore removed his robe. Cold air touched his bare skin, just as it cooled the sweat lining Luis Rodriguez's brow. The new welterweight champion had been persuaded to return to ringside, in a suit, to offer between-rounds colour commentary.

'Luis says he wants to see the fight anyway,' the television commentator Steve Ellis explained.

The American followed the retreating challenger around the ring for the opening twenty seconds. 'Moore is a stalker and certainly the better puncher,' Ellis suggested, 'although Ramos can punch.'

It looked, for a while, as if the featherweights might replicate the tactical battle that had made the preceding welterweight clash such a slow-burner. There was little action in the first three minutes, but, before heading to their corners, Moore and Ramos tapped each other respectfully on the head.

During the break the cameras cut away to Rodriguez, who was asked whether his 'stablemate', Ramos, could win. 'I think he's going to beat Davey Moore tonight,' Rodriguez said.

'You really do?'

'Yes.'

'Why?' the portly interviewer asked, wrapping his hand around the back of Rodriguez's neck as if to ensure that the new champion wouldn't suddenly disappear. 'How will he do it?'

'It feels real good, great. I feel happy because I have won the title,' Rodriguez replied, sidestepping the question. 'I think, anyway, he's going to win.'

'All right, Luis, you stay right with us and call some of the shots,' the man with the microphone said optimistically, as if Rodriguez had offered the first of many trenchant insights.

Moore and Ramos remained cautious, moving their heads as much as their feet in a concentrated effort to avoid being tagged. A burble of voices cut through the quiet hubbub at ringside. 'The sound you can hear in the background is Griffith talking to Rodriguez,' Ellis, the commentator, revealed. 'We'll pick up some of that conversation in a little while. They're talking about a rematch right now. We'll get Emile and Luis on in a little bit. Meanwhile, let's get back to this one. This one is a good one.'

The excellence of both Moore and Ramos was plain. Each worked behind a slick, fast jab that probed for openings. They were both keen to use combinations while moving fluidly and showing solid defensive skills. The difference was that Moore was more aggressive and ready to switch his attack to the body – while Ramos relied on the jab and his quick feet. Moore still landed first.

'Beautiful shot by Davey Moore,' Ellis yelled when the little champion sank a rattling left hook into the ribcage. 'He might have hurt Ramos.'

Moore doubled up with two swift right hands. Ramos connected with a right-hand bomb of his own. He then reeled off a couple of left hooks that sent Moore back onto the ropes. The crowd rocked in appreciation, sensing the coming fury. A small cut had opened up under Ramos' right eye, but he detonated another left against Moore's head. As they broke for the end of the second, Moore looked at Ramos, smiled and gently cupped the Cuban's head.

Griffith, looking smart but sober in a dark suit, stood beneath a neutral corner outside the ring. 'It's on everyone's mind, every-where,' the interviewer said, as Griffith ducked low so that he could answer the question above the bedlam, 'and so what about the return between you and Rodriguez for that title?'

'Well, tonight, I heard from Luis and his manager that I can have a return bout anytime,' Griffith said in his piping voice. 'And, believe me, I'm going to wait for this return bout.'

'Would you want to fight here in Dodger Stadium again?'

'I'll fight here again,' Griffith said. 'I'll fight Luis anywhere. Luis is a wonderful champ, but I thought I won the fight.'

'All right, Emile, you're a credit to the sport,' the tuxedoed man said as the bell for round three sounded.

In pound-for-pound terms, Moore probably hit as hard as anyone from the welterweight ranks down. If he could get to the body of Ramos, the challenger's darting head would begin to loll. But Ramos was as slippery as he was dangerous.

In the last twenty seconds of round three, Ramos was hurt again by a short, jolting hook but he fought back. They traded fiercely.

'Man, this is punching,' the commentator exclaimed at the bell. Ramos looked at Moore, and tapped his head as if to say that he had absorbed the power of his opponent. Moore tapped his own head in the same gesture.

Angelo Dundee went to work. The glow of Rodriguez's title win had already been set aside as Dundee urged Ramos on, before, spon-taneously, the trainer turned to the crowd. Gazing directly up at the cheap seats, he raised his hands beseechingly. The Cuban and Mexican *fanáticos* responded with a roar of: '*Ra-MOS, Ra-MOS, Ra-MOS!*'

Moore left his stool a few seconds early and wandered around his corner, drawing in breath. He seemed lost in the moment. The bell clanged again. Ramos moved towards him and their dark dance resumed.

The punches became increasingly heavy and, even though Ramos was still light on his feet and Moore cleverly deflected many of the blows with his arms and elbows, both fighters soaked up punishment. Moore drove Ramos to the ropes before there was an inevitable retaliation. 'Ooh, bam!' Ellis exclaimed as Moore shipped a big shot that made him list to the side. 'I don't see how this thing can go fifteen . . .'

Moore responded with a couple of right hands that threatened to pin Ramos and leave him wide open. But the Cuban was strong and he withstood another right hook and uppercut. Moore flashed a white gumshield of a smile at his opponent's courage and again rubbed his head appreciatively.

Huge swathes of the heaving crowd were dragged to their feet as Ramos set about Moore in round five. After some effective jabbing from the American, Ramos took control. A savage combination made Moore blink and step away, but Ramos was on top of him in an instant. A curt left and a right push sent Moore crashing to the canvas as if his legs had been cut away from beneath him. But the referee made a 'no knockdown' gesture and indicated that the champion had been shoved.

Moore's brief visit to the canvas galvanised him. He forced Ramos against the ropes and made his head shudder with a series of uppercuts. Ramos returned fire with even greater force and accuracy. Five successive jabs and a right cross made Moore sag and the mouthpiece flew from his mouth, like a pip being squirted from a squashed orange.

'Davey Moore is hurt,' Ellis cried out. 'This fight cannot go all the way. But don't sell Davey Moore too short. He whacks and, woah, did Ramos get hit! This is going to wind up as one of the all-time great boxing cards.'

Deep into the sixth round, blood seeped from a cut inside Moore's mouth. His gumshield had been cracked by the force of Ramos' punching and its splintered edges caused the bleeding. At the bell it was Ramos who offered a tribute first, and Moore tapped him on the head again in reply.

Moore spat out his mouthguard. It was smeared in red. Ketchum washed the blood away in a bucket but, seeing how badly damaged it was, he called for a replacement. It was no use. The spare mouth-piece wouldn't fit over Moore's teeth, which had been loosened by Ramos' fists. They had no option but to slide the damaged guard back into his swollen mouth.

Ramos nailed Moore repeatedly in the seventh, his left hand unerring against a weary target. The thin six-ounce gloves offered little protection from a fist smashing into flesh and bone. In the last thirty seconds, it was Ramos' turn to suffer as Moore unfurled a bar-rage of combinations.

'Hold on, boy,' Ellis shouted at ringside. 'Now Ramos is hurt!'

There was no cuddling or respectful head-cuffing from either fighter as they sought the sanctuary of their corners. Moore's train-ers worked on his cut, while Ramos looked dazed by the champion's ferocious will.

'They're giving Sugar a bit of the smelling salts,' Ellis confirmed. 'Waking him up a little bit. He took a lot of good right-hand jolts on the jaw.'

Ramos remained under fire. 'Oooo, what a hook,' Ellis hollered. 'Ramos is hurt again early in this round [eight]. It gives more time to uncork the right. There it goes. Look out below! There's the hook. Davey's letting them go, coming from behind. But look at the heart of this feller from Cuba.'

Moore ended the round taking the worst of a brutal exchange. The two fighters stood toe to toe, head to head, as their leathered fists blurred against each other. But Ramos' blows were deadlier and the *fanáticos* chanted, '*Arriba! Arriba!*'

Ramos pumped his left hand into the champion's face in round nine. Blood ran both from Moore's nose and mouth, as the cracked gumshield kept cutting him. His nose had been broken and he was battling to breathe. Ramos' left eye, meanwhile, had closed to a bruised slit.

On his stool, Moore looked up at the black sky as they poured water over his throbbing head. They wiped the blood away and tried to encourage him. Across the ring, Dundee spoke huskily to Ramos. He knew the end was near if the Cuban could maintain the fury of his attack.

The Springfield Rifle had not been silenced quite yet. Moore lived up to his nickname, sending tracer-like punches zinging into Ramos to welcome him to the fateful tenth round. 'Now Ramos is starting to bleed around the nose,' Ellis said. 'He was hurt by a hook and has puffiness under the right eye. This is one they're going to remember for a long time, whether they watch it in Tokyo, Japan, in Mexico City or the Philippines or wherever ...'

In the last minute of the round, Ramos set about Moore. He hit him repeatedly and then, at last, Moore sagged briefly to one knee when attacked on the ropes. But the champion was up so quickly that the referee didn't even have time to start a count. Ramos was all over Moore, winging in with blows from both sides. A devastating left knocked Moore down, making him tumble awkwardly on his back as his head snapped against the knotted lowest rope.

'He's absolutely hurt,' Ellis screamed. 'That was the knockdown. Moore on the floor.'

He was up at four and the referee counted to eight before he sent Moore back out into the fray, with twenty-eight seconds of the round remaining.

Moore threw a desperate left, which missed badly. He staggered and Ramos nailed him to the body, missing with a swinging right but again rocking Moore with another left to the head. The champion careered backwards and Ramos hit him with a couple of right hands. Moore slumped over the ropes.

Referee George Latka separated them and checked if Moore was fit to continue. He didn't spend more than a second before he summoned Ramos to fight on. The end was gruesome. Ramos was lethal. Seven punches flew from his fists, making Moore sag again over the ropes. Only the bell stopped the carnage.

Moore walked unsteadily back to his corner. The noise engulfing Dodger Stadium was raucous enough to induce another collapse but, somehow, he made it. The fading champion sat down on his stool and supported his arms on the ropes behind him. They wiped his face but everyone knew. It was over. Willie Ketchum nodded bleakly at Latke when asked if his fighter was done.

It took only seconds for Ramos and his corner to understand. He ran to the centre of the ring in ecstasy and relief, before he was swallowed up by his team and spectators who had climbed through the ropes. Ramos headed for Moore. As they clutched each other the two fighters were surrounded by a small crowd. Their embrace lasted just seconds before they were parted forever.

They had laid out a rubbing table for Moore in the locker room he shared that night with Griffith. The little fighter refused to lie down. Instead, he sat on the edge of the table and spoke to the reporters who thronged around him: 'I'll take the rematch – you better believe it. Look, you guys know that when I'm right nothing gets to me. Not nothing. I was off. It was an off night. That's it – plain and simple.'

Moore laughed wryly as the hacks gazed at him dubiously. 'Just like you writers, if only you'd admit it. You fellers can't write a lick some days. Well, that was me tonight. I just wasn't up to my best.'

But Moore consoled himself. 'Don't worry,' he said softly. 'I'll come back. We'll get him again.'

They drifted away to join the more upbeat gang of scribblers crammed into Ramos' locker room. Moore was left alone with Ketchum, his trainer Teddy Bentham and a few disconsolate friends. They kept on talking and Moore seemed no different from any other beaten fighter after a brutal contest. Bentham offered him an ice bag to press against his broken nose.

The invisible pressure on Moore's brain had intensified. The fighter was the first to realise something was awry when he lifted a hand to his throbbing head. Even the lightest touch made him wince.

Moore slumped back on the table. 'I gotta sleep,' he said in a slurred whisper.

Eddie Foy, who had helped work Moore's corner, was startled. 'Get a doctor, Willie,' Foy urged.

'My head, Willie,' Moore whimpered. 'It hurts something awful.'

Foy held him while Ketchum ran for the phone. By the time the manager returned to the room, having called for emergency help, Moore was stretched unconscious on the rubbing table.

An ambulance from White Memorial hospital arrived within ten minutes. The severity of Moore's condition was obvious. The paramedics inserted a tube into his mouth, so that his brain could be oxygenated, and packed ice bags around his head in an attempt to slow the swelling of his brain. The fallen champion was rolled onto a transfer table and wheeled down the corridor. They pushed him fast, knowing that every second counted, the wheels clattering along the echoing corridor.

Davey Moore was rushed past Sugar Ramos' dressing room. It was already empty. Ramos and Luis Rodriguez had left to celebrate their joint triumph. Emile Griffith was back at his hotel, nursing his dejection, and yearning for the night when he might win back his title from the Ugly One. They had no idea that Moore had slipped away into a coma.

The little man was lost to the world as, hurtling down the passage, his face masked and his eyes closed, they wheeled him hard towards the exit sign. An ambulance was waiting. The driver flung open the back doors when he saw the boxer. The engine coughed into life and the ambulance cranked into gear. They picked up speed and, racing through the darkness, the ambulance siren cut through the night. It made a forlorn and wailing shriek; but Davey Moore did not hear a sound.

Luis Rodriguez and Sugar Ramos went to a Mexican restaurant on Wilshire Boulevard. They were both so happy that they didn't know whether to sing or cry. Instead, they decided to get drunk.

'Easy, fellers,' Angelo Dundee quipped from the end of a long table filled with the fighters' supporters and friends. 'You're back in the gym on Monday.'

The two Cubans looked up from the tray of tequila shots lined up in front of them. They were such dedicated fighters that they wondered if Dundee was serious.

The trainer chortled. 'Got ya both,' he cackled. 'Go on, champs, have fun. After tonight you deserve it ...'

As everyone at the table banged their flattened palms against the wooden surface, making the glasses wobble and the cutlery fly into the air, they roared, '*Campeones, campeones!*' Ramos and Rodriguez knocked back the first of many tequilas. They looked in the mood to have as many shots as they had boxed world championship rounds that night.

Rodriguez picked up his next glass, handed another to Ramos, and then he paused. *El Feo* had such presence that everyone soon hushed. He raised his glass and tilted it towards the pair of boxing gloves pinned to the wall behind them. And then, quietly, he told everyone that those very gloves had once been worn by Benny 'Kid' Paret.

The Ugly One, suddenly grave, said the English name that Cuban fighters always love most: '*Kid* ...'

Sugar Ramos followed him. He raised his glass to the gloves and said, '*Kid* ...'

The eighteen other people around the table followed the two world champions. Together they held their shots in the air and murmured in unison: '*Kid!*'

They flung back their heads and felt the heat of the tequila burn their throats. And then, guessing that Kid Paret would have understood, they broke out into a hoarse chant again: '*Campeones, campeones!*'

Sugar Ramos would only learn the following morning, amid the blurring fog of a hangover, that his fists had pounded Davey Moore into a terrible silence.

Emile Griffith was the first of the six fighters on the Carnival of Champions to be called by the promoter George Parnassus. George the Greek knew how important it was to talk to Emile before the newspapermen chased him.

Gil Clancy answered the phone in Emile's hotel room. He had been looking after his fighter who, apart from a slightly cracked heart, was struggling with cramping in his legs. The cramps had been so bad in the locker room that, after the fight, Emile had had to be helped into the showers. A few reporters had queried the reason, and Clancy had blamed the excessively soft-padded canvas of the makeshift ring. But the trainer was more certain that the cramping had been caused by dehydration in the wake of Emile's battle on the scales. It was a dangerous business. Dehydration means that the brain is protected by less cranial fluid and more prone to damage when rattled by a hard punch to a dried-out skull. Clancy would ensure that they monitored Emile's weight more carefully next time.

All thoughts of weight loss and leg cramps disappeared as Clancy absorbed the shocking news from Parnassus. Moore was in a coma but, unlike Paret or Alejandro Lavorante, he would not undergo an operation. His brain stem had been badly bruised but there was no haemorrhage or clotting. Surgery would do nothing and so all they could do was hope that the swelling of his bruised brain would subside. The chances of Moore surviving were considered to be much less than 50 per cent.

'Christ,' Clancy said despairingly down the phone.

Emile looked up in concern. He saw how Clancy clutched the black receiver so tightly that his knuckles had turned white under the strain.

After he had put down the phone, Clancy sat down on the bed next to Emile. 'It's little Davey Moore,' he said. 'It's not good ...'

Clancy told him everything he knew. It seemed as if the neuro-surgeons at White Memorial had decided the bruising had been sustained in the very last round, when Moore had been knocked down so heavily that his head had snapped back against the bottom rope which was bolstered by a core of steel cable. They did not believe he would recover.

Emile did not say anything. With tears rolling down his face, he walked to the mirrored cupboard, opened the door and reached for his suitcase. Emile snapped it open on the bed and, without a word, began to pack methodically.

'I'll get us on the next plane home,' Clancy said.

Emile did not respond. He dressed himself in a black suit, splashed water on his face and dried his cheeks carefully. Emile then placed a black fedora on his head. He picked up his suitcase and walked out of his hotel room, closing the door behind him and Clancy with a soft click.

'*I kill a man and most people understand and forgive me ...*'

How long would forgiveness last, amid the tragedy of another death in the ring?

On Saturday morning, 23 March 1963, the *Los Angeles Times* ran a banner headline in black print: **DAVEY MOORE IN COMA, FIGHTS FOR LIFE.**

Moore's condition had deteriorated considerably since the previous afternoon, eighteen hours after he had arrived at the White Memorial hospital. A news bulletin issued by the medical authorities at 11 a.m. had suggested it was 'encouraging' that Moore 'had been able to hold his own in the night'. But as the day wore on, the fighter responded less and less to usually painful stimuli. Dr Philip J. Vogel, a professor of neurosurgery, told the waiting press that Moore's chances of survival were 'extremely poor'.

The *LA Times* suggested, 'the other fighters on the title card were shocked by the turn of events which led to Moore's collapse. Emile Griffith said he sympathizes deeply with Sugar Ramos and knows how he feels. Ironically it was a year tonight that Benny Paret suffered brain injuries and died following a knockout loss to Griffith in New York. Griffith sent a telegram to Ramos "trying to help him get through this".'

At the hospital, Ramos had repeated over and over again, '*Lo siento mucho* [I'm very sorry]' until, eventually, they sent him back to the Alexandria hotel. He sat glumly in the hotel coffee shop with Angelo Dundee, his manager Carlos Conde and Alfred 'Kid' Rapides, his full-time trainer. They were surrounded by reporters attempting to find out how Ramos felt about hurting Moore so catastrophically. His eyes still swollen and blackened by Moore's fists, Ramos shook his head stoically.

'What can you do about destiny?' he said in Spanish. 'Fighters go into the ring to win. But we're all comrades. We're not trying to hurt each other badly. Maybe people who don't understand boxing can't understand that outside the ring we are brothers. I don't know Moore well but we met at the weigh-in. He didn't act like a vain champion. He's just a very decent man. I like him.'

Ramos looked up at the reporters from out of his dark, puffy eyes. He tried to talk in English. 'Davey is good ... *hombre*.'

'We know he's a good man, Sugar,' a big-mouthed reporter said, 'but he's close to death now. Why?'

Ramos gazed at the wiseguy. It had been different the last time he had killed an opponent. Nobody had hounded him in Cuba. They understood that he had not meant it to happen. Then, finally, Ramos said, '*Fue del destino* [It was destiny].'

The next day, on Sunday afternoon, Sugar Ramos met Geraldine Moore in a private room on the fourth floor of the White Memorial hospital. The 26-year-old wife of Davey Moore retained her composure as the boxer in front of her cried softly. Dan Smith of the *Los Angeles Times* interviewed Mrs Moore later that day and she told him that the man who had battered her husband to the brink of death had been distraught.

'I am very sorry,' he said to her. 'I've been so anxious. I wanted to see you.'

Geraldine held the hands of the 21-year-old fighter. 'I want you to understand one thing,' she said to the boy called Sugar. 'I'm not blaming you. Both of you went into that ring to fight for the title. One of you had to be the winner and you were the lucky one this time. It was God's will.'

They spoke for fifteen minutes. The fighter only broke down again when Geraldine asked him to pray for Davey.

'I'm praying every night,' he wept.

'Please don't cry,' she said. 'It was God's act.'

As Ramos turned away to leave the hospital by a rear exit, to avoid the press, Mrs Moore called out to him. 'I want to wish you all the luck in the world,' she said. 'Keep your chin up.'

Davey Moore died in the early hours of Monday 25 March 1963. Geraldine was resting in a room down the corridor when his faint pulse disappeared entirely. All her previous calm was obliterated and she had to be sedated.

A few miles away, on his hotel bed, Ramos was grief-stricken when hearing the news later that morning. He had now killed two men in the ring.

Carlos Conde said Ramos was 'wordless. He doesn't know what to say or think. He doesn't know if he can ever fight again. We were supposed to leave for Mexico today but I don't know what we'll do now.'

It seemed as if the rest of the world, united in outrage, was convinced. The governor of California, Edmund 'Pat' Brown, demanded the 'complete abolition of this barbaric spectacle' and urged that a referendum should be held so that voters could choose to outlaw professional boxing forever from their state. In the Vatican City, *L'Osservatore Romano* produced a searing editorial linking the deaths of Benny Paret and Davey Moore: 'Here is another crime committed in the name of the boxing idol; another moral taint on our civilization ... [which] serves the childish myths of often unconsciously savage crowds.'

Jim Murray, of the *LA Times*, had been at Dodger Stadium. His writing was infused with anger. 'Does a "sport" which has been on parole deserve a full pardon when it proves again and again it hasn't changed? Do we swallow our conscience one more time and continue to sanction prize fights? Are animals more precious than human beings? Are duels at dawn more immoral than death in the evening? Do we sell tickets to an execution? Is this the 20th Century or the

Roman Empire? How many deaths and comas are over the legal limit?'

The *New York Times* was just as incensed. 'How long will this go on, this wretched business Pope John has rightly described as barbaric?' their editorial asked on 27 March. 'How many more Davey Moores do we need before we call a halt? How many more Kid Parets? How many more Alejandro Lavorantes? Where is the political leadership clear-sighted and courageous enough to say that we are fed up with the nauseating hypocrisy that permits this sordid business to be called a "sport" and that we intend from henceforth to brand as the crime it is in fact?'

On the day that they buried Davey Moore in Springfield, Ohio, a less pompous message was sent to the fighter's wife by Lucy Paret. A widow and the mother of three-year-old Benny Jr and six-month-old Alberto, Lucy decided to send a spray of lilies and simple note to Geraldine Moore: *'There is so much I would like to say to you. But please know you have all my sympathy and understanding in your loss. I am praying for you that God will give you the comfort you need at such a time. From Mrs Benny Paret.'*

Down in Greenwich Village, not far from the Cherry Lane Theatre where Freddie Wright, Emile Griffith and other gay men liked to meet in the spring of 1963, a young folk singer had just recorded his second album. *The Freewheelin' Bob Dylan*, set to be released in May of that year, would be a landmark record featuring 'Blowin' in the Wind', 'A Hard Rain's a-Gonna Fall', 'Don't Think Twice, It's All Right' and 'Masters of War'.

Dylan had heard Gil Turner sing his own composition, 'Benny "Kid" Paret', at a folk club a few months before. The song had made an impression on him; but nothing like the death of Davey Moore.

In a clarity of fury, amid a tumbling list of questions, the 21-year-old Dylan wrote a song he would never officially record – even if he would play it live whenever the dark mood gripped him. The first line of the song gave him his title and, not long after he finished writing it in a fiery burst, he played it out loud and sang his words in angry honour of a dead champion: '*Who killed Davey Moore/Why an' what's the reason for?*'

Dylan picked out all those who were responsible and had the referee, the crowd, the manager, the boxing writer and even Sugar Ramos, 'who came here from Cuba's door', lined up in front of him. Each of them, through Dylan, proclaimed their innocence, crying out 'Not I', one after the other. But, still, Dylan's raggedy, rasping voice persisted and, again and again, he sang his searing question: '*Who killed Davey Moore/Why an' what's the reason for?*'

Eighteen months after he was persuaded to pull on a pair of boxing gloves for the first time, Emile Griffith knocked down Osvaldo Marcano on his way to becoming national Golden Gloves welterweight champion. Later that same year, having given up his dream of designing ladies' hats, Emile made his professional debut on 2 June 1958.

Emile Griffith trained relentlessly in the gym. In his more furtive private life he preferred relaxing, or dancing up a storm, in the illegal gay bars and clubs around Times Square in New York.

September 1961. Benny Paret (left) looked slyly at the smiling world champion, Emile Griffith, before their second title fight. Relations between the two men were still relatively friendly. Yet, a few days later, at the weigh-in to their rematch, Paret mocked Griffith's sexuality for the first time. Paret won back his title that night after he had insulted a distressed Griffith as a '*maricón*' (faggot).

24 March 1962. On the morning of their third fight, again at the weigh-in, Paret taunted Griffith. 'Hey, *maricón*,' Paret said in a cooing voice, 'I'm gonna get you and your husband.' Ten hours later an enraged Griffith battered Paret. At ringside they could hear the sound of every punch, as if it was the distant echo of a heavy spade digging a grave. Paret was unconscious even before the referee, Ruby Goldstein, finally grabbed Griffith.

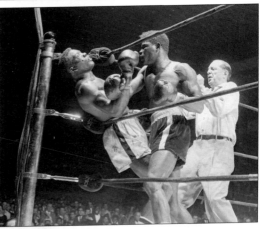

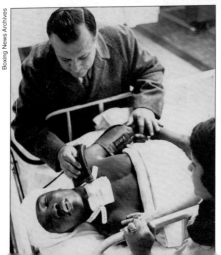

Benny 'Kid' Paret, in a coma, at the Roosevelt hospital in New York. His helpless wife, Lucy, and his manager Manuel Alfaro maintained a constant bedside vigil. Paret died on 3 April 1962.

Gil Clancy, a great trainer and a father-figure to Emile, tried to help his fighter recover from the tragedy of Benny Paret. He also took typical care of Emile before they went to work at a gym in White City, west London. Emile fought twice in London in 1964 – against Brian Curvis and Dave Charnley.

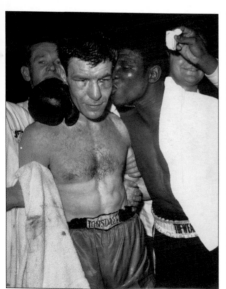

After he beat Curvis at Wembley in September 1964, Emile placed a consoling kiss on his opponent's bruised cheek. Twenty minutes later, startled British sports reporters walked into Emile's dressing room and saw him French kissing a gay friend in a much more passionate embrace.

Emile Griffith had one of the most imposing physiques in world boxing. His body was revered even more in gay New York.

In London in 1964, Emile hung out with Frank Sinatra and enjoyed himself at a gay bar in Soho called Le Duce. After he beat Brian Curvis he also went shopping for the gaudy jewellery he always loved.

On his second visit to London, the world welterweight champion was invited to make a speech at the House of Commons before, on 1 December 1964, he stopped Dave Charnley [right] on a ninth-round TKO. The party whips at Westminster would have been scandalised by the sexual habits of Griffith, but, as always, some secrets were best never told.

Emile Griffith was named Fighter of the Year in both 1963 and 1964. *The Ring* celebrated Griffith's domination of world boxing in March 1965.

Esther Taylor was Emile's girlfriend in the late 1950s and early 1960s. She remained a loyal and true friend to Emile – and, in 1971, she again refused to help his overbearing mother disrupt his private life. 'Emile was a good person.' Esther Taylor-Evans said in 2015. 'That's all that matters in the end.'

On 2 June 1973, Argentina's Carlos Monzon [right] won a narrow decision over Griffith to retain his world middleweight title. The verdict was jeered by the crowd in Monte Carlo. Monzon, who had not lost for nine years, admitted that, 'The fight was the hardest of my career. I'm going to rest for two days and I'll make a proper decision then if I should continue fighting.' Emile, in contrast, insisted he would win back his title.

Getty Images

Instead, the brutality of the ring began to diminish Griffith. Even after another victory in October 1974 against Benny Briscoe, the renowned hardman from Philadelphia, the old fighter needed to ice his swollen face.

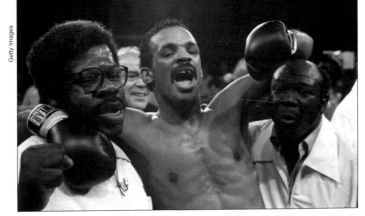

Emile experienced both tragedy and glory as a trainer. This was one of his happier nights when, on the right, he enjoys the fact that one of his fighters, Mark Medal, has just become IBF light-middleweight champion in March 1984.

Emile Griffith with Benny Paret Jr, in January 2005. Haunted by the fact that his fists had ended the life of Benny Jr's father, Emile finally gained some peace. The compassion of Benny Jr helped end the nightmare which had shrouded Emile's life for more than 40 years.

Emile and Joe Frazier at the premiere of the documentary *Ring of Fire* in January 2005. Joe had been best man at Emile's surprise wedding to Sadie Donastorg in May 1971. The marriage did not last long.

Herminio Rodriguez

In October 2012, Orlando Cruz became the first openly gay professional boxer. In his first newspaper interview after coming out, the Puerto Rican featherweight told Donald McRae: 'I have been living with this thorn inside me. I wanted to take it out of me so I could have peace within myself.'

In September 2013, while training for his first world title fight in Las Vegas, Cruz and his team took a late night break to watch a pay-per-view bout between Floyd Mayweather and Saul 'Canelo' Alvarez. Cruz is on the right, in the white t-shirt. He said: 'Four weeks tonight it's my turn.'

Herminio Rodriguez

The following morning Cruz went to church in Buffalo to pray. He had already decided to dedicate his historic world title fight to Emile Griffith.

March 2010. As the end closed in on him, Emile Griffith succumbed to a creeping form of dementia. He had taken too many punches to the head as a fighter – and had almost died when savagely beaten in 1992 outside Hombre, a gay bar near Times Square.

December 2012. Luis Rodrigo cared for Emile Griffith at the Nassau Extended Care Facility in Hempstead, Long Island. Emile eventually died in this same room on 23 July 2013. He was 75.

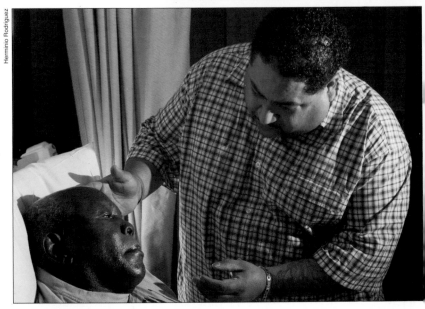

Herminio Rodriguez

CHAPTER ELEVEN

A Man's Man

Emile Griffith saw stunning bravery just before midnight at the Bleecker Street Cinema in Greenwich Village. On 29 April 1963 he was surrounded by extraordinary creatures blurring the differences between men and women so convincingly, or so comically, he could hardly look away. Black, Hispanic and white transvestites strutted prettily into the movie house. Emile thought they were more gorgeous than any of the Hollywood actresses he had met.

He saw a cracked kind of beauty, too, in ugly men dressed as trashy women. These were his people. They were rough and tough men who knew how to look after themselves but were happier laughing and shrieking once they had covered their heads with wigs, painted their faces in almost grotesque parodies of harlots and slipped into the ill-fitting hot pants and miniskirts favoured by the streetwalkers of New York.

A black drag queen called Miss Coco was one of Emile and Calvin's best friends. Miss Coco had huge shoulders, almost as wide as the fighter's, and rippling strength in his arms and legs. No one could mistake Miss Coco for a girl; just as nobody dared mock him. Miss Coco carried a boxcutter which she was not shy of flashing.

'Anyone mess with mommy,' she'd say in an extravagantly camp voice while waving her knife, 'and I got their name on this cutter.'

Miss Coco was brazen and a little scary. But she could also be sweet and polite. Emelda Griffith, despite avoiding her son's sexuality, welcomed Miss Coco into their Hollis home and served him giant plates of food. 'You have to love Coco,' she cooed, knowing that a cross-dressing hulk would not steal Emile away from her. Emelda had been wary and even jealous of Esther Taylor. Girlfriends threatened her; transvestites were, in a surreal way, more acceptable to Emelda.

Emile found it hard not to like everyone he saw at the Bleecker Street premiere of *Flaming Creatures* – a 43-minute-long film about transvestites, hermaphrodites and vampires. It had been made for $300 by Jack Smith, the experimental director. Smith's awed friends and fans – including Andy Warhol, Susan Sontag and Virginia Prince, the editor of the world's first cross-dressing publication, *Transvestia* – celebrated an already notorious film. *Flaming Creatures* would soon be seized by the New York City Police Department and become a landmark case in US censorship of 'obscene material'.

Warhol, who had just opened The Factory on East 47th Street, was fascinated by the flamboyant star, Mario Montez. He was also determined to copy Smith's cinematic style and had decided he would cast Montez, a Puerto Rican drag queen, as the hero/heroine in his future movies. Montez, whose real name was Rene Rivera, was only eighteen. With Smith's encouragement, he based his female character on Maria Montez, a movie star of the 1940s and '50s, the 'Queen of Technicolor', who came from the Dominican Republic and was cherished as a gay icon in B-movies like *Cobra Woman* and *Wicked City*.

Smith favoured 'simple-minded plots' and 'atrocious acting' as a way of elevating his trash-aesthetic beyond everyday competence. He kept his bemused viewers hooked in a grimy black-and-white fantasy world he called 'Montezland', in which the lovely Mario was surrounded by poorly lit, badly filmed and seemingly unrelated scenes full of cocks and tits, fans, flowers, hats, drug-taking trannies, masturbation, cunnilingus and extended orgies accompanied by crackly silent-movie music.

Emile didn't think much of the movies, which bored him, but at the afterparty he was smitten by the strange creatures. He could relax and be himself, his true self. The boxer carried out his business in the straight world, but he was essentially a happy person, a gay man in every sense of the word. Emile felt safe and secure in an inspiring underworld.

He wondered what it might be like to live life as Miss Coco or Mario Montez. New York State law still used the guideline that anyone wearing fewer than three articles of clothing appropriate to their sex could be arrested – for breaking the law according to Subsection 4 of Section 240.35 of the New York Penal Code. It was part of the city's campaign, under Mayor Robert Wagner, to 'clean up' New York and make homosexuals and transvestites 'invisible' before it staged the World's Fair in April 1964.

Great courage was needed to step out onto the streets in 1963 as a drag queen and face down the fear of abuse and arrest. Miss Coco and Mario looked more like champions to Emile than most fighters.

Late that night, in a corner of a murky club on East 4th Street, he was introduced to Virginia Prince, a male pharmacologist dressed as a middle-aged housewife. She looked more suited to slipping into a Tupperware party than wandering through Club 82, a drag club where men kissed transvestites on the dancefloor or sucked each other off in the toilets. But Virginia was like no man Emile had ever met. She exuded a biting intelligence that stood out at two in the morning.

As the founder and editor of *Transvestia*, Virginia helped start the transgender movement in America while offering men the chance to write about their conflicted feelings and appear in photographs, dressed as women, in her magazine. When she heard Emile was about to return to training in the Catskills, in preparation for yet another fight against Luis Rodriguez, Virginia smiled wickedly and suggested that the fighter should take a break and pop into Chevalier d'Eon Resort.

Emile looked at her in puzzlement. It was then that he heard the story of how an educated couple and Virginia herself ran a weekend refuge for ordinary men, who were often husbands and fathers, to dress up in private as demure housewives.

Tito Valenti, a highly competent court translator who just happened to be a transvestite, had started the safe house for cross-dressers. His wife, Marie, ran a wig boutique and, accepting of her husband's feminine persona, Susanna, she advertised her shop in *Transvestia*. Tito wrote a column for the magazine called 'Susanna Says', in which he dispensed civilised advice for aspiring cross-dressers: 'Let us, for heaven's sake, strive to forge a nice, clean cut, real person out of "the girl-within".'

Marie and Tito taught their friends how to dress, walk, talk, act and think like 'proper women'. Instead of the traditional drag-queen trick of slapping on the sleaze, Tito/Susanna and his real-life wife helped their male friends spend the occasional weekend playing the part of a cheerful and fulfilled housewife. In full transgender dress, they would dust and vacuum, play Scrabble and drink dry Martinis.

'You've got to be kidding,' Emile said to Virginia Prince in the depths of Club 82.

The blessed Virginia cackled. 'You've got a lot to learn, sweetheart,' she said, running her hand along the muscled arm of the two-time world champion.

Emile gazed in wonder at Virginia Prince – dressed in an immaculate Chevalier d'Eon outfit. Not every cross-dresser was lucky enough to look like Mario Montez, or wild enough to become Miss Coco. Emile had no desire to wear women's clothes, but he was convinced that the flaming creatures and the Scrabble-playing middle-aged men dressed as suburban housewives were the bravest people he knew. He was just a fighter; they were dreamers and radicals changing themselves and everyone around them.

*

Back up in the Catskills, at the Concord hotel on a spring afternoon in early May, Emile Griffith slumped down on a sofa. He faced Milton Gross of the *New York Post* and Red Smith, one of the great American sportswriters. Gil Clancy sat next to him, having persuaded Emile to talk to the press again. Emile had resisted at first. Gross had pushed him hard in the past about his sexuality. He also knew Smith would manipulate the conversation so that, eventually, they got back to Benny Paret and Davey Moore.

Famous old Red had once said: 'Writing is easy. You simply sit down at the typewriter, open a vein and bleed.' Emile was sure that neither the white-haired, bespectacled man in his late fifties, nor the tenacious Gross, would slice open their own veins. They had fixed their gaze on the artery that led into the wounded heart of Emile's story. As always the boxer, rather than the writers, would be left bleeding.

Smith was a skilled interviewer. He returned Emile to a steamy afternoon on West 37th Street in the summer of 1956 and had him describe the factory at Howard Albert Millinery. Emile relaxed and smiled as he remembered stacking ladies' hats in boxes with his cousin Edigo. Emile recalled stripping off his wet T-shirt as sweat rolled down his body. He had thought nothing of death then. Untouched by tragedy, he had felt no guilt. Emile might just have been a factory worker; but he had felt free.

Describing Emile as a 'ring enigma', Smith wrote, 'he has a small voice, and a precise manner of speech.'

Emile also admitted to Smith and Gross that his talented cousin Bernard Forbes, his regular cheerleader who had decided to turn pro, had just knocked him down in sparring. Forbes would win his only three professional fights convincingly before an eye injury forced his premature retirement in 1964.

It might have seemed strange, in the build-up to another rematch with Rodriguez, that Emile should voice his vulnerability. But Clancy pointed out that, 'when Emile isn't pressed he is inclined to take it easy. He doesn't get really dangerous until he's hurt. It's not smart to knock him down.'

They were immersed in the violence of the ring again; and Smith had his opening. He asked Emile about Davey Moore.

Emile hesitated. And then he surrendered and relived that awful night. Emile told the reporters how he and Moore had sat together in their joint locker room and talked at length. He thought Moore was one of the nicest men he had met in boxing. Emile's voice wavered as he admitted that, 'if Moore had fought before me, instead of after, I would never have gone on'.

But, when pressed, Emile scrunched up his face. 'I know I have to go on,' he said of boxing. 'It's better than having my family begging.'

'In a way,' Gross wrote, alluding again to Emile's sexuality, 'Griffith is begging for understanding because of the dual tensions beneath the gay façade of his calypso personality. "I'll always live with it," he said, meaning Paret, of course. "I try hard to get over it. People keep saying to me, 'Forget it. It's not your fault.' But it didn't happen to them." The twenty-four-year-old sustains himself with the thought that those same fists brought a broken family together, took it off relief, bought a $35,000 house in Hollis and is making certain all his brothers and sisters receive the education he did not get.'

Emile was guaranteed $37,500, compared to Rodriguez's $40,000, when they met again at Madison Square Garden. Boxing history also beckoned for Emile. If he defeated Rodriguez he would become the first boxer to win the world welterweight title on three separate occasions.

As the weeks passed Emile's old hunger returned in the Catskills. He was determined to atone for his defeat in Los Angeles. 'I thought I won that fight,' he said, 'but it wasn't one of my better performances. I landed some good body shots and I could feel Luis give way. Every time I trapped him in a corner Luis would grab me tightly in a clinch. This time I hope to fence him in so he's got no way out.'

The Ugly One always made him feel just a little mean. 'I'm not predicting the round,' Emile said, 'but I'll definitely win by a knockout. I'm feeling real good.'

*

El Feo sounded dark and brooding. He was also training in the Catskills, just fourteen miles from Griffith, in Greenfield Park. The new champion worked out in a modest hall at Tamarack Lodge. Rodriguez was unhappy that, when he faced Griffith again, just eleven weeks would have passed since he won the title. It was a painfully brief time to enjoy his new status – but Clancy and Albert had been canny in drawing up a contract that included an immediate rematch clause.

On the night of Rodriguez's greatest victory, and first world title, Davey Moore began to die. 'I am very sad about it,' Rodriguez said of Moore's death. 'But no one remembers I won my fight. The fight wasn't on [network] TV and then for one month we all just think about Moore. Now we just hear Griffith say he was unlucky. I won the fight but Griffith don't stop complaining.'

Rodriguez had spotted Bernard Forbes in the crowd. Griffith's cousin had watched *El Feo* spar in the week of the fight. 'He came to spy [on] me,' the Cuban said of Forbes. 'But after he see me work and he go back to his cousin, Griffith is quiet. He knows I knock him out.'

The Cuban sounded brutally certain and he spoke as if he had already forgotten the fate of Paret and Moore. 'This time I no just beat Griffith,' Rodriguez told Pat Putnam of the *Miami Herald*. 'I whip him. I'm gonna punch his big mouth many times. I'm gonna bloody his face, his eyes and his ears. I'm gonna hit him 150 times every round. He no talk after this fight. He no be able to talk. I destroy him.'

Griffith was neither mute nor fearful at the weigh-in on the morning of their Saturday night fight on 8 June 1963. Instead, he and Rodriguez smiled cheerfully as they both scaled 146½ pounds. The photographers urged the fighters to move their heads closer together in the traditional face-off.

'If we do that, we'll be kissing each other,' Griffith said as he eyed the Ugly One.

A shutter of hardness slid down Griffith's face. He stared malevolently at Rodriguez.

'Don't pay any attention to him,' Angelo Dundee told Rodriguez. 'He's just trying to give you the eye.'

One of the reporters said to Griffith: 'You were giving him the voodoo eye, weren't you?'

'I was not,' Griffith protested. 'I was giving him the grim face. We'd had enough of laughing and good-fellow stuff. I wanted him to know how I really felt – grim, very grim. It'll be a grim business tonight.'

The nature of boxing's grim business meant various forms of history were made in Madison Square Garden that night. It was the first time a ring was surrounded by four rather than three strands of rope. After Davey Moore's head snapped against the third and lowest rope in Los Angeles, a change needed to be made to protect all fighters. In the same way, Griffith and Rodriguez used eight-ounce gloves, rather than the less padded six-ounce mitts that had been the championship norm. A mandatory eight count would follow any knockdown and the fight would end if one boxer went down three times in a round. Those safety regulations were used for the first time in a world title fight as Griffith and Rodriguez went to work.

There were no knockdowns but the attritional contest fulfilled Griffith's prediction of a grim affair. In a mirror image of their first two bouts, the gruelling triptych was completed by a fight so close that there was dissent again over the scoring. Apart from the seventh, which Rodriguez dominated with imperious counter-punching, and the tenth in which he was hurt by Griffith, an argument favouring either fighter could be made after most rounds. The majority of ringside reporters scored the fight in favour of Rodriguez, but the verdicts that counted, from the two judges and the referee, took longer to be collected.

While they waited, Griffith and Rodriguez wrapped an arm around each other. 'There're no hard feelings after a hectic battle,' the commentator Don Dunphy said. 'Here comes Johnny Addie with the decision . . .'

'Ladies and gentlemen,' Addie boomed, 'Judge Tony Rossi scores it 8 to 7 to Griffith . . .'

Emile raised his arms and hugged Clancy.

'Referee Jimmy Devlin,' Addie continued, 'scores it 9 to 6 . . . *Griffith!*'

The new champion was lifted high into the air by Clancy. Emile could not contain himself. He closed his eyes and flung himself backwards. Howie Albert and Syd Martin reached out to support him.

The final score was read out as Griffith came back down to earth. 'Judge Joe Armstrong . . . ten rounds for Rodriguez, five for Griffith. The winner . . . and the first man to win the title three times . . . and the new welterweight champion of the world . . . *Emile Griffith!*'

An ecstatic Emile took Addie's round face in his hands and kissed him on the forehead. 'Emile Griffith has never been happier in his life,' Dunphy chuckled. 'Come here, Emile, c'mon. Congratulations.'

'Thank you very much, Don,' Griffith said. 'It was a wonderful fight with Luis.'

'Were you surprised it was a split decision?' Dunphy asked.

'I thought I had the fight won all the time,' Griffith said. 'I pressured him. I hurt him with the most punches and all he would try to do was get me with one punch – the right hand over my jab.'

'Well, I'm going to let you get your breath,' Dunphy said with a smile.

'But I'm not tired, Don,' Griffith protested. 'Just happy. It's all joy.'

'I don't blame you,' Dunphy said as he turned to Clancy. 'Now Gil, what about the future?'

'Well, Don,' Clancy said, 'as always, Emile doesn't dodge anybody. We'll go anywhere there is a good offer. He'll fight welterweights or middleweights.'

'Rodriguez again?' Dunphy asked.

'Why not?' Clancy said with an admiring nod. 'He's a great fighter ...'

Down in his locker room, Rodriguez said bitterly: 'The newspapers were right. I read this morning that if it goes fifteen rounds then they'll give Griffith the decision. I won it. I score it 8-6-2.'

There was a lull before a brightly numerate reporter piped up. 'Luis, that makes it a sixteen-round fight.'

'Okay,' Luis said grudgingly, 'make it 8-6-1. I still won.'

When Clancy heard Rodriguez's complaint he shook his head in relief. 'I would have died,' he said, 'if they'd taken the fight away from us.'

The number of people relying on Emile for accommodation, food, clothing, education and spending money had risen to seventeen. Apart from his mother, four sisters, three brothers, five nieces and three cousins, he still looked after Matthew. The ten-bedroom house in Hollis, Queens, was bursting with people. Emile did not like to plan ahead, but the clutter forced an alternative. He could not bear the thought of kicking anyone out of his home, and so the idea of moving into his own place, away from his family, became irresistible. Esther, in the last days of their relationship, had once warned him of his mother's controlling influence. She had not laboured the point, out of respect for Emile, and he had tried to dismiss it then. But the truth of Esther's insight could no longer be avoided. He needed to loosen his mother's iron grip on his life.

Gil and Howie had also badgered him for almost a year in an effort to weaken the family's dependence on his money. Howie kept two ledgers, which itemised contrasting strands of expenditure. He was happy whenever Emile spent money on himself, even when he was extravagant, because Howie knew how difficult it was for him to keep fighting. The second ledger contained many more entries, as Howie tried to keep track of all the money squandered on the others. It was depressing to see that four times the amount Emile spent on himself was consumed by everyone else.

Emile shrugged. If anyone wanted money, Howie should just give it to them. Gil always had another fight lined up for him. He told Howie and Gil to stop worrying, and to quit counting his cash.

They regarded it as a positive step when Emile announced his intention to buy an apartment. Of course, he was still more like a child than a man when it came to anything as practical as purchasing property, and he left it to Howie to find him a suitable place and negotiate the right price.

Howie picked out an upmarket apartment in Weehawken, along the shores of the Hudson, and across the water from midtown Manhattan. A short drive down the Lincoln Tunnel would bring Emile back into the heart of the city, but, most of the time, he could relax in his apartment and gaze at the New York skyline.

Emile enjoyed turning it into an outrageously camp refuge for him and Matthew. He spent $400 on a lavish circular bed, which measured eight feet in diameter and was dominated by a flamboyant headboard resembling a giant golden crown. A leopard-print bedspread was draped over the satin sheets. Emile had cupids painted on the walls of his lounge and bedroom, which were linked together by plush red carpets. French furniture, featuring ornate carvings and delicate motifs, dominated the apartment – at the centre of which stood a marble table. In the far corner, near a window overlooking the Hudson, on a sidetable supported by spindly legs, sat a pink Princess telephone. The look was completed by a white French poodle called Don Achilles, who trotted around the apartment like the queen of Weehawken.

Only the neighbours seemed elusive and uneasy. They shut their doors hurriedly whenever they saw Emile. Most of them never answered when he knocked politely in an attempt to introduce himself. The deluxe block seemed almost ghostly in its silent resistance of Emile's efforts to become a good neighbour.

He wandered down to the lobby, which was covered in expensive terrazzo tiles, and asked the Jamaican doorman how he might go about meeting his neighbours. 'They don't even know I live here,' he said.

'Oh, believe me, they do,' the doorman replied. 'They just never had no one like you living in such a fancy building. You must have noticed we're different to them.'

The doorman grinned and pointed at his own black skin. 'Maybe they got to get used to you,' he said, 'like they done with me.'

'Uh-huh,' Emile said sadly. 'So that's it.'

Later that month, on 28 August 1963, Martin Luther King was introduced on the steps of the Lincoln Memorial in Washington DC as 'the moral leader of our nation'. He spoke to 250,000 people who had marched on Washington in support of President Kennedy's pledge two months earlier to introduce civil rights legislation that would tackle discrimination in the United States.

King began with a reference to the Emancipation Proclamation, which had freed millions of slaves in 1863. As he lamented, in the rolling cadences and melodious oratory of a speech broadcast on network television, 'One hundred years later, the Negro still is not free. One hundred years later, the life of the Negro is still sadly crippled by the manacles of segregation and the chains of discrimination.'

Emile and Calvin Thomas sat in the gay splendour of their Weehawken refuge, and listened to King's unforgettable voice. 'There are those who are asking,' he said, '"When will you be satisfied?"'

King gave his communal answer. 'We can never be satisfied as long as the Negro is the victim of the unspeakable horrors of police brutality. We can never be satisfied as long as our bodies, heavy with the fatigue of travel, cannot gain lodging in the motels of the highways and the hotels of the cities. We cannot be satisfied as long as the Negro's basic mobility is from a smaller ghetto to a larger one. We can never be satisfied as long as our children are stripped of their self-hood and robbed of their dignity by signs stating: "For Whites Only". We cannot be satisfied as long as a Negro in Mississippi cannot vote and a Negro in New York believes he has nothing for which to vote. No, no, we will not be satisfied until justice rolls down like waters, and righteousness like a mighty stream.'

Emile lived in a deluxe pad in an exclusive apartment block, surrounded by wealthy white people, but the words resonated. He knew what discrimination meant. He felt the barbs of injustice. He felt slighted and wounded. Like Calvin, he buckled a little under the twin yoke of being black and gay.

'Let us not wallow in the valley of despair, my friends,' King cried out, as if talking directly to them.

'I have a dream that one day, on the red hills of Georgia, the sons of former slaves and the sons of former slave owners will sit down together at the table of brotherhood. I have a dream that one day even the state of Mississippi, a state sweltering with the heat of injustice, sweltering with the heat of oppression, will be transformed into an oasis of freedom and justice. I have a dream that my four little children will one day live in a nation where they will not be judged by the colour of their skin but by the content of their character.'

As King called for freedom to ring from 'the prodigious hilltops of New Hampshire' and 'the mighty mountains of New York' all the way down to every 'molehill of Mississippi', Emile and Calvin felt compelled to stand up. They were crying, but they were also laughing, thinking too of every secret bar in Times Square or drag club in a hidden corner of the sprawling city across the river.

'When this happens,' King exclaimed, 'and when we allow freedom to ring, when we let it ring from every village and every hamlet, from every state and every city, we will be able to speed up that day when *all* of God's children, black men and white men, Jews and Gentiles, Protestants and Catholics, will be able to join hands and sing in the words of the old Negro spiritual:

Free at last! Free at last!
Thank God Almighty, we are free at last!'

Cuba, and a fuzzy idea of freedom from capitalism, was at work in Lee Harvey Oswald's addled brain for years before two shots from his rifle killed John F. Kennedy on 22 November 1963. A former marine, who had defected to the Soviet Union for two-and-a-half years, Oswald and his Russian wife had been allowed to return to the US in June 1962. His disillusionment with the Soviet system meant that Oswald had come to regard Castro's Cuban revolution as an ideal form of Marxism.

Oswald's anger towards Kennedy had been sparked by the president's support of the botched Bay of Pigs invasion of Cuba. In late September 1963, Oswald took a bus to Mexico City in the hope that he would be granted a visa to Cuba, where he planned to defect. That aim was blunted when Oswald was told he could only gain entry into Cuba during transit to the Soviet Union – whose embassy in Mexico City stressed it would take months to process his application.

A dejected Oswald then headed for Dallas. Amid increasing feelings of alienation and disillusionment with America, and hearing of Kennedy's presidential visit on 22 November, he began to plot his assassination.

After the shooting, he was arrested just before midnight on a charge that he did, 'in furtherance of an international Communist conspiracy, assassinate President John F. Kennedy'.

The United States would never be the same again after those tumultuous few months in 1963. Martin Luther King's speech, and Kennedy's assassination, changed everything.

Oswald was killed thirty-six hours after his arrest when, leaving a police station in Dallas on his way to prison, he was gunned down by Jack Ruby, a strip club owner suspected of supplying weapons to rebel fighters in Cuba. Ruby's real name was Jacob Rubenstein and he had been boyhood friends with Barney Ross, one of the greatest fighters in history, who won world titles at lightweight, light-welter and welterweight in the 1930s. On the night earlier that year when Griffith regained his welterweight crown from Rodriguez at the

Garden, Ross had been called into the ring to receive the plaudits of the crowd.

Ruby's assassination of Kennedy's killer was captured on network TV. After Benny Paret, Lee Harvey Oswald was only the second man in history whose death was seen on live television. America had become a much darker place in the bloody autumn of 1963.

Emile Griffith was announced as the Fighter of the Year by the Boxing Writers Association in early December 1963. He had lost to Luis Rodriguez in March, on that devastating night at Dodger Stadium, but he had since won back his title and also defeated Holly Mims and Jose Gonzales. As a three-time world welterweight champion, he had entered the boxing pantheon. He would receive his award in January but, before then, on 20 December 1963, he faced Rubin 'Hurricane' Carter in Pittsburgh.

Two-and-a-half years later, in June 1966, Carter would be arrested for a triple homicide he did not commit. He would spend twenty years in prison, as an innocent man, in a travesty of justice Bob Dylan railed against in 'Hurricane', his second song about a boxer. Unlike 'Who Killed Davey Moore?', Dylan would record 'Hurricane' and include it on his album *Desire*.

Just before Christmas in 1963, Griffith was hit by a Hurricane. As a world champion, and having faced superior opposition, Griffith was heavily favoured even though he was moving up to middleweight to fight Carter. His managers were gearing him up for a tilt at the heavier and more lucrative title against the champion Joey Giardello. But he had never faced a puncher like Carter.

After a minute and forty seconds of serious trading, Carter landed a vicious left hook to the body that dropped Griffith in a heap. He took the eight count on his knees, battling for breath, before he staggered up. Heavy combinations made Griffith sag to the canvas again. His right glove pushed down against the lowest rope. Griffith got back on his feet at the count of eight.

The referee, Buck McTiernan, wiped Griffith's gloves against his white shirt and looked at him closely. McTiernan stretched out his left hand to stop the advancing Carter and then grasped Griffith by the shoulders. The proud champion lifted his gloves in ritual defiance – but he was still trying to understand what had happened. The fight was over.

It was the first time Emile had been stopped in forty-two fights and five-and-a-half years as a professional. 'A left hook sent Emile to dreamland and he never quite recovered from it,' the commentator suggested as the fighters embraced. 'Griffith is a real good sportsman after such a shock.'

Twenty-three nights later, on 12 January 1964, Emile was just as gracious, and embarrassed, as he accepted his Fighter of the Year award for 1963 at the Americana hotel in New York. He had agonised over his acceptance speech, trying to overcome hubris and humiliation, before deciding to tell the truth.

'Ladies and gentlemen,' he said in his singsong Caribbean accent, 'a funny thing happened to me on the way here. I met a guy named Rubin Carter and he looked down at me and said, "Get up, Griffith, that ain't no place for the fighter of the year."'

The boxing writers roared their approval and it took more than a minute before Emile could continue. 'I have some awards to give out to my managers Gil Clancy and Howie Albert and my cornerman, Syd Martin,' he said with a shy smile. 'They are extremely uplifting awards. In fact, they will be known as the Uplifters of the Year – and that is for lifting me off the canvas in Pittsburgh without dropping me once.'

Matthew was tall and lean. Emile cut a much more imposing figure, with his barrel chest and pinched waist, but he was just five feet eight inches tall. He had to look up to his slender boyfriend, whether he wanted to kiss him or remonstrate with him. Matthew was also good looking, and his slicked-back black hair had been cut by an expensive stylist. Wearing an imported Italian leather jacket, a crisp shirt, immaculately pressed jeans and a pair of new boots, he looked more than good enough to be the partner of a world champion. But, beneath the increasingly sophisticated surface of a mostly secret relationship, trouble brewed.

Emile might have been knocked out by the thunderous fists of Hurricane Carter but he still held the world welterweight belt. He was still earning big money. From early February to mid-April 1964 he fought three non-title fights in Australia, Italy and Hawaii. Emile needed to overcome his shocking loss to Carter and, even more pressingly, he needed to keep the prizefight cheques rolling in.

He met an old rival, Ralph Dupas, in Sydney on 10 February, and the outcome was very different from their first fight. Emile had failed to catch Dupas with any meaningful punch until the last round in Las Vegas in July 1962. His head had swarmed with Benny Paret that night, and Dupas had been as elusive as a summery bee dodging his swatting hands. In Sydney, he caught Dupas early, knocking him down three times in round two. Emile hit him even more viciously in the third, leaving Dupas stricken on the canvas. It took almost a minute for Dupas to regain consciousness and Emile paced up and down in agitation. Dupas was a tough old bird, fortunately, and he rose unsteadily and walked out of the ring on his own two feet. Another tragedy had been averted.

A farce followed. In Rome, the Italian press had depicted Emile as 'a killer', describing the Paret massacre and the Dupas knockout in chilling detail. His opponent Juan Carlos Duran, from Argentina, ran all night as if any other action against a lethal puncher would be madness. Emile was in no mood to repeat the trauma he experienced against Dupas, and so he restricted himself to jabbing his way into a wide lead. The Italian fans, expecting a gladiatorial battle, were incensed. They threw bottles and fruit to express their displeasure and, in the seventh round, the referee Fernando Pica called a halt. He ruled the fight a 'no-contest', even though Emile had won every round, as it would be too dangerous to continue.

Honolulu was next and Emile found the right balance. He knocked out Stan Harrington in the fourth round, but the punch did not endanger his opponent's life. Harrington was on his feet, smiling for photographs alongside the winner within minutes. Emile returned from Hawaii with gifts for all seventeen of his dependants. The Hawaiian shirts and hula skirts were a treat for everyone – apart from his mother. He had bought the very largest hula skirt he could find but Emelda scolded him. Chubby Checker needed at least two extra-large skirts to be stitched together so that they might fit around her huge tummy.

There were more serious problems. Emile had moved Matthew out of his Weehawken apartment and into his family home in Queens during all three trips abroad. He knew Mommy would feed Matthew and keep him out of mischief. She had succeeded in the first task, but failed to stop the vicious squabbling between Matthew and Emile's brother, Franklin. Emile was paying for Franklin to study law at the Hampton Institute, but he could not stop his little brother sniping at his sexuality.

Franklin and Matthew had never liked each other; and while Emile was away their mutual animosity intensified. Emile never discovered exactly what happened, but the fighting reached a point where Matthew apparently tried to run over Franklin. He was driving Emile's new silver Buick. Mommy told her world champion son that he had to sort out his life.

On the slow drive back to Weehawken, a distressed Emile warned Matthew that he would have to change. He could not go around aiming their car at anyone who angered him. Emile initially thought his boyfriend had absorbed his advice, but he almost swerved the Buick off the road when Matthew said it was time they parted. He had met a girl while the champ was gallivanting around the world. Matthew would move out of Poppyman's apartment and live with his new girl. Emile was hurt most by the fact that Matthew called him 'Poppyman', his pet name.

They got home to Weehawken and Matthew was silent as he packed. He was gone within an hour, saying, 'So long, champ, you been good to me ...'

As Emile looked around his gaudy but empty apartment, he felt utterly alone.

Emile Griffith and Luis Rodriguez completed their harsh quartet. There was, as always, little fantasy surrounding their title contest in Las Vegas on 12 June 1964. In the week of the bout, Jerry Izenberg wrote that, 'On Friday night, Rodriguez will fight Griffith for the world title. He is very good at this, because he has been fighting Griffith for four years. He fought him twice in New York and once in California and, now, every time a telephone rings Luis puts up his fists and looks for Emile. The title has changed hands twice in the stretch, small wars have begun over all the split decisions and the two of them have spent more time trying to dismember each other than any pair since the Montagues and Capulets.'

The Ugly One and Emile as boxing's answer to Romeo and Juliet had no romantic merit. Luis was older, bigger and tougher than the slim-hipped and much prettier young Latino men the world champion liked. They could only be rivals. Luis was married and he hoped that he and his wife would soon be joined from Cuba by his mother – to counter the hollering presence of Emelda Griffith.

Izenberg described how, during their third fight, Emelda, the 'Chubby Checker' of all matriarchs, had 'leaped menacingly to her feet in the fourth row' and unleashed 'the resonance of the *Queen Mary*'s fog horn' as she urged on Junior.

The reporter next to Izenberg quipped, 'I think Rodriguez can match Griffith, but I don't know if he can handle the mother ...'

Emelda joined him in Vegas only a few days before the latest rematch. Still grieving over the loss of Matthew, her son sounded lonely. Sitting next to the pool outside his cottage at the Thunderbird hotel on the Strip, Emile lamented to Huston Horn of *Sports Illustrated* that, 'I'm homesick. I don't like to be alone. I must have something to do, somebody to occupy my thoughts.'

The nightmares of Benny Paret had returned. Emile often woke in Vegas, drenched in sweat, sitting upright and staring wildly in fear that Benny would be looking down at him from his bedside. But the ghostly apparition that haunted his sleep was gone as soon as Emile opened his eyes.

His title meant more to him in his desolation. He had suffered so much, and caused so much suffering, that he resolved to hold onto it. 'I am the champion of the world,' he told Izenberg. 'It's the best thing I own in all the world. I am not going to let Rodriguez take it away from me again.'

The Cuban was based at the Sands hotel and, as Horn explained in his *Sports Illustrated* feature, 'mostly stayed in his room, dressed in blue pyjamas, balefully watching television, eating steaks (four a day at $7 each) and chicken soup with lemon juice, and waiting for sunset. When it was dark and cool he went to a horse racing track in Las Vegas and jogged around its mile-long perimeter, time and again. "Why do you run at night?" somebody asked him. "Because," he said with his infectious smile, "I fight at night."'

Angelo Dundee, monitoring Rodriguez's nocturnal training, had seen his career, and boxing itself, transformed earlier that year. On 25 February 1964, Cassius Clay had fought Sonny Liston for the heavyweight championship of the world. Apart from Clay and Dundee, it seemed as if no one believed that the mouthy challenger, who had just turned twenty-two, could withstand the sullen ferocity of Liston. The champion himself was convinced that, beneath his brash chattering, Clay was petrified.

A week before the fight, when seeing Liston in a casino, Clay had hollered: 'Look at the big ugly bear, he can't even shoot craps!'

Liston had walked over to Clay and, darkening and lengthening the *maricón* taunt lifted from the Paret handbook of insults, he spat out a warning: 'Listen, you nigger faggot, if you don't get outta here in ten seconds, I'm gonna pull that big tongue outta your mouth and stick it up your ass.'

Later, Liston sneered: 'I got that punk's heart.'

Clay surprised Liston and everyone else in the Miami Convention Center, where Griffith and Paret had fought for the first time three years before. He seemed able to hit the champion at will. A swollen welt rose up under Liston's left eye and blood trickled from a gash above his cheekbone.

Then, in the fourth round, Clay's eyes began to burn inexplicably. By the time he reached his stool for the break, Clay was almost hysterical. 'I can't see,' he yelled. 'Cut off the gloves!'

'Cut the bullshit,' Dundee said as he sponged Clay's eyes. 'We ain't quitting now. You gotta go out there and run.'

Those two simple instructions saved Clay and slowly, as his eyes cleared of a substance that might have been smeared on Liston's gloves, he landed hurtful punches again. By the end of the sixth round, with Liston utterly demoralised by such virtuosity, the champion quit.

Steve Ellis, who had commentated on the Moore–Ramos tragedy, stuck a microphone under Clay's screaming mouth. 'I shook up the world!' Clay yelped. 'I am the greatest thing that ever lived! I don't have a mark on my face and I upset Sonny Liston and I just turned twenty-two years old! I must be the greatest! I showed the world! I talk to God every day! I'm the king of the world! I'm pretty! I'm a bad man! I shook up the world! I'm the prettiest thing that ever lived! I shook up the world! I want justice!'

The following morning the new champion confirmed his conversion to Islam. Just over a week later, on 6 March 1964, Cassius Clay changed his name to Muhammad Ali.

'Clay means dirt,' he said, explaining his decision. 'It's the name slave owners gave my people. My white blood comes from slave masters, from raping. The white blood harms us. It hurts us. When we were darker we was stronger. We were purer. Superman is white. The president is white. Santa Claus is white. That's brainwashing, the biggest lie you ever told your children. Every year you buy toys and your children wind up thinking they came from some white man with rosy cheeks. They think everything good has to come from someone white.'

Emile, who was much blacker than Ali, felt uncomfortable. Had

Ali forgotten how Gil helped him against Sonny Banks, when he had been knocked down? And how could Angelo continue working for Ali when the new champion seemed to hate white people? The political backdrop of Ali's conversion to Islam confused Emile.

Dundee, in contrast, was sanguine. He adjusted to the new reality and was happy to call his fighter 'Muhammad'. Dundee might have been suspicious of the Black Muslims but he loved Ali – and felt secure in the knowledge that Ali respected him and would not countenance a change of trainer. They were as close as ever. Dundee also remained loyal to Rodriguez and Sugar Ramos, who was fighting again.

A day after he returned from Ghana, where Ramos retained his world featherweight title, Dundee went into a month-long training camp. He was determined to help Rodriguez, still the boxer who meant most to him, defeat Griffith. The closer they moved to the fight, the more Dundee tried to unsettle Griffith. He confronted the Nevada State Commission and demanded they force the champion to change his shorts.

'Griffith doesn't wear his trunks around his waist,' Dundee complained. 'He uses an oversized protective cup underneath to make them higher. They come all the way up to the ribs. My guy is a body puncher and nobody ever warned him about punching low – except against Griffith. He has to pull his pants down.'

Howie Albert, an expert in sartorial matters, reacted indignantly. 'It's ridiculous. Emile wears his pants the way everyone else does. The first time Emile hits him, Luis will run like a thief again.'

Clancy joined the chorus. 'If Emile doesn't force the action there won't be a fight. Rodriguez is just a dancer.'

Rodriguez glowered. 'I am not a dancer. I am a matador. I will kill the black bull.'

Griffith was infuriated. 'It's not a matter of race,' he told the scribbling sportswriters. 'It's the word he used – kill. *Kill* the black bull. Has he forgotten my accident with Benny Paret? Or does he really want to taunt me? Well, the bull will chase him down.'

The *Chicago Defender* reacted with a provocative headline: 'Rodriguez Also To Die After Insulting Emile?'

Jack Cuddy, in the accompanying article, drew a direct comparison with the controversy before the final Paret fight. He also quoted Albert who, apparently, had said: 'Emile hates this man – and we can't control him.'

On the night of the fight, Griffith looked more like a gay matador than a snorting bull. Huston Horn, in *Sports Illustrated*, was amazed. 'Emile, exuding aplomb, came into the ring wearing a white twill robe with aquamarine velvet collar and cuffs. When he drew on flamingo-pink boxing gloves the effect was startling.'

The fight was much less flamboyant. It was, yet again, an abrasive, dirty battle without frills or thrills. And the result was, once more, a split decision. Izenberg wrote that, 'These two have fought fifty-five rounds and they are no closer to a decision than when it all began four years ago. They tried hard to end it and all they got was a two-point spread and one of those points came off Rodriguez's scorecard for striking low in the second round. They have fought four times and Griffith, the puncher, has yet to take his man out. Rodriguez, the boxer, has yet to dance and sting and hook Griffith into submission.'

An era, just short of twenty years, was also ending. Live televised boxing had begun on NBC in September 1944 and their weekly *Friday Night Fights* had become part of the fabric of American life. Over the previous four years, ABC had taken over the production with *Fight of the Week* on Saturdays before, following Paret's death, reverting to the traditional Friday night slot. Griffith had been at the heart of ABC's live programming ever since he headlined their third card against Willie Toweel in October 1960. The decline of boxing had escalated after the Davey Moore disaster, and ABC had just announced they would no longer screen live ring coverage once their contract expired that September.

Dan Dunphy had commentated on a Griffith title defence for the last time. 'Most of the rounds were pretty hard to score,' he said chattily. 'The boys have now fought four times and I'm sure that, as in the others, this will probably be a controversial decision too. Here's Chuck Hull with the announcement.'

The immaculately coiffured Hull confirmed the obvious. 'Ladies and gentlemen,' he said into his gleaming microphone, 'we have a split decision. Referee Harry Krause scores 69 Griffith ... 67 Rodriguez.'

As Syd Martin peered over Hull's shoulder in an attempt to discover the news first, the tension rose. 'Judge David Zenoff,' Hull continued, 'scores 71 Rodriguez, 70 Griffith.'

That basic device, of delaying the announcement of the winner, had always been avoided by Johnny Addie at Madison Square Garden. But Hull worked the Vegas crowd. As an expressionless Martin went in search of Griffith, believing he had seen the final scorecard, Hull extended his dramatic pause.

'Judge John Romero,' he finally intoned, 'scored 70 Griffith, 68 Rodriguez ...'

Emile shrieked at the first mention of his name, and even before he heard Rodriguez's score. He knew that he had won, for Martin had tipped him off seconds earlier.

Albert and Clancy had already lifted the champion onto their shoulders when Hull completed the formalities. 'The winner, and still welterweight champion of the world, Emile Griffith!'

'He's being mauled by his handlers,' Dunphy yelled as he ducked through the ropes. Calvin Thomas was already ahead of him. The rotund figure of Emile's cherished gay ally ran towards him. Calvin's face was alight and Emile leaned over to kiss him. Calvin then hugged Emile before flinging his arms skyward as he did a jitterbug.

'I'm going to try and get Griffith over here,' Dunphy said as he grabbed Emile's satiny gown. 'Let's have the interview, boys. I want to congratulate you, Emile. Let's look at the camera, Emile.'

As his cornermen dragged him towards Dunphy, the commentator said: 'Congratulations Gil, Howard and Syd Martin. You all did a tremendous job with this young man. I have never seen him in better shape.'

'Thank you very much, Don,' Emile said. 'As you know, Rodriguez and myself are two of the best welterweights around today. Everybody says it's too bad we weren't five years apart.'

'Well, that's a very nice thing for you to say, Emile.'

'No, it's true,' Emile insisted. 'Luis tried his best. He hit me with some good punches but I was determined to defend my crown.'

'Emile, you're sort of a contradiction,' Dunphy suggested. 'During the fight you seemed awfully mad at Rodriguez and he was awfully mad at you. But now you're saying the nicest things . . .'

'No, Don,' Emile countered. 'He was man enough to apologise to me in the ring for what he said before about wanting to kill the big black bull. And I am man enough to accept his apology.'

'Wonderful,' Dunphy enthused, before turning to Clancy. They all knew that there would not be another rematch with Rodriguez and so Clancy said, 'I tell ya, we're open to any offer. I think a great match would be Giardello and Griffith for the middleweight championship. It would be a natural.'

'Well, that's an idea,' Dunphy said with a toothy smile. He knew that he and the ABC cameras would not be there, as boxing, without network television, was shunted to the darker fringes of mainstream society.

In a ballroom at the Thunderbird, hundreds of people anticipated the champion's arrival. Emile Griffith made them wait. They ate caviar canapés and drank champagne, which would be paid for out of his purse, but he needed to relax. Jerry Izenberg and Huston Horn, who had followed him to his cottage in the hotel grounds, told him Rodriguez had said: 'Maybe it's time I quit fighting welterweights. I beat the best welterweights but not Griffith. He got me again.'

'Luis is a gentleman,' Emile said, tucking into a tub of vanilla ice cream. 'It was a rough fight. I hit him low and I was sorry. We banged heads, he got cut and I was sorry. Once I had my glove under his throat and I wanted to hit him and then I said, "No." He had already apologised for talking about killing the bull. I was glad he did. Luis is such a gentleman. He's a real man's man.'

Howie Albert, smoking a cigar, smiled. He loved being the co-manager of a world champion and a slice of poetic licence seemed acceptable amid the celebrations. 'We've watched Emile grow, me and Gil,' he said. 'When he started going out with girls we told him to hold their hands, look into their eyes and tell them they were beautiful. He giggled at us. But, now, he doesn't. Emile's debonair.'

Emile and Calvin rolled their eyes at each other. Howie might already be tipsy.

His mother walked in from the bathroom where she had just poured bubbles into the steaming water.

'It's bathtime, fellers,' Emile said.

Izenberg and Horn packed away their notebooks, but the fighter gestured to them to follow him. He was happy to talk more while in the bath. He stripped off and stood in all his naked glory while Izenberg and Horn shuffled in embarrassment.

Emelda slapped junior on his bare backside. 'C'mon, mummy's boy,' she cackled.

'Ow, Chubby Checker!' Emile yelled, rubbing his stinging rear as if his mother had caught him with a better shot than Rodriguez had managed all night.

He sank into the foaming bath with a blissful sigh. The reporters leaned against the wall and watched in bemusement as the fighter finally sat up and hummed peacefully as his mother soaped his back. She then ran a sponge around his shoulders and over his muscled torso.

'Now, *this* is a real man's man,' Emelda said as she marvelled at her son's body. She turned to the writers, who looked as if they had been struck dumb by the sight of a 26-year-old world champion fighter being bathed by his mother. 'You boys have gone quiet,' she said.

Emile grinned at them. 'Mommy's right. You fellers never seen a naked man before?'

CHAPTER TWELVE

The Outsiders

The world champion was the only person drinking tea on a Saturday night at the Stork Club on Swallow Street in London. Frank Sinatra, sitting next to Emile Griffith, had just arrived for his first post-gig double Jack Daniel's in a frosted tumbler filled with ice. His 24-year-old daughter, Nancy, and her husband Tommy Sands, the singer, actor and fading teen idol, were knocking back shots too, alongside Gil Clancy and Howie Albert. The rest of the club seemed to be steaming drunk as Emile discovered another side of London. He had expected classy refinement and so, as if to remind everyone else, he lifted his little finger daintily and sipped from a bone-china cup. It was exactly how he imagined a British gentleman might enjoy taking his tea in a gentler setting in September 1964.

There was nothing quiet about the Stork Club. The music was so loud and the laughter so raucous that Emile could barely hear Sinatra. He just knew that, even after a concert at the Palladium, Sinatra was talking about boxing. Sinatra loved boxing so much that Emile sometimes wondered if they should have swapped jobs. Emile fancied himself as a singer, while Sinatra often imagined he could have been a fighter. His father Anthony, or Marty as he was called, or Saverio Antonio Martino Sinatra as he had been born in Sicily, had fought as a part-time pro in between working as a full-time fireman in Hoboken, New Jersey. Sinatra Sr had changed his name in the ring to Marty O'Brien, because he figured that Irish boxers were more likely to get a break. It did not help him much and he lost seven of his eight fights as a bantamweight before he retired in 1921 with broken wrists.

Frank learned from his father how to throw a jab, and he did well enough in street scraps as a kid in the Little Italy quarter of Hoboken. But he could sing like no one else and so Sinatra limited his ring activities to that of an avid fan who, as his fame and power grew, nurtured ambitions of managing and promoting fighters. He advised and helped Tami Mauriello, a meaty Italian New Yorker, to get a crack at Joe Louis' heavyweight title in 1946 – but Sinatra's aim of having a hand on the biggest prize in sport was shattered by a first-round KO for the 'Brown Bomber'.

Sinatra also promoted a heavyweight title eliminator between Jersey Joe Walcott and Joey Maxim in June 1947, and managed Cisco Andrade, a Los Angeles lightweight, who lost his only world title shot against Joe Brown. Andrade's last fight as a pro had been a seventh-round defeat against Davey Moore in March 1962 – exactly a year before Moore lost his life. Sinatra was still looking for his first world champion and he tried to persuade Clancy and Albert to let him buy a share of Griffith's contract.

It was not easy to turn down Sinatra, one of the most famous men in America, but Clancy and Albert refused. No one else understood Emile, or cared as deeply for him as a boxer and a man. Sinatra accepted the decision and still hung around with them. He loved being with fighters, even if Emile was like no boxer he had ever met. Sinatra didn't care about him being a fairy. Griffith was a great world champion.

The whole Sinatra clan, from Nancy to Frank's mother, Dolly, to his cousin Buddy Garaventi, was besotted with Emile. Dolly invited him regularly to dinner in Hoboken, where she would feed him pasta and tiramisu between bouts. When he fought in Las Vegas, Nancy and Tommy wore matching tops with Emile's name stitched on the back as if they belonged to his entourage. Nancy, eighteen months from her first big hit with 'These Boots Are Made for Walkin'', felt an instinctive bond with the sensitive boxer.

Emile nodded earnestly as Sinatra shouted out tactical advice for his fight in three nights' time against Brian Curvis. He knew he could handle Curvis, even if the Welshman would be the first southpaw he had faced. It was enough just to enjoy his English tea and sink into the sumptuous reality that he was friends with '*Frank ... fucking ... Sinatra*', as his buddy Calvin liked to say, and they were in the Stork Club in the heart of London.

A girl dressed in a skimpy outfit arrived with a fresh pot of tea. She also brought Sinatra another Jack on the rocks and leaned over so provocatively that he couldn't help but say hello to her breasts. There had been no point in her doing the same with Emile, and he was relieved that some London girls were as savvy as him in recognising a gay man. The English, surprisingly, were not as innocent or restrained as he had expected.

Homosexuality was, of course, still illegal in Britain. It would take another three years for parliament to act on the recommendation of the Wolfenden Report, published in 1957, which called for the decriminalisation of homosexuality. 'Homosexual behaviour between consenting adults in private should no longer be a criminal offence,' Lord Wolfenden argued in his committee's ground-breaking report into homosexuality and prostitution. 'Homosexuality cannot legitimately be regarded as a disease ... [and] it is not, in our view, the function of the law to intervene in the private life of citizens, or to seek to enforce any particular pattern of behaviour.' Ten years later, the Sexual Offence Act of 1967 finally decriminalised consensual sex between two men over the age of twenty-one in the privacy of their own homes in England and Wales. Homosexuality would remain illegal for years in Northern Ireland and Scotland – as well as in the army and the merchant navy.

Calvin, on his first trip abroad, paid for by Emile, had quickly found his sexual bearings in London. He had discovered a club in Soho, a short walk from the Piccadilly hotel, called Le Duce. It was rammed with working-class gay Londoners, who called themselves mods, dancing to soul and Motown records. There were enough pretty girls around – and Calvin told Emile knowledgeably that they called them 'dolly birds' in London – to stop the police raiding Le Duce too often. The dolly birds loved dancing to black music and they left the gay boys alone. It was a perfect place for Emile and Calvin.

Until his fight against Curvis was over, Emile knew that he could not go clubbing for long. But most nights, just as he trained almost every day in a gym in Shepherd's Bush, Calvin took Emile into Soho. It was a way for him to unwind before he got back to the hotel at 11 p.m. They rarely stayed for more than an hour because, even against a limited challenger like Curvis, Emile needed to store his energy.

They were just three days away from Tuesday's fight; but it was a Saturday night. Calvin had arrived at the Stork Club bang on ten-thirty. Everyone knew he was meant to escort Emile back to his hotel room. The champion needed his sleep. Even Sinatra sent him on his way with a regal wave. The discipline of fighters seemed even more commendable the drunker everyone else became inside the Stork Club.

Calvin and Emile were stone-cold sober. They knew what they were doing. It just needed the smallest of nods from the fighter to his closest friend and occasional lover to set them on the illicit path to Le Duce.

The narrow streets looked slick and black in the drizzle. Calvin and Emile walked fast, heads down against the threat of discovery as well as the rain. They had been surprised, having been told to prepare for freezing, wet weather, to discover that September days in London, especially in 1964, were warm and dry and framed by sunshine. But the closer they came to the fight, the colder the nights felt. It was almost as if the strange old city had changed its mood. The nights turned rainy and foggy, and the cramped streets linking Piccadilly to Soho seemed as confusing as ever.

Emile, however, loved their names. They left Swallow Street and headed north on Regent Street. After they had got lost again, they somehow found their way back to Brewer and then Berwick Street. The deeper they wandered into Soho, the more striptease joints and blue movie cinemas they saw. At first, being two young black Americans, they had been confused by the scrawled cards offering 'French Lessons', 'Model' or 'Large Chest For Sale' outside stinking stairwells. Calvin was the first to work out these were not adverts for linguists, artists or furniture shops. The seedy red lights were as much a giveaway in London as they were in Times Square.

They kept walking, more at ease after a week in town, until they turned right into D'Arblay Street, which seemed so grand. It sounded French rather than English but, once inside, everything was familiar. Gay men in London looked different, with their weird haircuts and surreal fashion sense, but the dark grime of sex was the same the world over. Emile and Calvin had found their place. The music was American. The urge was universal. They were home.

Brian Curvis had been ringside at Madison Square Garden on the night that Benny Paret slipped towards death. If Paret had won the title, he would have been expected to defend it against the Welshman. Two-and-a-half years later, as Curvis told the *Sunday Mirror* in a column written under his name, 'I have a date next week with a killer ... Emile Griffith, welterweight champion of the world.' The date was Tuesday 22 September 1964, and the venue was the Empire Pool, Wembley, London. But the tabloid's crude depiction of Curvis facing a 'killer' distressed Emile. His sexuality remained a taboo subject. Yet there were no limits on highlighting Emile's role in the death of Paret.

Curvis stressed that he felt no fear of Griffith; but his young wife was different. 'I get so tense,' Barbara Curvis told the *Mirror*. 'The worst part is not the fight. It's just when the lights dim, the spotlights come on, here's the fanfare and then that sudden, awful hush. It seems to last for hours ... but, oh, those punches. I'm sure I feel them more than Brian does. Listening to it on the radio is even worse. If the commentator says Brian has a small cut, you immediately think it's a great big gash. Your imagination runs away with you. So I'm not going to the fight. Friends are taking me to a quiet hotel to take my mind off it.'

In an attempt to soften perceptions of him as a murderous puncher, Emile arrived in London with a gift for Mrs Curvis. It was a flowery bonnet he had designed for her. 'I don't see anything strange about it,' Emile said after he had given the hat to Jack Solomons, the former Petticoat Lane fishmonger turned powerful fight promoter, to present to his opponent's wife. 'I don't see anything unusual about a fighter designing women's hats ...'

The London fight press gossiped privately. A boxer who was an aspiring milliner? It was black-and-white code for a simple truth.

'He's a bleeding iron,' one of Fleet Street's finest muttered out loud while they waited for Emile's first joint press conference with Curvis at the White City Stadium Sporting Club in west London. 'Iron' was cockney rhyming slang for homosexual: an iron hoof rhymed with 'poof', and was simply shortened to 'iron'. Emile, fortunately, knew less London street talk than he did Spanish insults like *maricón*.

The British press was not going to let Emile get away with revealing that the governor of the Virgin Islands had presented him with a medal and a citation: 'Your manly career in and out of the ring is a fine example to the youth of the Virgin Islands and to young men everywhere.'

He was pressed to explain why, being so manly, he was not married? 'I had been going steady with a sweet kid,' Emile said, without mentioning the names of either of his old flames, Matthew or Esther, 'but right now I'm in no mood to settle down. I guess I have another four good years of fighting left, and I'll still be only thirty then, plenty young enough for marriage.'

The *Sunday Mirror* had paid Emile for an 'exclusive' first-person account with the headline: 'How I Killed A Man In The Ring'. 'There's a memory lodged inside my brain that will never leave me even if I live to be a thousand,' the article began. 'The memory will be heavy in the air when I step into the ring at Wembley to defend my world welterweight title against Brian Curvis. I know I will have to live with my label – The Man Who Killed Benny Paret – for the rest of my life. Not so long ago, it looked like wrecking my career and my life . . . When we got together around the weighing scales, Benny whispered in my ear. In Spanish, he called me a sissy. Other people heard him, too, and after he died they said I'd been so mad I'd wanted to kill him.'

Before he described some of his nightmares of Paret, he suggested that, 'I thought that victory would kill me, too. I couldn't get Benny off my mind. In the day I saw him everywhere. At night I couldn't sleep without pills. I wouldn't train. I wouldn't do anything. I didn't think I would ever snap out of it.'

He was less forthcoming when facing the entire press pack. Emile missed luncheon invitations, skipped interviews and avoided additional press conferences. The *Sun*, which had just been launched as a newspaper a week earlier, in broadsheet form on 15 September 1964, suggested that, 'Emile Griffith became a moody, I-want-to-be-alone fighter as he sweated out the hours before staking his world welterweight crown against confident Brian Curvis at Wembley tomorrow night.' They used a photograph of Emile looking sullen in a black bowler hat.

Emile stripped down to his sparkling white underpants at the weigh-in on Great Windmill Street on the morning of the fight. He wore the silver chain that Calvin had given to him as a gift. Curvis, grinning helplessly, as if dazzled by Emile's underwear which looked pristine in comparison to his old stripy boxer shorts, accepted the champion's hand after they had both stepped off the scales. Emile stared down at the challenger with a sombre expression. He no longer saw any novelty in a title fight weigh-in.

At Wembley, and to heighten the sense of fighting for his country as well as himself, Griffith's white robe featured a small American flag on its breast pocket. As he walked calmly around the ring on that dry but chilly Tuesday evening, Emile was commended by the BBC's commentator, Harry Carpenter, as 'a cool and a confident world champion'.

Frank Sinatra watched from ringside and the old tug of danger was still obvious. Unlike the changes enforced at Madison Square Garden, the Wembley ring was squared by three rather than the safer four ropes. The two fighters' hands were also covered by six-ounce gloves, rather than the more cushioned eight-ounce variety, which had become compulsory in world title fights in America.

'Over 10,000 people in this Wembley stadium are now hushed and tense, as people always are before a world championship fight,' Carpenter said in a broadcast that would be screened the following night on the BBC's midweek *Sportsview* programme. 'Over in the distance, the strains of a Welsh song rise from the darkness as this tremendous number of supporters for Curvis begin to urge and encourage their man. Miners have left the pits only hours ago. They clearly took time off to wash the grime from their faces and then they caught a train and they've come to London to cheer on their man from Swansea – Brian Curvis of Wales, the British and Empire welterweight champion. All over this stadium, Welshmen are wearing Welsh rosettes in a demonstration of patriotism we haven't seen in a boxing arena for a good few years – perhaps not since Turpin had that immortal night with Sugar Ray Robinson thirteen years ago.'

Randolph Turpin was a mixed-race British middleweight who had stunned everyone when he defeated Robinson on points in London in 1951. But the lack of recent British success at world level was underlined when seventy-year-old Ted 'Kid' Lewis was called into the ring. Gil Clancy applauded Lewis enthusiastically, knowing that the tubby little white-haired man who called himself the 'Aldgate Sphinx' had featured in world title fights at welterweight, middleweight and even light-heavyweight. Carpenter pointed out that

Lewis was also 'the last British fighter to contest the world welterweight title. He lost it in 1919 – forty-five years ago.'

Patriotic fervour reached such a pitch that tradition was overturned and the champion was introduced first. Griffith bowed so politely to all four corners of the ring that he just needed to doff a bowler hat to complete an utterly genteel response to the indignity of having to precede the challenger. Curvis, however, looked very anxious.

Griffith started cautiously, wary of the Curvis left hand, which had helped the Welshman to an impressive 30-1 record that included a victory over Ralph Dupas at Wembley two years earlier. The champion soon settled into his familiar relentless rhythm. Griffith punched mostly to the body, as if he wanted to avoid excessively dangerous head shots, but he still peppered Curvis with his fast jab.

By the end of round five the Welshman's left eye was cut and starting to swell. A jolting right to the ribs made Curvis gasp. An even harder punch, another right that landed with sickening force just below the heart, dropped the challenger. Curvis, supporting himself on one knee as he waited for the count to reach eight, looked in trouble. He got to his feet and was saved by the bell, which rang just seconds later. 'This crowd is stunned by that sudden whiplash right hand to the heart,' Carpenter said into his microphone. 'The Welsh supporters have gone very, very silent. Griffith has turned into a bogeyman.'

Curvis took his beating from the bogeyman stoically – but when round nine ended he looked deflated. On his stool, as they towelled down his dejected face, Curvis' right eye was even puffier than the left.

'He's felt the force of Griffith's punches and he's a little apprehensive,' Carpenter said of Curvis. 'He's not producing all the fire and the fury that he has in some other fights – because he's up against an extremely competent craftsman in Emile Griffith.'

As the cameras switched to the opposite corner, Carpenter marvelled at the sight of Griffith. 'You might have noticed the build of this man. He's got extraordinary shoulders and a 44-inch chest that comes down to a 27-inch waist. He's just beautifully built.'

Gay men and transvestites in Times Square would have been whooping – had the BBC been screened into the bars and clubs where the world champion was revered most. Yet there was nothing statuesque about Griffith's fluidity as, midway through the tenth, he moved in quickly and let rip with a big left hook that dumped Curvis back on the canvas. The Welshman only made it up again at the count of nine. His head had begun to loll, but Griffith, still avoiding lasting damage, stuck to body-punching. A right hand sank into Curvis' gut and made him hunch over in pain at the bell. He had survived another round.

Curvis had his best round in the twelfth, but it simply spurred on Griffith. He knocked Curvis down for a third time just before the end of round thirteen. 'Griffith is again the master,' Carpenter said. 'Curvis' legs and arms seem to have turned to paper ... oh, what a punch to the solar plexus ... a right hand and Curvis is so hurt.'

He staggered up once more, at nine, and Carpenter exclaimed: 'That bell must come as such a welcome relief to Brian Curvis.'

Once it was all over, and Curvis had made it through fifteen rounds, Griffith tapped his opponent admiringly on the head. He wrapped his left arm around Curvis and walked him back to the Welsh corner – only to be interrupted by the referee, Harry Gibb. As the sole scorer of the fight, under British rules, Gibb lifted Griffith's right arm as the obvious winner.

Calvin Thomas was into the ring quicker than Clancy, Albert and Martin. Wearing a candy-striped shirt, he rushed over to Emile – who kissed him. Calvin reached out to hold Emile's face in his hands. It was a surprisingly intimate gesture as, tenderly, he gazed at Emile, checking that there were no more than a few small cuts and bumps on the face he loved. Emile rubbed Calvin's arm in a reassuring way. It was a rare display of deep affection between two gay men in a world championship ring.

Emile turned to find Curvis again. Eventually, surrounded by cameramen whose flashbulbs popped, Emile wrapped his right arm around Curvis. He pulled his opponent towards him and kissed him on the left cheek. Emile kept his lips pursed against Curvis' bruised and swollen face for as long as the Welshman would allow. It looked as though Emile believed that his kiss had the power to take away all the hurt etched onto the face of a beaten man.

Alan Hubbard, a young sportswriter for United Newspapers, followed the hacks down the long corridor leading to the fighters' dressing rooms at Wembley. His work was distributed from a London office to various provincial newspapers. That night, Hubbard was on a ten-thirty deadline. He needed as many quotes as he could get from both Griffith and Curvis before filing his final report for the late edition of the following morning's *Sheffield Telegraph*. All the writers, led by Reg Gutteridge, felt as if a cocked gun was pressed to their heads. Their editors had already screamed down the phones for copy.

Gutteridge was the coolest of them all, for he was more experienced and had been through the horrors of World War II. On D-Day, he had jumped out of his tank and landed on a mine, which blew off his left leg. His hopes of becoming a boxer were over, but Gutteridge did not lose his sense of humour. There were occasions in later years when, if bored on a beach holiday, he would sometimes hide his prosthetic limb under his towel near the edge of the water before hopping around on one leg shouting: 'Shark! Shark!'

At Wembley, with Gutteridge walking fast on two legs, they careered towards the winner. It would be easy to get words of disappointment from Curvis, but they needed to hear from the champion. Hubbard pushed his way nearer the front as they reached Griffith's dressing room. Gutteridge opened the door and they sauntered in – only to stop in shock. Silence settled over all of them as they stared in disbelief.

In a corner of an otherwise deserted room, Emile Griffith, the world welterweight champion, sat on the lap of another young black man. They were locked in a passionate embrace, kissing each other deeply, tongues buried in each other's mouths. Emile was naked from the waist up and oblivious to his visitors.

Seconds slid past before Gutteridge made an incredulous snort and the two men broke apart. Emile looked across at them, and then stood up. He still carried the marks of battle on his face. The far lesser-known figure of Calvin Thomas turned away. He knew he had better find Gil and Howie to keep the press boys happy. Emile, in the meantime, would handle them.

The champion ignored the fact that he and Calvin had been rumbled. Instead, Emile nodded politely to the writers and waited for the first questions. He was sure that no one would dare ask him about the kiss. And they couldn't write about it. Who would believe them? Their night editors wanted punchy quotes rather than dressing-room gossip they would never be allowed to print in the national newspapers. It was impossible even to repeat a profanity in the pages of the British press. A reported kiss between two black men would have half the country choking on their morning cornflakes or toast and marmalade. It was also illegal.

Hubbard, who became sports editor of the *Observer* decades later, let his friend lead the way. Gutteridge asked Emile a routine question. What had he thought of Curvis and the Wembley crowd? It seemed the best way to get everyone back on the straight and narrow.

Emile was an old pro and, as if the kiss was already forgotten, he spoke about his courageous opponent and the wonderful Welsh fans who, incredibly, had sung more loudly each time their man had been knocked to the canvas. 'What a crowd,' Emile said with a wry smile. 'What a night . . .'

The kiss was never mentioned in print until Hubbard wrote about it in a different century, after Griffith's death in 2013.

Instead, on a night that was still unfolding on 22 September 1964, Emile and Calvin left Wembley in a rush to hang out with Sinatra's gang at the Stork Club for an hour. Emile was feted and exalted. They managed to escape just before midnight. It was past closing time and, as they hailed a cab, all the pubs were already blackened and shut for the night. But they knew where they were heading. It had become a familiar route to D'Arblay Street and Le Duce. They were in the mood to dance, and kiss some more, not necessarily each other, as Emile and Calvin were open to new experiences. A couple of sleazy white London boys, among the mods of Le Duce, would round off an interesting night. They were ready to party.

Emile was back in London, and at Le Duce, nine weeks later. He was invited to make a speech at the House of Commons before, on 1 December 1964, he stopped Dave Charnley on a ninth-round TKO in that same ring at Wembley. The party whips at Westminster would have been scandalised by the sexual habits of the world champion, but, as always, some secrets were best never told.

London, Le Duce and a French kiss in a Wembley dressing room belonged to Emile and Calvin.

Gay sex, in 1964, was still illegal in forty-nine out of America's fifty states. Illinois remained the lone exception. Gay men and lesbians could be dismissed from their jobs or denied housing and other benefits on the grounds of sexuality. Their persecution was often undertaken most aggressively and systematically in New York, supposedly the country's most liberated city.

On 17 December 1963, the *New York Times* had printed a rambling and skewed 5,000-word feature, beginning on the front page, which explored 'the homosexual problem' apparently engulfing the city. In a story written by Robert Doty, and headlined 'Growth Of Homosexuality In City Provokes Wide Concern', the *Times* complained that, 'sexual inverts have colonized three areas of New York. The city's homosexual community acts as a kind of lodestar, attracting others from all over the country.'

Doty suggested that, 'The old idea, assiduously propagated by the homosexuals, that homosexuality is an inborn, incurable disease, has been exploded by modern psychiatry. In the opinion of many experts it can be both prevented and cured. It is a problem that has grown in the shadows, protected by taboos on open discussion that have only recently begun to be breached.'

The *New York Times* claimed that there was 'overwhelming

evidence that homosexuals are created – generally by ill-adjusted parents – not born. Leaving the subject to bar-room jesters, policemen and the homosexuals themselves can only perpetuate the mystery and misconception that have grown in the dark.

'The homosexual has a range of gay periodicals that is a kind of distorted mirror image of the straight publishing world ... homosexuals are traditionally willing to spend all they have on a gay night. They will pay outrageous prices to be left alone with their own kind to chatter and dance together without pretence or constraint.'

A campaign to rid New York of all 'undesirables' and criminal elements before the 1964-65 World's Fair intensified. In October 1964, Ed Koch and Carol Greitzer, the First Assembly District leaders of the city's apparently enlightened Democratic Party, demanded action with regard to 'the problem of homosexuals who congregate on Village Square at Eighth Street and the Avenue of the Americas'. Koch told the *New York Times* he had met the city's police commissioner, Michael J. Murphy, and formulated 'plans to increase surveillance of Greenwich Village to curtail homosexual loitering and solicitation'.

Homosexuals were targeted as criminals, and over a hundred men a week were entrapped for 'solicitation' by New York City policemen who, pretending to be gay, propositioned them in restrooms and at bar counters. Gay bars and clubs in the Village were raided and shut down – and homosexuals were harassed on the streets of New York's most bohemian neighbourhood.

Freddie Wright knew that, because of the Village crackdown, he would have to start working more around Times Square. He was moving to midtown and into Emile Griffith's territory, where he'd soon forge a friendship with the fighter that would endure for decades.

Freddie called himself a Village person – a Village girl. He was more than a barman. Freddie was a part-time hustler. When he needed some extra cash, he would slip out from behind the bar and do a little business. Freddie was willing to use his hand and his mouth, but he always let the clients know his limits in a charmingly blunt way. 'You're not fucking me,' Freddie would tell them in regal fashion.

The straight men, all those husbands and business executives, flooded the places where Freddie worked. They were hustle bars where the straights loved sneaking over for a night. The bar boys hustled, the dancers hustled, the drag queens hustled, everyone young and wild hustled. Freddie saw all kinds of men with all kinds of desires. Some were from out of town, on a business trip, and it seemed as if the straighter they looked, the kinkier their fetish. Freddie thought it was amazing that middle-aged straight men would be after the drag queens with big dicks.

'Why would you want them to fuck you?' Freddie sometimes asked the clients. 'It blows my mind.'

He finally caught on; and saw that the johns thought they were getting the best of both worlds when they had sex with transvestites who looked like women but felt like men.

Freddie was an amateur hustler, who only did a little sex work on the side. He was far more interested in becoming a dancer, a DJ and a female impersonator. Freddie was hard-working and clean and he avoided all the pills and the coke and heavy drinking that clogged the Village. Every now and then he might smoke a joint but, for the most part, he saved himself for dancing, dressing up and partying.

When he was behind a bar in the Village, men always hit on him: 'I'll buy you a drink, gorgeous . . .'

'Thank you, baby,' Freddie smiled. 'I'll get myself a soda.'

The johns knew that a simple soda would not get Freddie drunk and more likely to turn a trick for free – and so the reaction was always indignant.

'I'm not buying a fucking soda!'

Freddie shrugged. 'That's fine. You offered, but I just wanted a soda. Calm down, honey.'

After Freddie moved out to work in midtown, they were merciless whenever he returned to the Village.

'So you left us to become an upper-class sissy,' the bitchier queens sniped at him.

'Hello,' Freddie said quietly. 'I'm working. I'm not up there hustling.'

Freddie had met Kathy Hogan, fast establishing herself as the Queen of Midtown, and the owner of numerous gay bars running between 42nd Street to 50th Street. Midtown was much nastier and raunchier than the Village, where Freddie had worked the bars among largely educated and predominantly white crowds. Porn movie theatres lined both sides of 42nd Street, and the majority of drag queens were black or Latino men dressed for business rather than just pleasure. Most of Kathy's joints were on 46th Street and Freddie soon proved himself to be indispensable.

Kathy looked after Emile in midtown. She didn't care that he was a famous world champion. Kathy just thought he was a sweetheart. Emile sometimes seemed lost, vulnerable and exhausted. He would retreat to one of Kathy's joints and, if he was not in the mood to party, he'd find a stool in the corner and put his head down on the bar counter. Emile could fall asleep, and Kathy would amble over and gently remove his cash and jewellery, his stylish jacket or coat, and keep them safe in her office.

Most of the time, Emile visited Kathy's bars for outrageous bursts of fun. Calvin was almost always with him and Freddie watched their double-act with amused affection. Calvin spoke about boxing and his Christian faith with as much relish as he eyed the boys lining the bar, while Emile would introduce every new young Hispanic conquest as his latest 'cousin' or 'nephew'. They were contradictory and enigmatic; but Freddie assumed that there must be no other way in the macho world of professional boxing. He thought such discretion a less kinky quirk compared with the white businessmen and suburban husbands who liked picking up chicks with dicks.

Freddie was out, proud and happy to let everyone know that, with him, there were no secrets. At the same time, he was never judgemental of Emile. He was a revered world champion who also happened to be infamous for killing Benny Paret. How could he be as free as Freddie?

In March 1965, the *New York Times* profiled Emile as an unlikely boxing champion who, as the headline suggested, 'still likes to mix hats with gloves'. Describing him as 'an articulate twenty-seven-year-old with the highest television ratings in boxing,' the *Times* featured a photograph of Emile using a pair of clippers to trim a fluffy ladies' bonnet on the head of a mannequin. 'Familiar as he is with the world of pillboxes, ostrich plumes, "chicken coop" netting and other millinery items,' Griffith was locked into boxing. He was preparing for the tenth defence of the welterweight crown he had first won from Paret in 1961.

'For a long time after Benny died,' Emile told the *Times*, 'I was holding back. But in the last year or so I've been punching freely. I try to think Benny's death was fate. I try real hard. But I always know I was the guy in the other corner that night.'

Freddie Wright could not lift his eyes from the striking sight of a world boxing champion tending to a ladies' hat in the pages of America's most renowned newspaper. His gaze fixed on the mournful face of his new friend. Emile, whose laughter usually boomed around Kathy Hogan's midtown bars, looked hauntingly sad in the black-and-white print.

Sonny Banks had been the first man to floor Muhammad Ali – back in February 1962, when the eventual winner of their fight was still called Cassius Clay. Three years and three months later, Banks was knocked out in the ninth round of a bout against Leotis Martin, a rising heavyweight prospect, in Philadelphia.

Martin was a brutal hitter from the streets of Philly – but Banks fought with raw desperation. Bill Conlin described the dramatic ending in the *Philadelphia Daily News*: 'A tremendous brawl came down to a frantic ninth round where Martin was out on his feet. Then he threw one textbook straight right that caught Banks on the left temple. I can still hear the bass drum sound of Banks' head hitting the mat. And I can still see them, bearing him to the locker room on a stretcher.'

Lucien 'Sonny' Banks was twenty-four years old when he died three days later, on 13 May 1965.

The months, and the fights, blurred. One followed the other in a ceaseless procession as Emile Griffith fought again and again. Eight bouts were crammed together between 26 January 1965 and 3 February 1966. He lost two decisions in non-title ten-round fights to Manuel Gonzalez and Don Fullmer. Griffith had already beaten Fullmer and, when it mattered, in his final defence of his world welterweight title, he outpointed Gonzalez decisively in December 1965. He travelled to Houston, Honolulu, Salt Lake City, Fresno, London again, and Las Vegas once more, while squeezing in a trio of trips to his home at Madison Square Garden. Griffith was again voted the Fighter of the Year in 1965.

He had racked up fifty-six fights, with a winning record of 49-7, as he tried to make history by becoming only the third welterweight champion, after Sugar Ray Robinson and Carmen Basilio, to jump a division and take the world middleweight title. Griffith had to relinquish his welterweight crown to challenge Dick Tiger, an excellent Nigerian exiled in America, for the champion's middleweight belt. He liked Tiger, and few expected him to be able to withstand the power of the much bigger man. But on 25 April 1966, in the Garden, Griffith knocked Tiger down in the ninth and went on to became a world champion for a fourth time as, after fifteen close rounds, he was the undisputed winner on points.

Emile went on *The Ed Sullivan Show* and, after he sang impressively, as the *New York Post* confirmed, 'the new middleweight champion signed a lucrative contract with Columbia Records. They will put Emile on wax and heavily publicise his new recordings. He is being booked to appear on the Johnny Carson and the Merv Griffin shows. There is rhythm to this young man, who is so many things, and an eagerness in him that makes him a completely different personality than so many others who earn their living with their fists. But there is also gentleness in him, which makes him a paradox of our time.'

He was also strapped for cash. 'After fifty-seven professional fights, including twelve title bouts, you'd figure the flashy Virgin Islander was a wealthy man,' Tim Moriarty wrote in the *Jersey Journal*. 'He isn't. That's the primary reason Griffith has agreed to make the first defence of his newly won middleweight crown against Joey Archer at Madison Square Garden on July 13 [1966]. Emile needs the money – to buy more suits, more paintings, more jewelry, and to keep those thirteen hungry relatives living in the manner to which they have become accustomed.

'Generous to a fault, that's Emile. In addition to caring for his large family, he is also a soft touch to any guy with a hard luck story. He has reached a point where he must keep fighting in order to pay all his bills. Other bouts are being lined up fast for Emile, who needs all the money he can get his hands on to pay for those Italian silk suits – and to keep the wolf from his relatives' door.'

Griffith beat Archer on points to retain his new title. His outrageous lifestyle, and thinly veiled sexuality, was soon the subject of another long *Sports Illustrated* feature called, in a knowing wink, 'Camping Out With The Champ'. 'The wall-to-wall carpet in poinsettia red is what first strikes you when you enter the living room of Emile Griffith's apartment [in Weehawken],' the 7 November 1966 profile began. 'The style is parvenu modern or, in the hip phrase, high camp. Lady, a six-month-old Doberman pinscher, whines from the bathroom. Don Achilles, a white poodle, barks from the kitchen. Don recently had his hair shorn. Griffith, who did not care for the styling, spent three hours with a pair of shears carefully recasting the dog's image. But Griffith does not notice the dogs. He is busy singing: *"She brings out the tiger in me/And she makes me feel like a man."*'

The Weehawken apartment seemed to bring out the queen in Emile. Milton Gross, in *Sports Illustrated*, made careful note of

Emile's 'hip-hugging plaid trousers, as mod as anything on Carnaby Street, his black suede, ankle-high boots zippered up to the sides, a heavy gold bracelet on one wrist and rings on his fingers. There are as many sides to Griffith, who has won a world boxing title four times, as there are gewgaws in his apartment. On one wall, for instance, above a love seat, is a large oil painting, in dainty shades, of flowers in a vase. Only inches away are three reminders of the fighter he is. One is the *Ring* magazine belt awarded to him for outpointing Luis Rodriguez to become the first man to win the welterweight title three times. Another belt is for kayoing Benny (Kid) Paret, the first time Griffith won the crown. A third one is for regaining the title from Paret. Ten days after this last fight, Paret died.'

Gross thought Griffith was 'courteous, gentle and gregarious' – but Gil Clancy, sitting in on the interview, said, 'he can also be bitchy. The slightest thing can set him off. We can have some violent arguments but, ten minutes later, he's forgotten them. He laughs easily, he cries easily.'

Griffith protested at being too closely examined. 'I'm not a butterfly you can put a pin in and study,' he told Gross. 'I'm still like a little baby, but I'm a grown man.'

Gross wrote sympathetically about his financial travails. 'If Griffith seems flighty or flouncy to outsiders, he is a bedrock of solidity for a fatherless family – a family that plagues and bleeds him with demands that would crush almost any other man. They call him Junior, Sonny, Uncle and Poppy, and he embodies all these relationships for his mother, three brothers, four sisters, five nieces, in-laws and "loving cousins" for whom he is the sole support. At one time he has fed, clothed and educated as many as seventeen people while trying to create an identity of his own.

'Sometimes it seems to be a race between Griffith and his mother to see who can spend money faster. He has more than fifty suits and eight tuxedos. He owns five heavy 18-carat gold bracelets, two of which spell out "Emile" in diamond chips. He has more fancy sports jackets than he remembers, at least twenty-five pairs of shoes and two dozen sweaters. He drives a tan 1966 Lincoln Convertible, complete with tape recorder, stereo and TV.'

Emile had fought twenty-six times since 'the accident' of Paret's death. Yet, as Gross concluded, 'he can no more forget that terrible day than he can give up leopard-skin bedspreads, pink phones, and gold bracelets.'

He looked away from Gross and down at the jangling, gold jewellery on his wrist. 'You know where I got the idea for these bracelets?' Emile asked. 'I saw one on Benny's hand once. It looked so nice there.'

Esther Taylor had not seen Emile for years but she still read about him. It was hard to miss one of the most famous men in America – who had, for years, called her his girlfriend.

One of her ex-boyfriends, the first guy she had gone out with after Emile, had always laughed mockingly. 'Don't you know he's gay?' he asked Esther.

'Get outta here,' Esther snapped.

Some men were so jealous they would say anything to undermine Emile. Yet the thought nagged at her sometimes, and so much of it made sense when she reflected on their relationship, but Esther preferred to think of Emile as her friend and, yes, her old boyfriend.

Life had changed anyway. She was with Charles Evans now, her future husband, and Esther was happy. Charles came from the same Harlem neighbourhood as both her and Emile, but they had all moved on. Charles and Esther were together – but Emile would always remain a vivid part of her past.

At night, in seamy terrain stretching from 42nd Street to 48th Street, they became known as the Three Musketeers. Emile Griffith, Calvin Thomas and Freddie Wright were a distinctive trio. They were rarely apart on a Friday and Saturday night in New York City. Freddie had started working at a club on 45th Street. There was a huge dance-floor covered by a circus top and Freddie turned himself into a trapeze artist. He swung dizzyingly from one side to the other on his trapeze, flying over the dancers, as Emile and Calvin roared along with everyone else.

There was more danger on the outside. Bottles would sometimes be thrown at them when they turned into a gay club and a zealot yelled: 'Hey, you nigger faggots, we know what you're doing in there.'

The musketeers just ducked and laughed. They knew that no one would yell 'faggot' if they came face to face with Emile and recognised him. He did not fit the stereotype of a homosexual man. Emile Griffith broke the mould and, for his courage, he was celebrated. He was cherished. He was loved. He gave them all hope amid the suffocating repression.

At prime time, 10 p.m. on Tuesday 7 March 1967, CBS screened a documentary called *The Homosexuals*. It was the first attempt by network television to address homosexuality since a local station in San Francisco, KQED, had aired a programme that laboured under the title of *The Rejected* in 1961. Fronted by Mike Wallace, *The Homosexuals* purported to be a balanced analysis of a debilitating but curable illness.

'Homosexuality is an enigma,' Wallace said in the opening frame of a documentary screened right across America. 'Even in this era of bold sexual mores, it remains a subject that people find disturbing, embarrassing, and there is a reluctance to discuss it. Yet there is growing concern about homosexuals in society, about their increasing visibility. In preparing this broadcast, CBS commissioned a survey by the Opinion Research Corporation into public attitudes towards homosexuality. We discovered that Americans consider homosexuality more harmful towards society than adultery, abortion or prostitution.'

CBS claimed that, 'Most Americans are repelled by the idea of homosexuality. Two out of three Americans look upon homosexuals with disgust, discomfort or fear – one out of ten feels hatred. A vast majority believe that homosexuality is an illness. Only 10 per cent say it is a crime and yet – here is the paradox – the majority of Americans favour legal punishment, even for homosexual acts performed in private between consenting adults. The homosexual responds by going underground.'

Wallace and his team relied on the findings of 'scientific experts', like the psychiatrist Charles Socarides, who argued that, 'The fact someone is homosexual, a true obligatory homosexual, automatically rules out the possibility that he will remain happy for long. The whole idea of the "happy homosexual" is to create a mythology about the nature of homosexuality.'

It was implied that Socarides, rather than being a crank with a warped agenda, was an eminent scientific thinker, for Wallace introduced him as a 'New York psychoanalyst at the Albert Einstein School of Medicine'. Wallace suggested that, 'many psychiatrists now believe that no man is born a homosexual. Homosexuality begins to form in the first three years of life ...' He also underlined Socarides' insistence that, 'Homosexuality is in fact a mental illness which has reached epidemiological proportions.'

Socarides' own son came out as gay over twenty years later – and in 1996 Richard Socarides was appointed as President Bill Clinton's liaison officer for the US's gay community. But, in 1967, his father believed that, 'the average homosexual is promiscuous. He is not interested in, nor capable of, a lasting relationship like that of a heterosexual marriage.'

Wallace was an acclaimed television anchor and, in an effort to appear balanced, *The Homosexuals* included gay voices. Gore Vidal was interviewed and stated that, 'There's a certain homosexual who has written the only good women characters in the American theatre. So the idea that the homosexual is a seditious person trying to absolutely destroy the family structure of the United States is nonsense.'

Vidal, tellingly, did not feel able to name Tennessee Williams as a homosexual on national television. Other gay men were also interviewed with their faces hidden or obscured. 'This man is twenty-seven,' Wallace said of an interviewee who stood behind a fern plant so that his identity was masked. 'He is college-educated but he was unable to hold down a job because of his inability to contain his sexual inclinations. He has been in jail three times for committing homosexual acts. If he is arrested once more he faces the possibility of a life sentence. He is now on probation and in psychotherapy.'

The man tried to explain the reasons for his homosexuality. 'I had a very domineering mother,' he said in a crackly interview. 'She was a very sweet tyrant – but a tyrant nonetheless. The love I had was kind of killing. I was mocked by other children . . . I now know that, inside, I am sick. I am not just sick sexually. I am sick in a lot of ways.'

In contrast, Jack Nichols, renamed 'Warren Adkins' in the documentary, emerged as confident and articulate. Nichols stressed that he would never wish to renounce his homosexuality and that he had no anxieties about why he had become a gay man. 'It really doesn't concern me very much. I never would imagine that if I had blond hair I would worry what genes or chromosomes had caused my blond hair. My homosexuality to me is very much in the same category. I feel no more guilt about my homosexuality than a person with blond hair or dark skin or with light skin would feel about what they had.'

Nichols praised his 'warm and understanding family' because 'they accepted me as a person. They don't think of me as some kind of creature. I am very lucky.'

Yet Wallace concluded the hour-long programme with a grim message. 'The dilemma of the homosexual: told by the medical profession he is sick; by the law that he's a criminal; shunned by employers, rejected by heterosexual society. Incapable of fulfilling a relationship with a woman, or for that matter with a man. At the centre of his life he remains anonymous. A displaced person. An outsider.'

The next morning Jack Nichols was fired from his position as a sales manager for a Washington hotel. Nichols' acceptance of his sexuality had meant that, despite changing his name in the documentary,

THE OUTSIDERS | 267

he had not tried to disguise himself on screen. His employers responded by fulfilling Wallace's slanted description and shunned him. Nichols, for daring to speak the truth about himself, had become just another 'displaced person', and 'an outsider' in mainstream America.

Emile Griffith, locked in public silence and public denial of himself, felt just as displaced in America. He was still an outsider in his own country.

CHAPTER THIRTEEN

Stonewall

The damage spread slowly, like poison, inside Emile Griffith. He had been taking blows to the head as a professional boxer for ten years when he first felt the creeping impact of an invisible sickness. Emile stared at the mirror and, if he lowered his gaze, the illusion of perfect health remained. He had turned thirty on 3 February 1968 and his body still resembled a sculpted marvel of rippling power. Emile lifted his eyes and his face was worn. The cost of all he had endured in the ring had begun to leave its mark.

There was scar tissue above the thickened eyebrows, and his nose appeared flatter than before, but you needed to look more deeply to see how his vitality had ebbed away from the surface. The skin on his face was still taut, but life no longer poured out of him. His features were just a little duller and there was a drained gauntness around his eyes, which no longer gleamed. It was easier to imagine the punishment he had absorbed beneath those darker, cloudier irises.

He felt muffled in his head, as if his brain had been lined with raw cotton, but he thought it might just be a looming cold. The cold never came; and his head cleared for a while. Emile was still fractionally slower. He noticed it once they had settled into camp at the

Concord hotel in the Catskills, as he began training to defend his world middleweight title on 4 March 1968. Kiamesha Lake felt like home and it was less lonely having Joe Frazier training alongside him. But the swarming ambition of Joe, closing in on the world heavyweight title, made Emile look like a blurry silhouette shuffling through the old routines.

Emile was attempting to hold onto the title he had lost to Nino Benvenuti but then won back in a rematch in September 1967. Their rubber match, in one of the trilogies that shaped Emile's long and varied career, promised to be another exhausting battle for supremacy. He was about to climb into the pro ring for his sixty-third fight.

Joe, six years younger at twenty-four, had a perfect 19-0 record. He had knocked out seventeen of his opponents on his fast march towards the heavyweight title. There was a freshness and violent spark to Joe Frazier that was long gone from Emile.

When they ran along the mud-blackened shores of the lake, with the water as flat and lifeless as a grey stone in the half-light, it was easy enough for Emile. He was much the lighter man, and the better runner, and it was hard for Joe to keep pace with him. It suited Emile to ease back a little, to keep Joe company, and he had enough breath in his body to keep chattering away to the panting heavy-weight, who communicated in grunts and mutters as they jogged through the biting February cold. Joe didn't waste words but he liked listening to the fluting singsong of Emile's incessant high-pitched patter.

They both wore woollen skullcaps, heavy tracksuits and thick gloves on the freezing dawn runs. Emile almost disappeared beneath his fluffy hat, pulled low over his head, like an old bird trying to bury itself in the warmth of a puffy bundle of feathers. Joe was more con-spicuous. At five feet eleven-and-a-half, he was nearly four inches taller than Emile, and yet he resembled a squat and menacing figure as he ran. Joe only broke his dogged rhythm with an occasional flurry of jabs and hooks at the icy air.

It was different in the ring. Joe fizzed with ferocity, the punches careering into his hapless sparring partners with unerring force. He fought with a bristling intent which meant that no one could hold him at bay for long. When it was Emile's turn, the pace was sedate. He handled the journeymen lined up against him without any difficulty. Only Emile and Gil Clancy could see that his reflexes were more clogged. He still had the jab to measure the distance between him and his rivals but, once he had opened them up for a swift combination, it took Emile a split-second longer to spot the gap. He missed most chances to nail his sparring partner and simply went back to outjabbing him with superior technique and experience.

'The sharpness will come back against Nino,' Gil reassured him.

Emile wished Benvenuti no harm. The debonair and handsome Italian, whom people in boxing dubbed 'The Intellectual', was the son of a fisherman from the port of Trieste and, with his obvious intelligence and curiosity, he had developed a taste for literature and beautiful women. He could also box brilliantly and, during their first world title contest in April 1967, in *The Ring* magazine's eventual Fight of the Year, Benvenuti floored Griffith in round two. The champion got up and, in the fourth, he knocked down Benvenuti with an overhand right. Griffith had a glaring opportunity to stop the Italian but he was not fast enough and Benvenuti recovered. That failure to capitalise on a clear opening cost Griffith his title, and caused him weeks of misery. Life as a former champion seemed unbearable.

'I feel naked without my title,' Emile had said sadly. His disappointment accounted for his unusually tetchy mood in the build-up to the rematch five months later. Emile had watched film of the first fight over and over again, tormented by his fourth-round failure to stop Benvenuti. 'Stupid, stupid,' he'd wailed as the television footage played on a loop in his darkened hotel room.

'Are you going to give Benvenuti a good fight this time?' a reporter from the *Chicago Defender* asked before the rematch on 29 September 1967.

'No,' Emile growled. 'I'm going to make love to him. I'm going to put my arm around him and we'll waltz a little. What do you think?'

His irritability was rooted in the fact that he had trained harder for the second Benvenuti fight than he had done in years. Emile felt mean and on edge. It helped him in the ring at Shea Stadium in Queens, his old borough, and his conditioning made the difference as he regained his championship on points after sending The Intellectual toppling to the canvas in the fourteenth round.

The decider would be staged at the new Madison Square Garden on 4 March 1968, in a double bill, with Griffith fighting alongside Joe Frazier. It had been a wrench when they closed down the haunted old building where Benny Paret had fought his last fight exactly six years before. The Garden, an uptown venue on 8th Avenue and 50th Street, moved into Emile's midtown Manhattan turf, on Pennsylvania Plaza, stretching from 31st to 33rd Streets and between 7th and 8th Avenues. Teddy Brenner, the old matchmaker, was emphatic that Emile had to headline the opening night of boxing at the revamped Garden.

Griffith and Frazier would be paid $175,000 each – while Benvenuti was guaranteed $80,000 and Buster Mathis $75,000. Those fight purses made it plain who Brenner regarded as the real draws in New York.

Emile liked watching Joe spar in preparation for the most important fight of his emerging career. The heavyweight's opponent, Mathis, was also unbeaten, with a 23-0 résumé; but they shared a tangled rivalry. Joe had lost only one amateur fight in three years, between 1962 and 1964, and that defeat had been against Mathis. They had met again in the 1964 Olympic trials and, once more, Mathis stole the decision. 'All that fat boy did was run like a thief, hit me with a peck and backpedal like crazy,' Joe complained.

There was a change of luck in the end and, when Mathis was injured, Joe was called into the Olympic team for the Tokyo Games. He won heavyweight gold, despite breaking his thumb, but Joe still seethed that Mathis had beaten him in their two previous bouts. They would settle it in the Garden.

Everything had changed in heavyweight boxing. Muhammad Ali had been world champion for three years when, on 28 April 1967, he refused to be inducted into the US Army and drafted to fight as a soldier in Vietnam. Seven weeks later, on 20 June, Ali was convicted of draft evasion, sentenced to five years in prison and fined $10,000. Ali appealed successfully against the jail term but he was banned from boxing.

The World Boxing Association held a series of bouts to decide who would contest the title stripped from Ali. Joe refused to participate in the elimination tournament – out of loyalty to Ali. He was certain he could whip anyone they eventually put in front of him. Frazier against Mathis, in the meantime, had the makings of a grudge fight and the New York State Athletic Commission, as well as the boxing authorities in Maine and Massachusetts, declared that they would recognise the winner as the new world champion.

Joe would take care of Mathis and allow whoever wanted to call him the heavyweight champion of the world to go right ahead. It wouldn't take him long to wipe out every other contender. And then, one day, he and a returning Ali would make some real money together in a defining fight.

One of Frazier's closest friends, Gypsy Joe Harris, who would fight Emile later that year, started to call him 'Smoke' because of his blisteringly hot ring workouts. It was lengthened into a crackling nickname. Smokin' Joe Frazier was about to turn his fire onto Buster Mathis.

Emile and Joe had moved to Harlem from large families and contrasting backgrounds – the Deep South for Joe and the Virgin Islands for Emile. Joe's past was even more complicated because he was one of fourteen children, rather than a mere eight in Emile's family, and he suffered far more racism and impoverishment. Joe said in later years that, 'I was born into animosity, bigotry and hatred. We had water for white folks, and water for coloured folks.

White lines, black lines. I came from Beaufort in South Carolina and it was tougher than Georgia, Alabama and Mississippi. I had to work on the land from when I was seven. My parents really suffered back in them days.'

Frazier took the Greyhound bus, 'the dog', from the South to Harlem. He eventually ended up working in a Philadelphia slaughterhouse. 'I was the drain man. My job was to make sure the blood went down the drain. But sometimes, early in the morning, I'd go down that long rail of meat and work on my punching. That's how [Sylvester] Stallone got the same idea for *Rocky* – just like he used the story about me training by running up the steps of the museum in Philly. But he never paid me for none of my past. I only got paid for a walk-on part. *Rocky* is a sad story for me.'

Back in 1968, *Rocky* was not even a scintilla of an idea for a ham-fisted film. The first of the *Rocky* series was released in 1976 but, eight years earlier, Joe and Emile forged a more layered friendship. They were opposites in many ways, for Joe was a macho man and Emile was more like a future member of the Village People; but they were both fighters. Emile had already won five world titles as a boxer and so it didn't really matter that he was so much more effeminate than Joe. If you knew what it meant to kill a man with your fists, Joe reasoned, it didn't matter what you did in your personal life.

They were humble fighters, with simple needs and pleasures. Emile and Joe liked to win fights, make money, look after their families and sing songs as if they were great soul crooners.

The press were still fascinated, notwithstanding the restraints of the era, by Emile's love life. As he followed the world champion both before, during and after his victorious second fight against Benvenuti, Gilbert Rogin of *Sports Illustrated* revealed how the boxer was affected by a boyfriend. 'When a soulful young man, whom Griffith describes as his son, speaks, the fighter may be unexpectedly moved to tears,' Rogin wrote. '"The day of the fight I couldn't sleep," Griffith said when it was all over. "I tried but I was edgy. So I looked at TV all day. Cartoons, as usual. Then Madsu my son came in with the sneakers I was going to wear in the ring if it was raining. 'Fight until you drop,' Madsu said. Tears came into my eyes. I felt like fighting for the first time since ... my accident. I hate talking about it."

'He was referring to his third fight with Benny Paret, who died thereafter. Griffith was locked in a bathroom in the Sheraton-Tunney near LaGuardia airport, holding a drink in his right hand. His victory party was on the other side of the door. With his left hand Griffith picked a hair from Benvenuti's chest out of his teeth. It had been that kind of fight. "He was actually biting me in the ear in the ring," Griffith said, outraged. "Once he even pinched my butt and looked at me and laughed."'

Emile knew what to expect in their conclusive bout – as Joe did when he faced Mathis for a third time. Big Buster, who weighed forty pounds more than Smokin' Joe, spoke briefly at the final press conference. 'I'm very elated about this fight,' Mathis said. 'I don't know why he signed for it, but he did. He will regret it.'

Joe was far more riled by the smack talk dished out by Mathis' manager, Jimmy Iselin, who warned that, 'Frazier is too slow and too dumb to ever figure out a classy stylist like Buster. He's in for a whuppin'.'

Smokin' Joe didn't trade much in pre-fight rhetoric. He stared at Mathis and Iselin for a long time before turning to the microphones. 'I'm just pleased to be fightin' in the new Garden next to my friend and a great world champion in Emile Griffith,' Joe said politely. He then switched his brooding gaze back to his opponent. 'Your manager actin' as if he's gonna fight,' he said.

'I'll do my talking in the ring,' Mathis replied. 'I won't be a Cassius Clay ...'

Joe jabbed a finger in Iselin's direction. 'You doin' all the talkin'. You actin' like the big man. Now, when that bell rings and it's just me and him [Frazier nodded curtly at Mathis] ... who's gonna do the fightin'? We gonna learn a lot about all of us in the new Garden.'

*

The deepest lesson was learned in the penthouse lounge of a five-star Manhattan hotel late that night. Joe Frazier had been beaming, and singing sweatily up on stage, hollering into his microphone as if he really was the Godfather of Soul, when the band struck up the first notes of 'It's a Man's Man's Man's World'. It was a song that he and Emile Griffith both loved and Joe really believed he could sing it with just as much raw truth as James Brown had done in his seminal 1966 recording.

Emile stood alone in the furthest corner from the stage. If they had both been winners that night, Joe would have called Emile up on stage. They could have both cried out the words which tore at Emile in a way that he could never really explain to Joe. But the harsh truth had been embedded in Emile's face when, twenty minutes earlier, he'd hugged his friend and told him how happy he was that Joe had won.

Griffith had tried his heart out against Benvenuti. The fight had been even until the ninth round, when Benvenuti's stabbing left jab carved out an opening. He ripped in a big right hand that rocked Griffith and left him on the ropes. Another thunderous right unleashed a terrible storm in Griffith's head. He fell as if he had been stricken. Somehow, he dragged himself up. For the rest of the round, he clinched and backed away in a desperate attempt to avoid the knockout. All his experience and desire saved him.

Benvenuti dominated the next three rounds. Just before the bell rang to start the thirteenth, Gil Clancy urged his champion to find something deep within himself. Like a brave old warhorse driving himself on for one more great effort, Griffith responded, and in the championship rounds, as the last three were called, he poured out everything. He attacked Benvenuti with relentless body-punching. In round fifteen, The Intellectual's legs wobbled and his head dropped as Griffith tore into him.

The new Garden was turned into a roaring pit as Griffith's fans were matched by the huge contingent of Italian supporters, who chanted, '*Nee-no ... Nee-no ... Nee-no!*', as if sheer volume would keep

Benvenuti on his feet. They were still trading at the bell, with Benvenuti just holding off Griffith's surging assault.

It took a long time for the referee and two judges to check their scorecards. But, finally, they had a decision. Referee Johnny LoBianco and Frank Forbes both scored the fight 8-6, with one round even, in favour of Benvenuti. Al Berl had it 7-7, with one shared round, and he decided that the lone knockdown meant that Benvenuti should also get his verdict. Griffith had lost his world title on a narrow but unanimous decision.

Smokin' Joe Frazier had provided a much more conclusive ending – knocking out Mathis with his trademark left hook after a clubbing series of combinations.

There was a hushed pause before, on stage, Joe began to sing 'It's a Man's Man's Man's World' with his throatily rasping impression of James Brown. The heavyweight looked over at his forlorn friend, knowing that Emile had only come to the party for his sake. After such a devastating defeat, Emile had the look of a man who wished he could crawl away into an empty room. But, still, he had turned up to congratulate Joe on his victory. Joe felt humbled and emotional as he started to sing about a man's world – which would mean nothing without a woman or a girl.

Joe looked out into the hushed room and, even if he was not really a great singer, he found a grainy tone and texture in his voice as he sang directly to Emile. The words tumbled out of him and the ending was strangely chilling. After Joe had sung the chorus again, his hand stretched out to Emile and he crooned, almost conversationally, that he sympathised with a man 'who don't have a woman'. And then he sang the last two haunting lines again and again – about being lost in the wilderness, and in bitterness.

It was hard to tell whether tears, or just sweat, rolled down the face of Smokin' Joe Frazier.

After it was over, and Joe had flung down the microphone, he walked across the dancefloor to find his buddy. Smokin' Joe was as straight as the end of a sharpened axe, and he had no understanding of Emile's other life in a different world, but he felt only sympathy for his fallen friend.

Joe embraced Emile and held him close. 'You'll be back, champ,' he promised.

For the next fifteen minutes, until Emile finally made the lonely trip back to Weehawken, Joe never left his side. There were women who wanted to dance with him and men who wanted to pump his hand and slap his broad back. Joe made them all wait.

'You're a great fighter, champ,' he finally said as Emile stretched out his hand to say goodbye.

America felt an even lonelier country for Emile when, on a Thursday evening in New York, exactly a month to the day since he had lost his world title, he heard the shattering news. Just after 6 p.m. on 4 April 1968, at the Lorraine motel in Memphis, Martin Luther King was assassinated. He was shot by a middle-aged white man, James Earl Ray, who had planned his execution for weeks. Ray used a Remington rifle, which he had trained on King from a rooming house across the street. When hit by the single bullet, King had been standing on the balcony of his usual room, 306, at the Lorraine. He uttered his last words just moments before he was killed.

'Ben, make sure you play "Take My Hand, Precious Lord" at the meeting tonight,' King apparently said to the musician Ben Branch, who was due to perform after King spoke in Memphis that night. 'Play it real pretty.'

The bullet from Ray's gun smashed into King's face, breaking his jawbone and severing the jugular vein which leads from the head to the heart. The civil rights leader was rushed to St Joseph's hospital but, at 7.05 that evening, he was pronounced dead. He was thirty-nine years old.

The *Washington Afro-American* reported that King had predicted his tragic fate to his wife, Coretta. 'This is what is going to happen to me also,' King had supposedly said to her on the day, four-and-a-half years earlier, that John F. Kennedy had been assassinated. 'I keep telling you. This is a sick society.'

Emile didn't know how to do anything else for a living but fight and so, in June 1968, he went back out on the road. He was due to meet a seasoned pro in Andy Heilman, who had lost only three of his forty-three bouts, in Oakland, California, on 7 June. Two nights before the fight, alone in his hotel room, Emile watched television. The local channels all focused on the likelihood that Robert F. Kennedy, JFK's younger brother, who had just swept to victory in the California and South Dakota primaries, would run for president later that year. Bobby Kennedy looked like he was on his way to the White House.

Gil Clancy checked on Emile just before 10 p.m. and suggested he get a good night's sleep. He needed to be rested and ready for Heilman who, at the age of twenty-nine, clearly saw a surprise victory over Griffith as his path to the big time.

'Lights out, champ,' Gil said.

Emile was tired and yet he slept fitfully. He felt dispirited and alone, bereft of his title and drifting from one fight to the next, from one boy to another. Weariness and regret trailed him.

He climbed out of bed early the next morning and, in a reflex gesture, snapped on the television. It would be better watching a few cartoons while he waited for Clancy to arrive and check on his weight.

Emile stared blearily at the screen. He was still on the news channel and, before he could flip over to the cartoons, the latest American nightmare unfolded.

Bobby Kennedy had been gunned down at the Ambassador hotel in Los Angeles. It was the same hotel where Emile had stayed on the night that Davey Moore had lapsed into a coma; the same hotel where Emile had nursed the loss of his welterweight title against Luis Rodriguez. He remembered how he had cried as he packed his suitcase silently and headed out of the Ambassador and flew straight home to New York.

Emile sat on the edge of his bed in a more modest hotel in Oakland. He watched the news of the latest American tragedy. Bobby Kennedy had been shot just after midnight. Four hours after the election polls had closed, he was declared the winner of the California primary. He had addressed his jubilant campaign supporters in the Empire Ballroom of the hotel and, being hustled to a press conference so that his quotes could be included in the final morning editions, his aides had taken a shortcut through the kitchen of the Ambassador. It was then, just as he walked down a narrow corridor flanked by an ice machine and followed by a large group of people, that Kennedy was hit.

Sirhan Sirhan, a 24-year-old Palestinian from Jordan, had stepped out from behind the ice machine and aimed his small-calibre revolver right at Kennedy in anger at his support of Israel. Three bullets ripped into Kennedy before the men around the senator leaped at Sirhan and brought him down. One of that group was George Plimpton, the writer who had helped found *The Paris Review*, and who was renowned for his participatory brand of sports journalism. Plimpton, in one of many attempts to convey the painful difficulty of elite sport, had sparred three rounds with Sugar Ray Robinson and Archie Moore for *Sports Illustrated*. He helped pin down Sirhan while the gunman was stripped of his weapon.

Early that morning Kennedy lay close to death at the Good Samaritan hospital on Wilshire Boulevard. Doctors had carried out emergency brain surgery for three hours – but the prognosis was bleak. The most damaging bullet had entered his head just behind his right ear, while he had also been struck in the neck and an armpit.

Finally, twenty-six hours after he had been shot, Bobby Kennedy died at 1.44 a.m. on 6 June 1968.

Griffith's bout against Heilman was postponed to Tuesday 11 June. Death stalked so many of his nights in the ring.

It was not easy motivating himself for a twelve-round non-title fight, with the country in turmoil. Griffith performed fitfully, but the gulf in their abilities was mirrored in two scorecards which gave him victory over Heilman by 8-4 and 8-3, with one round even. The referee, Vern Bybee, somehow scored it as a draw but, in a majority decision, Griffith had racked up the fifty-fifth win of his career.

Emile did not celebrate that night. He went back to the hotel and, with Gil and Syd Martin, caught the red-eye early the following morning to New York and the old Idlewild airport, which had since had its name changed to honour the first of the Kennedy brothers to have been assassinated. Every flag at John F. Kennedy International airport had been lowered. The country was in mourning; and so too was Emile Griffith, a lost and lonely soul to whom even winning had become a joyless exercise.

Freddie Wright loved Emile as a friend, as a brave and inspirational man whose life was shrouded by difficulty and sadness. He knew that Emile's existence as a gay man was framed by constant secrecy and evasion, which meant he lived an essentially melancholic life studded by moments of outrageous happiness. Emile was still a sucker for craziness. He liked wearing pink suits and clubbing all night in the seediest joints he, Freddie and Calvin could find. Emile seemed child-like in his bubbling pleasure and joy, then, only to retreat into the tangled repudiations of his sexuality as soon as he was in the conventional world.

The double life he led, as an ageing former world champion boxer and a gay black man caught between the hedonism and repression of homosexuality in late 1960s America, tore at him. It was impossible for Emile to live a balanced and serene life. He also struggled living alone, even if he resorted to surrounding himself with five dogs in his apartment, and so Freddie and Calvin made sure they kept him company. It was one of the reasons why Freddie didn't fuck around with either of his friends. He could get plenty of sex elsewhere. His friendship with his fellow Times Square musketeers was too important to squander.

Anonymous sex, with a passing stranger, was easy to find. They all got off on the grimy thrill and, even if it felt empty afterwards, the lack of emotional intimacy stripped away the complications. The passing hunk was gone and quickly forgotten. But as ordinary human beings, as men who just happened to be gay, they all yearned for something deeper and more lasting. Relationships were hard, just as they were for straight couples, but the difficulties were increased by the illegality of any gay partnership.

Police harassment and entrapment of homosexual men continued even as the free-sex revolution exploded across America. Civil rights advocates acted with increasing authority and belief while, in 1968, the first national gathering of women's liberation movements was held – in Chicago. Black Americans, and women all over the US, rose up against repression. Yet the clampdown on homosexuality remained stringent.

Pete Hamill, who had written so eloquently about Benny Paret and Emile Griffith as a columnist for the *New York Post*, addressed the inequities of a typical entrapment and interviewed the wife of a man arrested in a bathhouse. Hamill was straight, and married, but he despised injustice and deceit – whether it was evident in a boxing ring or a bathhouse. He described the entrapment in stark detail.

An undercover policeman, stripped down to his underwear, moaned theatrically as he clutched at his groin. He seemed distressed and a forty-year-old man, who worked in the city as a tailor, turned to him anxiously and asked if he was ill or in need of any help. That simple approach resulted in the tailor being arrested for attempting to solicit the attention of another man. The ensuing shame and uncertainty about the tailor's future was obvious – but Hamill described the sobbing of the man's devastated wife in a way that undermined the police department's claim that they were carrying out 'a necessary public service'. He concentrated on the despair of a woman who felt desperate that her husband, whom she considered to be a good and kind man, had been entrapped and seemingly ruined by the threat of a jail sentence.

Amid such oppression the idea of Emile coming out in public as a gay man would not just have invited disbelief. It would have been a criminal act which could have resulted in his imprisonment. Freddie, who was not famous or lauded, could be open in ways denied to Emile; and so he never judged his friend's avoidance of the truth. Instead, he understood the vulnerability of Emile. He even understood why Emile was so overjoyed when, just a few days after he returned from Oakland, he was reunited with Matthew.

His old boyfriend had pulled out of a planned marriage to the woman for whom he had left Emile. Matthew turned up, unexpectedly, at the Weehawken apartment on a sultry Friday evening. Emile thought Matthew looked gorgeous and he struggled to stop himself from crying when his lost lover kissed him.

'I'm back, Poppyman,' Matthew said, convinced that Emile would never turn him away. He was right. The old champion had been floored all over again.

The year 1969 was meant to be lucky. Emile and Freddie knew gay men in New York who were convinced that they would finally experience freedom from fear and repression. It was, according to the Chinese calendar, the Year of the Rooster. They cackled over that one. The Year of the Cock would be an unforgettable year. Even those two digits, 69, had worked as a gay sex code. Sixty-nine belonged to them, signifying two men performing oral sex on each other simultaneously, and so it was easier to feel lighter and more hopeful about a new year at the very end of an increasingly dangerous decade.

There had been assassinations and ring deaths, the fear of nuclear apocalypse and Communist infiltration in Cuba and Vietnam, and yet there had also been an explosion of defiance and liberty. People wanted to have sex and get stoned. They wanted to be free from conformity and consumerism. 'Free love' and 'let it all hang out' were meaningless mantras, but a wider rebellion ripped up the straight-laced compliance and submission of the 1950s. Men grew long hair and slipped into hip-huggers. They wore jangling jewellery and flowery clothes. Women burned their bras and let hair sprout on their legs and under their arms.

That blurring of sexuality was especially evident in music as Mick Jagger, Marc Bolan and David Bowie cultivated androgyny and flirted with bisexuality – while Lou Reed, with the Velvet Underground, wrote songs about transvestites, heroin and sex as an integral part of Andy Warhol's Factory where Mario Montez and Candy Darling were his cross-dressing queens.

On Broadway, *Hair*, which had opened as a musical in April 1968, was in the midst of a run of 1,750 performances. It celebrated, in the form of its hippie anthem, 'the dawning of the Age of Aquarius' as a time of 'harmony and understanding'. There was a clear allusion to a celebration of homosexuality. In Greek mythology, Ganymede was the most beautiful boy on earth and Zeus, the decidedly macho supreme god of the Greeks, could not resist him. He seized and transported Ganymede back to Olympus where Hera, Zeus's consort, was so jealous of the boy that she plotted against him. Yet Zeus ensured that Ganymede would remain immortal by turning him into a constellation called Aquarius. The Age of Aquarius had since become an astrological term – which meant nothing to Emile and Freddie. They were happier just talking about the Year of the Cock.

Hypocrisy and violence still undermined New York. In a public park in Kew Gardens, a quiet middle-class area of Queens, late-night cruising had become a regular event. As bathhouses were crawling with cops, and bars and clubs kept being raided, stealthy fun among the trees and bushes began to occur after midnight. The neighbourhood men of Kew Gardens formed a vigilante group to hunt down the queers of Queens in a concerted effort 'to protect our wives and children'.

Few women and no children were seen in the darkened park after midnight. The gay men who took an illicit stroll through the woodland area had no interest in meeting any ladies or kids. They were looking only for a fleeting male encounter in the black woods. Some of the cruisers conceded that they understood a secluded neighbourhood's disquiet at the fact that sex was being pursued in one of their prettier parks at the dead of night. But the vigilantes of Kew Gardens acted more personally.

A group of forty men, carrying sticks and walkie-talkies as if they were soldiers rather than middle-aged husbands and dads, stalked the park at night. They shone torches into bushes and behind trees and spoke excitedly into crackling radios to coordinate their efforts to catch a faggot or two. When they did flush out a couple of cruisers, the Kew bruisers were surprised. The gay men did not run away. Many of them looked into the blazing torchlights and asserted their right to be in a public place. The disputes turned ugly.

Gay men continued to use the park at night, in defiance of the neighbourhood mob. The vigilantes returned with saws and axes. They hacked at the trees, chopping them down in concentrated fury as they razed the woodland area to the ground. Concerned neighbours tried to stop the carnage. One man was attacked with an axe. The police were called but, on arrival, they just chatted to the vigilantes and watched them cut down the trees. By the end of the night they had driven all the gay men away. Their own park was decimated.

Elsewhere in the city, the NYPD was hard at work. In June 1969, five gay bars had been raided in Greenwich Village and three of them, Tel-Star, The Sewer and Checkerboard, were forced to close permanently. Freddie had often taken Emile and Calvin to Tel-Star because, still being a 'Village girl' at heart, he liked enticing his friends out of Times Square so that they could sample diverse attractions around Christopher Street, Waverly Place and the suitably named Gay Street.

On their way to Tel-Star, Freddie had confronted Emile gently about Matthew. Freddie was convinced that Matthew was ripping off his generous friend. The relationship seemed doomed as they bickered.

'What's the deal with this kid?' Freddie asked Emile.

Emile turned stony. 'That's my business, Freddie,' he said.

Freddie nodded. 'You're right,' he said.

He resolved to say nothing more, even if it pained him to see his friend being conned. It felt better to make Emile laugh and take him to Tel-Star without Matthew.

That option, in the summer of '69, was gone. Freddie had seen it all before – whether heartbreak or a police raid. He had been working for a while as a go-go boy at the Stonewall Inn, on Christopher Street, the only gay bar in town where it was permissible to dance. The mob ownership of Stonewall, and the Mafia's links with the police, secured that dancing licence. But it did not prevent Stonewall from also being invaded by the cops on Tuesday 24 June. Freddie was happy it had been on his night off. He was not afraid. He would dance on a metal stand and shake his mamba again at Stonewall that very weekend.

Stonewall Inn, 51-53 Christopher Street, Greenwich Village, New York, Saturday 28 June 1969

Midnight had come and gone. Friday night had been swallowed up and the Stonewall Inn was heaving with men in the early hours of that steamy Saturday morning. Freddie Wright was happy to be wearing only a tiny G-string as he raised his lean and sinewy black arms high above his head. He could feel sweat rolling down his bare, shimmering skin as, staying true to his promise, he shook his scantily clad mamba while he danced frenetically on the go-go stand at the front of the first dance-floor.

Freddie, the most popular go-go boy at Stonewall, was the dancer everyone saw once they had made it past 'Blond Frankie', who studied every new visitor from behind a slatted window carved into an imposing double wooden door. The muscular bouncer had worked at gay bars across New York and it was said that he never forgot a face. Blond Frankie, whose real name was Frank Esselourne, had a knack of spotting an undercover cop who might be trying to get into Stonewall for a night of entrapment. He would stress that Stonewall was a members-only club and send the disguised cop on his way. A retaliatory raid might happen a night or two later, but the police would usually have tipped off 'Fat Tony' Lauria, who had turned the Stonewall restaurant into a gay bar in 1966.

Fat Tony was a small-time mobster. His father, Ernie, was the real mafioso. Ernie Lauria operated among the high ranks of the mob and he affected a veneer of respectability. He had sent Fat Tony to a Catholic prep school, but that choice had not done him much good. Ernie was disgusted that his son seemed high on drugs most of the time and had opened a fag bar.

At least Fat Tony and his co-owners, including Ernie Sgroi, were making a sizeable profit from the Stonewall. Sgroi, whose father Ernie Sr ran the Bon Soir, the gay club where Barbra Streisand sang so often, chose his staff cleverly. Apart from Blond Frankie, the Stonewall was kept under control by its formidable manager, Ed Murphy, also known as 'The Skull'.

A very fat, bald man, whose grey beard was matched by his grey suit, The Skull's sinister Buddha-like presence was enough to keep everyone in check. He rarely had to say much to make his point as, seated at his usual table, he sent a glaring warning to anyone trying to pull a fast one.

The only way of getting into Stonewall was via a nod from Blond Frankie or The Skull. If Blond Frankie didn't like someone, or he remembered 'a bad face' from a previous encounter, the wooden door stayed shut. Once it swung open, the bouncer ensured that all visitors signed the 'members book' to gain entry. No one used their real name and, instead, Stonewall seemed full of gay men called Mickey Mouse, Frank Sinatra, Donald Duck, Elizabeth Taylor, Charlie Brown, Dorothy Friend and Judy Garland.

More members than usual were called 'Judy Garland' that weekend because a few days earlier, on 22 June 1969, the actress had died of a drug overdose in London. Her body had been flown back to New York, and on Thursday 26 June over 20,000 people, many of them gay men who regarded her as an inspiration, had walked past her coffin at a funeral home in Manhattan. Signing in as 'Judy

Garland' at the Stonewall that Friday night and Saturday morning was just another way of paying tribute to the woman who, as a girl, had played Dorothy and worn those sparkly red shoes while singing 'Somewhere Over the Rainbow'.

Ever since *The Wizard of Oz* had first been screened, in 1939, gay men had referred to themselves as 'friends of Dorothy' – warmed by her affection for the lost and rejected, like the Scarecrow, the Tin Man and the Cowardly Lion who, living a lie, finally admitted that, 'I'm afraid there's no denyin', I'm just a dandy lion ...' In the daffodil and dandelion dens of gay New York, as homosexual bars were tagged in the city's press, there was always a place for Judy Garland and her forsaken boys.

Inside Stonewall, all the walls were painted black – some said it was Fat Tony's way of hiding the dirt. The windows were covered by black drapes. Even the floor was black, sticky with spilt drinks and body fluids, while it was so dark behind the two bar counters that none of the customers seemed to notice there was no running water. A tub of warm water was brought in from outside at the start of each night – but it turned grey and cold long before midnight as glasses were given a grimy rinse every now and then. Stonewall dysentery was a nasty side effect for some of the inn's unluckier members.

No one cared much just before one in the morning as Freddie danced frenetically. On the second and far larger dance-floor, deeper in the bar, other go-go boys strutted around in glittering steel cages. Freddie liked the freedom of dancing without bars. He was proud that everyone saw him first and that he danced to an audience of young men who were white, black, Hispanic and Asian. There were drag queens and trannies, lesbians and straight girls, but, mostly, it was gay men who lived rough and partied hard. Some of the homeless street kids sneaked in so they could get a few drinks for free, while young hippies, working-class men and hustlers made up the majority of the crowd. Freddie liked Stonewall because, unlike Julius' around the corner, that fancy gay restaurant for the famous and middle-aged, he danced to a mixed and noisy crowd.

Maggie Jiggs, one of New York's best-known transvestites, ran the bar, where the drinks were cheap, if watered down. Whenever there was a brief lull in the music, Maggie would yell out something crudely amusing: 'Hey, girl, I hear you got a new plate of false teeth from that fabulous dentist you been fucking!'

Freddie was impressed most by Storme DeLarverie – the drag king of Stonewall. Storme dominated the jukebox area of the bar as a member of the Jewel Box Revue, which regularly went on tour and consisted of a dozen men dressed beautifully and seductively as women – and one biological female. Storme, wearing a top hat and tuxedo, introduced the girls one by one and invited the whooping audience to pick out the one real Jewel Box woman. Unless they had seen the Revue before, no one got it right. They pointed at any one of the glamorous girls, thinking that she had to be a woman, only to be stunned when the truth was revealed. The girls were all men. Only Storme looked like a man. He spoke like a man. He moved liked a man. Storme even scowled and scratched like a man. As the audience screamed in disbelief, she confirmed she was a fiercely butch lesbian. Storme DeLarverie was the best gender-bender in the business.

Storme and Freddie had become close friends. He regularly accompanied her to the only lesbian bar in the Village, for Freddie liked hanging out with smart and funny people. The best go-go boy in Stonewall was open to meeting anyone who had a good brain and a big heart. Storme had both, even if she, or 'he' as even Freddie called him, could be scary. No one messed with Storme – who sang with a husky baritone when he did his male impersonations. Unlike the drag queens, who always impersonated famous women, Storme the drag king was always himself.

Freddie was still dancing on his stand, as Storme stalked the jukebox floor, when the raid began at 1.20 a.m. Plain-clothes policemen from the First Division Morals Squad banged on the double doors. 'Police!' yelled their leader, Deputy Inspector Seymour Pine. 'We're taking the place!'

Blond Frankie knew that the NYPD's Sixth Precinct received a $2,000 weekly pay-off from Fat Tony and the boys. They could afford it when Stonewall raked in almost twelve grand over a busy weekend. The two-grand bribe was always enough to ensure that there would be a tip-off a few minutes before a raid. Blond Frankie would give a signal to The Skull and the searing white lights would be turned on in warning. There would be just long enough to tone it down and hide the drugs. This time, however, there had been no phone call.

Pine and his boys poured past the bouncer into the first dance room. They got an eyeful of Freddie Wright writhing and gyrating before, in the middle of a rhythmic beat, the music cut off and the lights blazed on.

Pine and his officers spread out quickly. 'C'mon, you bunch of faggots,' one of the policemen shouted, 'up against the wall.'

It was the typical routine. A search for drugs was followed by an examination of the transvestites. Anyone who gave some lip would be taken away for a night in the cells. The atmosphere, however, was different. The more abusive the police became, the more belligerent the reaction. Whether it was the mood after Kew Gardens and the latest crackdown on gay bars in the Village, or the death of Judy Garland, something stirred in the sweaty dive of Stonewall.

'Move out of my way,' a policeman sneered at Storme DeLarverie as he went to check the transvestite-girl IDs.

'I'm not moving,' the drag king said. 'This is my job ... and you're disrespecting me.'

Freddie almost whooped up on his stand. He loved the way that Storme, the daughter of a white man and a black mother in New Orleans, lingered over her clearly enunciated use of 'disrespecting'.

The policeman shot back some crude insults. He, plainly, did not know he was dealing with a woman as he railed against Storme being a 'fucking faggot' and a 'goddamn queer'.

Storme would not back down and the policeman cursed. The drag king then nailed the cop with a blow that made Freddie yelp. It was the kind of punch that would have impressed Emile Griffith, the champion of them all in Stonewall and every other gay bar across town.

At last, Freddie thought, a cop got back what he gave. Storme, like Emile in the ring, had decided to fight.

Chaos broke out across both dance-floors. The police were yelling and swearing, but Storme was defiant. She would not back down. The cop rubbed his bruised mouth and then, glaring and spitting in anger, he reached for his handcuffs. Two other officers pushed Storme roughly down on a table, just a few feet from Freddie's bare feet, and cuffed the lesbian's hands behind her back.

Storme was still yakking away, telling the cops to stop 'disrespecting' her and inciting the transvestites around her to holler in support.

Pine, as the officer in charge, was taken aback by the sheer gumption. Normally a gay crowd melted away meekly in an effort to avoid arrest. But the Stonewall crowd was dangerously provocative. His efforts to disperse the masses and to send the least offensive kids out of the bar were resisted.

'We ain't going,' a young gay man said quietly. 'You can't make us . . .'

His friend next to him shouted at Pine. 'We've had enough of this . . .'

'Enough of what?' Pine said threateningly, jangling his cuffs. He felt ready to arrest the whole lot of them.

Pine's aim, to target Fat Tony and the Stonewall owners by finding a haul of drugs big enough to shut down the joint, had become messy. He didn't like the mood of this crowd. They were mocking and heckling. He decided it would be best to get the hulk who had hit one of his men before things turned even nastier.

Freddie had clambered down from his stand in an effort to reach Storme. He was blocked by Pine while three of the cops wrestled with Storme. They finally got him off the dance-floor, while Pine and two other policemen cuffed three vocal transvestites.

A crowd had gathered on Christopher Street as news spread of the raid and the altercation inside. Queens and transvestites yelled at the policemen who had been called as back-up – either taunting them with exaggerated wit or shouting out good-humoured backing for their boyfriends and girlfriends inside. There was no threat of violence as the curious spectators waited to see what would happen next.

It was only when Storme was dragged out of the club, fighting all the way, that people began to realise that something surprising had occurred.

'Leave him alone, pigs!' a gay man shouted.

'Get the fuck out of the way, faggots,' one of the sweating cops snarled as he grappled with Storme.

'Let her go, let him go,' the crowd chanted. 'Let her go, let him go!'

'Love you, Storme!' someone else yelled.

The treatment of Storme became rougher as they hauled him towards a police car; and the crowd's humour soured. There was anger and defiance when Storme was hit over the head by a club. He swore at the cop and the crowd roared.

Pine ordered the paddy wagon and three police cars, filled with arrested dancers from Stonewall, to 'get the hell away' before a riot broke out. They were just forcing Storme into the last car when a Stonewall regular called Gino, a working-class gay man from Puerto Rico, picked up a cobblestone. Gino hurled the huge stone and it landed on the trunk of a police car.

Storme escaped and the crowd felt emboldened. 'Let's get 'em!' someone cried and the gay men and transvestites, the lesbians and gender-benders stormed the police in homage to Storme and Stonewall.

Even the back-up police were overwhelmed as scuffles between irate gay men and bewildered cops spilled out of the club and onto the street. There was violence everywhere as the police lashed out in desperation. Dave Van Ronk, the famous folk singer and a straight man who had been passing with two girlfriends, was knocked down, kicked and handcuffed by the NYPD as they tried to restore order.

They were helpless against a crowd who unleashed decades of anger in a single night. Bottles and coins were hurled at the policemen.

As Pine bellowed at his men to retreat, the crowd blocked the paddy wagon and the police cars. They ignored the blaring sirens and began to rock the wagon and the cars. Someone used a knife to slash the tyres of the vehicle that had been reserved for Storme. The policemen looked terrified.

Pine had no option. He and his men raced back inside the Stonewall Inn, where they barricaded themselves until they were rescued by all the forces the Sixth Precinct could send.

Freddie Wright, still wearing nothing but his G-string, watched them disappear inside the gay bar. On the street outside he stared back at the crowd, the lost and the damned of New York City. Freddie did not know whether to laugh or cry with pride. His people were fighting back as if the spirit of Emile Griffith, a five-time world champion, had entered every one of them.

The Stonewall riots spread across New York. They lasted six days, as gay men, lesbians, transvestites and transsexuals took to the streets to protest against oppression and police brutality. There were marches and demonstrations, pitched battles with police and fierce confrontations with homophobes.

'We'll never be the same again,' Freddie Wright, the go-go king of Stonewall said simply. 'Everything's changed now. We're out – and we're proud.'

CHAPTER FOURTEEN

Wedding Fever

Mercedes Donastorg's red hot pants emitted so much heat they were practically smoking. They stunned Emile because he was a hot pants connoisseur. When he strutted around in a shimmering pair he got so many wolf whistles and catcalls it made him feel like he was the king and the queen of the hotties. Everything changed on the night he saw Mercedes, or Sadie as she was called, in sultry hot pants on the dance-floor at Bambousay, a nightclub in Charlotte Amalie, on the island of St Thomas.

Sadie was young, beautiful and very raunchy. She had a pretty face, gorgeous coffee-coloured skin, an amazing body and a radiant smile. She was an even better dancer than Emile – a fact which shocked him as much as her hot pants. Emile walked over, quickly, to introduce himself. Sadie knew he was the most famous man from the Virgin Islands and, not long out of her teens, she could not resist him easily.

Two nights earlier, on 17 October 1970, Emile had outpointed Danny Perez over twelve rounds at the Lionel Roberts Stadium in Charlotte Amalie. He was on a winning five-fight roll after a year earlier, to the very night, he had failed to win back the world welterweight title from Jose Napoles. The drop down in weight, to the division where he had made his name, was too hard to negotiate successfully in his early thirties and he had lost a unanimous decision to Napoles, yet another Cuban champion.

Emile had no thoughts of boxing as he danced with Sadie. He loved the way she looked, as sensual as she was languid, and he remembered that he liked girls too. They danced to soca and soul, to calypso and funk, and Sadie moved so effortlessly it seemed surprising that her skin gleamed with a sheen of perspiration. Eventually, the dance-floor cleared as she did a limbo dance that defied belief, bending backwards so far and so low as she inched her way beneath a burning bar that the rammed club roared. Emile led the celebrations and, finally, whisked her away to a dark corner.

'Tell me about yourself,' he said. Sadie, being so young and happy, allowed a short life story to tumble out of her. She had grown up in Charlotte Amalie before, while still in grade school, she had moved with her family to New York. Sadie had eventually become a professional dancer, working with the June Taylor Dancers, who opened and closed *The Ed Sullivan Show* on CBS every Sunday night. But she had come back home for good because she missed island life.

Emile clapped his hands in delight. She had danced on *The Ed Sullivan Show*; he had sung on *The Ed Sullivan Show*. Clearly, they were made for each other.

'Will you marry me?' he asked.

Sadie's eyes opened wide in amazement. 'You got to be kidding,' she said. 'You don't even know me.'

'No, no,' Emile exclaimed. 'That's what I want. I want you. I want to marry you.'

Sadie didn't say 'yes', then; but she didn't say 'never', either. Emile told her he would be back, as soon as he had taken care of some business back home, and had dispatched his next opponent. He didn't tell Sadie that he needed to break up with his boyfriend, too, before he could ask her again to marry him. Emile had been in that prickly conundrum before. He had once warned Matthew that he was thinking of marrying Esther and an almighty squabble had broken out. Emile had never really wanted to marry Esther; but, this time, it felt different. He decided he would explain everything to Matthew, calmly and firmly, as soon as he got back from boxing Nate Collins in Daly City, near San Francisco.

He had shocked himself with his proposal to Sadie. Emile had always been an impulsive and often reckless man. He was neither introspective nor analytical, and so he allowed many of his choices to be shaped by his mood. Emile had been in a deep funk for a long time. His usual sunny outlook had darkened in recent years. The rigours of boxing marked him more deeply with every fight and he felt worn down by the same old problems. Gay America had begun to liberate itself, but Emile remained tightly shackled.

The fight game was not the Stonewall Inn; and his family could not be defied as fiercely as the NYPD had been challenged by the cross-dressing and gay rebels of the Village. Boxing was as conservative and macho as always. His mother was still controlling and manipulative; Franklin was just as angry and judgemental; and Matthew caused him familiar grief. Even as America finally began to change, it seemed as if Emile was doomed to remain locked in the same old puzzle. He wanted a way out. He wanted peace at last.

Emile had spoken about marriage often enough with Esther, but he had never uttered the word with any conviction. It felt different with Sadie. She seemed so full of hope and light that he thought she might help him discover his old delight in life. He didn't think for long about whether it was possible for a gay man to live happily as a straight husband with a much younger woman. Emile just plunged in and trusted that, with Sadie, he would free himself from Matthew, Emelda, Franklin and the pain of his double life. He decided all this within an hour of seeing Sadie for the first time in his chaotic life.

Emile was due to fly to California on Saturday 7 November 1970, and he stayed home on Friday night while Matthew went out drinking. He was woken early that morning by Matthew and his buddies kicking up a racket in the living room. They were playing seven-card stud poker and arguing between hands. Emile got out his suitcase and began packing for his latest trip. He might as well head out to the airport to escape the noise and, as soon as he was back from the West Coast, he would tell Matthew it was time.

A shot suddenly reverberated around the apartment. There was a cry and a brief muffled silence. Emile ran to the living room. He saw Matthew holding a .38 revolver, his face drained of blood, while he stared at a kid, Monseratte Deloen, who had fallen onto the leopard-print couch. He was bleeding but conscious; and Matthew was crying.

'It was an accident,' he whimpered to Emile. 'I didn't know it was loaded.'

Emile moved quickly. He called for an ambulance and the police. The wounded boy would be all right, but Emile knew he had to report the shooting. The kid was taken away to hospital and Emile raised the bail to keep Matthew out of prison. He also accepted a $1,000 bail fee to act as a material witness.

A strange calm settled over him when he flew to San Francisco on a later flight that night. Emile would be spared an agonising conversation about Sadie with his reckless boyfriend. Matthew had gone too far this time, even if the police had indicated that he would probably escape with a warning and avoid jail. That certainty soothed Emile. It almost felt as if fate had cleared a path for him to turn away from his chaotic old life and find himself anew with Sadie.

Three nights later, on Tuesday 10 November, he boxed beautifully to outpoint Collins while earning a modest $12,500 purse. Emile knew that everything had changed in the middleweight division. On the night of the shooting, Nino Benvenuti and Carlos Monzon, a beast of a fighter from Argentina, had met in Rome. It turned out to be 1970's Fight of the Year, and Monzon had won the title on a bloody TKO.

Emile was sorry for Nino, but their friendship had complicated matters. Nino had been avoiding another fight with him. Monzon was different. Clancy had already called Monzon's manager and had been assured that, once a rematch with Benvenuti was won, the new champion would fight Emile for the WBA and WBC world middle-weight titles.

By the time he arrived home a few days later, the apartment had been cleaned. Matthew was waiting, all packed up and ready to leave. At least the kid had the decency to wait for Emile to get back to say goodbye. The boy who had been shot had agreed not to press charges and Matthew was free. He told Emile that, at twenty-eight, it was time he finally grew up. Matthew had decided to get back together again with his former girlfriend. She would help straighten him out.

Emile felt a sudden ache as he embraced Matthew. They had been together, on and off, for ten years. It had been a crazy time, and full of love too. Emile did not explain that he was taking the same route, into the arms of a woman, in a bid to change himself too.

'Okay, champ,' Emile said softly as he kissed Matthew on the forehead. 'You take care . . .'

'You too, Poppyman,' Matthew said, knowing that it was finally over.

Sadie Donastorg might have been the hottest dancer in Charlotte Amalie but she was also a respectable schoolteacher with strong values. She refused to be swept away on the next plane back to New York City. The very idea of marriage still made her laugh and flush at the dizzying speed with which Emile had moved. Sadie wanted to be wooed before she would even consider his crazy proposal.

Emile flew back and forth to St Thomas, in between fights, and it made him proud to tell everyone he was visiting his future wife. Deep down, the idea of falling in love with a woman, even the lovely Sadie, terrified him. Gil and Howie were thrilled, especially after the shooting fiasco, that he had finally met a girl he wanted to marry. Their happiness proved how much they wanted him to give up his Times Square life.

Chubby Checker, his mommy, was different. She was convinced he was making a terrible mistake. It didn't matter that Emile's new sweetheart was an island girl. She sounded like trouble. Emelda screamed at Junior in the hope that he would come to his senses and not do anything so crazy.

All his lingering doubts, when Emile was away from Sadie and being berated by his mother, or tempted by a night out at a gay strip bar like Stella's, on 47th Street, disappeared on St Thomas. Sadie was one of the stars of a dance revue called Prince Edward & His Slave Girls. She was the sexiest Slave Girl on the island and Emile loved watching her before he took her to Bambousay for even more serious dancing.

Emile was travelling to the Caribbean so often that Gil and Howie, working hard to get him a shot at Monzon, decided he had better combine fighting with love-making. They arranged a bout for him at the Lionel Roberts Stadium on 5 March 1971. His sparring partner, Juan Ramos, was persuaded to step into the ring. Emile went easy on him until, yearning to go clubbing with Sadie, he brought an end to the virtual exhibition by stopping Ramos in the seventh round.

Late that night, Sadie gave him the news for which he had been waiting. 'Yes,' she said; and 'yes' again. She would move to New York; and she would become his wife. Emile was suddenly certain of everything. He yearned to be a family man. He longed to be calm and ordinary at last.

There was nothing serene or normal about the Fight of the Century when, three nights later, on 8 March 1971, Joe Frazier met Muhammad Ali at Madison Square Garden. Ali's record stood at 31-0, with Frazier's an equally flawless 26-0. The bad blood between them was dark and poisonous.

Ali had been in the wilderness for three long years as he remained true to his principles. 'I will face machine-gun fire before denouncing Elijah Muhammad and the religion of Islam,' he insisted.

Broke and vilified, and banned from the ring, Ali had often phoned Frazier, his eventual replacement as world champion. 'Ali would be calling every other day,' Frazier recalled years later. 'He'd say, "You got my title, man! You got to let me fight you!"'

Frazier regarded Ali as a friend, as well as a future rival with whom he could make millions of dollars. They were both black men, who had suffered in different ways, and Frazier was sorry for Ali. He loaned him some money and even requested a meeting with President Richard Nixon at the White House. The heavyweight champion of the world wielded such power at the start of the 1970s.

Nixon listened carefully while walking the champion around the presidential garden. Frazier made their exchange sound very simple. 'I said to Nixon: "I want you to give Ali his licence back. I want to beat him up for you." Nixon said, "Sure, I'd like that." He knew what he was doing and Ali got his licence back.'

Ali returned to the ring on 26 October 1970. He had been banned for three years, seven months and four days, but his slashing fists were still fast enough to cut open Jerry Quarry's face and force a third-round stoppage in Atlanta.

Oscar Bonavena was next, less than two months later, and the Argentinian helped fill the Garden by calling Ali a *maricón*. Ali admitted to a group of British sportswriters after the fight that he had persuaded Bonavena to use the Benny Paret slur as a way to sell more tickets. Bonavena, a wayward fighter, was lucky he had Gil Clancy in his corner. But it was a dull affair until the fifteenth round, when Ali knocked down Bonavena three times to win by a TKO.

The victory secured Ali his coveted shot at the title. Interest in his fight against Frazier was so vast that both men were paid $2.5 million, and Ali set to work in an effort to upset Smokin' Joe. As easy as it was to love Ali, as the bravest, funniest and most significant sportsman of the twentieth century, he was cruel. Demeaning Frazier as 'flat-nosed' and 'backward', as a gorilla and an Uncle Tom, Ali's banter was malevolent.

Initially, Ali was amusing. 'Joe Frazier is too ugly to be champ. He's too dumb to be champ. The heavyweight champion should be smart and pretty like me. Ask Joe Frazier: "How do you feel, champ?" He'll say: "Duh, duh, duh." He can't talk. He can't box. He can't dance. He can't do no shuffle and he writes no poems. Like my poem says:

> Joe's gonna come out smokin'
> But I ain't gonna be jokin'
> I'll be pickin' and pokin'
> Pouring water on his smokin'
> This might shock and amaze ya
> But I'm gonna destroy Joe Frazier.'

The joking soon stopped. 'Joe Frazier is an Uncle Tom,' Ali ranted. 'He works for the enemy. Joe Frazier is the white people's champion. He's a traitor.'

Joe was wounded. He had experienced more racism in the South than Ali had done as a middle-class kid. Joe called Emile and voiced his rage. How dare Ali tell such vicious lies about him?

'Take it easy, champ,' Emile said. 'We know he can't stop talking.'

'I'm gonna shut him up,' Smokin' Joe seethed.

Teddy Brenner and John Condon at the Garden received over 1,200 applications for press accreditations from around the world. They kicked out Diana Ross and Dustin Hoffman for posing as journalists, and Condon only stopped escorting Frank Sinatra from ringside when he received proof the singer was photographing the fight for *Life* magazine. Burt Lancaster also found a legitimate way to secure a press pass as, despite never having reported on a fight before, he worked as a colour commentator for the closed-circuit broadcast.

Reg Gutteridge and Alan Hubbard, the two British boxing writers who had been startled by the sight of Emile kissing Calvin Thomas in his Wembley dressing room in 1964, were asked by Condon if they'd like to meet Lancaster at the weigh-in. Accompanied by Colin Hart of the *Sun*, Gutteridge and Hubbard agreed enthusiastically. They had seen Lancaster's erotic tour de force on the beach with Deborah Kerr in *From Here to Eternity*, and remembered him as a macho hunk in *Trapeze* alongside Gina Lollobrigida.

'Hey, Burt,' Condon called out to Lancaster. 'I want you to meet some limey friends.'

Lancaster turned away from Ali and Frazier, who had stripped down to their trunks. Hubbard was startled to see that Lancaster's mouth was smeared with red lipstick, his cheeks were rouged and his eyebrows were pencilled delicately. 'Hi, fellers,' the actor crooned. 'Don't you just love their muscles?'

'Fuck me,' the unreconstructed Gutteridge whispered to Hubbard. 'He's a bleedin' iron.'

Clancy had one of the best seats in the house, working Frazier's corner, opposite Angelo Dundee in Ali's camp. Eddie Futch, Yank Durham and Clancy let Frazier fight his natural way and all the anger and resentment poured out of him. 'I was mad as a junkyard dog at Ali,' Frazier said later. 'I used to watch him on television, talking about me, and I'd say: "God, give him to me. I want him so bad."'

It was a brutal fight. Afterwards, Frazier's face was bruised and lumpy. He had won clearly on points, and had knocked down Ali with a devastating left hook in the fifteenth round, but he still felt sore all over. Ali was in far worse shape. They took him to Flower Fifth Avenue hospital for X-rays because his jaw was so badly swollen it looked broken. Ali refused to stay in overnight. He did not want anyone to be able to say that Joe Frazier had put him in hospital; and he decided to meet the press.

'Just lost a fight, that's all,' Ali said in a muted voice. There was dignity and grace in the defeated former champion. All his garrulous venom towards Frazier was gone, at least for a while.

'There are more important things to worry about in life,' Ali shrugged. 'Probably be a better man for it. News don't last long. Plane crash, ninety people die. It's not news a day after. My losing's not as important as ninety people dying. Presidents get assassinated, civil rights leaders get assassinated. The world goes on. You'll all be writing about something else soon. You lose, you don't shoot yourself.'

A reporter interrupted Ali's solemn monologue. 'Joe said he didn't think you wanted to fight him again.'

Ali looked up. His puffy face turned into a grimacing smile. 'Oh,' he said softly, 'how wrong he is.'

Emelda Griffith was determined to challenge a young rival for her son's attention. Emile was back in the Caribbean, planning his future bride's departure for New York, when his mother returned to battle.

Esther Taylor-Evans, working under her married name, could hardly believe it when she answered the phone and heard Emelda's familiar voice. Chubby Checker was seething with resentment. She started talking fast and hard to her son's old girlfriend as if she had seen Esther only days, rather than years, before.

Emelda could not contain herself. The distress poured out of her. Junior was getting married – in the biggest mistake of his life – to a young fluffy girl who Emelda neither liked nor trusted.

Breath snagged at the back of Esther's throat in surprise. She was happily married to Charles Evans. They had a son and she owned a dress shop in Greenwich Village. Life was sweet for Esther. But, still, the thought of Emile wanting to marry someone else, besides her, made her pause. If he was ever going to marry anyone, Esther always assumed it would have been her. Her old pain did not last. She knew how much happier she was with her own husband and, instead, she felt anger rising inside her as Emelda began to lay out her plan.

'Esther,' she said, 'you should come back ...'

The words rolled out of Chubby Checker. Together, they could convince Emile to give up his new floozy. Emelda would be happy to have Esther back in Emile's life. They would be together again – just like the old days.

Esther cut in with two blunt words. 'No way,' she said.

It was Emelda's turn to be surprised. She tried again, attempting to flatter Esther into changing her mind by reminding her how she had helped Emile in the past. He needed her now. They would be happy again.

'No,' Esther said even more sharply.

There was a long silence and Esther began to wonder how Emelda had even tracked down her number. She must have got it, somehow, from Emile in her bid to regain control of her son's life. Esther thought that she would never plot against her own son in such a way – even if he wanted to marry a murderer. She would talk to him rather than scheme against his possible happiness behind his back.

'Why not?' Emelda eventually asked.

'I'm married,' Esther said.

'But not to Junior,' Emelda said with her peculiar logic. Even Esther's new life should not preclude her from returning to woo Emile away from his latest love. 'Come back, Esther . . .'

'No,' Esther said as she repeated herself. 'There is no way, whatsoever, I would ever do that to Emile . . .'

On 8 May 1971, the world heavyweight champion had a date at St Peter's church in Monticello, with a glittering wedding reception held afterwards at the Concord hotel in upstate New York. Joe Frazier was proud to be the best man at Emile Griffith's wedding. Joe always knew that Emile was a real dude. You didn't become a five-time world champion without being brave and manly.

It felt like they were back in a training camp as they made the same journey up to the Catskills and stayed in their usual rooms at the Concord. Yet, instead of running alongside the freezing lake at dawn, they danced and sang and partied in a room crammed with beautiful women. Joe took Emile aside to tell him that, in Sadie, he had found himself a real fox. She was a good woman.

'You're gonna be happy, champ,' Smokin' Joe reassured the groom.

Emile was far closer to Calvin Thomas, and Freddie Wright, but it seemed more appropriate to have a world champion, rather than a queen, as his best man. He and Calvin had seen too much together around Times Square, and kissed each other too often, to stand side by side at the altar. And Freddie was camp enough to divert attention from the bride – he could have starred instead as a pouting, cross-dressing bridesmaid. Calvin and Freddie understood why Smokin' Joe had to be best man. It made sense in the straight world and, as Joe sang again that wedding night, in 'A Man's Man's Man's World'.

Sadie Griffith looked up in wonder at her handsome husband. 'Let's dance, baby,' she said.

Slowly, as Joe sang the aching words made famous by James Brown, Sadie held Emile as they shuffled around the hotel dance-floor. It was hard to understand the groom's expression as his best man hollered that a man's world meant nothing without a woman or a girl.

Esther Taylor-Evans turned the pages of *Jet* magazine in wonder and surprise. The wedding of Emile Griffith and Sadie Donastorg looked a grand affair. It also looked like an occasion as happy as it was lavish. Emile was smiling in every photograph that *Jet* printed of him in its excitable celebration of his marriage. He was still one of the most famous black men in America and so *Jet*, which catered for a 'Negro' readership, could exult in a large spread.

Years earlier, Esther might have thought she should have stood prettily alongside Emile in those wedding photographs. But not now, not when she was married to another man, and content in her own life as a wife and mother. She could share in Emile's celebration from a distance – and wonder how Emelda, the Chubby Checker of controlling matriarchs, might have conducted herself on a day of conflicted emotions.

Emile had, somehow, broken free of his mother, at least for a while. Esther looked down at her copy of *Jet* and smiled back at her old boyfriend.

*

Marriage could offer sanctuary from doubt and fear. In the 1970s, just as in previous and later decades, untold numbers of gay men became husbands and fathers. Emile loved Sadie; and she loved him back even more fiercely. He was kind and good and she, in turn, offered him happiness and hope. It was also true that, as for other gay or bisexual men, conventional married life provided a barrier against gossip and bigotry. All the slurs about Emile being a *maricón* could be blunted by a young wife at home.

Emile enjoyed talking about Sadie and, preparing to return to the ring for the first time since his wedding, he complained to the venerable sportswriter Jimmy Cannon that, 'Gil Clancy broke up my honeymoon with this fight.' He was back in training to face Max Cohen at the Garden on 26 July 1971, and Emile told Cannon that Sadie was protecting his trainer. 'What kind of cruel thing is it to break up a honeymoon? But my wife said, "Don't be mad at Gil."'

The old fighter chuckled as he explained how Sadie had brought a new discipline to his life. 'My wife will do anything to help my boxing. She told me if I do things like going out and coming in later than Gil wants me to then she will call him. She wants me at home, getting my rest.

'I never liked getting up in the morning – but it's worse now. I still like boxing, just not waking up early. I have two clocks. One is on my side of the bed, the other is on my wife's side. I'm supposed to get up at six-thirty but she sets her clock for six. Sadie did this even before we got married. She would be in the Virgin Islands and I'd be in New York. She would call me and say: "It's time to get up. I love you. Bye."'

His changed life chimed with renewed ambition. Emile wanted to be a world champion again. 'It's like having the world in your hand when you're the champion,' he told Cannon. 'I feel naked without a title.'

Emile's decisive victory over Cohen meant that he had won ten successive bouts in twenty-one months. It was a run made even more impressive by the fact that his victims were not all journeymen.

He had beaten a former world champion in Dick Tiger, for the second time, and Tom Bogs was undefeated after fifty-four bouts when he was knocked down twice by Emile in his home country of Denmark.

He had to go back out on the road again because Carlos Monzon would only fight him in Buenos Aires. Emile was intrigued to visit a new continent, and it suited him not to be cooped up at home with Sadie. It felt better when he went away and then, after a long training camp and a fight, he returned home to see her face shiny with happiness that he was back. That arrangement was less satisfying for his wife because, with no friends in Weehawken, her world narrowed. She only got out of the apartment when doing chores at the supermarket, the dry-cleaner's, the drug store or walking Emile's dogs. Sadie had hoped to travel with her husband, but he argued that a fight camp was no place for a woman. The truth remained that he liked seeing his gay friends, from time to time, in secret hideaways.

Emile soon became consumed with Monzon because the champion had not lost for seven years, since October 1964. Monzon had fought eighty-four times and had suffered only three defeats. There was a brooding darkness to Monzon, a surly and menacing figure. He was also a striking man, with inky black hair and flashing good looks, but there was something unsettling about him. Dave Anderson in the *New York Times* suggested, 'Monzon had the smouldering appearance of a volcano about to erupt. With his high cheekbones, he resembles Jack Palance, the actor ... he often appears bored and impatient.'

There was also violence in Monzon, whose love life was tempestuous, and he carried a brute of a right hand. As a kid in Santa Fe, where he was born and still lived, Monzon had used that vicious right hand to settle hundreds of street fights. He had been less happy shining shoes, selling newspapers and delivering milk. Monzon wanted big money, fast, and he was ready to hurt anyone who stood in his way. He had lost none of that vicious certainty when Griffith arrived in Buenos Aires in September 1971.

'I will knock out this old man,' Monzon promised. He was twenty-nine; Griffith was thirty-three.

Griffith was intent on becoming the first fighter to win a world title three times in two different weight divisions. He started well against a cautious Monzon and, for two-thirds of a fight scheduled for fifteen rounds, he led on all the scorecards. Moving into the eleventh, the contest changed. Griffith was subjected to a blatant poke in the eye from Monzon's thumb and he cried out to the referee. Monzon clubbed him savagely with his right hand, as if showing how much he resented that protest. Griffith began to wilt and in round fourteen the crowd chanted, '*Mon-zon, Mon-zon!*' as the champion dominated. A left hook to the body was followed by a crunching right cross that made Griffith clinch desperately.

Monzon shoved him away and a series of straight rights backed Griffith into a corner. He swayed helplessly as Monzon pummelled him with piston-like lefts and shuddering right uppercuts. Griffith bent over and used his arms to cover his face and head as Monzon rained down his destructive blows. The referee waved an end to the carnage.

Griffith looked battered but he tried to sound upbeat. 'Monzon is a great fighter and a great champion,' he said. 'I don't feel too bad about losing because I know I lost to the best in the world tonight.'

It was only when pressed to consider walking away forever that Griffith bristled. 'I have no intention of retiring,' he insisted. 'I'm willing to fight any top-ten middleweight out there to qualify for a rematch with Monzon. I still believe I can beat him.'

Another year had passed, and another gay pride march beckoned for Freddie Wright. Since Stonewall and the riots, 28 June had been enshrined in the New York calendar as an anniversary to be marked. It felt to Freddie as if he and everyone else who had been at Stonewall that night had witnessed a seismic change in the gay community and America itself. The riots had been reported initially in a comic vein. The *New York Daily News*, the most widely read newspaper in the United States, had chortled over its racy headline in the immediate aftermath of Stonewall: 'Homo Nest Raided, Queen Bees Are Stinging Mad'.

Stonewall's influence endured for years, even if it had seemed enough, back on that hot summer night in 1969, to see a black man, a raging queen, mincing up Christopher Street, screaming theatrically, 'Let my people go!' as the police tried to force gay men and transvestites into their paddy wagons. A joint homage to Martin Luther King and gay liberation could be even more inspiring than it was humorous.

As Storme DeLarverie, the drag king, told the writer Charles Kaiser years later, 'Stonewall was the flipside of the black revolt when Rosa Parks took a stand. Finally, the kids down there took a stand. They said it was a riot; it was more like a civil disobedience. Noses got broken, there were bruises and bunged-up knuckles, but no one was seriously injured. The police got the shock of their lives when those queens came out of the bar and pulled off their wigs and went after them. I knew, sooner or later, people were going to get the same attitude that I had. They had just pushed us once too often.'

The first march, exactly a year on from Stonewall, started out as a nervous parade. Just two hundred gay men, transvestites and lesbians gathered in Greenwich Village behind a single banner that proclaimed 'Christopher Street Gay Liberation Day 1970'. By the time the marchers reached Central Park, the parade had swelled to over two thousand gay people who, realising that they weren't about to be assaulted by the bewildered onlookers, had stepped off the sidewalks to show their solidarity.

They were welcomed by Frank Kameny, a former astronomer who lost his position in the US Army because of his sexuality and had led the first gay picket line in 1965. That inaugural homosexual protest, outside the White House, had consisted of ten people. Kameny was startled to see thousands celebrating Stonewall – for it vindicated a 1968 essay he had written entitled 'Gay Is Good': 'It is time to open the closet door and let in the fresh air and sunshine; it is time to discard secrecy . . . to live your homosexuality fully, joyously, openly, and proudly, assured that morally, socially, physically, psychologically, emotionally, and in every other way: *Gay is good*.'

The same old pain remained. Nine months after Stonewall, Deputy Inspector Seymour Pine, who led that raid, had gone back on the attack. He led his vice squad into The Snake Pit, another Village gay club, and when the same resentment rose up he proceeded to arrest 167 people. Diego Vinales, a young gay man from Carlos Monzon's territory, Argentina, panicked once he was taken into police custody. His visa to remain in America had expired and, worried that he would be extradited, Vinales jumped from a window of the Sixth Precinct. His attempted escape ended as he impaled himself on the metal spike of a fence.

In 1970, *Harper's Bazaar*, featuring dynamic young writers like David Halberstam and Seymour Hersh, published a 10,000-word attack on homosexuality written by the Chicago academic Joseph Epstein. Warning *Harper's* fashionable readers that 'homosexuality is spreading', Epstein concluded that, 'Nothing [my sons] could ever do would make me sadder than if any of them were to become homosexual.'

The *New York Times* produced a trenchant response. That august newspaper had endured immense difficulties with the subject – but, on 17 January 1971, their Sunday magazine allowed the established novelist Merle Miller to come out on its front cover in a thoughtful article called 'What It Means to Be a Homosexual'. Miller's landmark essay sparked over 2,000 letters – with the overwhelming mood echoed by a reader who wrote, 'I've always reacted with horror and indignation at words like "kike", "dago", "spic", "nigger", and yet for every time I've said homosexual, I've said "fag" a thousand times. You've made me wonder how I could have been so cruel, so thoughtless, to so many.'

Progress continued in a steady trudge. In 1971, Frank Kameny, the army astronomer turned activist, became the first openly gay candidate to run for Congress. He lost the race to win the District of

Columbia's election of a non-voting congressional delegate, but it had been another step forward for gay people at a time when homosexuality was illegal in many states and still classified as a 'psychiatric disorder' by the American Psychiatric Association (APA).

In 1972, Bob Fosse's film *Cabaret* showcased a positive depiction of homosexuality in a decadent Berlin, amid the rise of the Nazis. The lead role was played by Liza Minnelli, daughter of a certified gay icon in Judy Garland, which added to the impact.

Yet the Mafia's control of New York's gay bars and clubs had not lessened since Stonewall. Freddie had found another dancing gig at the Gilded Grape, an 8th Avenue tranny bar, run by Matty 'The Horse' Ianniello, a mobster who controlled a 'smut cartel' of around eighty dubious establishments. They stretched from porn theatres to titty bars to gay clubs in and around Times Square.

Just before the third anniversary of the riots, in June 1972, Edwin 'The Skull' Murphy became strikingly interested in gay riots. He had not yet come out as gay; but The Skull, who had managed the Stonewall Inn with iron control, formed the Christopher Street Festival Committee and persuaded the marchers to change the direction of their parade. Instead of starting in Greenwich Village and heading for Central Park, Murphy used his persuasive influence to forge a new route. The 1972 march ended up in the Village, so that Murphy's bars could make plenty of cash selling food and drink to the revellers. It was an indication that money might be more important than bigotry.

There were more encouraging moments as the snaking masses approached the Village, led by Storme DeLarverie and Freddie Wright. The mother of Monty Manford, the president of the Gay Activists Alliance, waved a banner next to her son, his friends and Dr Benjamin Spock. Jeanne Manford's sign carried a simple message: 'Parents of Gays United in Support of our Children'.

People cheered a middle-aged straight woman more loudly than the most outrageous queen on that parade. Men and women ran up to hug and kiss her. 'Will you talk to my mother?' someone shouted.

Jeanne Manford did much more. She and her husband, an esteemed doctor, set up the Parents and Friends of Lesbians and Gays, which would become one of America's largest and most powerful lobby groups.

Freddie Wright raised his black fist and said softly, 'Hallelujah!' As Bob Dylan had promised them in the Village eight years earlier, the times, really, were a-changing.

Emile kept up the old routine. After his world title loss in Argentina, eight more bouts in twenty months secured his next tilt at Carlos Monzon. On 2 June 1973, at the age of thirty-five, he would face the champion in Monaco. Emile had fought ninety times as a professional, but he settled down again at the Concord hotel for an arduous training camp. The venue for his wedding reception only seemed to hold boxing memories.

He saw less and less of his lonely wife. Sadie was bereft without him but Emile needed to win back his title. He also needed to carve out his old twin life, with two different groups of men, both fighters and lovers, to feel whole again. Emile was worn and damaged by the fight game; but the thought of beating Monzon roused him like nothing else had done for a long time.

Emile often found it easiest to express himself with fighters. After he had lost to Monzon he boxed a kid called Armando Muniz, a handsome 24-year-old Mexican, who had built a huge following on the West Coast. In early 1972, Muniz was still unbeaten after seventeen contests and he was touted as a possible world champion. His nickname was '*El Hombre*' (The Man). Emile exposed him as a boy.

By the eighth round, Muniz's face was a dark and purple canvas. His left eyebrow had split open and blood ran over the swollen mouse and down his battered face. Muniz looked ready to quit but, with compassion running through him, Emile turned from tormentor to supporter. He switched his attack from the head and only jabbed to the body. 'Don't give up, kid,' he urged *El Hombre*. 'Keep punching.'

The crowd had never seen anything like it and they rose to both fighters during the final two rounds. Muniz lost badly on all three scorecards but he said later that, 'I didn't mind because it was an education. I learned what prizefighting was all about from Emile.'

Monzon, in contrast, was pitiless. And so Emile trained hard in the Catskills. He ran and sparred and watched the film of their first fight. 'Griffith sat in his chair in the darkened room as the rounds went by,' Vic Ziegel wrote in the *New York Post*, 'said very little, pressed his fists together in front of his face and pushed his thumbs against his lips. His eyes were so wide open he looked like a kid watching his first horror movie.'

Emile was absorbed in hatching a new plan and Ziegel noticed that, 'Gil Clancy leaned forward, scribbling furiously on a yellow pad. What could he have been writing?'

Clancy did not consider Monzon to be a great fighter. He was convinced Emile could beat him and become a six-time world champion. The trainer mapped out the perfect strategy to outwit a champion who could be slow and sloppy.

In Monte Carlo, from the first bell, Griffith brought ceaseless pressure to bear on Monzon. He outworked him and, fighting up close, catching him with heavy body punches, he negated Monzon's greater reach and power. Even when Monzon landed one of his big shots, Griffith took the blow. It looked as if Monzon, still only thirty, had begun to age in the ring. After ten rounds, as Graham Houston reported in *Boxing News*, 'Monzon was in real danger. There was blood on the champion's white gumshield and red weals on his back when he had been forced repeatedly into the ropes ... Monzon's corner were anxious.'

It was only in the fourteenth round that Monzon hurt Griffith. He unloaded a barrage of punches that rocked and wobbled a tiring Griffith. But the challenger made it through to the final bell.

Emile celebrated wildly, and prematurely, for a narrow but unanimous decision was announced in Monzon's favour. 'The crowd greeted the verdict, announced after a long delay, with jeering and catcalling,' Houston reported. 'Gil Clancy clapped his hand to his forehead in amazement.'

Nino Benvenuti, working for live television, was scornful. 'If Monzon won, I don't know anything about boxing. He did nothing. Griffith made the fight.'

Monzon admitted that, 'The fight was the hardest of my career. I knew I had won it but I'm going to rest for two days and watch film of the fight. I'll make a proper decision then if I should continue fighting.'

He had not lost for almost nine years but Monzon sounded dejected. Emile, in contrast, was defiant. 'I had him under control every round except the fourteenth. I'd take another crack at him but I don't think he'd give me one. I know I can be a world champion a sixth time – even if I wait until I'm in my forties like the "Old Mongoose", Archie Moore.'

Emile flew back into JFK and, as always, he called home on a pay-phone as soon as he was through passport control and customs. There was something soothingly familiar about slipping a quarter into the slot and hearing the ringtone once he had punched in the final digit of his home number. He sank back against the booth, leaning his head against the metal stand while waiting for Sadie.

Finally, without an answer, he hung up. Emile hailed a cab and headed for Weehawken. The yellow taxi raced through the Lincoln Tunnel, making good time on a night when there was little traffic.

The lights in the apartment were switched off and Emile, quietly, put down his suitcase, hung up his hat and coat and slipped off his shoes. He could wait until morning before he gave Sadie the perfume he had bought at Nice airport – as his way of saying sorry for all the weeks he had not seen her. It was then, as he switched on the side lamp, that he saw the white envelope on the table. It was a note from Sadie, her handwriting on the outside looking as pretty as ever.

Sadie had gone home for a while. He understood. She needed to see family back on St Thomas. Yet, reading on, the words hurt him more than the fifteen rounds he had shared with Monzon. This was a much more lasting pain than a punch in the face. This was the punishing truth.

Sadie explained that she was leaving for good. She still loved Emile but their marriage had not turned out as she had expected. Sadie knew Emile had another life and it made sense for her to go home to Charlotte Amalie and become a schoolteacher again. She had arranged for the dogs to be looked after and Emile could pick them up whenever he was ready. They would stay in touch, and remain close friends, but it was time for them to part. Sadie sent him a final line of luck and love.

Life was stranger and more confusing than ever. He missed Sadie already, even if he had hardly missed her during the previous ten weeks. How could that be? Emile felt alone and, suddenly, very old.

Freddie Wright's wedding was full of joy. The go-go dancer and aspiring female impersonator held his arms high in the air, waggled his svelte body and yelped: 'It blows my mind!'

He had cheerfully described himself as a slut for so long that it seemed surreal to imagine settling down at last with one person. His mother had known the truth long before he did. Freddie had tried to keep it from her for a long while, and it was easier to be evasive when she moved to Connecticut. But his mom had seen him hanging out with Dante Rodriguez before she left Queens.

She liked Dante; and Freddie liked him too. But there was nothing sexual between him and Dante. They were just close friends – in a similar way to Freddie and Emile.

Dante was a soldier, a marine, and he was married, with kids. Dante loved fooling around, but it was hard for him to come out as he was from Puerto Rico. Every Hispanic tough guy was just waiting to hiss '*maricón*' at anyone who was open-minded enough to like boys as well as girls. It seemed as if Dante had a real crush on Freddie's brother. Freddie just said 'Mmm-hmm' and 'Uh-huh' whenever he was told that his brother and Dante would get married one day.

Freddie still had special times with Dante, when they were club-bing or just talking, but he flushed when his mother spoke plainly about his friend just after they'd had 'the big talk'. For years Freddie had been putting off the moment. He didn't know why, as he had been out on the streets for years. But at home, with his mom, maybe out of respect for her, he never spoke about his sexuality. It was the only time he was a little like Emile in evading the truth.

He knew he owed it to her, and to himself, to talk honestly at last. He took the train up to Connecticut and felt bold and brave. A year earlier, on 15 December 1973, the American Psychiatric Association, the good old APA, had finally decided, in a unanimous 13-0 vote by its board members, to remove homosexuality from its roster of mental illnesses. The revelation, that you were not mentally sick if you were gay, made the front pages of most newspapers across America. Freddie did not need a bunch of shrinks to tell him that he was gay and sane. But he still owed it to his mom.

She listened quietly to Freddie and then, leaning over to kiss him on the cheek, she said simply: 'Son, I know. You're my child and I know.'

Freddie was glad that his mother squeezed his hand. But she took his breath away when she said: 'The feller you hang out with ... Dante? You're in love with him and he's in love with you.'

'Yeah, right!' Freddie exclaimed. His mom might be under-standing but her imagination must be running a fever. Dante Rodriguez? Never. Dante was a married marine being chased by Freddie's brother.

He kissed his mother back and they had a sweet afternoon together. She didn't say anything else about Dante but, three months later, she was proved right.

Out of nowhere, Dante phoned him. He got straight to the point. 'I want to marry you ...'

Freddie laughed. 'Yeah? Tell me when, baby ...'

It was so obvious Freddie regarded the call as a joke that Dante kept their conversation brief. When he next phoned, a few weeks later, he told Freddie he had picked out a date for their house wedding. He had even discussed it with his wife, Rosie, and she understood. Freddie could come and live with them. She thought it would be a good way of keeping Dante at home.

'You've got to be kidding?' Freddie exclaimed, echoing Sadie's reaction when Emile had proposed to her so suddenly. There was a long silence and then Freddie spoke again. 'I thought you were joking around.'

'No,' Dante said. 'I liked you from the moment I first saw you.'

Freddie sat down. He needed to stop his head spinning. 'What about my brother?'

'I like your brother,' Dante said, 'but he's not my type. Not like you.'

Dante then said one plain sentence, with words as simple as they were pure, which touched Freddie deeply. 'You are carefree and wild – but you got a good heart.'

'Yes,' Freddie said, 'I will marry you, Dante . . .'

Freddie and Dante held a house wedding and friends from all over came to celebrate their commitment. When Freddie screamed, 'It blows my mind!', he was thinking most about his mother. How could she have known about him and Dante before even he did?

'That's why you should always listen to your mother,' she said with a wise smile.

It was hard for Freddie's brother. He had already had a wedding dress made for himself, in the hope that Dante would propose to him. But, in the end, he gave that same wedding gown to Freddie. He was crushed with disappointment but he loved Freddie. He would be his brother's matron of honour.

Their cousin, Norman, agreed to perform the wedding ceremony. It would not be legally binding, but it meant as much to Freddie as any other bride to exchange marriage vows. Freddie would leave Queens and move out to Hoboken, New Jersey, and live with Dante, Rosie and their kids. They already called him 'Uncle Freddie', so it would all work out fine.

Emile grinned. They should have all guessed that Freddie, who always did everything his way, would end up living in Frank Sinatra's hometown – with a husband called Dante.

Freddie wore his brother's wedding gown and a strawberry blonde wig as he walked down the stairs in a stately march, with everyone applauding. And then, reaching the makeshift altar, Freddie Wright looked happily at the man who was about to become his husband.

CHAPTER FIFTEEN

Soweto Blues

On a Tuesday night thick with fierce February cold, Emile Griffith went back to work. It was the second week of the second month of a new year, 1974, and the streetlights shed a gauzy yellow over the snowy Boston sidewalks. Puffs of Arctic breath slipped from Emile's cracked lips as he made the short walk from his hotel to the Boston Garden. Gil Clancy was with him, as always, and Howie Albert too. Calvin Thomas and Bernard Forbes, Emile's cousin, completed the small entourage.

The big purses were gone. Emile could have won the title against Monzon the previous summer, but the judges ignored his last great performance in favour of an exhausted champion. He had been fighting for peanuts ever since. Howie had got him $15,000 for his latest bout. Fifteen grand for a five-time world champion. Fifteen grand to be taxed and shared and used up before the month was gone.

At least Emile was getting five thousand more than the 21-year-old kid in the opposite corner. Tony Licata was unbeaten and a roaring Boston favourite. He was number seven in the world middleweight rankings, while Emile had slid down to four. Emile had fought twice since his defeat to Monzon. He had beaten Manuel Gonzalez in Tampa, but dropped a decision to Tony Mundine, a grizzled

Australian, in Paris. In Boston, he and Licata would scrap over a shiny bauble called the North American Middleweight Championship.

Emile knew it would be a fight over something more desperate. Could a faded former champion hold off a promising kid?

It was so cold in the locker room that Emile kept on his fluffy hat, his heavy sweater and purple corduroy jacket, woollen pants and black boots still crusted with snow. Small puddles formed on the cement floor as the dirty snow melted. Clancy was convinced that the shady promoter, Sam Silverman, and Willie Pep, the greatest defensive fighter in history who had become Licata's trainer, had purposely turned off the heating. Why else would they be in danger of hypothermia, while Licata and Pep worked out in a snug Dressing Room 11 – reserved for the home fighter? Clancy moaned so much that Silverman sent over a heating engineer. The man banged at the pipes and used a shifting spanner to crank open the frozen radiator taps. Warm air seeped into the room.

'See,' Clancy hissed at Silverman.

'Whadd'ya mean?' Silverman yelled. 'I just seen we fixed your fuckin' heating. Ya got no excuses.'

Licata was apprehensive. 'The day before a fight like this is tough,' he said. 'I couldn't even go out today. Too cold. And, besides, I had Griffith on my mind.'

Willie Pep considered himself a Svengali and, to add to his mystique, he talked fast out the side of his mouth. 'Tony Licata,' Pep said, 'respects Emile Griffith. In fact, he used to read about him. But a lot of people read about me.'

Pep, the best featherweight in history, had lost only eleven of his mammoth 241 professional fights – but the last of those had been to a bum called Calvin Woodland, who had an 8-4 record in 1966. Boxing got everyone in the end. It didn't matter if you were Willie Pep or Emile Griffith.

'Licata can make it easy for himself,' Pep said with whispering confidentiality. 'All he has to do is jab and move. The kid ain't lookin' for glory. He's lookin' for a win.'

Mike Lupica, of the *Boston Phoenix*, saw that Licata 'mouthed silent words, followed by a furtive sign of the cross'.

Afterwards, once Licata had overcome his nerves to win a unanimous decision over twelve rounds, he said, 'I learned an awful lot from Emile tonight.'

Lupica was still a young writer but he understood an ancient business. Griffith had 'fought his fight by memory. All the ring trickery and guile, all the sweet motion, were from other arenas in other years ... he was thirty-six years and nearly 100 fights old now. He had seen it all too many times before: the flash and glitter of the young opponent, the cold house and the empty seats, the slicksters and the cigars.'

There had been just a small crowd in the Boston Garden, 2,800 frozen souls hollering for Licata as a way of trying to get warm, but Clancy knew more about boxing than any of them. 'If you were to ask me who landed the most effective punches,' Clancy said, 'I honestly think it was Emile.'

Lupica acknowledged that, 'Griffith broke cleverly off the ropes time after time to land quick and effective combinations, and slyly ducked under wild hooks ... but Licata has become a Silverman pet and a Boston favorite, and it was going to be very difficult for Clancy's fighter to win a decision.'

Griffith shrugged. 'It would not have made any difference what I did – but I don't think he won.'

Lupica described a poignant sight. 'Griffith sat on a chair in his dressing room, naked and tired and old, a white towel draped carelessly over his knees. He was always a squat man, but that has begun to unravel, with hints of paunch in the belly and chin. He softly recited the litany of the man who has lost a prizefight. "I would like to try waltzing with him again," Griffith said with the tiniest of grins.

'Griffith's manager, Gil Clancy, classy and without venom, stood a few feet away and, already, he was talking rematch. It is the nature of the game. "I would have a rematch any place a promoter wants to give us money." This is how the managers of thirty-six-year-old middleweights think.'

All the Friday night heroes had gone. The silvery-voiced Don Dunphy and Gillette's *Friday Night Fights* had been consigned to the sport's glorious past. Even Saturday night boxing on prime-time television was a wispy memory. Luis Rodriguez, *El Feo* or the Ugly One, had retired in 1972, after 121 fights. Nino Benvenuti hung up his gloves in 1971 and Dick Tiger a year earlier. Joey Archer had been sent into retirement by Griffith in 1969, while Gaspar Ortega quit the ring in 1965, Gene Fullmer in 1963, and his brother Don ten years later in '73. Ralph Dupas had fought his last bout in 1966, the same year that Rubin Carter went to the penitentiary for twenty years on a mistaken conviction of murder.

'Emile is the only one left,' Gil Clancy told Phil Pepe of the *New York Daily News* in November 1974.

Pepe anointed him as 'the last of a vanishing breed', who had first climbed into the professional ring on 2 June 1958. 'His contemporaries are gone, dead, retired, missing, one of them fighting for his freedom from a New Jersey penitentiary. Only Griffith goes on. Tonight he will fight for the ninety-eighth time, the twenty-fifth time in Madison Square Garden. His purses have amounted to more than $2 million.'

Clancy hailed his fighter's worldly fame. 'Emile's very big in Europe,' he told Pepe. 'They love him. Believe me, he stops traffic in Paris and Rome.'

No one else had headlined twenty-five events in the Garden, or fought as many world championship rounds, but Griffith was up against a 24-year-old roadblock of a fighter called Vito Antuofermo, who cared nothing about ring history. An Italian from Bari, fighting out of Brooklyn, Antuofermo's record stood at 26-1-1. He was yet another mean and hungry challenger and, in comparison, Tex Maule noted in *Sports Illustrated*, Griffith had been 'a reluctant dragon. "I was perfectly happy working for Howie Albert in his hat shop,"

Griffith said. "I am not the violent type." He has had a flamboyant, exciting and tragic boxing career. His skill at turning out women's fancy creations led to a story that he was homosexual and Griffith had to fight that rumor along with his opponents. "I am a friendly man," he said not long ago. "People may say bad things about me, but they are wrong."'

It was the same every time he went back to the Garden. Benny Paret, amid all the old questions, flooded his head.

Maule suggested that 'the memory ravaged him' and Griffith nodded. 'I would have nightmares about Paret. I would dream I met him on the street and I would say hello and he would put out his hand and I would take it and it would be cold and clammy. I would wake up screaming.'

He had spent the two million grand he had made in the ring and Griffith insisted he would keep fighting. His family depended on him.

Antuofermo was a good fighter, full of brash aggression, but he was not a ring great. A few years later, he would draw with Marvin Hagler in a world title fight – but he was stopped in the rematch and also lost twice to the British middleweight Alan Minter in his two other world championship attempts.

Griffith drew him in at the start and, ducking under the Italian's roundhouse swings, nailed Antuofermo with a right-hand cross. Blood spurted from a cut but Griffith did not pressure him enough. Antuofermo shrugged off the punches Griffith landed just below his heart and sometimes shook the veteran with blows that made the sweat beads fly from the bald spot on the older man's head. All three judges scored in favour of Antuofermo.

'After the fight Griffith sat quietly in his dressing room, swigging water from a polka-dotted ice bag,' Maule wrote. 'His face, which had none of the graffiti of forgotten punches marking most old boxers, was smooth and oddly peaceful. He thought he had won, but he was not unduly disturbed that he had not.'

Clancy, in contrast, was seething. 'They don't count body punches anymore, do they? He was hitting the kid all the time to the body and those blind so-and-sos didn't see it. He wins the fight.'

Asked why he had not attempted to stop Antuofermo when he had jolted him in the first round, Emile smiled sadly. 'I guess I don't have the killer instinct anymore ...'

Emelda Griffith, sitting next to her son, started to cry. 'Don't be so upset, Mommy,' Emile said.

As her tears fell, he used his old pet name and offered her his water bottle. 'Here, Chubby Checker, you take this. It's not the end of the world.'

'What now, Emile?' another hack asked on that grim November night in 1974.

'I go back to work, man. Anyone who wants to fight me, I will fight. Emile Griffith is not finished.'

It took sixteen hours to fly the 8,000 miles from JFK in New York to Jan Smuts airport in Johannesburg. Sixteen hours to mull over everything that had happened during the last fifteen years. Emile Griffith had fought Willie Toweel at Madison Square Garden in October 1960. He had signed, just a few days earlier, to fight Elijah Makhathini in Soweto on 9 August 1975. Emile had never heard of him. He just knew that the more he fought, the more difficult the names of his opponents became to pronounce. Antuofermo was hard enough. Mak ... Makha ... Makhathini was a mouthful he could never get right.

'Just call him "Tap Tap",' Clancy advised him. 'That's his nickname.'

'Tap Tap?' Emile smiled. 'I like that.'

'Yeah?' Clancy scowled. 'This feller is meant to have a hell of a left hook.'

'It's more than a Tap Tap?' Emile exclaimed, almost childish in his giggling amusement.

Clancy warned Emile that Makhathini had beaten a former world champion in Curtis Cokes. He had also defeated two other seasoned

American fighters in Willy Warren and Billy Douglas. Yet Emile was more interested in seeing Willie Toweel again.

At Emile's lowest, after Benny Paret had died, Willie's letter had arrived from South Africa. Emile had read his letter so often over the years he could remember the first lines.

> Champ, I wanted to write to you for a few days now. Ever since I heard the news about Benny Paret you are on my mind. I can't think of anything else. I know how you feel. It happened to me as well.

Willie helped him find a different word for death. It was a different word to killing.

> Accidents happen, champ. They're not always our fault. This is not your fault.

In all Emile's painful interviews since April 1962, the death of Benny Paret had become 'the accident'.

> I learned how to forgive myself, Emile, and you must do the same. You and me have to learn to roll with the punches in this life. They are often harder to deal with than the ones we got in the ring ... Good luck, champ. Your friend, Willie Toweel

Emile had answered Willie's letter, but he couldn't put down on paper everything he wanted to say. He just thanked Willie and asked how he was doing. How was his family?

Six months later Willie replied. He told Emile he was doing okay and that he had just begun to train fighters. His family was beautiful and he hoped all was well with Emile and his mom. Willie told Emile how proud he felt following his career. He told him to keep punching, and to keep smiling.

Emile never got round to writing back. But the opportunity to see

Willie meant Emile said little when he was asked if he knew what he was doing in flying to South Africa. People in New York looked angry or frightened when he told them. *South Africa!*

Had he not heard of apartheid? Did he not know how they treated black people in South Africa? Did he have a conscience?

Emile knew Willie Toweel had a conscience. He was a white South African, but he was a good man.

Gil spoke to Maurice Toweel, Willie's brother, the promoter who ran boxing in South Africa from his wheelchair. Maurice assured him that Emile would be welcomed by everyone.

Emile flew to Johannesburg on Tuesday 29 July 1975. Gil, who had a whole stable of boxers to train, would join him on Sunday, six days before the fight. The promoter, Gladstone Nhlapo, would meet Emile at the airport and get him safely to his hotel in the centre of town. It was the most prestigious hotel in the whole of Africa. Only white people, very rich white people, stayed at the Carlton, but it would be different for Emile. They would treat him not only as an honorary white but as an international superstar.

'A what?' Emile had asked in confusion when Gil read him the telex.

'An international superstar,' Gil shrugged.

'No,' Emile said. 'The other thing ...'

'An honorary white?' Gil murmured as his face scrunched up in dismay.

Gil mapped the murky terrain they needed to cross in Johannesburg. Apparently, it was like the South, Alabama and Georgia and Mississippi, but worse. Black and white people were kept strictly apart. Emile would stay in a swanky hotel in white Johannesburg and he would fight in the black township of Soweto. All he needed to do was focus on Tap Tap, do his job, pocket the purse, and get the hell out of there.

'Clancy, you had better not leave me on my own for too long over there,' Emile muttered with an uncertain smile when they had said goodbye at JFK.

Hours later, amid the low drone of the plane, Emile looked out of a blackened window. He had been a professional fighter for seventeen years and, during 101 paid bouts, he had fought all over the world.

His hundredth fight had been in Cali, Colombia, two months before. On 31 May 1975 he had fought a raw young boxer, Jose Luis Duran, from Argentina. It was a joke when they announced a split decision. One judge had it 96-95 for Griffith, and another had the same score in favour of Duran. Clancy cried out angrily when the third judge called it 97-94 for Duran. Emile just shrugged.

He fought next in Largo, Maryland, against Leo Saenz. He was a Maryland boy, from Baltimore, just thirty miles away, and, like Paret, he called himself 'Kid'. On 23 July, six days before he flew to Johannesburg, Emile knew far too much for an American Kid, who came into the fight with an impressive 22-1-1 record. Emile won a near shutout.

'I hope we do it again soon,' Emile said encouragingly to Saenz after the fight.

'Not too soon,' the Kid replied with a queasy smile.

In boxing there are five crude categories of fighter. There are champions, contenders and prospects and, below them, opponents and no-hopers. Emile had belonged to the first three sets almost all his seventeen years in the ring. He had been a fine prospect, a contender and a five-time world champion before he became a proven contender trying to win back another title. Over the last year – and neither Gil nor he admitted it – he had been scaled back to an opponent. He was no ordinary opponent. He was still a 'name'. If a kid could get past Emile Griffith, he was on his way to becoming a serious contender and, maybe, a champion.

Tap Tap would be another test. Tap Tap would almost certainly be more dangerous than he sounded. The battered fighter closed his eyes and, somewhere over an invisible stretch of North Africa, he fell into a fitful sleep.

*

The Carlton hotel on Commissioner Street in downtown Johannesburg was a beautiful skyscraper which looked like an upside-down Y. A five-star, 600-roomed palace, the Carlton seemed the equal of any sumptuous hotel in New York or Los Angeles. Emile agreed it was as grand as any hotel he had seen.

He did a lot of nodding and agreeing. White South Africans were keen to have him praise their country. Did South Africa not have the best weather in the world? The late winter days in July were so warm and crisp, and the sky such a stunning shade of blue, that Emile nodded his agreement. And how about the people? Were they not friendlier than anyone else he had ever met? How about the food? Wasn't it delicious? And weren't South African girls the prettiest in the world?

That last question caused an embarrassed change of subject – almost as if the questioner suddenly remembered that Emile Griffith was a black man, rather than an honorary white, and sexual relations between different races were a crime punishable by a prison term.

He liked a lot about the country, and the people, but South Africa spooked him too. The Carlton hotel was full of black people. But every single one of them, apart from Emile, worked as a waiter, a cleaner, a maid or a gardener. All the guests were white, and all the menial workers were black. They were called 'boys' and 'girls'. When he arrived, Emile squirmed as he was told not to lift his suitcase. The 'boy' would do it. Emile looked at the black porter and realised that the 'boy', in his mid-thirties, was almost as old as him.

Emile made a point of talking to the hotel's black staff and, at first, they were overwhelmed. Some of the 'boys' and the 'girls' covered their mouths, to hide their helpless grinning or shyness, but after a while they exuded more typical exuberance. They looked very happy, and Emile felt humbled. How could they be happy when they were not allowed to live in Johannesburg? How could they be happy catching black trains and black buses back to Soweto? How could they be happy when their children could not attend a white school? How could they be happy without electricity and running water and the vote? How could they be happy when a bridge crossing the railway, like the one leading to Johannesburg's train station, was divided into two – one side for whites only, the other for non-whites? How could they be happy when park benches carried a similar warning – *Whites Only*? Emile was taken for a walk around Joubert Park and he wondered whether he, as an honorary white, would really be allowed to sit on a park bench.

His confusion grew when he realised that boxing made up different rules. Gladstone Nhlapo, the promoter of his fight with Tap Tap, was a black man. Willie Toweel also took him on a tour of the various gyms where he trained fighters. Black and white boxers gazed at him in awe. And before every training session he was immensely moved. Willie made them all pray in a circle. Black and white fighters gathered together, wrapping their arms around each other, lowering their heads in unison. Willie's voice rang out as he welcomed Emile, 'my friend, my brother', and asked that every fighter would be protected by the Lord.

Willie trained more black fighters than he did white boxers. He treated them all the same, and he just laughed when he said he ignored the law and brought some of his black boys home to the suburbs so that they could get proper rest and a good meal, cooked by his lovely wife, Alida, before a big fight. Alida helped teach them English and Willie sorted out their chaotic lives. He had saved so many fighters from prison or death. Willie would rush to a police station or a courtroom to make a personal plea on behalf of a fighter – assuring the cop or the magistrate that his boxer was 'a very good boy', whom he would personally supervise. Willie was an old charmer and, usually, he got his boys free.

The black fighters shook their heads in wonder when they told Emile that Willie broke the law time and again by driving them home to the townships. Every other white man they knew was terrified of Soweto or Alexandra, Katlehong or KwaThema. Willie just drove straight in, bouncing along the rutted dirt roads. He became so familiar with the townships, and so comfortable, that Willie would drive in with his wife and children. He would leave them in the car and go inside a fighter's home to talk to the parents or to listen to a family problem, which he would try to solve.

'Man, Willie,' Emilie said, 'you're quite a guy ...'

'I try, champ,' Willie grinned. 'But hey, isn't this an amazing country?'

The press could not resist interviewing Emile and Willie together. At a Carlton hotel press conference, Emile wore a gleaming white tracksuit.

'Hey, Emile,' Willie said, shielding his eyes from the glare, 'you're whiter than white. Do you want to blind me, man?'

Emile laughed and threw a mock punch at Willie, dressed in his best black suit.

'Fifteen years ago Emile Griffith and Willie Toweel were too busy trying to punch each other on the nose to engage in idle chat,' Rory Brown wrote in the *Rand Daily Mail* on 31 July 1975. 'Yesterday, in a luxury Johannesburg hotel, it was all different. Two men, worlds apart in colour and background, found time to renew an old acquaintance and reminisce over the time they tried to knock each other cold. A common bond, albeit a violent one, linked the two men – one a black man from the Virgin Islands who, in seventeen years, has won and lost five world titles, and another, a white South African, who has won and lost the British Empire lightweight title.'

Brown reminded his readers that, 'There is another bond that links the two men – but one they don't like to talk about. They both had the misfortune to kill a man in the ring. Hubert Essakow died in hospital several days after a fight with Toweel on 19 March, 1956 and Benny "Kid" Paret died two weeks after losing the world welterweight title to Griffith on 24 March, 1962. "Don't talk about Essakow," Toweel said yesterday. "After Hubert's death, and it still haunts me, I never again punched my weight." Griffith said: "Don't talk about Paret. Let's talk about Willie. He made me a man in the ring. He was a smart boxer and he gave me plenty of trouble in the early rounds. For me the Toweel fight was make or break."'

Willie returned the compliment. 'Emile was the strongest man I ever fought. On top of that, he had a sneaky right hand that comes out of nowhere. The right that put me down in the fourth round was the hardest punch I ever took. But I spotted Emile ten pounds that night. I should fight him now that I'm middleweight ... all my weight these days is around my middle.'

The banter began. 'Hey,' Willie shouted, 'do you know why I never forget the date of my fight with Emile? It was my mother's birthday. You guys should meet Emile's mom. She's amazing!'

Emile broke into a hilarious imitation of Chubby Checker screaming for him – '*Juuunnnee-or! Juuunnnee-or!*' Willie and Emile had them rocking with laughter.

It was more sombre a few days later when, on Saturday afternoon in Willie's car, Emile turned to his friend. He asked Willie how he coped with Hubert's haunting death. Willie did not say anything for a long while; and then he asked Emile if he would join him for mass the following morning. He took mass every day, Willie said, and it helped him.

They picked up Gil at Jan Smuts airport early the next morning. Willie and Emile took the trainer, who was also a Catholic, to church. It was a Sunday and Willie had cleared it with the priest that Emile could join him before the main service. Black people, by law, were not allowed to worship in a white church.

As the car rolled through the suburban streets, with Gil chatting to Willie, Emile sat in the back and looked at Johannesburg on a stunning morning. The bleached yellow of the winter grass matched the scarred gold dumps surrounding the city. Everywhere he looked, Emile saw white people driving cars while black servants walked. The women carried bags on their heads, balancing them with stately grace, while the men strode past the palatial homes. Those 'boys and girls' were about to work in the gardens and kitchen of their white masters and mistresses. He felt sad when the servants at the Carlton insisted on calling him, a fellow black man, 'master'. Emile didn't want to be anyone's master.

It was peaceful in the Catholic church. Willie led them to the front pew. When the moment came, and they could walk up and take mass, Emile listened quietly while Willie said the litany of names he repeated every day ... moving from Papa Mike to his mother, Diana, her sister Mary, to his brothers and sisters, Jimmy, Vic, Maurice, Alan, Fraser, Maureen and Antoinette, to his wife Alida and their children Natalie, Samantha and Gabrielle.

Emile heard his own name, and Gil's, being said softly by Willie, who then murmured another before he took mass. 'And Hubert,' he said. 'Hubert Essakow.'

The tears rolled down Emile's face as he followed Willie's lead and, lighting a candle for those he loved, he said the names of all his family, and Gil and Howie, and Willie too. Then, just like Willie had done, he murmured another name. 'And Benny,' he said. 'Benny Paret ...'

Another kind of battle had broken out in the days before Gil's arrival. Gladstone Nhlapo, the promoter, had been contacted by a government official. He was reminded that, under apartheid's Group Areas Act, Emile would not be allowed to have Gil in his corner. The only white men who would be permitted into Soweto on the day of the fight, apart from the police, were the referee and three judges.

'I can't go anywhere without Clancy,' Emile wailed, explaining to Gladstone that his trainer had been in his corner for every one of his 101 previous fights and all his amateur bouts as well.

'I'm sorry,' Gladstone said. He told Emile some distressing stories about the security police and detention without trial. The South African government was a dangerous enemy.

'I don't care,' Emile said. 'I'm not fighting without Clancy.'

The story made headlines. 'Griffith has threatened not to go through with the fight if Gil Clancy, a white man, is not allowed in his corner in Soweto,' the *Rand Daily Mail* confirmed.

Mr Justice Klopper, the chairman of the South African Boxing Board of Control, said that his organisation could not intervene. 'It would serve no purpose. They knew of Regulation 15 and the Group Areas Act when they applied for the fight. Even the Minister of Sport, Dr Piet Koornhof, cannot make an exception.'

Emile reacted angrily. He was sick of the discrimination that had clogged his life as a black man and, especially, as a gay man. 'I've had a warm welcome in South Africa but I don't like racism or any prejudice. I think everyone, regardless of colour or creed, should be given the opportunity to see the fight. If Clancy's not in my corner I want to go home.'

Gladstone Nhlapo, on behalf of Emile and Cosmopolitan Promotions, wrote to the Transvaal Boxing Board of Control. Wilf Garforth, the head of that provincial body, responded sharply. 'I cannot ask the minister to break the law. I will not stick my neck out on this issue. If the promoters want an exception to be made they need to approach the government. Maybe they can negotiate a compromise.'

Emile Griffith stood up to the might of apartheid. 'I don't believe in this law,' he said, 'and I am not negotiating. I tell you one thing straight – no Clancy, no fight. You can lock me up or send me home. I know what's right and wrong. And this law is wrong. I refuse it.'

Willie Toweel looked at him in wonder. They could say all they liked about Emile being a fairy. He was, instead, a warrior.

Gil Clancy backed his fighter to the hilt. They were not out to cause trouble, but they would not shift from their principles. 'I think you had better listen to Emile,' he told the scribbling reporters. 'He's no politician. He means what he says.'

As the controversy escalated and the news was reported internationally, Prime Minister John Vorster, Piet Koornhof and the South African cabinet became increasingly uncomfortable. The sports boycott against apartheid had begun to bite and white South Africa's favourite sports, rugby and cricket, faced years of isolation. Emile Griffith was a renowned fighter and his comments were an embarrassment. They could hardly lock up an honorary white, from New York, and so they buckled.

Koornhof, as Minister of Sport, gave his permission for Gil Clancy to enter Soweto between the hours of noon and 6 p.m. on the afternoon of 9 August 1975. The fight was back on.

'Man,' Willie Toweel said admiringly to Emile, 'you really beat them. 'Scuse my language but, boy, that was one hell of a knockout punch.'

Jabulani Amphitheatre, Jabulani, Soweto, Saturday 9 August 1975

One of the many crazed anomalies of apartheid meant that, while the Group Areas Act prevented white people from entering Soweto, another law stopped any black man from becoming a ringside official at a township fight. The referee and the three judges had to be white – and received special dispensation to officiate township boxing. Stanley Christodoulou would be in charge in the ring while Len Hunt, Wally Snowball and Chris Myburgh were the three judges.

As a boy Len used to sneak into the Bantu Men's Social Club in Eloff Street, then the busiest street in Johannesburg. Black people were called 'Bantu' or 'natives' and, in the days before apartheid's crackdown intensified, workers gathered there. In the 1950s Nelson Mandela, who then practised as an attorney, and Walter Sisulu were members of the Bantu Men's Social Club. Mandela's love of boxing was deepened in that steaming enclave, because the fights staged at the club were usually thrilling battles.

The men at the Bantu Club got used to young Len, the teenage boxing enthusiast, and once he had paid his ten-shilling entrance fee, they hid him away at the back. It was illegal for a white boy to be there and Len risked arrest every time he went to watch the fights. But he so loved the atmosphere, and the gripping boxing, that he took the risk every week. As an adult he quickly worked out that the only way for him to watch black boxing was as an official and he became a referee and a judge.

Stanley Christodoulou was the son of Cypriot immigrants who grew up in the tough neighbourhood of Brixton, on the western fringes of central Johannesburg. He would eventually become one of the world's best boxing referees, who controlled over a hundred world title fights around the globe – featuring Roberto Duran, Marvin Hagler, Tommy Hearns, Barry McGuigan, Eusebio Pedroza, Evander Holyfield and Saul Alvarez. But, as a Greek boy in Brixton, Stan had to fight Afrikaans kids who mocked him as an outsider. On the dark side of the Johannesburg tracks, he developed a keen interest in boxing.

He loved reading *The Ring* and listening to the boxing on his wireless. Like every other boxing-mad kid in Johannesburg, he paid a visit to Willie Toweel's amateur gym. Willie went out of his way to look after Stan. The Lebanese and the Greeks both took their licks in white South Africa. Like the Portuguese, they were used to being called 'white Kaffirs'.

Willie could tell that boxing pulsed deep inside Stan and so, one day, in 1963, when the kid was just seventeen, the old fighter asked him if he would like to watch a real war in the ring. Stan looked at him with big eyes. 'Come on,' Willie said, 'I'll show you.' He took Stan to the black location of KwaThema, just outside Springs, not far from where Willie had grown up on the unforgiving East Rand.

Stan could not believe how exhilarating it was to watch a fight between two black boys. Joe 'Axe-Killer' Ngidi and Carlton Mongogotlo went at it hammer and tongs, hell for leather, in a ding-dong battle. The worn old words poured out of Stan, sounding fresh and true, on the drive back to Johannesburg. He asked Willie if he could join him next time he went to the boxing.

'I'm going tomorrow, kid,' Willie said, 'to Standerton.'

There was a kerfuffle when they arrived at the location in Standerton. One of the white officials had not turned up. They were a judge short.

'Stanley,' Willie said calmly, 'do you want to be a judge?'

Willie was the referee and Stan, petrified at ringside, was lost. He looked helplessly at Willie who, coolly, started giving him little signals to help him work out who was winning. Stan's gaze soon shifted to the fighters. He learned that he could read a fight. It came easily to him and he judged all eight bouts.

A year later, in 1964, there was a riot in Soweto's Orlando Stadium after a bout between the 'Axe-Killer' and 'Kangaroo' Maoto. Bottles and bricks were thrown into the ring and the white officials were chased out of Soweto. Boxing was suspended for the next three months before a meeting was held at Hillbrow police station.

'Who wants to go back to the townships?' the senior police chief asked.

Only one white official raised his hand – Stanley Christodoulou.

Inside the Jabulani Amphitheatre, eleven years later, the atmosphere was similarly intense. The venue was packed with 5,000 fans and the doors needed to be barred to keep out any more people trying to squeeze in to see the great Emile Griffith and the Zulu slugger, Tap Tap Makhathini. Tap Tap's most vociferous supporters were in the Zulu heartlands of Natal; but he was also wildly popular in Soweto.

Len Hunt showed Emile and Gil into their dressing room. Noise rolled down from the venue and Len hurried away to take up the first of his judging duties during a long afternoon.

Gil didn't need to say much to Emile, apart from reminding him about the Tap Tap left hook and encouraging him to keep up his work rate. It felt very different from Madison Square Garden, the Las Vegas Convention Center and Wembley in London.

Tap Tap, the local fighter, walked second to the ring. It was another sign of how Emile's status had been downgraded but he didn't mind. They would soon be alone between the ropes.

The roar built gradually, deepening into a bellow that was then lifted by the high-pitched ululations of township women who had already seen the approaching Zulu army. There were around thirty bare-chested Zulu men wearing tiny leather pouches and white fluffy legwarmers. Brandishing their shields and waving their assegais, they stomped their feet in tandem with the drumming. Again and again, they lifted their legs and brought their naked feet crashing against the floorboards. The building shook as the crowd stood to catch sight of the men, who also sang an achingly beautiful Zulu song. Emile picked out a hooded fighter in the middle of the troupe: Tap Tap Makhathini.

It was a ring entrance like no other and the Zulu impis, or warriors, galvanised Makhathini. The South African fought with controlled aggression, catching Griffith with heavy rights and his feared left hook. Tap Tap hit hard, with draining force, and it turned into a one-sided beating. Griffith was still canny enough to slide away from the worst punishment, but even the four white men, who understood his place in ring history, could not soften the truth. Their judgement was unequivocal. Tap Tap Makhathini was a comprehensive winner on points.

Len Hunt had given Tap Tap little chance before the fight; but by the end of the first round he knew it was going to be brutal. He admired the bravery of Emile and, afterwards, he felt compelled to seek him out.

Gil Clancy welcomed Len into the stark dressing room. There were no showers and Emile cut a forlorn figure as he towelled himself down. He nodded to the ringside judge, gesturing for him to take a seat. Len complimented him on a good fight. He knew it was a small lie, for Emile had been a shadow of himself, but Len wanted to pay tribute to a world champion he had loved as a boy.

Len was deeply impressed by the grace and class of Gil, while Emile was more muted. After a while, Len stood up and said he would allow them to finish changing. He had just one small favour to ask of Emile.

'Yes, champ?' Emile said, as if in a daze.

Len produced a boxing book. Would Emile do him the honour of signing it?

'Okay,' Emile said. Len could see the bald patch on the top of Emile's head as he hunched over the book. His hand shook slightly. To break the silence while Emile scrawled his name, Len asked when he had won his first world title.

Emile looked up at him blankly. He could not remember. 'Gil?' he said with a slurry voice. 'When did I become champ?'

'1961, Emile,' Gil said patiently. 'The first Paret fight – in Miami.'

'1961?' Emile echoed. His look of incomprehension chilled Len Hunt to the bone.

Emile handed back the book and the pen. 'There you go, champ.'

The lost old champion gazed at his trainer. '1961?' Emile said again to Gil, as if the last fourteen years had been beaten out of him. 'No kidding?'

CHAPTER SIXTEEN

Hombre

The end came on a sunlit evening early in August 1977. Emile Griffith finally accepted it was all over in a Long Island living room rather than a bloody boxing ring. He sat facing Gil and Nancy Clancy in a familiar ritual. The trainer and his wife liked to watch the sun set over their yard while sipping dry Martinis. It was a civilised way to conclude a rare day when Gil was not working in a stinking gym, trying to get a fighter to move his feet or switch to the body.

Emile was a regular visitor to the Clancy home and, after twenty years together, he and Gil were closer than ever. They had travelled the world and been through the fire of 112 professional bouts together. They had experienced glory and defeat, and death.

Since his defeat to Tap Tap Makhathini, Emile had won four, drawn one and lost five of his ten fights. His most recent bout, and loss, had again been in Stade Louis II in Monte Carlo. The bill, on 30 July 1977, had been headlined by Carlos Monzon, world middleweight champion for almost seven years. Monzon had been knocked down in the second round by Rodrigo Valdes. He prevailed in the end, winning on points, but he was done. Clancy knew Monzon would never fight again.

It seemed fitting that another great former champion should box for the last time on that same promotion. The main preliminary bout had been between Emile Griffith and Alan Minter. The European champion from London, who would eventually hold the world title for a brief period, was a tall southpaw. Minter was a very good fighter, but he would not have beaten Griffith ten years before. He knocked Griffith down and dominated large chunks of the contest. Clancy urged on Griffith once more, and the old lion roused himself for a final tilt at glory. Griffith won the last two rounds, but lost the fight.

'Emile,' Gil said, his voice thick with emotion in his living room, 'it's over. You're retiring.'

'No, no,' Emile protested. 'One more fight, Clancy. Against someone who's not a tall lefty.'

Gil shook his head. 'That's it, Emile. You've got nothing more to prove.'

Emile only really believed it was over when Clancy's voice cracked. Nancy handed him a tissue, and Gil dabbed his one good eye. Emile had never seen his trainer cry before.

They both knew the damage that boxing caused. The third fight between Joe Frazier and Muhammad Ali, the 'Thrilla in Manila' in October 1975, had uncovered the darkness yet again. Ali said it was 'the closest thing to dying' – while Frazier, who had beaten up his enemy remorselessly, was plunged into near blindness when his only working eye was sealed shut. For years, he had fooled the doctors. Whenever they tested his eyes, Joe was letter-perfect. 'I learned the eye chart by heart,' he cackled.

In Manila, towards the end, Frazier could not see much out of either eye. After fourteen rounds, Ali also wanted to quit. 'Cut 'em off,' he said, looking down at his gloves, unable to bear another round. Angelo Dundee spoke urgently to him, pointing at the blind, spent figure of Frazier.

Slumped on a stool before the fifteenth and deciding round, Joe protested angrily when his trainer, Eddie Futch, would not allow him to answer the bell. 'Eddie, please,' he begged. 'Don't you stop this fight.'

'It's over, Joe,' Eddie said softly.

Gil Clancy and Eddie Futch were cut from the same compassionate cloth. Emile knew there was no point arguing.

'Okay, Clancy,' he said. 'You're the boss.'

Emile asked if he could use the phone. He dialled up Chubby Checker. 'Mommy,' he said, 'I'm at Clancy's. He's said it's time to retire. I'm not fighting no more.'

He sat down again. 'Gil,' Emile finally said. 'Thank you.'

Emile and Calvin Thomas hired a pink limousine that night. He wore a pink jumpsuit and teased his hair so it stood up straight. Emile looked a scream. There was no point feeling miserable. He had been fighting as a pro for nineteen years. It was enough. They were in the mood to celebrate.

The pink limo scooted around to the Gilded Grape on 8th Avenue. Freddie Wright was shaking his mamba again as a dancer, a DJ and a barman. Freddie worked all over the city. But they loved it most when he was at the GG. The wildest transvestites there gave them the most riotous welcome.

'*Emile!* You cocksucker! Where you been?' Giselle, the gorgeous tranny, screamed in delight when the fighter, Calvin and Freddie sauntered over to the bar.

'I'm back, baby,' Emile said, almost shyly. 'I'm back for good.'

Luis Rodrigo was slim, cute and seventeen. He had been born in Puerto Rico and had moved to the Bronx twelve years before. Luis reminded him so much of Matthew that Emile could not easily divert his gaze in the Hudson County Youth Detention Center in Secaucas, New Jersey. Emile could tell he was lost and troubled. Of course, that description applied to almost every inmate in a juvenile jail, but Luis stood out to Emile.

The kid spent a lot of time on his bunk, staring at the ceiling, waiting for his six-month sentence to pass. He was back in Secaucus a second time for breaking and entering a property. Emile eventually sat down on Luis's bed and, rather than bawling him out, offered a Hershey's bar. Luis accepted the candy suspiciously and waited for a long lecture. The new corrections officer, however, was very different. He was a strapping black man and the gold badge on his brown uniform said *Emile Griffith*.

The name meant nothing to Luis. He munched his candy bar dolefully while Emile asked why he was back in the clink.

'I keep getting invitations for free board and lodging,' Luis said.

Emile told him to keep on going if he wanted to be a smart ass. But he was pretty sure Luis had a good head on him. Emile advised him, with a smile, to use it.

'Do you have any idea what it's like to be in a place like this?' Luis sneered. 'Do you know anything?'

Emile stood up, remembering Mandal, where he had lived on St Thomas. He seemed more sad than angry. 'Maybe we'll talk another day, champ.'

The former world champion continued his rounds. He had only been in the job two months but he liked it just fine. Emile thought he might do some good because, as far as he could see, most of these kids needed compassion rather than punishment. He had said as much when he was first offered the job. It came right from one of the top men in New Jersey.

Chris Jackman, who would soon become state senator, was the speaker for the New Jersey General Assembly. He was also an ardent fan of Emile Griffith. When Jackman heard that Emile needed a job he invited him for lunch. The Democratic Party representative thought the boxer should not have to work another day of his life but Emile was emphatic. The routine and a steady pay packet would help him.

The whole sorry story tumbled out of Emile. For the first year of his retirement he had just gone over to Howie Albert's office whenever he needed more money. That was pretty much every week, and

Howie just signed him a cheque for however much he asked. Emile had turned forty in February 1978, and by the summer of that year he felt vaguely embarrassed that he still needed to go to Howie's office for a hand-out. Maybe it was time he took charge of his nest egg, as Howie had long been making big payments on his behalf – like the $13,000 for Chubby Checker's new kitchen.

'How much have I got left, Howie?' Emile asked one sweltering summer morning at the hat factory.

There was an awkward silence. Howie eventually told him the truth. Emile had not earned a dime since he had fought Minter the previous summer – and he had been in the red long before that last throw of the dice in Monte Carlo. Gil had not taken a full share of his purse as co-manager and trainer for the last five years of Emile's career.

Howie and Gil had been propping up Emile for a while. They were happy to keep going but Emile, a proud man, wanted a job. He helped out as an assistant trainer at the Solar Gym on West 26th Street. He knew so much about boxing that a long line of fighters asked to work with him. But it would take years to establish himself as a professional trainer. After he sold the Weehawken apartment and moved to a cheaper place in New Jersey, he still needed paid work.

Jackman suggested all kinds of fancy office jobs, but Emile wanted something meaningful. When he finally heard about the correctional officer gig, he jumped at the chance. He figured he knew a lot about trouble, and a lot about kids.

Emile felt so proud when he received a wage packet after his first month in uniform that he ordered a gilt-edged plaque. It meant even more to him when he saw that Gil Clancy, who had accepted a new position as the matchmaker at Madison Square Garden, kept the plaque permanently on his desk:

To my Dad, Gil
The best Trainer in the World
Your son, Emile Griffith

Emile liked to call Gil 'my Irish pop', and Howie 'my Jewish pop'. He felt lucky to have had two fathers over the last twenty-one years. They made up for the absence of his real dad.

Luis Rodrigo had lost his father when he was just four years old. His dad had been a foreman on a construction site and had fallen from the fourth floor and broken his back. He died in hospital and Luis's mother, Maria, had moved the family to the Bronx. Emile read the kid's case history and understood a little more about Luis.

Everything changed when the director of the detention centre, William Mullaney, asked Emile to bring in some fight footage for their weekly movie night. None of the boys knew he was a multiple world champion and Mullaney was convinced it would do wonders for them to understand the significance of their newest correctional officer.

Emile chose his second fight against Nino Benvenuti at Shea Stadium in September 1967. It was one of his sweetest nights, winning the world middleweight title a second time. That night also marked the moment he became a five-time world champion.

The recreation room in Secaucas grew hushed and reverent when the lights dimmed. In the shadowy gloom, the boys cast furtive glances from the screen to Emile and back again. They were in the presence of a sporting legend. The huge wingspan of Emile's formidable shoulders remained, even if he had lost his hair and his face had grown much rounder in twelve years. When the verdict was announced in his favour the boys whooped as if they had been transported back in time to Shea Stadium.

They surrounded the old champ once the lights came back on and lined up to shake his hand.

'Sign right here, champ: "To Belty",' the toughest kid in the joint said loudly as he held out his arm.

'Soap and water will take it right off, Belty,' Emile smiled.

'It's okay, champ,' Belty said. 'I don't wash much. And no more after you sign this arm.'

Only one kid hung back. Luis Rodrigo, the boy Emile liked most. A few weeks before, Emile had tried to tell Luis a little about his former life, as a boxer, in the hope that he could prove to the kid he had met enough tough guys to last him a lifetime.

'Yeah, yeah,' Luis had dismissed him then.

As the recreation room emptied in a babble of excited voices and shadow-boxing impressionists, Luis looked at Emile. 'You really were a champ.'

Emile nodded and smiled. For the first time in a long while, he felt proud to have been a fighter.

Sadness crept over them when Luis's six months inside came to an end. 'So this is it,' Emile said, 'the day you get discharged?'

'Yeah,' Luis said, feeling desperate that he would never see Emile again. 'I'm going home to my mother.'

'I don't ever want to see you back here again.'

'No, Emile, you won't,' Luis said. He turned away and walked back to his cell, to pick up his bags.

Emile called out. 'Luis?'

'Yes, Emile?'

'Would you like to be my adopted son?'

Luis looked at Emile in confusion. 'What?'

Emile repeated the question and, this time, Luis answered quickly: 'Hell, yeah!'

The 41-year-old man and the seventeen-year-old boy gripped hands. 'You had better call your mother,' Emile said.

'Adoption' was the only way in which Emile would feel comfortable living with a young man. As much as he needed the company and love of Luis, he could not bear the thought that the outside world might consider that they were gay. Luis could not be his partner. He would have to become his 'son'. In the same way, he had often called Matthew his 'nephew'. Emile could never articulate the reasons for his confusion – just as he could not confess to anyone, at least until then, that years earlier he had been molested on St

Thomas by a strange man who had called himself little Emile's 'uncle'. Family names and sexual secrecy were bound together inextricably in Emile's jumbled head.

It took months of meetings and discussions, with family and social workers, before Maria Rodrigo agreed to a surreal arrangement. She loved her son but, in the end, she agreed to the 'adoption'. Emile was hard to resist and Luis needed an older man, a father-figure she was advised, to guide and love him in the years ahead.

Luis could, at last, live with Emile in his apartment on Glenwood Avenue, in Jersey City. The fighter had met the love of his life. They would be together for the next thirty-three years, until the end for Emile.

Boxing was a bruising business. Deals were cut, like a sliver of flesh, and deals were broken, like a busted nose. Emile had made his first successful foray into training when he answered Gregorio Benitez's call to help his son in Puerto Rico. Wilfred Benitez was a gifted fighter who had began boxing as a pro when he was just seventeen. As soon as he moved up to welterweight, his dad, who trained him, called Emile. Gregorio Benitez was a student of the fight game and he remembered Griffith at his welterweight peak. He had never seen a better conditioned fighter and he hoped that magic would rub off on his son.

Emile was in Wilfred Benitez's corner when the young Puerto Rican won the WBC welterweight title from Carlos Palomino in San Juan. The deal was that Emile would work as chief trainer when Benitez defended his title against Sugar Ray Leonard, the glittering new star of boxing. But Benitez senior changed his mind. He would return to the corner. Emile was out, and the promise of money was gone.

Once Luis moved in with him, the charms of the juvenile detention centre waned for Emile. He quit his post in Secaucas but Emile needed to earn a living. He trained his boxers in the day and, at night, worked as a cheerful bouncer at O'Hara's tavern, which catered for office workers and college students in Jersey City. His old boxing itch intensified.

All his knowledge of life, and death, was wrapped around boxing. He was a good cornerman, too, and Gil and Howie beamed like proud parents as they watched him bring the same commitment to training as he had to fighting.

Emile did not forget the terrible dangers. Exactly a year after his last fight, against Alan Minter, the English middleweight also hit tragedy. On 19 July 1978, Minter had flown to Italy for a European title match against Angelo Jacopucci. Near the end, Minter's eyes were swollen. But he had done more damage to Jacopucci and Minter stopped him in round twelve. Later that night they met in a local restaurant and shared a few drinks.

Afterwards, they shook hands outside and Minter watched Jacopucci lean over a bridge spanning a river. The Italian vomited, but Minter, a hard man, left him to it. 'One drink too many,' he said to his friends.

A day later, having collapsed into a coma, Angelo Jacoppuci died in hospital. His fatal head injuries had been discounted by the ringside doctor, who was charged with manslaughter.

Minter did not blame himself. It could have been him spewing into the river and then sliding towards death. They all knew the risks. Minter fought on and he was a proud world champion. 'I wanted Jacopucci's children to know that their dad lost to a champion and not just some mug,' Minter said.

It could be a horrible and forsaken business, but Emile clung to boxing. He taught his fighters to protect themselves and he encouraged them to work hard. Lives were on the line, and Emile looked after every fighter who came to him.

In mid-November 1979, Gil asked Emile to assist a hard-hitting prospect from Port Arthur in Texas. Wilford Scypion had turned twenty-one earlier that summer and his record as a middleweight stood at 12-0. He had won every fight by knockout. Scypion was trained by Kenny Weldon, but this would be their first test outside of Texas. Mike Jones, a friend of Gil's who managed Scypion, thought the Texans could do with some New York savvy in their corner.

Jones would have loved to have called in Clancy but that was impossible. Clancy was the matchmaker for Madison Square Garden and had retired, at least for a while, from training. He could not bear working with any fighter besides Emile. In his spare time, Gil had become CBS's expert analyst for all their televised boxing shows. He advised Jones that Emile would be the best man for their corner.

'It'll be good for you,' Gil told Emile. 'And you'll earn a few bucks too.'

'Okay, Clancy,' Emile said. 'Whatever you say ...'

Felt Forum, New York, Friday 23 November 1979

Emile had to step back inside the new Madison Square Garden because the Felt Forum was a 5,000-seat indoor theatre attached to the arena. As boxing's popularity ebbed, it become more practical to stage most fight promotions in the Forum rather than the main venue. Emile sensed Benny's spirit in the Garden on that unseasonally warm Friday night.

Wilford Scypion was a softly spoken black kid and he looked happy to have Emile in his locker room. Weldon and Jones, the lead trainer and manager, bustled around Emile, thanking him for his help.

'No problem,' Emile smiled. 'Gil's told me all about the other guy.'

Willie Classen was the other guy, a 29-year-old Puerto Rican who lived in the South Bronx. Before becoming a professional fighter, he had been 'the tumbler man' at a laundry in Manhattan. His job was to remove the sheets and towels from the dryer. Willie made better money on the streets. There were drugs, deals and fights, and Willie ended up doing time inside. When he came out of prison, he resolved to dedicate his life to the ring. His first wife, Gloria, hated boxing but Willie was adamant: 'I won't look at a woman who tells me boxing is not my sport. I will die in this sport.'

By late 1979, Willie had lost six of his twenty-four bouts. Unlike Scypion, he had fought high-calibre opponents in Eddie Gregory (who became Eddie Mustafa Muhammad) and Vito Antuofermo. In August 1978, when they went to the scorecards against Antuofermo, Willie thought he might get the nod. After they gave the decision to Antuofermo, who was managed by more powerful people, Willie spoke bitterly. 'They don't give black people no breaks in this place. You gotta knock 'em dead or you don't win. Titles are not made for guys like me.'

He still flew to Italy a few months later and beat Jose Luis Duran, who had sneaked a decision over Emile in Colombia. That had been Emile's disappointing one hundredth fight, and so it was obvious that Willie knew his way around a ring. It was the reason why Gil had chosen him as Scypion's first New York opponent. He was tough and experienced, but unlikely to shock Scypion.

In April 1979, at the Felt Forum, Willie had taken a beating from John LoCicero. He was knocked out and suspended from boxing by the New York State Athletic Commission. Willie would only be allowed to return to the ring once he had passed an EEG. While he waited for his brain scan, he started packing bread on the shelves of a supermarket called Pathmark in the Bronx. Everyone liked Willie at Pathmark, where he worked on Aisle 16. He was quiet and helpful, even though he only earned $3.10 an hour.

On 5 October, Willie's manager, Marco Minuto, was called by the British promoter Mickey Duff. Did Willie fancy fighting in London against an English middleweight called Tony Sibson? Neither Marco nor Willie had ever heard of Sibson – whose scheduled opponent had made a late withdrawal. Willie needed the money. He agreed to fight for $3,000. Willie would arrive two days before the bout. Marco figured that one day would be enough for Willie to shake off the jetlag. They did not breathe a word to Duff or the British Boxing Board of Control that Willie was still suspended from boxing in New York.

Sibson, who eventually sent Alan Minter into retirement, stopped Willie in two rounds. Duff shrugged. It hardly looked as if the bum had tried before Sibson smashed him to the canvas.

Clancy and Duff discussed Classen over the phone. Duff thought Classen had no heart; but Clancy knew Puerto Rican fighters. At home, in San Juan or New York, their pride would never allow them to just quit. Willie Classen's nickname was 'Macho'. Clancy was sure that, in his hometown, Classen would give Scypion a real test.

Marco Minuto haggled over money and finally they got $1,500 to fight Scypion. Once that had been settled, Willie applied to have his New York licence reinstated. He was examined and he grunted when asked if he had lost the fight in London on cuts. Willie could not let them know he had suffered a heavy knockout just seven weeks before. He was granted his licence and the fight was on.

Emile allowed Kenny Weldon, head trainer in his high platform shoes, to take charge. He changed into his gear for the fight. Emile wore black gym shoes, dark trousers and a white training top with a striking motif on the back. The index finger and the thumb of a black hand were joined together to make a little 'O' of affirmation. It was the kind of positive signal Emile liked to give all his fighters.

As he walked with Scypion and Weldon to the ring, it felt like the old days. People called out his name, but Emile chose not to wave back. He felt the attention should be on his fighter.

Scypion wore white trunks, while Willie Classen was clad in soft red with yellow trim around the waist. Emile noticed how Classen puffed out his chest and held his gloved fist high when the ring announcer introduced him in grandiose style: *'Willieeee ... "Macccchoooo" ... Classennnn!'*

Emile glanced over at Gil and shrugged. Why did Latino fighters love being 'Macho'?

As the ring emptied, and Emile ducked between the ropes to take his seat just below Scypion's corner, he waved to John Condon in the middle of the front row. The old Madison Square Garden publicist was the television commentator for the night, assisted by Davey Vasquez, the featherweight prospect.

They started quietly but, by the third round, it turned serious. After heavy trading, Scypion made Classen reel back. The Texan then nailed him with a right hand. Classen was down, on his hands and knees, as referee Lew Eskin started counting. Emile knew Classen would get up even if, just as the Puerto Rican was back on his feet at '. . . eight', some wiseguy yelped, 'He's going down.'

Classen bobbed and weaved and Scypion missed some big shots. Emile clapped encouragingly as the Texan settled back into his ominous rhythm. 'There's a lot of action in the ring now,' Condon shouted. 'He has Willie Classen in a lot of trouble. Classen is hanging on.'

Scypion punished Classen, who had been backed into a corner, with two thunderous blows to the head. 'Classen's legs have gone completely,' Condon warned.

Yet all his Puerto Rican pride, missing in London, surged through Macho. He fought back.

The round ended. Scypion stared hard at Classen and then nodded vigorously. It was a way of commending his opponent's bravery. Classen wandered towards Scypion's corner and his trainer raced across the ring to steer him back in the right direction.

Weldon wiped Scypion's face, and Emile pulled back the waistband on the trunks of his fighter so that he could draw in breath. 'Relax, champ,' he said in his soft singsong, 'you're doing great.'

A Latino band struck up a jaunty melody. It was toe-tapping stuff in between such violent hitting.

'Any kind of good, sharp punch will do the job now on Willie Classen,' Condon suggested midway through the fourth round. 'What do you think, Davey?'

'Well, Willie's an unusual fighter,' Vasquez countered. 'He can throw some bombs when you least expect it. So you can never really count him out.'

'He's taking quite a bit of punishment,' Condon replied. 'So he's going to have to get some new juice out of his battery to come back in this fight.'

'Yeah,' Vasquez said, 'if the battery's dying out, he's in trouble.'

Scypion rocked Classen with a nasty left hook. It seemed unsurprising that, at the bell, Classen again walked to the wrong corner.

A card girl in a tiny red miniskirt and tight black top ducked through the ropes so that, in high heels, she could walk around the ring holding up a sign with a number – just in case anyone forgot they would start the fifth round next. It would never have happened at the old Garden.

Emile glanced at Classen's corner. They seemed panicky, waving a big towel in his face while he asked for water. 'There's no rush,' Emile said to Scypion. 'Look for the combinations. Don't waste any punches.'

Vasquez, watching round five as Classen fought with renewed energy, agreed. 'Scypion has a tremendous left hook and left uppercut – but Willie Classen, when he puts them together, bangs pretty hard himself. Scypion can't just walk in on him. He has to be very careful.'

A right uppercut made Classen's head nod sickeningly. 'He looks a little dazed,' Condon confirmed.

'He's still fighting, he's still trying,' Condon said more brightly as Classen fired back. Scypion was precise, remembering Emile's advice, hitting Classen with measured blows.

Another smooth Latino rhythm blasted out between rounds and, at the sound of the bell for round six, Willie Classen got up and danced in his corner. The words '*El Macho*' shimmered on his red trunks.

Vasquez suggested that Classen was no longer fighting with 'the same kind of style, desire and energy of a year ago. He's lost something.'

As if stung by the commentary, Classen threw a flurry of punches. Scypion held on, for the first time, and the Forum roared. They wanted Classen, the boy from the Bronx, to come back.

'Scypion might have been hurt,' Condon exclaimed as the Texan back-pedalled.

'He was hurt by a left hook and that's why he's moving around,' Vasquez said. 'He's trying to clear his head.'

'Classen knows it,' Condon yelped. 'Classen pours it on.'

Scypion was smart. He crowded Classen in a neutral corner, allowing him little space to punch. Scypion barrelled his head into Classen's chest and tied him up. The danger, for the black Texan, passed.

A funky organ solo boomed around the arena and the crowd whistled as a different ring-card girl, dressed in lacy red with a short black bob, strutted around with a yellow 'Round 7' sign. Emile leaned on the ropes, listening to Kenny Weldon's instructions, while Classen's corner waved their huge red towel in his face.

The expressionless Scypion made Classen miss time and again, and peppered *El Macho* with his jab and salty combinations. Scypion was more than just a brutal KO artist. But Davey Vasquez could see tiredness creeping over both fighters as they faced 'these last two rounds'.

'Three rounds, Davey,' Condon corrected gently. 'Eight, nine and ten.'

'I've had too many bouts,' Vasquez joked.

Classen forced the pace in the eighth, and stalked Scypion. The Texan lost his mouthpiece. 'If he gets hit in the mouth,' Vasquez said, 'he might be in trouble. It's amazing. In the early rounds it looked like Willie was out of gas. It looked like he was going home early. And now, all of a sudden, he perks up.'

Scypion switched to boxing, keeping Classen at long range. Then, just as Classen closed the distance between them with ten seconds left in the round, Scypion hammered him to the body.

'Close the show, champ,' Emile said before the start of the ninth.

Scypion came out, blazing away on the inside, and hurt Classen up close. With a minute left in the round, he backed up the Puerto

Rican in the corner so that Classen was jammed against the sponsor-covered stake. Scypion connected with a blurring series of right hands.

'Willie Classen is hurt,' Condon screamed. 'He's ready to go down but he's up against the ropes.'

Scypion paused and looked purposefully at the referee, willing him to stop it. Lew Eskin finally stepped in and made Classen take a standing count.

'I can see myself in there,' Emile said to Mike Jones, Scypion's manager, in the seats below their corner.

Scypion hesitated and then referee Eskin waved him back in with twenty seconds left.

'He's hurt,' Vasquez warned, looking up at Classen. 'He's hurt, John.'

'He's hurt plenty,' Condon agreed.

'They ought to stop it.'

Scypion went back to work, thudding punches into the helpless form of Classen on the ropes.

Emile, remembering the sight of Benny Paret pinned to the ropes before he slid down in woozy imitation of a crucifixion, gripped Mike Jones by the arm.

'I see myself in there,' Emile repeated hoarsely, horror thick in his throat.

'One good punch will do it,' Condon yelped as Scypion threw and missed with a haymaker.

Classen reeled into another corner and Scypion made him hunch over with a right to the ribs.

'There's the right hand,' Condon said. 'That could be the one.'

Another two rights came winging in, just as the bell rang. Classen slumped onto the bottom rope.

'He's out on his feet, John,' Vasquez said. 'There's no way this should go on.'

Classen's cornermen steered him back to his little wooden stool.

The referee stood over Classen but, working as a scoring judge, he scrawled another round in favour of Scypion rather than checking on a barely conscious man.

The music started up, as frisky and sunny as if it was blasting out at a beachside bar rather than in a boxing slaughterhouse. Emile clung to the ropes, standing over Scypion. He could not look away from Willie, whose head twitched as he tried to find his gumshield.

On the television monitors they watched, in slow motion, the series of rights with which Scypion had scythed so much life out of Classen. They mirrored those terrible right uppercuts Emile had smashed into Benny's head.

'There's the first right hand,' Condon said as, on his screen, he watched Classen's head wobble.

'Second right hand,' Vasquez said grimly.

'That's the one that really did it,' Condon suggested.

'Here's the third right hand,' Vasquez murmured. 'He's out of it right now.'

In the slow-motion footage, Scypion turned again to the referee, as if to plead for mercy for Willie.

'One round,' someone screamed. 'Go get him, Willie baby!'

At the bell, Scypion was off his stool quickly, striding towards the centre of the ring.

The referee looked at Classen again, and held up his hand to stop Scypion.

Classen then stood up, and Eskin gestured to Scypion. The fight was not yet over. Emile turned away and climbed down from the ring.

'The bell rang and Willie Classen just sat on his stool,' Condon said in surprise.

Classen was already back on the ropes. Scypion hit him again, and then followed with a right cross that looked as if it had knocked Classen into oblivion.

'Two right hands and that's the end of it,' Condon said bluntly as Scypion wheeled away, his arms raised in triumph.

Relief spread deep inside Emile. He moved quickly to Scypion. The savagery had ended.

Mike Jones celebrated with his fighter. They gambolled in the ring, while Emile stepped back. He could see Classen lying on the wrong side of the ropes. Classen was motionless.

The bell rang again, and the announcer shouted into his microphone. 'After twelve seconds of the tenth round the winner by KO ... *Wilford Scypion!*'

Emile tried to towel down Scypion and to keep him still, but the jubilant Texan strode away to soak up the applause. He raised his lethal right hand again.

'Thirteen fights, thirteen knockouts,' Condon said as he turned back to yet another replay of the end.

'Willie didn't know where he was at,' Vasquez said. 'They should have never let him out the corner that last round.'

'Willie Classen is still lying on the apron of the ring, on the far side,' Condon acknowledged. 'There is Wilford Scypion, as happy as can be, but Willie Classen is in a little bit of trouble.'

Chaos gripped the Forum. The doctor and a small crowd huddled around the fallen boxer. Willie Classen's manager, Marco Minuto, cut the gloves from his hands. They still could not rouse the fighter. The doctor called for an ambulance to be sent to Madison Square Garden. It was a dire emergency but the ambulance never arrived. After a thirty-minute wait a sports administrator, Richard McGuire, ran out into the street. He spotted another ambulance on 8th Avenue and, racing into the traffic, flagged it down.

The ambulance belonged to Cabrini hospital, but McGuire insisted they take the dying fighter to the closest medical centre. Five minutes later, amid a screaming blue siren, they rushed Willie Classen to Bellevue hospital.

Emile wanted to get out of the Garden as fast as he could; but he saw the devastation in Wilford Scypion. He hung around and yet there was little he could say.

Gil Clancy found him. They embraced and Gil said, 'I'm sorry.'

Scypion wanted to fly back to Houston that night. But he needed to see Willie in hospital.

Emile looked away. On the night of the Paret fight, the Cuban's cornermen had turned him away. They refused to let him see Benny in his hospital room.

Suddenly, he could stand it no longer. Emile stretched out his hand to Scypion, telling him to stay strong, and said goodbye to everyone else. They all understood why he could not stay.

Gil had Emile pull his hood over his head in the hope he would avoid any waiting reporters. Emile slipped out of a side entrance and headed for his car. Luis was waiting for him. They needed to be together.

Two hours after he had been battered unconscious, neurosurgeons at Bellevue hospital removed a large blood clot lodged between Willie Classen's brain and the dura mater, the outer membrane, in an attempt to relieve the unbearable pressure. The fighter remained in a deep coma.

Wilford Scypion visited his vanquished opponent. He and Kenny Weldon saw Willie's third wife, Marilyn, waiting in the hallway. Kenny urged Wilford forward but the fighter could not face her.

Five days later, at 7.42 p.m. on Wednesday 28 November 1979, Willie Classen died. The official cause of death was an acute subdural haematoma following a succession of heavy blows to the head.

Emile Griffith was soon confronted by reporters. 'I'm so sorry for Willie,' he said simply. 'I'm so sorry for Wilford. I know what he's feeling right now.'

As Dave Anderson wrote in the *New York Times*, 'Wilford Scypion will always be haunted by this memory. For the rest of his boxing career, perhaps for the rest of his life, Scypion's toughest opponent might be himself. The tragic irony of the Texas middleweight's situation is that Emile Griffith worked his corner in the fatal bout at the Felt Forum.'

Anderson pinpointed the eerie parallels with the tragedy of Benny Paret in the old Garden. 'It flashed at me, too,' Emile admitted to Anderson, 'but I tried not to think of it.'

He did not convince anyone. 'Emile Griffith has always tried not to think of it,' Anderson wrote of Paret's death, 'but the memory is always with him. For weeks after that fight, Griffith had a recurring dream. He would see Benny Paret walking toward him and he would say: "How are you, Kid?" and reach out for Paret's hand. But instead of taking his hand, Emile Griffith would wake up in a cold sweat.'

Mike Jones, Scypion's manager, explained how deeply Emile had been affected by another fatality. 'In the fight, right near the end, he twice said, "Oh my God, I see myself in there." Afterwards, Emile wanted to comfort Wilford. But he was so upset he left early.'

'I kill a man and most people understand and forgive me . . .'

How long would forgiveness last, amid the tragedy of yet another death in the ring?

Willie Classen's body had been transported from the Bellevue hospital to the Ortiz funeral home in the Bronx, which had tended to the corpse of Benny Paret in April 1962. Classen's funeral was expected to be held at the St Joan of Arc Catholic church before he would be buried at St Raymond's cemetery. Yet the service and burial were delayed. The management of the Ortiz funeral home would not release the body until a $2,000 bill was paid to cover costs of the Paret service. Those charges had never been settled and, seventeen-and-a-half years later, the undertakers decided to take a stand against fallen boxers.

The money was raised, in memory of Benny Paret and Willie Classen, and the Puerto Rican middleweight was buried a week later.

The fight game remained in purgatory. Senator Roy Goodman issued an immediate suspension of all boxing in New York until a detailed investigation had been completed. His special committee eventually concluded that Classen's death had been a 'preventable tragedy', which was 'a glaring indictment of an archaic and inadequate system of boxing supervision'. The sport would only be allowed to recommence in New York once a six-point programme to protect fighters had been implemented. These included a stipulation that it become mandatory for all ringside physicians and supervisory officials to receive neurological training, while an ambulance needed to be on site at every promotion. CAT scans for boxers would become obligatory and a computerised boxer identification system had to be accelerated in order to track a fighter's history of knockouts.

For six weeks, until 19 January 1980, boxing venues in New York remained dark. The blackout, however, was clogged with voices. Most were accusatory, some were defensive. As referee and match-maker, Lew Eskins and Gil Clancy were subjected to intense scrutiny. 'I'm sorry I made the match,' Clancy admitted. 'But it was a competitive fight. I don't want to single out Marco Minuto, Classen's manager, but I wouldn't have let the guy go out there for the last round. He's very inexperienced. I think 50 per cent of managers don't have the minimum standards we need in boxing.'

Eskins, still suspended from boxing, stressed his credentials. 'In the first fight that night, I was booed because I stopped a fight with two seconds left in the round. I stopped it because the kid was unable to defend himself. I did my job later on as well. I checked Classen and he seemed lucid.'

The referee remembered that, before Paret had been left comatose in 1962, he had knocked down Griffith. 'The bell saved Griffith. But who's to say that if Paret had won that night he would not have been hit by a truck after celebrating his victory. I keep asking, "Why did it have to be Willie Classen? Why did it have to be me?" There are no answers. It's just fate.'

In those torturous weeks, Luis held Emile whenever the old champion cried. He held him, too, when Emile was at last able to talk to him about Benny. Slowly, as friends and lovers, Emile and Luis helped each other. Emile voiced other haunting memories. He told Luis how he had been abused by his threatening and mysterious 'uncle', the man who had forced him to do unspeakable deeds when he had been just a simple boy on a sunlit island. Luis, in turn, found the courage to talk for the first time about the sexual molestation he had also suffered as a boy. They became stronger together.

They eventually moved to an apartment on Highland Avenue, in Jersey City, which they shared with one of Emile's gay friends, Eddie Hernandez. It helped having Eddie pay some of the rent, and Emile and Luis had their own bedroom. But some family members still despised them. Franklin, Emile's younger brother, remained contemptuous of gay relationships. They were more shocked when Luis's teenage brother, Angel, also lambasted Emile.

Angel slipped a note under the apartment door. Emile, who was at home on his own, read it first. The letter was just a few scrawled words on a sheet of lined paper torn from a school workbook. 'Why are you living with these faggots instead of being with your family?' Angel asked his big brother.

Luis found Emile hunched up in a corner of their bedroom. The great old champion was distraught. At first he turned away, feeling angry and shamed all over again.

It seemed as if the ghosts of the past would never leave him, as the same old dilemma rose up again and again, taunting him in new ways.

'*I kill a man and most people forgive me. However, I love a man and many say this makes me an evil person.*'

Luis loved Emile and he refused to be pushed aside. He wrapped his arms around his lover. Emile began to sob. Luis cried too but, afterwards, he felt clearer in his head. It was time he changed. He had dabbled in drugs and Emile had often tried to persuade him not to get wasted. Luis, for too long, had been a boy. It was time that he cleaned himself up and looked after Emile, rather than the other way around.

'I'm going nowhere without you, Junior,' Luis told Emile.

'Me neither, champ,' Emile replied.

They headed back into New York City, to the parade of gay bars and clubs in and around Times Square. Emile loved the atmosphere as much as ever and his extravagance remained boundless, despite his inconsistent earnings. Luis would tell him that he didn't have to buy champagne for everyone, but Emile just shrugged and laughed.

'These are my friends,' he said, relieved that in the sanctuary of his gay world he could embrace, rather than deny, the people who meant so much to him. 'These are our friends.'

Luis, in all the partying, lost his slim body and grew to twice his original size. But they had great fun and Emile would think nothing of hiring a limousine to take them straight to Stella's or Sally's Hideaway, where Freddie Wright did the most incredible female impersonations. He was a better Diana Ross than Diana Ross herself. They danced and hollered along to the old anthems. 'I Will Survive', with Freddie as a young Gloria Gaynor, always had them roaring at a time when gay New York was ravaged by AIDS.

Death still stalked Emile and the ring. He worked with a fighter, Juan Ramon 'Bambino' Cruz, whose opponent, Isidro Perez, died six days after their fight, again at the Felt Forum, on 30 September 1983. It was a savage irony that Fred Bowman had also died, in March 1982 – thirteen months after he had lapsed into a coma following his bout with the same Isidro Perez.

Emile's real uncle, Murphy Griffith, was in the corner on the terrible night in November 1983 when his fighter, Ray 'Boom Boom' Mancini knocked out Duk-koo Kim of South Korea in the fourteenth round of a vicious contest at Caesars Palace in Las Vegas. Kim died four days later and everyone wanted to know, again, how Emile felt, and to hear his memories of Benny Paret.

After that trilogy of interlinked fatalities, Emile told Luis it was time he sold 'the death belt'. He could no longer bear to keep the belt he had retained the night Benny had slid away into his coma and death.

*

Boxing also helped. Emile trained lots of fighters and the money started rolling in again. He and Luis had been struggling and they had moved back to Hollis, Queens, where Chubby Checker still lived in the house that Emile had bought decades earlier. She was happy to have her boy home, even with his 'son', so that she could try to regain some of her old control over Emile.

At least there was always another upcoming big fight. Emile found it easy to help James 'Bonecrusher' Smith, a mild college graduate, make his mark in the heavyweight division. Smith was an awkward stylist, rather than a real bone crusher, but Emile plotted a strategy to help him wait until Frank Bruno, the hugely popular and unbeaten London heavyweight, punched himself out in their Wembley battle. Smith then knocked out Bruno and eventually earned himself a multimillion-dollar title shot at the fearsome Mike Tyson.

Emile took Bonecrusher to Vegas to face Tyson in March 1987. The young heavyweight was a wrecking ball of a world champion, but he was also a ring historian. His reverence towards Emile Griffith was curiously touching, and he paid homage to the former champion's achievements and longevity in the ring. Tyson did not come close to stopping Smith. It was a tedious affair but Emile was happy. His fighter was unhurt and Emile took home a cheque for $90,000. It was like being a world champion fighter again.

That Tyson purse, in 1987, constituted a landmark moment in Emile's relationship with his family. He was bold enough to confront his mother. He told her that he loved her but, for once, he would not share his ring earnings. Emile would use the $90,000 to set up a trust fund for Luis and himself. He had no idea what the future might hold, but he was certain that he and Luis would remain together. Chubby Checker was unhappy; but, finally, it was time Emile looked after himself and the man he loved.

Emile loved going to Stella's and Sally's, to Hombre and Katz's, because he always found Freddie. If he was not working as a bartender, Freddie would be DJ-ing or performing as a drag queen. Freddie made sure that he kept a close eye on Emile. As the years passed, and Emile became older and more forgetful, he drank even harder. Freddie knew that, when Emile started drinking, he would also certainly end up very drunk unless good care was taken of him. It was the easiest way Emile had of blunting the enduring confusion inside him.

'No more, baby,' Freddie would say softly to Emile. 'It's time we got you home. I'm calling Luis.'

Emile also looked after Freddie. He and Calvin were in a bar once, where Freddie worked, and it was a busy afternoon. Freddie was working his skinny butt hard, racing up and down the counter to keep everyone served. Someone yelled: 'Hey, faggot, I been waiting a long time.'

Emile didn't want anyone being called a faggot or a *maricón*, let alone someone he loved, like Freddie. His whole life had been defined by that word and its terrible consequences. The old hurt rose up inside him.

'*I kill a man and most people forgive me. However, I love a man . . .*'

'Listen,' Emile said quietly to the man, 'that's my friend. Don't call him a faggot.'

'Who the fuck are you?' the guy sneered as he stood up.

Freddie could not quite believe it but, before he could even blink, Emile had knocked down the much younger man. Emile looked at him for a moment and then went outside for a walk, to cool off.

A couple of kids stood over the man. 'Don't you know you who're messin' with?' one of them said.

'Aw, he's just a faggot too,' the guy said, after checking that Emile had disappeared.

'Hey, man,' the second kid cackled, 'that's Emile Griffith.'

The bruiser sat up, his eyes widening in surprise. 'What? That's Emile Griffith – *the boxer?*'

'No,' Freddie said sharply. 'That's Emile Griffith, the five-time world champion boxer.'

When Emile came back to his seat, the man walked over and offered his hand. Emile took it, but he did not smile.

'I'm sorry,' the man said. 'I had no idea. Let me buy you a drink.'

Emile shook his head. 'No, I don't want anything. It's just that you called my friend a faggot and you had no right to do that.'

'I won't do it again,' the man said, looking like a chastised boy.

'Thank you,' Emile said quietly.

There was much laughter, too. Freddie entertained them with a life like no other. He was no longer with Dante Rodriguez, his divine Puerto Rican husband, but he had a knack for making people fall in love with him. Emile, Luis and Calvin were beside themselves with mirth at Freddie's latest escapade. He had just completed a show at Bon Soir in the Village. He was so convincing as a woman that a guy came up to him and said, seriously, that Freddie was his kind of girl. He clearly had no idea that Freddie was a man. He was in for a big surprise, Freddie chortled when he told the story to his friends, later that night.

'You're very cute,' Freddie told his Bon Soir admirer.

'Where do you live, gorgeous?' the man asked.

'I live in Jamaica, Queens, honey,' Freddie smiled.

'Would you like some company in Jamaica, Queens?' Freddie's fan asked.

'Why not?' Freddie said. 'It could be fun.'

Freddie was right. It just turned out to be a little different from how he had imagined. Once they got back to his place, he fixed them a couple of drinks, moved into the bedroom and turned the lights down low. But Freddie was not a liar. He always wanted to be upfront. So, as he and the Bon Soir man yakked away, he turned to the mirror and began to remove his false eyelashes. He then took off his long blonde wig.

The man leaned forward in surprise. Freddie, keeping eye contact with him in the mirror, then reached down into his dress and lifted the stuffing from his bra.

'Wait a minute,' the guy yelled. 'You're a man?'

'Yes, honey,' Freddie said coyly. 'What did you think I was?'

'My God,' the man said. 'I thought you were a real woman.'

'Thank you, sweetie,' Freddie said. 'I'm flattered.'

At this point in his story, Freddie paused for a long time. Emile, who had been laughing hard, banged his fist on the table. 'C'mon, Freddie,' he cackled. 'What happened next?'

Freddie took them back to his bedroom. The man stood up and walked over to the wigless Freddie. 'Well,' he said, 'that's real funny, because I have a surprise for you.'

'What's up?' Freddie said, in bemusement.

Freddie paused and, again, Emile didn't know whether to scream or laugh. He ended up doing both when Freddie revealed the truth. 'The guy came up real close and, bam, he told me he was a woman.'

Freddie's gang exploded in noise and disbelief. A female impersonator had ended up with a lesbian dressed as a man. They had fooled each other.

'So what did you do?'

'We went to bed, of course,' Freddie said casually.

'You fucked a *woman*?' Calvin yelped.

'You know what?' Freddie said in a whisper, while arching an eyebrow. 'It was pretty good . . .'

On a sleepy July afternoon, in 1992, Emile needed to shake off the jetlag. He and Juan Laporte, his Brooklyn-based Puerto Rican fighter, had just arrived at Newark after a twenty-six-hour flight from Sydney. Laporte was a very good boxer, but he was also a 32-year-old campaigner after fifty bouts. They had gone all the way to Australia so that Laporte could face Kostya Tszyu, a venerable amateur champion. Tszyu had only fought three times professionally before he met Laporte in Sydney. Yet he was such a good fighter, who would soon become a hugely respected junior-welterweight world champion, that he was too good for even a wily old fox like Laporte.

It had been so cold in Sydney that the humid warmth of Newark felt beautiful. Emile had spent much of the flight consoling Laporte.

Tszyu was seriously good and he was also much the bigger man. A day after the weigh-in, he had scaled fifteen pounds more than Laporte, who had originally been a featherweight.

The fighter offered his trainer a lift to Queens when they landed. 'It's okay, champ,' Emile said.

Emile was in need of a drink and some Times Square sleaze. He embraced Laporte and sauntered over to the taxi rank.

A yellow checker cab snaked into view. Emile climbed in. 'Eighth Avenue and 41st Street, champ,' he said cheerfully.

Emile was heading for Hombre where, hopefully, he would find Freddie in the mood to pour him some serious shots. He needed the haze of drink and a little seamy fun to snap him out of his exhaustion.

Hombre, as Benny Paret would have told him, was Spanish for man. Emile was in a mood for the company of a few young Latino men. He loved Luis but it would be good to see some Hispanic boys doing a sultry dance. Emile would be home in Queens soon enough.

He rolled out of the cab and headed for Hombre. A stray queen yelled his name, but the bar was quiet on a Monday afternoon. Emile looked around. No sign of Freddie. He had a couple of drinks. Still no Freddie.

'It's Freddie's day off,' another barman told him.

'Damn,' Emile sighed. 'Line me up a couple more . . .'

It was late by the time he stumbled up the stairs, hauling his suitcase behind him. At least he had not done his usual trick and forgotten it at the bar. The gleaming neon lights outside made him blink. He felt very drunk. Emile looked left, and then right, hoping to spot a cab that would take him back to Queens, Luis and his comfortable bed.

Emile did not see the fist as it smashed into the side of his skull. He said later that it felt as if a small fireworks display had exploded deep inside his head. Dazzling colours lit up his brain. These were not the black lights of unconsciousness he had seen just before a murderous hitter like Rubin Carter knocked him out in the ring.

Still, it was one hell of a punch. He staggered forward, as the effects of the drink kicked in, and another blow caught him. There was more than one man out to get him.

They said the word, then, and it tore at him. 'You fucking *faggot* ...'

He got up and bunched his small hands into black fists. Emile was nobody's faggot. A blurry group of snarling men closed in on him. He lashed out and felt the thwack of his fist against a hard skull. His fingers throbbed but he was sure the guy's head felt a lot worse. There was no more time to think as they were all over him then. There could have been six of them, or more, because all Emile could do was cover his head with his arms and absorb the punishment.

They hit him for so long, and kicked him just as hard, that any thoughts of fighting back were gone. All he could do was curl up in a ball and wait for the beating to end. He felt his bones crack and his skin burst open. Blood, hot and sticky, poured out of him. He was still conscious when they rolled him over. He moaned in agony when they hunted for his wallet and watch. They tore off his rings and chain and picked up his suitcase. He was left on the street, a red pool of blood leaking from his head.

Emile did not know how long he lay there, not far from Hombre, or even if he was helped to his feet. All he could remember, later, was walking blindly down 8th Avenue, weaving past terrified people.

He passed out and someone, at last, helped him. He did not know how he got home.

Luis was asleep in bed when he heard a crash downstairs. He grabbed a baseball bat, fearing a burglar, and barrelled down the stairs. He switched on the light. He looked down a further flight of stairs, leading to the basement. It was then that he saw Emile, clinging to the banister.

The old champion, the man Luis loved like no other, looked broken. His right arm, seeping red, was wrapped around the banister. His bald head was worse. It was caked in dried blood, but looked as if it might burst open at any minute. Luis ran towards him: 'Junior!'

Emile fell, ripping up part of the banister as he tumbled down towards the concrete floor. Luis lunged out and caught him. Luis saved Emile before he broke his neck. He cradled Junior and saw how his clothes were torn and filthy, covered in dust and blood. His right foot was the size of a melon.

Luis carried Emile up the stairs and laid him out, covering him with a blanket. He called Emelda, Chubby Checker, babbling that they needed her.

Emelda was soon there. 'Junior! Junior!' she screamed. 'What happened to my boy?'

Emile opened his eyes. 'I fell, Mommy,' he whispered. 'I fell.'

Carefully, Emile's mother and his lover undressed him. They managed to bath him and wipe away the blood. They lowered him into the bed he shared with Luis. His eyes were closed.

'Let Junior rest,' Emelda advised.

They cleaned up the mess and found a pouch containing $800 in his underwear. Emile had hidden the balance of his fight purse from the Kostya Tszyu bout in his secret hiding place. The muggers had not got his money, but they had stolen much of his life.

Luis and Emelda watched over him for two days, trying to help him drink water, but not really knowing why he was sleeping so much. They were desperate when Juan Laporte called.

'Where's Junior?' Laporte asked.

'Junior's sick,' Emelda cried into the phone. 'He's very sick, Juan ...'

Laporte could not believe how ill his trainer looked when he arrived. He screamed at Luis and Emelda. Why had they not taken him to hospital?

An ambulance took Emile to Queens general hospital. His kidneys had been badly damaged in the assault. They were barely functioning. He also had a spinal infection. Emile Griffith was slipping away.

He was rushed to a specialist unit at Elmhurst hospital in Queens. In intensive care, he was hooked up to a humming kidney machine.

Thin tubes were fed into his arm and his flared nostrils. He did not move while he was monitored constantly by specialists.

Luis, Emelda and Juan Laporte stayed at his bedside, and they were soon joined by Gil Clancy and Howie Albert. His old managers were distraught.

'Why was he in a gay bar?' Howie asked, as if he could not quite believe that Emile had kept to his old ways.

Laporte, a proud Puerto Rican fighter, insisted Emile was not gay. He just liked hanging around with gay people; and he got rolled by some brutal muggers.

'All that matters,' Gil said softly, 'is that he makes it ...'

The old trainer leaned over his stricken fighter. It looked as if he was about to kiss him goodbye. But the bond between a boxer and his cornerman ran deep. As if they were lost deep in battle, in the last round of a ferocious championship bout, Gil murmured a simple instruction: *'Fight, Emile, fight ...'*

Seven months after the attack, Emile Griffith finally started to heal. At home he could talk and walk around. He was able to dress and feed himself. Life would never be the same but, somehow, he had survived.

A faded version of the old mazy patterns of Emile's world resumed. He watched fighters in the gym, he went to see Calvin and Freddie. People still arrived from around the world to interview him. They always asked him about Benny Paret.

Emile didn't want to talk about Benny, and he began to forget all his other fights. The names and the nights under the hot lights became a dark blur. His mind started to slip, and the shutters of confusion cluttered up his head. Emile could not remember much anymore.

The first hazy flickers of dementia had emerged years earlier, but the attack turned its previously scattered warnings into a steady march of deterioration. Emile was losing his mind slowly, inexorably.

He still had a little time left and he made the most of it. He went to the fights and to boxing conventions and dinners. Emile smiled a lot and called everyone 'champ'. He only looked dazed and a little frightened whenever anyone asked anything more searching, about his love life or Benny Paret. The ghosts clung to him, reminding him of the worst times of his life, even as he began to forget everything else. It seemed as if he would never shake free from that haunting Saturday night in the Garden, on 24 March 1962.

Forty-two years later, in 2004, Emile Griffith found serenity. His great friend, the compassionate and amusing writer Ron Ross, who had written his wry and gentle boxing biography, called *Nine ... Ten ... And Out!: The Two Worlds of Emile Griffith*, met with two film-makers, Dan Klores and Ron Berger. They wanted to make a documentary about Emile's third fight with Benny Paret. Ron and Gil Clancy sat down with Emile and talked it through. It felt like the right time. The documentary would not probe his sexuality, and it was a way in which Emile might try to close the wound.

Emile agreed and the shooting of an enthralling and moving documentary called *Ring of Fire* began. All the old faces and voices filled the screen. Even though his speech was slurred and his memory was shot, Emile did well alongside Gil and Howie and all the great old boxing writers like Jerry Izenberg and Pete Hamill, Jimmy Breslin and Ron Ross. The commentary of Don Dunphy and the *Friday Night Fights* echoed as if they had come back to life.

It was not the time or the place to talk about Calvin, Freddie or Matthew. Luis featured briefly, as Emile's adopted son, but it was not appropriate to talk about drag queens or transvestites. Instead, Dan Klores persuaded Lucy Paret and her eldest son, Benny Paret Jr, to revisit the night they lost their husband and father.

The film-makers hoped that Lucy might meet Emile. The fighter was willing to face her, but Lucy refused. She could still not bear to look at Emile Griffith. His fists had taken her husband's life away.

She was asked if she ever dreamed of that night. 'Dream?' Lucy said, raising her sad eyes. 'I stopped dreaming a long time ago.'

Benny Jr was different. It would be hard but, yes, he was willing to meet Emile. Ron Ross and Gil Clancy, with Dan Klores, sat down with Emile. They explained that Kid Paret's son, Benny Jr, would talk to him. There would be no pressure to film a staged scene.

They settled on Central Park as a neutral setting. Emile caught the bus, to settle his jangling mind, and he agreed at the last minute to have a small microphone pinned to his shirt. He was told where in the park he would find Benny. If either of them decided it was too much, they could walk away. The documentary was already shot. This would be more a chance for them to discover if it would help to meet.

Klores filmed him from a distance. He was too far away to give Emile any instructions. The old champion was on his own.

Emile wore a black leather jacket, a grey tracksuit and white trainers. He walked through Central Park on an early winter afternoon. Emile slowed and hesitated when he saw a man waiting for him at the appointed spot. He was a black man, in his early forties, with a strong frame and a kind face. A tiny gold stud glinted in his right earlobe.

The man approached him. 'Mr Griffith,' he said, extending his hand. 'It's a pleasure ...'

Emile held the man's hand. The boxer kept shaking it while, all the time, he looked into the face in front of him. 'It's my pleasure to see you, sir,' Emile said.

The handshaking continued, solemn and ceremonial. Eventually, Emile spoke. 'Are you ...' he started to ask, pointing at the man.

Emile stopped and then managed to continue. '... the Kid's son?'

Benny Paret Jr could not talk. He tilted his head to the left and nodded, as his mouth twitched silently. He and Emile were still shaking hands.

Emile tried to talk. There were no words. He could not remember exactly what he wanted to say.

Time passed, and Benny Jr came to Emile's rescue. 'I want you to know,' he murmured, 'there are no hard feelings here.'

Emile let out a great sigh, as if the buried pain of forty-two years could finally be exhumed and then exhaled. He took a step towards Benny Paret's son.

Benny Jr opened his arms in welcome, and Emile sank into his chest. His words were muffled, but audible through his tears.

'Thank you,' Emile said, clapping Benny Jr on the back, his smooth forehead suddenly furrowed with deep lines. 'Thank you, sir.'

Holding each other, Benny Jr quietly patted Emile. 'I didn't go in there to hurt no one,' Emile cried.

Benny Jr cupped Emile's bald head in his right hand. 'I know,' Benny said.

Emile stepped back so that he could look at Benny Paret Jr. 'But things happen,' he said simply.

'I know.'

They parted. 'It's just ... I always wanted to meet you too, you know.'

'So have I,' Benny Jr replied.

'With your mommy,' Emile said.

'My mom?' Benny murmured.

Emile looked deeply, full of hope, at Benny and Lucy Paret's son. 'It's hard for her,' Benny Jr said.

'I understand,' Emile nodded. 'It's very hard for her. I understand.'

Benny Jr, wearing a smart brown polo-neck sweater, looked at the man who had shared a ring three times with his father. He found the right words to comfort Emile. He found the right words to end the darkness.

'But one thing I can say is that there are no hard feelings. She's ...' Benny Jr said in his gentle voice. He stopped. And then he said it again: 'There are no hard feelings at all.'

Emile sagged a little, but he stretched out his hand again. Benny Jr grasped it. 'Thank you,' Emile said.

Emile let go of Benny's hand. His eyes were closed and his head was down, but he still found his target. His bunched right fist reached out and, with affection and respect, he punched Benny Jr softly on his chest, near the heart. It was a champion fighter's gesture to a fallen champion's son. Emile reached out to bring Benny Jr close to him. He was still crying, but with tangled happiness. The two men, aged sixty-four and forty-two, held their embrace for a long time. They were bound tightly together by boxing, by life and death, and, in the end, by forgiveness and love.

Emile & Orlando

San Juan, Puerto Rico, Friday 12 October 2012

Orlando Cruz listened intently while I read to him a quote from Emile Griffith: 'I kill a man and most people forgive me. However, I love a man and many say this makes me an evil person.'

On the balcony of his apartment in San Juan, Orlando's face almost crumpled as he absorbed the haunting words said four years earlier. He sank back into his chair, and gazed at the falling rain.

The previous week, Orlando had become the first ever professional boxer to come out and confirm in public that he was gay. The 31-year-old Puerto Rican featherweight had made his historic announcement on Telemundo, the Hispanic television network. He and I were in the midst of his first newspaper interview as an openly gay man, for, as soon as the story broke, I knew I had to write about him.

Emile Griffith's story had been in my head since my South African boyhood, when he had stood up to apartheid before losing to Tap Tap Makhathini. I had since learned much about his trilogy of fights with Benny Paret, and gained some understanding of his conflicted sexuality. It provided a stark backdrop to Cruz's revelations, which had made news around the world.

Eventually, Orlando spoke in Spanish as he reflected on the social context of Emile's words. 'It shows the hypocrisy of the world,' he said. 'He probably wanted to say those words in the 1960s and not later. But, fifty years ago, Emile was not living in the moment we are now. He was not as lucky as me.'

Orlando nodded when I asked if he knew the tragic story of Griffith and Paret. 'Of course,' he said. 'Griffith was gay, but he could not do what I did. It was only years later he could admit to being bisexual. I understand. I know the history of boxing, and the pain of that fight. Griffith could not come out. I now have the chance to be different – to be the first boxer in history who can say he is gay. That is a powerful statement but it's also why I was afraid of saying it.'

Exactly fifty years had passed since Paret taunted Griffith as a *maricón*, and yet it seemed as if little had changed. Until Cruz made his announcement most people still regarded the idea of a gay boxer as oxymoronic. The two words, 'gay' and 'boxer', simply not did not fit together.

Boxing was not alone. In 2012, there were no publicly 'out' gay professional sportsmen playing American football, basketball or baseball. Justin Fashanu, until then, was the only professional player who had come out as a homosexual man in British football. Fashanu might have been a million-pound striker but Brian Clough, one of the greatest managers the game has produced, demeaned him at Nottingham Forest as 'a bloody poof'. Fashanu ended up hanging himself in 1998.

In September 2012, just weeks before Cruz's revelation, a taboo subject had returned. Yunel Escobar, a Cuban player for the Toronto Blue Jays, had worn black stickers beneath his eyes during a Major League Baseball game. They contained the words, '*Tu eres maricón*' – 'You are a faggot'.

When asked against whom his taunt was directed, Escobar shrugged: 'Nobody.'

Escobar could not understand why he had caused offence. 'I have friends who are gay,' he protested. 'The person who decorates my house is gay. The person who cuts my hair is gay. Honestly, they haven't felt as offended about this. It's a word [*maricón*] without meaning.'

Orlando shook his head. 'He is wrong. That word carries the same meaning now that it always did.'

The boxer reflected on his lush and sweltering island's brutal homophobia, as well as the bravery of those who refused to deny their sexuality. In recent times, there had been eighteen murders of gay men in eighteen months in Puerto Rico. The deadly vitriol still ran deep.

'I decided to be free,' Orlando said with piercing clarity when asked why, unlike Emile Griffith, he had come out. He ignored the drops of rain glistening on his bare torso. Bam-Bam, a cheerful sausage dog sitting on the fighter's lap, looked up attentively, as if he was listening to familiar words from his master.

'They can call me *maricón* or faggot,' Orlando said as he tickled Bam-Bam behind the ears, 'and I don't care. Let them say it because they can't hurt me now. I am relaxed. I feel so happy. But to make this announcement to the whole world I had to be very strong.'

Orlando's tattooed arms flexed while he deflected Bam-Bam's urge to lick his face. He was besotted with the little dachshund, but Orlando was also fiercely concentrated as he explained the struggle he had finally won over fear and prejudice. 'I have done well as a boxer,' he said before switching to Spanish. 'I've only lost two of my twenty-one fights. I won those other fights but, all this time, I have been living with this thorn inside me. I wanted to take it out of me so I could have peace within myself.'

Orlando glanced down and it was easy to imagine him searching for an invisible wound, the same wound that had scarred Emile. 'You can't see it,' he said of his hurt, 'but it was here.'

He tapped his heart and recalled his bleakest moment. 'People have died because of this,' he said. 'I am proud to be Puerto Rican, just like I am proud to be a gay man. But I was sad and angry a long time because there are two doors to death over this one issue. There is suicidal death – when a gay man cannot stand being unaccepted and takes his own life. And there is homophobic murder. In both these situations I want to be a force for change.'

Orlando was such a warm and friendly man, and an unassuming fighter, that his words carried a jolting impact. He made it sound as if he had personal experience of tragedy. '*Sí, sí,*' he murmured. 'I lost one friend who was murdered by people who hated gay men. I was very angry then because homophobia ended his life in the most violent way. But I was also angry because, at the time, I was hiding my secret.'

The rain fell harder. He stood up, almost reluctantly, as if not wishing to break the spell of his confession. 'Let's go inside or we will look crazy – sitting in the rain.'

Orlando gathered his boxing paraphernalia – scooping up the gloves and headguards, his trunks and socks – and ushered us inside the condominium.

He sat on the kitchen worktop, not quite believing how life had changed in the last few blurring days. 'It's emotional, but I am also excited. I think I can be an example for people in the same position. I have received letters from people saying they have been afraid to come out of the closet because of what their families might think. Now, they say, I have given them courage.'

Seven nights from then, on 19 October 2012, he would fight for the first time as an openly gay man in Kissimmee, Florida. Kissimmee sounded like a sweetly coy name for a gay fighter called Cruz to make his first appearance in the ring as a self-confessed homosexual. But boxing's brutal undertow remained.

While Bam-Bam crunched his dog biscuits and lapped noisily from his water bowl, Orlando licked his dry lips. Boiling down to the 126-pound featherweight limit, and only days from fighting Jorge Pazos, a durable Mexican, he had to ration every morsel of food. Despite his raging thirst, he would soon step into the rustling sweat-suit to help him shed more ounces during afternoon training.

It seemed strange that he should have invited such scrutiny so close to a fight of this magnitude. If he beat Pazos, his hopes of fighting the world's best featherweight, the WBO world champion, Orlando Salido, would feel deliciously close to fruition. But a loss would be disastrous. Was it difficult coming out so close to an important fight?

'No,' Orlando said. 'I have been a professional fighter for twelve years and I have been hiding this secret all that time. Believe me: that means there is so much less pressure on me. All the time I was fighting and thinking when would be the best time to show my real self. It started in 2001 when I told my parents.'

Orlando laughed. 'You should have seen me,' he said, remembering the moment he told his mother he was gay. 'I was crying! She was crying! She said: "It doesn't matter. You are my son. I love you." That made me cry some more.'

He sighed, his breath leaving him in a muted hiss of resignation. 'My dad is more difficult because of the macho thing. Now, it's better. He supports me but . . .'

The fighter shook his head. 'My parents are separated. My dad lives in Miami but I'm glad he will be at the fight to support me. My mother and I will fly together to Orlando. She was always more sympathetic – she's a special friend. And my sister and brother have been great. They have known for a long time.'

His phone rang repeatedly, but Orlando had been so engrossed that he waved dismissively at it. Eventually, he picked it up. 'Oh,' he said, 'it's my trainer. The two o'clock call . . .' He was told that they would train again at 3 p.m. It had been a long day.

Orlando had set his alarm for 4.30 that morning. Thirty minutes later he had slipped out into San Juan's sultry blackness. 'I thought then about the fight against Pazos. If I win then the next fight is for the world title. But I had time to think about everything. I moved to New Jersey two years ago because my manager wanted me to get disciplined. There are too many distractions in Puerto Rico. In New Jersey I started the psychological process of being able to come out. After a while the psychiatrists say: "Are you ready?" I say: "Not yet." A few months later they ask the same question. I was nervous a long time because it's a big step to be the first in history. Even six months ago I was worried how people would take it. I had to wait until I was physically and emotionally prepared.

'It was a big surprise to lots of people in boxing. But Miguel Cotto [the great Puerto Rican light-middleweight, who is the same age as Cruz and his former team-mate on the national amateur team] said beautiful things in support of me. Miguel suspected I was gay but I could never discuss it with him.'

Would his coming out help other gay boxers follow the same path? 'I don't know. Probably in other sports it will happen. But boxing will still be difficult because it is so macho.'

Orlando named Muhammad Ali as his favourite fighter. I did not tell him that Joe Frazier had been Emile's best man. Instead, he covered his face in embarrassment when I suggested that, in his humble way, he had made the kind of history that usually belongs to a monumental fighter like Ali. Orlando had not risked jail, like Ali did in refusing to serve in the US Army in Vietnam, but he had broken boxing's last taboo.

'Thank you,' Orlando said before lightening the moment with a quip. 'Even women in Puerto Rico were surprised. They used to say to me: "Oh, you are beautiful!" Now they say: "Oh my God! You are gay! I'm *sorry*!" But they accept it. They are still nice and warm.'

When did Orlando discover he was gay? 'Before the 2000 Olympic Games in Sydney I tried to deny it to myself. I dated girls as a straight man. I had sex with girls. It was only after I came back from the Olympics that something changed inside me. But, still, I didn't want to accept the truth about myself.'

At the sound of his doorbell, Cruz jumped up. 'You're going to meet my father-in-law,' he said.

Jim Pagan was a ring veteran. He arrived at the condo with a weathered face and a quiet gravitas. Orlando told me how Pagan had trained him since he was seven years old. 'Twenty-four years,' he exclaimed.

Another more emotive bond tied the two men together. 'I went out with Jim's daughter for five years,' Orlando said. 'Her name is Daisy-Karen and she has supported me. Just like Jim.'

I asked the trainer how he felt now that his daughter's former boyfriend had come out as a gay man. 'We have great respect for each other,' Pagan said in gravelly Spanish. 'Orlando is a very good person.'

Orlando laughed. 'Not always,' he said, switching back into English. 'He once told me to fuck off and leave his gym. I had no discipline as a kid. But I always came back to him. He's my second father.'

Walking in tow with Pagan's sons – one who hoped to become a professional fighter, while the other dreamed of playing baseball for a living – Cruz led us to a gym at the far end of the complex. It was neat and clean and without any of the grit and stink of Pagan's boxing gym in downtown San Juan.

Inside, Orlando skipped with a rope and then smacked his fists into Pagan's raised pads. They made eerie shadows when silhouetted against the fading afternoon light; but the old tattooed beat of their pad-work called up an enduring love of boxing. He was just another fighter preparing for a dangerous battle.

Later, I asked Orlando if he felt nervous. 'Not yet,' he said. 'The worst is two hours before the fight. Oh my God! Then there are big nerves. I go very quiet. But as soon as the knock comes on the locker-room door I am fine. And next Friday I will be ready.

'Pazos is a tough, typical Mexican. We respect each other. When they asked him about me he says he doesn't care about my sexual preference. He knows I am a good fighter. I am the same towards him. I keep my private and professional life separate but for one thing...'

Orlando looked up, his eyes shining in his sweat-streaked face. 'If I am inside or outside the ring I just want to be me. And, now, I'm happy I can do it. I can be true to myself.'

I wished him luck and we said our goodbyes. I had just reached the glass door and was about to step outside when Orlando called my name.

'Next year,' he said, 'when this fight is over and I have recovered, can you take me?'

I looked at him in confusion. 'Can you take me to see Emile Griffith?' he said quietly. 'I would be so proud to meet him.'

*

In Boca Raton, Florida, I met Ron Ross, Emile's boxing biographer, and he entranced me again with his stories and memories. He also warned me that Emile had declined markedly in the past few months.

'I can't even bear to visit him now,' Ron said sadly, his usual warmth chilled by the dementia pugilistica that had ruined a five-time world champion. 'It's no longer Emile,' Ron said. 'But thank God for Luis ...'

Ron had read my interview in the *Guardian* with Orlando Cruz and he was impressed by the Puerto Rican. We laughed as I explained that, when he fought Jorge Pazos in Kissimmee, I had followed the fight at the dead of night on Twitter. The world had changed, but the old boxing obsession remained. Ron patted me on the back, kindly. 'We're addicted,' he smiled.

The pressure bearing down on Cruz was immense as his previous anonymity had been replaced by sudden fame around the world. Yet his margin of victory was decisive on all three scorecards – 118-110, 116-111, 118-110. He had moved a huge step closer to the title fight he had craved so long.

When I flew to San Juan, Orlando was jubilant. 'I had to win. I would have let down myself and my people if I had lost. But it was my moment, my opportunity. And I was very happy the crowd respected me. No one said anything bad. That's what I want – for them to see me as a boxer, an athlete and a man.'

A short man, at only five foot four, Orlando seemed to soar up into the clouds. 'I'm getting my title shot,' he exclaimed. 'Can you imagine it? A gay man fighting for a world title!'

Emile Griffith had fought so many world title fights – but the difference was clear. He had never been able to publicly declare his sexuality as a fighter. Orlando would make history.

'How is Emile?' he asked suddenly.

I repeated Ron Ross's words. It did not sound good but I would talk to Luis and, perhaps, sometime in 2013, I would take Orlando to meet Emile, his new inspiration in the ring.

'Please tell them,' Orlando said. 'I am going to dedicate my world title fight to Emile. I must do it.'

On a freezing morning in December 2012, fifty years since Emile Griffith had fought Benny Paret for the last time, I sat on a small sofa in the old fighter's apartment. Luis Rodrigo stretched one of Emile's world championship belts over his knees in a drab brick building on Washington Avenue in Hempstead, Long Island. Emile and Luis's tiny dog, a Chihuahua called Princess, burrowed her head under the belt. She was searching for Luis's hand so she could lick it.

'She misses Emile,' Luis said as he scooped up Princess. 'Ever since he's gone to the nursing home she's been looking for him.'

Emile had been in the Nassau Extended Care Facility, a few blocks away, for more than a year. His dementia, after so many blows to the head, had become so entrenched that he could no longer talk. Ron Ross had been right. Emile lived in a shadowy world of silence and sleep.

The quiet was broken twice a day when Luis went to visit his lover and the man who had officially adopted him in 2005. Luis called Emile his father, but he was more than just an adopted son. He loved and cared for Emile when everyone else had gone. There was little money left, and no glory, and Luis worked two jobs. During weekdays he was based in the post room at Dan Klores' production company in Manhattan. In the wake of *Ring of Fire*, Dan had offered jobs to both Luis and Benny Paret Jr. For a long time they worked alongside each other, before Benny Jr returned to Miami to look after his mother.

'We became good friends,' Luis said of Benny Paret Jr. 'He lost his father, I lost mine. We had a lot in common. We both loved boxing. We were both hard-working guys. Even today we keep in touch.'

Luis also worked as a delivery boy for Domino's Pizza. He drove all over Hempstead delivering pizza, even at the dead of night when the customers were drunk and riotous. Luis needed the money and he still had time to visit Junior. Every morning, before he went into New York, he dropped by the care home to see Emile. And then, before he began his pizza shift, he returned to visit Emile.

Luis looked tired. He still laughed a lot, especially when showing photographs of him and Emile from the early 1980s.

'Man,' he exclaimed. 'Look how thin I am! Damn, what happened?'

Luis had become a very large man, but his physical bulk matched the size of his heart. In the apartment where he and Emile had lived so long, before darkness obliterated everything in the boxer's punched-out brain, he was part of a love story. Only love could possibly drive him on to care so much for the empty shell of Emile.

At one point that Saturday morning, Luis broke down. 'Sometimes I say to myself, "Why him?"' he murmured, his voice cracking, his head falling into his hands.

Luis soon regained his composure. 'He was such a strong individual and I hate to see him like that,' he said. 'I'm doing all the talking. Before, he would ask me about my day and we'd have a joke and we'd watch the boxing together and go out to a bar. It's not easy. This is a man that has won so many world titles. He had full health and we shared a deep experience of life together for over thirty years. To see him in this condition really hurts. But it's part of life. We all get old. Even Emile Griffith gets old. At least we had so many happy times.'

We spoke in detail about Emile's sexuality. 'The straight world to him was the place where he did his business,' Luis said. 'He was Emile Griffith, the boxer. In the gay world, he would unwind and feel very comfortable. One of the reasons he went to the gay bars was that he felt safe. People loved him. People were so proud of him. He represented them. And so Emile always walked into a gay club or bar through the front door. He never used a side door. He showed a lot of balls – because there was so much oppression of gay people. He and Calvin and Freddie and their friends went through so much.'

In a *New York Times* interview with Bob Herbert on 14 April 2005, all the tangled complexity knotted up inside Emile. *Ring of Fire* had just been made and Emile told Herbert that, before he fought Paret for a third time, 'I got tired of people calling me faggot'. The article was called 'The Haunting of Emile Griffith', and Herbert ended by suggesting that, 'he looked as if he wanted to say more. He told me he had struggled his entire life with his sexuality, and agonized over what he could say about it. He said he knew it was impossible in the early 1960s for an athlete in an ultra-macho sport like boxing to say, "Oh, yeah, I'm gay." But after all these years, he wanted to tell the truth. He'd had relations, he said, with men and women. He no longer wanted to hide. He hoped to ride this year in New York's Gay Pride Parade.'

It was almost the closest Emile came to confirming his sexuality. Three years later, in 2008, Emile spoke to Ron Ross as his friend wrote his upbeat biography. Emile allowed himself to be heard in the prologue to a book called *Nine . . . Ten . . . And Out!*: 'I killed a man but did not go to jail. I was angry at him – oh yes, very angry – because he trashed me and insulted me in a very terrible way. He called me a – a faggot. It wasn't just what he said, but the way he was ridiculing me, making a fool, a joke of me in front of a roomful of people who respected me. But even though I was angry, hurt and upset, I never wanted to kill him. The thought never even crossed my mind. But it happened. We are in a cruel business.'

In the prologue to a book that merely skirted Emile's sexuality, an old quote was then developed and amplified in Emile's voice: 'I keep thinking how strange it is, though. I kill a man and most people understand and forgive me. However, I love a man and to so many people this is an unforgivable sin: this makes me an evil person. So even though I never went to jail, I have been in a prison all my life.'

On a telling page near the end of Emile's touching but mostly sunny biography, Ross lingers over a scene in which the fighter studies a poster publicising his appearance at a Stonewall Veterans' Association meeting in May 2005. Beneath a headline of 'GAY BOXING CHAMP EMILE A. GRIFFITH', the poster confirmed that 'he has fought more world championship rounds [339] than any other world champion in history . . . our special guest speaker is the legendary middleweight boxing champion Emile A. Griffith Jr, who is also quietly gay'.

Emile looked at the poster for a long time before he turned to Luis. 'Why are they calling me gay?' he asked.

'Because you're the vice president of the Stonewall Veterans' Association,' Luis answered patiently, 'and you already said you were gay. You said it in your movie [*Ring of Fire*], you said it to the newspapers, and, anyhow, it was never a secret from a lot of your friends and people who knew you.'

Ross quoted Emile's strangely wounded reply in full: 'Okay, but why do they have to make such a big deal about it? Why do they have to advertise it and make me sound like a freak?'

Years later, with Emile lost in dementia, I asked Luis about that bizarre exchange. Emile, I knew, had always stayed true to his sexuality through his deeds and actions. I also understood why he had not been able to confess his real identity in the 1960s and 1970s, when he was a world champion boxer in a grimly repressive time for homosexual men. But why had he remained so circumspect in the twenty-first century, especially after lending his full support to the Stonewall Veterans' Association – where his friend Freddie Wright was such an iconic figure?

Luis smiled sympathetically. 'The Caribbean culture does not easily accept a gay lifestyle,' he said. 'It's like the Latino culture. Franklin, Emile's brother, never really accepted us. But Gloria, his sister, always told me she knew Emile was gay, even as a little boy. But, as a gay man in the 1960s, you could get locked up. My father had to be careful.'

It was strange to hear Luis describe Emile as his father; but their love ran so deep that it did not seem appropriate to probe any inconsistencies. Luis seemed, suddenly, so happy. I muzzled my questions, and simply listened.

'When I think about my dad, I think of the kindness, the selflessness. He impacted my life and other people's lives too. Emile was there to fight for what was right – racial, sexual – it didn't matter. He would say, "Don't mess with my friends." If he was to start all over again he would remain the same person.'

Luis nodded emphatically before looking down at Princess, snoozing on his lap. 'Hearing you talk about South Africa reminds me what Emile said. He told me he had fought in South Africa and he said, proudly, "I brought the government of apartheid to its knees." He said: "No Gil, no Griffith. I am not going to fight without him. I don't care for your laws." The officials looked at each other, clueless as to what to do. So they allowed Emile and Gil to break the South African law, for one night. Emile told me all about that, and about Willie Toweel and everything. So it makes perfect sense you are here now.'

We reached the Paret tragedy and Luis was compassionate. 'Benny Paret was actually an okay guy,' he said. 'I know his son is a very good guy. It's just that Benny Paret came out of that very macho Latino world. Benny was not educated and Emile suffered so much afterwards. But it was better in the later years. Once he made peace with Benny Jr he had some freedom.'

The room was quiet. Outside, on the streets surrounding the Nassau Extended Care Facility, there was a similar hush. On a sleepy Saturday afternoon the snow was piled high on the sidewalks. The occasional swish of a car driving along the icy street broke the silence, but, mostly, there was a deathly stillness.

Luis had disappeared down the hall to receive the latest of his twice-daily updates on Emile's unchanging condition. The old fighter lay on his back, his head propped up by a couple of pillows. His eyes were open and they stared straight at me. I did not see much life inside Emile as I gazed back at him. I moved away, towards the line of photos decorating the wall to his right. Emile kept staring straight ahead.

I saw the familiar faces, belonging to fighters I would spend the next few years writing about, from a time when boxing meant so much to millions of people. I saw Luis Rodriguez, *El Feo*, the Ugly One, a magnificent fighter. I saw Nino Benvenuti, the handsome Italian, 'The Intellectual', who had shared a trilogy of fights with the man lying in the bed next to me. I saw Willie Toweel, who had written the letter that had helped Emile in his darkest days. I saw Joey Archer being nailed by a brutal right uppercut from Emile. I saw the real Emile, the man who beamed down from the walls whether he was at an International Boxing Hall of Fame celebration or in his last public position as vice president of the Stonewall Veterans' Association at the Lesbian-Gay-Bisexual-Transgender Community Center in Greenwich Village.

Luis returned to the room, as bright as ever. 'Hey, Junior,' he said, 'look who's come to see you.'

He bent down to kiss Emile on his smooth, round face. 'C'mon, champ,' Luis said. 'Give us a smile.'

Emile's expression remained frozen. 'Take Emile's hand,' Luis eventually suggested, 'and tell him what you told me this morning.'

I got over my shyness and spoke to Emile about Willie Toweel, Tap Tap Makhathini and Orlando Cruz. I told him how I had met Gil Clancy in Las Vegas in 1999, and how that gripping interview had shaped so many of the ideas I had for this book. I said I would be back, maybe in time for Emile's next birthday on 3 February 2013, when he would turn seventy-five.

Emile's skin looked very black against the white bed linen and his mustard-yellow T-shirt. I still held his small hand. Luis leaned over and stroked Emile's vacant face.

'Hey, champ,' he said. 'Don read Willie's letter. You remember the letter, Junior?'

Luis paused. 'Did you see that?' he asked as he looked up in surprise. 'Did you see Emile smile? It's gone now but I saw it. He heard us. He heard us . . .'

I was not sure if Emile smiled, but Willie was one of the few survivors left from a lost era of boxing. Gil Clancy had died in 2011. Howie Albert was gone. Calvin Thomas too, and Luis Rodriguez. Emile and Willie were still with us, at least in shadowy form, and it felt important to talk to them.

Johannesburg, South Africa, Thursday 8 August 2013

Emile Griffith had died sixteen days earlier, at the age of seventy-five, on 23 July 2013. He slipped away peacefully in his sleep. Emile

Griffith had died sixteen days earlier, at the age of seventy-five, on 23 July 2013. He slipped away peacefully in his sleep. His funeral took place on Saturday 3 August at St Thomas the Apostle Church in Hempstead – and he was buried later that day at St Michael's Cemetery in Queens. Those who loved him most spoke less of their grief than of the release death gave him from dementia. His extraordinary boxing career and life was celebrated in hundreds of moving obituaries around the world.

The boxing writer Robert Ecksel reflected the mood when he wrote: 'Champion, gentleman, sexual pioneer, even the subject of an opera, Emile Griffith embodied class in a sport where classlessness sometimes seems the norm.'

Willie Toweel looked at me blankly when I told him about his former opponent. Willie picked up the photograph again. It was a black-and-white shot of him fighting Emile at Madison Square Garden in October 1960.

'Willie Toweel,' the old fighter said with a warm smile, as he tapped the image of himself.

'Yes, Willie, that's you,' his wife Alida said patiently. 'And that's Emile Griffith.'

'Emile Griffith,' Willie said, echoing the name. He looked down fondly at the photograph again. And then he tapped himself in the snap. 'Willie Toweel,' he said proudly.

Willie and Emile both suffered from dementia, but there was a striking difference between the two men. Emile had resembled a man in a waking coma; but the 79-year-old Willie looked physically well and happy. He also had an appetite like a strong old horse with a very sweet tooth.

'No, Dad,' his daughter Natalie said, 'no more biscuits for you. Those are meant for Don.'

Willie had almost demolished a plate of cakes and biscuits as if he was in his fighting prime, mowing down one opponent after another. Natalie steered him back to his seat on their patio, and she and her mother spent the rest of the morning telling me about

Willie. I, in turn, told them about Emile, and how much Willie's letter had meant to him. It felt as if I had given a small gift to Alida.

'Do you hear that, Willie?' Alida asked, her face shining with joy. 'Your letter to Emile, it helped him.'

Willie nodded and beamed. He pointed to the biscuits again. 'No, Willie, it's lunchtime soon,' Alida said.

She explained that, just like Emile could never forget Benny Paret until he lost his mind, her husband had honoured the memory of his fallen opponent. 'Willie prayed for Hubert Essakow every single day of his life. The day didn't start until he had been to mass and prayed for Hubert and the whole family.'

I drove up the road to see Willie's nephew, Alan Toweel. Alan, just like his father, Alan Sr, who had been in Willie's corner throughout his career, was a boxing trainer. Over lunch he suggested that, 'My dad got Willie through the Essakow tragedy. It was so traumatic for Willie and only my dad could help. In Willie's first twenty-one fights he had fifteen knockouts. After that he could only knock out seven guys. He would not want to knock out anyone. Willie was such a good boxer he could use just his jab to get through a fight. He went through such pain – like Emile Griffith. I can't believe Emile's gone. Shame . . .'

It was a distinctive South African word, 'shame', signifying sympathy. I suggested to Alan Toweel that there was no sadness in the passing of Emile Griffith. The consuming sorrow had been felt most acutely when his dementia took hold. Those who loved him had grieved the loss of Emile then. A few weeks before, when I heard the news from Ron and Luis, there was relief that his open-eyed oblivion was over.

'It was time,' Ron Ross said simply. 'Luis is hurting, but it's a release for them both.'

Earlier that week I had flown to Durban to stay with Stan Christodoulou and his wife, Mary, on my way to meeting Elijah 'Tap Tap' Makhathini. Stan had been the referee in Soweto on the night Emile lost to Tap Tap. He still officiated as a referee and a judge at world title fights featuring the best boxers today, like Gennady Golovkin and Saul 'Canelo' Alvarez. Stan understood the meaning of Emile's life and death.

'He was a great fighter,' he said, 'and a brave but complicated man.'

Tap Tap Makhathini and I could not talk in the same detail outside his small shop on a dusty road near the black township of Stanger, ninety minutes from Durban. My Zulu amounted to a few words and Tap Tap still spoke rudimentary English. He did not have access to the internet and he could not read much either. Tap Tap was surprised to hear that Emile had died a few weeks before. But he was utterly shocked when I asked him, through a translator, if he knew that Emile had been gay.

His shook his head. 'Shame,' Tap Tap said, but I accepted it as less a judgement than an acknowledgement of how lonely a life Emile Griffith must have led as a gay boxer.

Tap Tap's mind seemed in perfect working order. He wrapped his hands around mine and thanked me for remembering him. And then he held up both his thumbs and said, at the very same time, 'Emile Griffith!'

In September 2013, every sparring session at the Northwest Buffalo Community Center was a grim battle. Orlando Cruz knew how hard he would have to fight when, in Las Vegas, a month from then, he challenged Orlando Salido for the WBO world featherweight title. Salido had boxed professionally for seventeen years – since he was fifteen – and had won the IBF and WBO world featherweight titles. He was the same age as Cruz, but Salido had been through fifty-three fights – thirty more than the Puerto Rican.

Released from the shackles of secrecy and guilt about his sexuality, Cruz worked with new intent. 'Salido's had his time,' he murmured in Spanish. 'Now it's my time. People think I'm not strong enough. They doubt me. They wonder if a gay man can win a world title.'

Cruz shrugged. 'The sceptics will see what I am capable of on 12 October.'

He was still brooding over his chief trainer Juan De León's rough treatment of him, and it was not long since he had sworn vehemently at his trainer. Cruz peeled the bandages from his hands. They were soaked after two hours of training. The mess of boxing shoes and bags strewn around him belonged to the world of a fighter rather than a gay icon.

Sweat ran down his sunken face like tears, and he cackled at the melodramatic picture he and his mother had made when he first told her he was gay. He had sobbed then about not being able to come out in two worlds, Puerto Rico and boxing, built on machismo. As Salido hurtled towards him, his mind was less cluttered.

Cruz understood how the fight would smudge the boundaries between the personal and professional. He implied that Salido, as a Mexican, might be troubled by facing a gay fighter. 'My coming out made it harder for him. He will have it in his mind that he's fighting a homosexual for the world title. He's professional with me, but Mexicans often have something homophobic in them. It's the machismo culture. Salido won't want to lose to a gay man. But he'll fall into the trap by being macho. I'll let him come at me, and I'll show him then. The only language I will use is spoken by my fists. They will do my talking.'

Cruz was also motivated by the memory of Emile Griffith. Our plan for me to take him to see Emile had been foiled by our hectic lives and the fighter's death. A Saturday night in Vegas, in October 2013, would mark a more sombre memento from Cruz to Griffith.

'I'm fighting for my family, my team, everyone who wrote to me around the world since I came out, as well as the gay-lesbian-bi-transgender community,' Cruz said. 'They all brought grains of sand to the dream I've built. But I want to dedicate this fight to Emile Griffith. He had to live with the stigma of being black when there was such prejudice. And he was gay. He suffered from double prejudice – and the second was even worse because he kept it secret so long. He was a brave man, a great champion.'

De León joined us in a stark dining hall next to the gym. Cruz rolled his eyes at me as he listened to his trainer. 'I love this kid,' De León said, 'but I was hard on him today. You know how important this fight is to Orlandito. Last October he released something he was holding inside for so long. He's free now.'

The trainer remembered Cruz beating up a fighter who had taunted him for being gay. 'Orlando had already confessed to me,' De León said. 'I had no problem. A couple of my cousins are gay or lesbian. I accepted him and we kept it secret. But this guy in the gym knew the rumours. When he and Orlando sparred he was kidding around. Orlando said: "Keep your hands up because I'm hitting you." But this fighter kept taunting him. He said: "Do what you gotta do, you fucking gay ..."'

De León glanced at Cruz who said: 'He called me *maricón*.'

I heard the pain Emile Griffith had felt against Benny Paret. It seemed to echo, more than fifty years later, in the husky Latino voice of Orlando Cruz.

'Oh, Orlandito,' De León sighed, 'you opened up on him.'

The trainer pumped his fists: '*Ba-ba-ba-bam, ba-ba-ba-bam!* Orlando got him in the corner and said: "I'm gonna fuck you up ..." *Bam-bam-bam!* "How does it feel? A fucking gay beating you up?"'

De León's eyes widened. 'It reminded me of Griffith against Paret. That's how angry he was.'

The truth, even when smeared with hurt and violence, mattered to Cruz: 'I had a lot of pain in me. I carried a persecution complex.'

De León confirmed that, 'Back then Orlando didn't get on with my fighters. He thought they were all laughing at him because there was so much gossip. He would say: "What you looking at?" I would say: "Hey, Orlandito, people can look at you." So that's why, when the guy called him *maricón*, Orlando cut loose. But the next day they both apologised and started working together. That's Orlando's strength.'

Cruz smiled. 'I'm much more tranquil now. My mind is on the fight. It was the same with my two other fights after coming out. I was calm and won easily. I'm a gay man – and a fighter. This gives me calm.'

He had felt jittery when, three months earlier, he proposed to his partner, Jose Manuel Colon, on Facebook. In that video posting, he sounded nervous: 'I'd like to say, and share it with your friends, and my friends: "Do you want to marry me?" It's an important step, a step I've thought about, a step we've thought about . . .'

Jose, a year older than Cruz and an engineer, accepted and told the boxer: 'I love and adore you.'

Cruz looked dazed as he remembered his unusual proposal. 'I came in after a long run and just did it. It was very spontaneous. Life is much more positive for me now. I have my boyfriend. I'm much more confident. My marriage can happen soon but a world title fight is a once-in-a-lifetime chance.'

Marriage between gay men was still banned in Puerto Rico, as in many states of America, and their struggle was not over. We left the gym and crossed the street for lunch at the house belonging to De León's brother. Over steaming bowls of soup, Orlando played with De León's baby niece, throwing her gently into the air as she squealed excitedly. 'I would love to have kids,' he said.

Orlando and Jose knew that they would have to marry in New York and adopt children away from Puerto Rico, where the notion of gay parents is illegal. But Orlando echoed the little girl's laughter as he turned her into a small aeroplane and flew her around the kitchen. His battle with Salido seemed an age away.

Just after ten o'clock that Saturday night in downtown Buffalo, New York, Orlando Cruz looked wistfully out the window as our car sped through the deserted streets. After a brutal day in the gym, sparring twelve rounds against four different opponents, he yearned for an escape.

'There are only four gay bars in Buffalo,' Orlando said, switching from Spanish to English, 'and they're not so exciting. But ... you know ...'

Orlando laughed because he had just spent an hour in one of those bars, but we were sworn to secrecy. In the backseat my friend Amrai Coen, a young German writer for *Die Zeit*, and I exchanged knowing looks. Amrai was a woman who knew little about boxing but, researching a feature, she had been following Orlando for months. She understood that he was not meant to step inside a bar before a world title fight – but he had not drunk anything and he needed a respite from the pressure and months of monastic training. Orlando reminded me of Emile Griffith, slipping into a Times Square gay bar for a break.

Juan De León was waiting for us at home in the suburbs of a blue-collar city deep in New York State. We were late and so we raced through the darkness. That night, Floyd 'Money' Mayweather was set to earn $70m for fighting the unbeaten Mexican, Saul 'Canelo' Alvarez. We would watch Mayweather, on pay-per-view television, in a late-night taster of everything that awaited Orlando in Vegas.

'It's been my dream all my life,' Cruz murmured as he considered his title fight. He sounded like a typical fighter; and he also looked like one as the streetlights cast an eerie glow across his battered face.

Orlandito, as De León called his 32-year-old fighter, smiled when Amrai and I disappeared into the trainer's kitchen soon after we arrived. It felt rude not to accept De León's offer of a shot of tequila and cognac to get us in a big-fight-night mood. Orlando remained in the sitting room, drinking water, while we knocked back the hard stuff.

There was a cruel beauty to Mayweather's work as he speared blurring combinations into Alvarez. The raucous anticipation in De León's living room quietened as the Puerto Rican boxing men showed appreciation of a master of their vicious trade. Cruz was the most concentrated of all as he studied Mayweather. Amrai and I kept drinking.

At 2.15 a.m., in the cool air outside following Mayweather's decisive win, Cruz stretched out his hand. 'Four weeks tonight ... it's my turn.'

On my last day in Buffalo, Orlando suggested we go to church. He arrived late, having slept in, but he grinned. 'It's better I go to church than a gay bar,' he said as we walked into St Joseph's where Juan De León's eleven-year-old son, Angel, was an altar boy. I found it hard to shake stark thoughts of everything Cruz would face against Salido – especially when his head was bowed in silent prayer. The hymns rolled on – and Orlando sang quietly, 'Lord, I'm Coming Home'. When we were asked to link hands, he held mine tightly while the priest prayed for those facing danger, or darkness.

Encouraged to turn to each other and say, 'Peace be with you ...', Orlando shook my hand and said the words sincerely. He was a fighter, and so he also winked.

A month later, in Las Vegas, the tension was palpable. At the final press conference for HBO's pay-per-view event, the veteran promoter Bob Arum held court. He recalled his promotion of Muhammad Ali and hailed Orlando Cruz as another pioneer, who would wear pink-streaked gloves and multicoloured trunks that looked more like a skirt. Arum suggested that, even recently, a fight featuring a gay boxer would have led to 'a thousand protesters. But boxing, and the world, is a much better place now.'

On the podium, and wearing a smart charcoal-grey suit, Cruz smiled and spoke clearly in English. 'Today I'm making history ... and on Saturday I'll be the new world champion.' Salido cut a contrasting figure in a black tracksuit. The old Mexican warrior's usually granite-like face kept twitching. But he did not sound frightened when he said: 'It's going to be a war.'

Away from the hoopla, Cruz knew that he would make history as the first publicly gay fighter to challenge for a world title.

'Everything I've been through has taken me to this point,' Orlando said in one last moment of private reflection before we parted in Vegas. 'It's the most important fight of my life. I'm a gay man, but I'm also a boxer. My two worlds have come together and I will fight with all my heart. The world knows the truth about me as a man. Now the world will see the truth about me as a fighter. I want to win this for me but ... and I know you understand ... I also want to win this for Emile.'

Thomas & Mack Center, Las Vegas, Saturday 12 October 2013

Michael Buffer, tanned as always in his tuxedo, was ready for the money-shout. He stood in the middle of the ring, a silver-haired master of the microphone, and began the ritual welcome with his trademark mix of velvety smoothness, rolling cadences and guttural pronunciations.

'For the thousands in attendance,' Buffer crooned, 'and the millions watching on HBO pay-per-view ... ladies and gentlemen, from the Thomas & Mack Center, Las Vegas, Nevada ...'

The venue rocked in anticipation before Buffer did his party trick: '*Leeeeeet's ... Git ... Ready ... To ... Rumbleeeeeeeeeeee!*'

Buffer held the 'e' in 'rumble' for a long time before, finally, and only slightly red in the face, he remembered the fighters. He introduced the challenger first.

'Fighting out of the blue corner, wearing with pride the rainbow colours. His official weight 125 pounds, his professional record twenty victories, including ten KOs, only two defeats, with one draw ...'

Cruz wore a sleeveless blue satin robe, trimmed with pink, and trunks in the rainbow colours of the gay, lesbian, bisexual and transgender community. He had been hunched over, almost touching his toes, as he listened to the start of Buffer's announcement. When the veteran ring barker reached the moment, Cruz rose up proudly to hear his name being shouted out as a world title challenger.

'From Quintana, Puerto Rico ... *Orrrrrrrlandooo... El Fenómenoooooo ... Cruzzzzzzzzzz!*'

At the sound of 'Puerto Rico', Cruz stared at the lights above the ring and raised his right arm. The flamingo pink glove shimmered. The gay man who called himself '*El Fenómeno*' shook his way out of his robe. His upper body was bare by the time the final 'z' in his surname had been stretched towards breaking point by Buffer.

I was used to boxing in Las Vegas but I felt suddenly apprehensive. My head carried the ghost of Emile Griffith. All the tragedies of his ring career echoed again. Benny Paret, Davey Moore, Willie Classen and so many other fallen fighters could not be forgotten. But I thought mostly of Emile and how courageous he had been in and outside the ring.

Buffer had turned towards the stony-faced Mexican. 'Fighting out the red corner, wearing silver with blue,' he said, pointing to Orlando Salido. 'His official weight is 126 pounds. As a professional his record stands at thirty-nine victories, including twenty-seven knockouts . . .'

The acclaim of the Mexican fans gathered in intensity, drowning out Buffer. But he switched to Spanish and a guttural Hispanic roar as he celebrated Salido and *Me-hee-co*. It was back to English for Buffer's final flourish. 'Two-time featherweight world champion . . . *Orrrrrrrlandooo . . . Siriiiiiii . . . Saaaallidooooooo!*'

Salido, wearing a red headband emblazoned with his nickname, 'Siri', bounced up and down. He looked very serious, even though it was obvious that 80 per cent of the crowd were supporting him over Cruz.

Around fifty people had crammed their way into the ring, but all the cornermen, the promoters, the managers, the officials, the producers, the friends, the flag-wavers, and the pouting, big-breasted ring-card girls, finally slunk away. There were just eight men left in the ring – the two fighters, their head trainers, referee Kenny Bayless, a blazered official, Buffer and a television cameraman.

Bayless gave his instructions to the boxers as Cruz looked up at the rafters, avoiding eye contract with Salido. 'Now gentlemen,' Bayless said, 'we went over the rules in the dressing room. I have cautioned you to keep this fight clean at all times, to protect yourselves at all times. And what I say, you must obey.'

The referee looked directly at Cruz, who was giddy with nerves. 'Good luck to the both of you,' Bayless said. 'Now touch 'em up.'

Cruz touched his black-and-pink gloves against Salido's blue pair. But the challenger still refused to look at the champion. The crowd booed Cruz as he and Salido retreated to their corners. I hunkered down in my seat, next to Amrai Coen, my friend from *Die Zeit*. She shook her head and smiled nervously. We were both gripped by trepidation.

Juan De León and Cruz bumped chests, in a very manly way, and Salido flexed his jaw manically, as if preparing for a bloody feast.

The rainbow colours bounced under the lights as Cruz danced in his corner. At last, the bell rang.

Cruz, as always, fought as a southpaw, his right hand taking the lead behind his high guard. Salido boxed out of an orthodox stance. Twenty seconds passed before Cruz snaked out a couple of right jabs. He was understandably tentative against such an experienced world champion. Punches began to fly, but Cruz ducked under most of them. A couple landed near the end of the first round, and Cruz dropped his hands and pulled a little macho face to insist that he had not been hurt. Salido went low, punching Cruz below the belt. The Mexican was warned by the referee, who checked on Cruz.

'Okay?' Bayless asked. Cruz spread his hands and shrugged. They backed off for the remaining thirteen seconds, but Salido had shaded the round.

The second opened encouragingly for Cruz and he peppered Salido's face with fast jabs. Another low blow from Salido came winging in and he was rebuked again. As if in reply, Salido cracked a big right hand against the side of Cruz's jaw. A roar went up and Salido stepped in to land a left hook. A rhythmic chant of Salido's name resounded, but Cruz, backing away, stayed out of trouble.

There was more intent from Cruz in round three and he punched crisply, as Salido banged away at his body before connecting with a sneaky right uppercut. Cruz's face had begun to redden but he also made Salido miss under intense pressure. The same pattern continued in the fourth, with the punches becoming harder as Salido dominated. All Cruz's combinations seemed to bounce off Salido with little effect, as the champion marched him down.

Cruz suddenly switched tactics and, at least briefly, stood toe to toe with the Mexican and traded. Salido hurt him with shots to the body and the head. But the gay fighter would not crumple. He fought back and clipped Salido with a left that made the Mexican reel back. Cruz was still the aggressor at the bell.

Round five was the best yet for Cruz. He began to fight on the inside and managed to wrest back some control. A crunching right hand from Salido made Cruz blink, but he fought on, proving his toughness, and won the round. He pushed his head lightly into Salido's face as they parted, as if warning the Mexican that the balance of the fight might have tilted.

Boxing, however, is a cruel business. Salido struck Cruz with such a heavy right to the head that the Puerto Rican looked shaken after a minute of the sixth round. Salido backed him into a corner and, feigning nonchalance, Cruz waggled his tongue. The champion punished him for his impertinence, going downstairs with savage body punches before switching back to the head. His hitting was vicious and accurate and Cruz needed to draw in breath. Salido clubbed him again.

There would not be a pretty rainbow finish for Cruz in his quest to win the world title for himself, and for Emile Griffith. Salido dug in hurtful body shots, which made Cruz's lolling head an easy target in the seventh. With two minutes left in the round, a right cross and then a withering left uppercut dropped Cruz. He was down on his haunches as the referee began to count.

The impact of the punch spread through Cruz and he slid onto his knees, helplessly. Kenny Bayless crouched down and spread his arms wide. It was over.

Salido raced around the ring, his arm raised in victory. His son was soon passed into his arms and he held the little boy in delight. On the far side of the ring, in a lonely corner, a dejected Orlando Cruz sat on his wooden stool. His face was etched with pain. He had been knocked out. The dream was over.

A victory party had been planned for Orlando but, late that night, he stayed away. He remained on his own in his hotel room, nursing his hurt and disappointment, understanding the brutality of boxing all over again. I was sorry for Orlando, and I would have loved a sweet ending to this story. Yet it was in keeping with the dark truth of boxing. The challenger had been no match for the champion. He had suffered and lost to the better fighter.

In time, Orlando would feel whole again. He had lost the fight, but he had won a far more important battle against himself and the world at large. He had come out, as a gay boxer, and fought bravely in a world title contest. Orlando Cruz had still made history on another bruising night in the ring.

Freddie Wright and I completed our last interview in New York. We spent a few hours talking in a small, atmospheric apartment on 42nd Street, just around the corner from 8th Avenue and the Port Authority Bus Terminal. The apartment belonged to Freddie and Emile's friend, a transvestite from Alabama called Gina Demain.

We had covered a lot of terrain in the short time I had known Freddie. Our first interview, the previous year, in 2013, had been held in the chaotic anonymity of the Port Authority coffee shop. Slowly, trust had developed and Freddie had shared memories of his enduring friendship with Emile and Calvin Thomas – as well as telling me about his own life in a way as amusing as it was trenchant.

Freddie was not a boxing connoisseur, but he was interested in Orlando Cruz. He had witnessed Emile's struggles for so long that he found it heartening that a new boxing narrative had been forged. He was pleased, too, that the Puerto Rican featherweight recovered from the beating given to him by Orlando Salido. A month later, on 14 November 2013, Orlando Cruz and Jose Manuel Colon married in a legal wedding ceremony held in Central Park. Both men, husbands together, wore white jackets, black ties, white shirts, black trousers and shoes. Each of them had a little black handkerchief sprouting from the pocket of their gleaming white jackets. They looked a happy match.

A year later, as daylight disappeared across New York, Freddie told me of his own illegitimate wedding to Dante Rodriguez in the 1970s. It was a witty story, topped off by Freddie wearing a long blonde wig and his brother's wedding gown, but it spoke most of courage and resilience. Freddie also remembered his equally unlikely union, as a female impersonator, with a lesbian who dressed as a man.

'We laughed,' Freddie said dryly, 'when she saw that I was a man and I worked out she was a woman. A gay man and a lesbian – we ended up going to bed that night. We stayed together five years and we've got two children. She lives in Queens, and her name is Jo-Anne. I still see her and the kids. She lives with her female lover and when the kids came of age we told them about our real selves. It was cool. My boy is twenty-one, and my girl is eighteen.'

In 2014, at the age of seventy-one, Freddie said, 'The feller I go with now, he's pushing it. He says, "C'mon, Freddie, let's get married." I say: "I been there" – even though it wasn't legal. We've been together many years now. His name is James Roman. Jimmy. Let me show you his picture.'

Freddie flashed a photograph on his phone. 'Cute, huh?' he said, proudly.

'Jimmy has his own place up in the Bronx. We can walk to each other's apartment. We met in a bar where I used to work, on 41st Street. He was seventeen. I figured he was old enough to drink. We talked and I knew he was the one, but I never approached him. He chased me down. He had all these other people but he said, "I like you." And I said, "Well, you're kinda cute." He said: "Just kinda?" We went from there.

'From the start I told Jimmy straight. "You're number one. You're the main horse. But I got a couple of ponies on the side. This is how I am. But when the moment comes and you walk through the door

then all the other boys knew that you, Jimmy, are the one for me."
Until this day they know it. I always been honest. You either accept
it or you don't. Jimmy accepted it because he was a hustler too. He
had to make his living. It's a love story.'

Freddie, the go-go dancer, found himself at the heart of the
Stonewall riots. He relived that momentous night, paying homage to
the magnificent drag king, the lesbian fighter, Storme DeLarverie,
who died in a Brooklyn nursing home in May 2014. 'Oh Storme!'
Freddie exclaimed. 'Storme sounded like a man. Storme looked like
a man. Storme walked like a man. Storme punched like a man. But,
baby, she was one hell of a woman.'

There had been so much exotic colour in Freddie's life – and yet
hurt and death lingered too. 'You cannot have been a gay black man
in the 1950s, the '60s and the '70s without feeling the most extreme
prejudice. I've been called everything. Nigger . . . faggot . . . *maricón*.
I look at these young gay people, these young black people, and they
have no idea. It was worse for Emile. Oh my God . . . *Emile!* Can you
imagine how hard it was for Emile? A world champion five times
over. And he got called a *maricón*? Can you imagine the hurt?'

Freddie brightened. 'I was just glad he had peace with Luis in the
end. Luis matured over the years. He was very good to Emile. He
has a big heart.'

I had travelled to Hempstead a few days before to see Luis again.
He had lost a lot of weight and, while still missing Emile, he seemed
content. Luis had swapped Domino's Pizza deliveries for a night-
time job as a taxi driver – and he still worked in Manhattan in the
day at Dan Klores' production office. He had helped raise the
money, with Ring 8, the former boxers' association in New York, to
unveil a tombstone in Emile's honour at St Michael's cemetery in
Queens.

Freddie remembered Calvin Thomas too. 'Calvin stayed at my
house when I lived in Harlem. He had a boil on his back. I would
say, "Calvin, go to the doctor," because I saw it when he was sleeping. He was in pain. I'd say, "Go, go . . .," and then one time it was

so bad that at 3 a.m. he said, "I'm going to the hospital." Instead, he came here to 42nd Street and he was talking to the guys and hanging out. Then he went to this hotel where he used to take his friends. That's where they found him in the hotel bed the next morning, dead. The poison had run through his system. If he had gone to the hospital and got it taken care of, he would still be here today. Emile was so upset he didn't make it to the service.'

Darkness spread across New York City. Freddie had walked me past the old site of Hombre, the gay bar where Emile had almost been beaten to death in 1992. We were back in Gina's apartment and Freddie, who still helped black and Hispanic men diagnosed as HIV-positive in his day job, looked weary. He had lived through a sexual revolution and survived the catastrophe of AIDS. His old friends, Emile and Calvin, were gone. But Freddie was still a dancer and, in his own way, a fighter.

He turned back one last time to the memory of Emile, his thin face streaked with pride. 'Back in the day we were the Three Musketeers . . . me, Calvin and Emile. I would definitely say Emile was the quietest of us all but, you know, he was the one who had the most to shout about. He inspired so many people when we were persecuted by the law, and hounded by the police. Emile might not have shouted out his sexuality, but he stayed true to all of us. He lit a fire in so many people.

'You could say it was often a sad life, because Emile had a lot of tragedy. He was haunted. But there were many moments of craziness, and joy. He was always struggling with himself and his reality, but he would do such wild, fun, crazy things. Emile and Calvin would pull up in a limo and he'd come out in this pink jumpsuit, with wild hair, and find me shaking my mamba at a gay joint like the Gilded Grape. We would just laugh and dance and all the pain got washed away for a while.

'Emile lived in two worlds. He was a great fighter and they loved and respected him in boxing. In his other world, in my world, he made gay people feel so proud – especially because he was a world champion boxer. We not only respected and liked Emile. We *loved* him. Yeah, he lived two lives but each one should be remembered. Each one should be celebrated.'

Freddie paused to snap on a small lamp because the room where we sat was shrouded in near darkness. The light shone on his weathered face as he looked up. Freddie spoke softly, but urgently, as if talking to his friend and the great old champion one last time: 'Emile Griffith . . . what a man.'

Another year had disappeared; and another hard winter had finally ended. On a Saturday afternoon in the spring of 2015, at home in Stone Ridge in New York State, Esther Taylor-Evans allowed the tangled memories to unfurl from deep inside her. I had not even been born when she first called herself Emile Griffith's girlfriend. And so the surprise of being tracked down to talk about Emile, and their strangely poignant relationship, pulsed through her. Esther had not spoken about Emile to anyone outside her family and so, after a wary start, it was as if a lid had been lifted on a tumultuous past.

'I was probably the last one to know Emile was gay,' Esther said with a wry little laugh. 'I never saw him with any gay people. Yeah, there were times when I did see him with young men, but I never put two and two together. It was 1960, '61. My head just wasn't there at that time. If I was to think about it and look back, I'd say: "Yeah, of course . . ." But not at that time. He always hid the fact that he was gay – especially from me. There were a lot of rumours and my ex-boyfriend would say that Emile was gay and I always said, "Get out of here!"

'When I was seventeen we started going out. He was real fun; he always dressed well and he was a fabulous dancer. I was okay as a dancer, I kept up. He was a real busy person, especially once he got in the limelight, so I only really saw him when we went to places, out for dinner and stuff like that. He was too busy for a real courtship. It was hinted that maybe we would get married but nothing was formal.'

Esther paused as she reflected on the elusive nature of their relationship, and how little she had really known about Emile when, during that giddy time, he was her boyfriend. She had only learned snippets of the truth in a different century, when she had read Ron Ross's biography and then seen *Ring of Fire*. It was as if she had been introduced to a totally different person from the boy she had loved.

She listened intently when I told her much more about Emile and his life with Calvin Thomas and Freddie Wright. It seemed to me as though Freddie and Esther would have got along beautifully, united in a shared love and respect for Emile. She was struck again by how little Emile had told her about himself. 'He never talked about being in a home (on his boyhood island of St Thomas) and he never reflected on anything deep about his past or his sexuality. It was strange. You would think you would talk about it when you get to know people and become so close to them. But it never happened. Emile could never talk openly and we have to accept it. He had a lot of pain in his life . . .'

We swapped more stories, surprising each other with new revelations, and Esther actually cried out when I told her about the further tragedies that had darkened Emile's life. She knew nothing about the death of Davey Moore, on the night he and Emile had used the same locker room at Dodger Stadium in Los Angeles, so close to the first anniversary of the Benny Paret tragedy. Esther had also not known that Emile had been in Wilford Scypion's corner when the Texan battered Willie Classen into a coma and then death.

'Oh my God,' she cried, her voice suddenly cracking with horror, 'oh no . . .'

She could hardly believe that one man had suffered and been haunted by so much death in the ring. Esther did not like boxing and it was evident that any residual anger was directed towards the fight game rather than Emile hiding his sexuality from her. She had found Gil Clancy and Howie Albert to be 'pleasant enough', but

Esther then asked me a pointed and uncomfortable question: if they loved him so much how could they allow Emile to fight 112 times as a professional?

When I had interviewed Clancy in Las Vegas in 1999, he had argued that Emile felt lost without boxing. It gave meaning and structure to his complicated life. Even when Clancy insisted that he retire from the ring, it was inevitable that Emile would be pulled back to the corner as a trainer. He did not believe he could do much else outside of boxing.

His old girlfriend sounded unconvinced. She found it tragic that Emile had been battered so badly that dementia had taken hold of him in the end.

Esther still remembered, vividly, the build-up to the defining tragedy of Emile's life. 'Our relationship continued until just before that last Benny "Kid" Paret fight. That was when the rumours were out that he was gay and that's why he wanted me as his cover story. He just called me up and said, "I need you for some publicity shoots because they're trying to say I'm this way." And I said, "Of course, Emile ..." He didn't say that they're accusing me of being gay and I'm struggling with my sexuality. He just said, "They're putting a spin on it which I don't like." I was happy to help him. Absolutely. Why not? Emile was such a sweetheart.'

Did she really not mind when Emile pretended that she was his girlfriend and peddled the bogus line that, one day, they would be married? 'No, not at all,' Esther said quietly. 'Emile was a good person. That's all that matters in the end. And, afterwards, once the Kid actually died, Emile was devastated. He was such a kind-hearted guy. He didn't want to hurt nobody. But, more than anything, it was the sadness that he had died and the Kid had left a family behind. Nobody wanted him to die ... but people can be cruel.

'I was with Emile one time when he got abused about it. We were out one night, and that was the only time I ever saw him lose his temper and shout at someone – and that's because he was so haunted by the Kid. I found it heartbreaking to watch the film about him and

Benny. I can see now that Benny "Kid" Paret was a sweetheart of a guy as well. It was the media that hooked it up as a grudge fight – and so I felt for his wife and son.'

Esther helped me understand the perplexing enigma of Emile Griffith a little better when, in calm yet unstinting detail, she described his relationship with his mother. 'He was a momma's boy,' Esther said simply. 'He loved his momma very much. She was a controlling figure in his life and she had a very important impact on him. But he was crazy about his mother, too. He loved her. It made it difficult for me and for everyone else in his life. With me, his mother would sometimes be okay and sometimes she wouldn't be okay at all. She was just a very controlling person. When Emile and I were going to go away, she would stop it. She would be the one that went away with him. And if Emile was going to buy something special for me, she got it. I didn't. It's all a long time ago, so I don't resent her. It's just the way she was with Emile.'

Were Emile's problems with a conflicted sexuality connected to his mother? 'Yeah,' Esther murmured. 'I would say so.'

She then told me the bewildering story of how Emelda had tried to persuade her to return in a combined effort to block Emile's surprise marriage to Sadie Donastorg. 'I said, "No . . ." She tried again and I said, "No way am I doing that. No way, whatsoever." She was controlling and manipulative and I don't know if there was anyone she would have wanted Emile to be with in place of her.'

Esther laughed when I asked if she had been surprised by Emelda's call. 'God, yes! How many years had passed! I don't even know how she got my home number – probably from Emile. I was married. But I would never have done that to Emile. I wouldn't do that to my child, even if he was marrying a murderer . . .

'I ran into him about a year later. My son was about three, so it would have been around 1972. Emile was great and I don't think he ever knew his mother had called me. We just enjoyed seeing each other again. It was always nice to be around Emile. He was well then, he seemed to be doing okay.'

The next time Esther saw Emile he was lost in the depths of dementia. Death was closing in on him. 'His son [Luis] got in touch with me and we went to see him in the hospital. He didn't recognise me at all. My sister went with me and he looked at her as if he was trying to figure out who she was ... but he was blank with me. His body was fantastic. He did not look like an old, shrivelled man. But his mind had gone and I was very sad seeing him in that condition. But then you think of all his fights. He was so good-looking and such a happy man when we were young and he ended up an empty shell.'

Esther saw Emile once more, in the company of her husband, Charles Evans. 'It's a three-hour drive from our place to him down in Long Island, but I'm glad we made it – even if my husband was very upset to see him. We had grown up together in Harlem, all of us, and Charles remembered all Emile had meant back in those days as a black champion. It hit Charles hard to see Emile in that condition. But I felt his death was a release in the end. He had a lot of pain ... oh my God. Can you imagine what it was like for him? To be gay and a boxer ... no wonder he buried that secret so deep inside him all his life.'

I apologised for asking Esther how old she had been when she ended her relationship, if not her friendship, with Emile. 'Oh, I'm old now. It doesn't matter,' she laughed gaily. 'But I would say that, up until the age of twenty-one, I considered myself his girlfriend.'

As our interview wound towards its end, Esther said that she was still intrigued by how I had tracked her down. It was not through Luis but, rather, via a circuitous route. I had seen a small tribute she had written in the comments section of an online obituary. Her words were understated but crammed with meaning. Her married name, Esther Taylor-Evans, took a long while to provide a link. But, finally, I had seen it twinned with a website of a charity called A Thousand Moms.

The opening words on the website established an immediate focus:

'I was placed in a system and diagnosed as different – sick – simply because I was confused about my sexuality.' (Source: Child Welfare League of America)

'My boyfriend's father would give him up for adoption if he knew he was gay.' (Source: New York Times)

'Too often, Lesbian, Gay, Bisexual, Transgendered and Questioning (LGBT/Q) youth in foster/adoptive care experience rejection, from their families, from their peers, from society. The results are among the highest rates of social problems – most alarmingly, teen suicide.'

At first, as I told Esther, I could hardly believe the coincidence that Emile Griffith's girlfriend, the innocent young woman who had provided his furtive homosexuality with a cover story, had ended up fifty years later working with lesbian, gay, bisexual and transgendered teenagers. But I had quickly valued the link between his past and her present; and I had been encouraged to email A Thousand Moms. One of its co-founders, Fred Elia, had then spoken to me on the phone and promised to bring Esther and me together.

'Oh, Fred, what a sweetheart,' Esther smiled, using the same adjective she had applied to both Emile and Benny Paret. 'You know, I'm a social worker and I was teaching people how to be foster parents. I got together with this gentleman and said, "Do you know what? There are no avenues for gay kids to be fostered. We should do something about it." And we did. We started it up about five years ago and it's still growing. I was the one who actually named it. We were just sitting round and talking about it and I said, "We need a thousand moms ..." The name just stuck and now we give training to foster parents and teach them how to handle it when a child is gay ...'

Esther was quiet for a few moments when I said it appeared less an irony than a moving completion of a circle in her connection with

Emile Griffith. She might not have known he was gay when she was his girlfriend and he was on the way to becoming a five-time world champion boxer, but it seemed curiously touching that, fifty years later, in her mid-seventies, she should be committed to helping the community of people where Emile Griffith had felt most at ease.

'You know what?' Esther eventually said, her voice tinged with wonder. 'I never thought about it in that way. I just did it because it felt right. But I know exactly what you mean. I hope he would have been proud of me if he had known – just as I have always been proud of Emile. Yeah ... I like it. We've come full circle in the end. We made our peace.'

NOTES & SOURCES

PREFACE: Talking to Ghosts

I am indebted to Luis Rodrigo who was generous with his help and the many hours of his time whenever I visited Hempstead, Long Island, to see him. The particular December day, in 2012, which provides the basis for the preface was also made special by the way in which it was documented by the Puerto Rican photographer Herminio Rodriguez, who I had met a few months earlier when we worked together on the Orlando Cruz interview in San Juan. It was published in the *Guardian* on 18 October 2012.

Herminio helped with translation during the Cruz interview and he also provided a penetrating insight into enduring homophobia in Puerto Rico. I asked him to join me with Luis and Emile Griffith in Hempstead. His photographs are the last taken of the great old fighter before his death the following year.

I interviewed Mike Tyson for the *Guardian*, in a feature published on 24 January 2014. He cackled and grew even more animated as he began to tell me about his inspiring encounters with Emile Griffith. Tyson knew I'd been working for years on a book about Griffith. After his personal stories of how Griffith had bolstered him in the past, there were a surreal few minutes when we sat together and he read my chapter breakdown and I tried to explain how I had structured this book.

Tyson's encyclopaedic knowledge of boxing was at its most irresistible when he zipped from one great old fighter to another, from 'Kid' Chocolate to Luis Rodriguez, from Benny 'Kid' Paret to Carlos Monzon.

He spoke in detail about one of his favourite fighters, Panama Al Brown – the freakishly tall bantamweight of the 1920s and 1930s who had a tempestuous affair with Jean Cocteau.

'Can you imagine?' Tyson said his eyes widening at the unlikely pairing of a Panamanian fighter who became the first Hispanic world champion in boxing history and a French experimental writer and filmmaker, 'Panama Al and Jean Cocteau! Only boxing gives you these characters ...'

Yet not even Panama Al Brown, Tyson agreed, could match the lifestory of Emile Griffith.

CHAPTER ONE: Facing a Killer

Key interviews for this chapter were with Bert Blewett, Stanley Christodoulou, Gil Clancy, Len Hunt, Jerry Izenberg, Ron Jackson, Billy Johnson, Hank Kaplan, Ron Katz, Bobby Miles, Ron Ross, Esther Taylor, Alan Toweel Jr and Alida Toweel. They stretched across more than twenty-five years, for I interviewed Hank Kaplan in the late 1980s, and Gil Clancy in Las Vegas in 1990. The others were all carried out in 2013-14 with this specific chapter in mind.

Newspaper and magazine research included the relevant issues from 1956 and 1960 in the *New York Amsterdam News*, the *New York Daily News*, the *New York Herald Tribune*, the *New York Post*, the *New York Times*, the *Chicago Defender*, the *Rand Daily Mail*, *The Ring* and *The Star* and the *Washington Post* – all housed at the British Newspaper Library.

Further research at the Hank Kaplan Boxing Archive in Brooklyn in 2013-14 was invaluable as the magnificent boxing archivist featured so many bulging files on Emile Griffith as well as less-celebrated boxers like Willie Toweel and Hubert Essakow.

One of my favourite places over the last three years looked like an ordinary room in New York. It was tucked away down a corridor at the Brooklyn College Library but, as soon as you hit the buzzer, the doors swung open and you walked into the world's most amazing boxing archive. You signed in and then, with a deep breath, stepped back into ring history and decided where you'd like to be for the day, in what year and with which fighters, among a collection of 500,000 photographs, 2,600 books, 300 audio and videotapes, 1,200 posters, hundreds of scrapbooks and, best of all, 790 boxes of newspaper clippings about boxing from 1890 to 2007. For this chapter the key years were 1956 and 1960.

Each morning, on my way to the Hank Kaplan Boxing Archive, I walked past the Avenue H subway, where the Q train ran, and slipped inside a downbeat Brooklyn diner. While waiting for my ritual bagel and coffee I scanned the news-stand crammed with cheap gossip magazines. The *New York Times*, the *Daily News* and the *New York Post* were kept in small piles on the bottom shelf. I always thought of Hank Kaplan then, and remembered how different life had been for him and the fight-game.

Jahongir Usmanov, a research assistant in Brooklyn, once told me how Kaplan had set about building his archive. He began every day in Miami in the same way. Kaplan sauntered down to the news kiosk on his street corner and bought three copies of every newspaper. All the leading US publications – the *New York Times*, the *Washington Post*, the *Los Angeles Times* and the *New York Herald Tribune* – were available at his news-stand.

Kaplan did not check whether the papers contained boxing features, reports and news stories. It was a given that, every day, boxing was covered heavily in the major American newspapers. If Emile Griffith was fighting Willie Toweel, then Kaplan would cut out every article about the fight in all the papers. He did this three times with each piece.

One copy would be stored in his Griffith file, another in the South African boxing folder and the third would be reserved for whoever else featured prominently – whether it was Gil Clancy in Griffith's corner or Alan Toweel opposite him.

In 2013-15 there were few boxing stories in the *New York Times* or any of the other dailies. American newspapers simply don't cover boxing. Only on one or two days a year, in a piece tied to Floyd Mayweather and Manny Pacquiao, did boxing warrant a surprise mention in the sports pages.

It was a different world at the Kaplan collection. Every day it proved itself to be an irresistible treasure box of detailed history. It opened to the public in April 2012, after the entire collection was donated by Kaplan's daughter, Barbara Haar. Kaplan, born and raised in Brooklyn, always wanted his archive to be housed by his home college. The Brooklyn librarians honoured his life's work in exemplary fashion.

This opening chapter, like every other in this book, was shaped partly by the research I carried out at the British Newspaper Library and in Brooklyn. This was supplemented by reading various fascinating books on the period. I would like to especially highlight the contributions of the following:

Ron Ross's *Nine...Ten...And Out!: The Two Worlds of Emile Griffith*, Willie Toweel & Peter McInnes' *Somebody Ring The Bell!*, Troy Rondinone's *Friday Night Fighter: Gasper 'Indio' Ortega and the Golden Age of Television Boxing* and Peter Heller's *In This Corner...!*

I would normally be suspicious of books with exclamation marks in their titles – but this quartet provided an invaluable supplement to my research.

But the chapter was driven most by the first-person accounts provided by the interviews. Ross, Clancy and Kaplan were especially helpful in evoking the era of boxing in New York in 1960. Clancy, Ron Katz and Billy Johnson also told me much about Teddy Brenner.

Willie Toweel's mood in New York, his tragic fight with Hubert Essakow and his past family history were shaped by personal family notes – which Alida Toweel shared so generously with me. Interviews with Alida, her daughter Natalie and with Alan Toweel Jr taught me much about the family and Willie as both a man and a fighter. Ron Jackson, South Africa's premier boxing historian, was very kind and helpful. He had been at the tragic fight between Toweel and Essakow as a boxing-mad teenager and he knew both men. Ron became especially close to Willie and he provided compelling insights into his friend both in and outside the ring. Len Hunt and Stan Christodoulou were also invaluable interviewees for this chapter.

Bobby Miles, who knew Emile and Calvin Thomas, provided me with wonderfully rich and detailed stories about their friendship from 1958 to 1960 – as well as explaining much about Griffith as a fighter and Clancy as a trainer.

The definitive account of Emile falling into boxing at Howie Albert's hat factory was provided by my friend Ron Ross – who wrote about this surreal scene in his Griffith biography. Ron also shared so many first-person memories and anecdotes about this time and the relationship between Griffith, Clancy and Albert.

In the same way, Alan Toweel Jr told me much about his father, Alan Sr, and his two uncles, Vic and Willie Toweel, as well as offering details of the offer Brenner made to Maurice Toweel to stage the fight in Madison Square Garden.

CHAPTER TWO: Date Night

Key interviews for this chapter were with Bert Blewett, Jim Garcia, Jerry Izenberg, Ron Jackson, Billy Johnson, Ron Katz, Ron Ross, Nick Stone, Esther Taylor-Evans, Alan Toweel Jr and George Zeleny.

Newspaper and magazine research included the relevant issues in the *New York Amsterdam News*, the *New York Herald Tribune*, the *New York Times*, the *Chicago Defender*, the *Rand Daily Mail*, *The Ring* and the *Star* – as well as the Hank Kaplan Archive.

Esther Taylor was particularly helpful in detailing her relationship with Emile – as well as her feelings towards boxing and the Griffth family.

My friend George Zeleny, an eminent boxing historian, provided me with complete footage of Emile Griffith's fights against Wille Toweel, Gasper Ortega and Florentino Fermandez. George counts Rodriguez as one of his favourite fighters, so he was a great ally in setting the scene for my writing about *El Feo*.

Troy Rondinone's *Friday Night Fighter* was again useful in research for this chapter.

I found Charles Kaiser's book, *The Gay Metropolis*, to be indispensable in the way in which it detailed homosexual life in New York in the early

1960s. It is a book that is as authoratitavie as it human. David Carter's *Stonewall* and Bryne Fone's *Homophobia* were also useful in setting the backdrop to this section of Chapter Two.

My interviews with Jim Garcia, Nick Stone and Freddie Wright provided personal details of gay New York in 1960.

Ron Ross shared much with me about Emile's family and his past in the US Virgin Islands – and he also wrote perceptively about the fighter's youth in *Nine...Ten...And Out!* He also explained exactly how the Albert-Clancy managerial partnership worked.

CHAPTER THREE: The Ugly One, The Kid & His Girl

Key interviews for this chapter were with Brin-Jonathan Butler, Gil Clancy, Angelo Dundee, Thomas Hauser, Jerry Izenberg, Billy Johnson, Hank Kaplan, Ron Ross, Nick Stone, Esther Taylor-Evans and George Zeleny.

Newspaper and magazine research included *Boxing News*, the *New York Amsterdam News*, the *New York Herald Tribune*, the *New York Times*, the *Chicago Defender*, *The Los Angeles Times*, the *Miami Herald*, *The Ring* and the *Washington Post* – as well as the Hank Kaplan Archive.

I was lucky enough to interview Angelo Dundee in 2005 and his memories of Luis Rodriguez, boxing in Cuba, Emile Griffith, Gil Clancy and Muhammad Ali added greatly to this chapter. They worked in tandem with Clancy's anecdotes about Griffith's first fights against Rodriguez and Benny Paret.

Muhammad Ali's biographer, my friend Thomas Hauser, was a great help to this chapter and the sections on Miami, Angelo Dundee and Cassius Clay.

Brin-Jonathan Butler shared much of his knowledge of Cuba, and Cuban boxing, and I shared a memorable afternoon with him in Spanish Harlem watching his documentary *Split Decision*.

Dan Klores and Ron Berger's exemplary documentary *Ring of Fire* offered riveting background to this chapter – especially from Lucy Paret.

Dan Berry's *City Lights: Stories about New York* contains a short but evocative chapter on Benny and Lucy Paret.

This was where the Kaplan archive became invaluable. I just needed to read the dense typewritten notes Kaplan compiled about Paret's past, in the week he was buried in Miami a year later, or dig into the files of Cuban boxing history, to reach somewhere far more meaningful than a fight programme or newspaper article. Almost as if he was guiding me from the grave, Kaplan's archive steered me in the direction of so many exiled Cuban fighters from the early 1960s – whether it was Rodriguez in Miami, Isaac Logart and Paret in New York or Sugar Ramos in Mexico City.

Billy Johnson, a sports historian, with a particular interest in boxing, shared his detailed files on Paret and Manuel Alfaro.

George Zeleny provided complete fight footage for Griffith v Rodriguez I, Paret v Jordan and Griffith v Ortega I.

CHAPTER FOUR: Glory in Miami

Key interviews for this chapter were with Gil Clancy, Angelo Dundee, Thomas Hauser, Jerry Izenberg, Billy Johnson, Hank Kaplan, Ron Ross, Esther Taylor-Evans and George Zeleny.

Newspaper and magazine research included *Boxing News*, the *New York Amsterdam News*, the *New York Herald Tribune*, the *New York Times*, the *Chicago Defender*, the *Los Angeles Times*, the *Miami Herald*, *The Ring* and the *Washington Post* – as well as the Hank Kaplan Archive.

I also re-read Thomas Hauser's *Muhammad Ali*, Dave Anderson's *Ring Masters* and Peter Heller's *In This Corner* – as well as the Ross and Rondinone books and Carter, Fone and Kaiser on homophobia.

Of course the dark heart of Emile Griffith's life centred on the brutal trilogy of fights with his bitterest rival, Benny Paret. It was moving to follow the explosive saga through the expansive yet steadying influence of Kaplan. He was with me every step of the way, long before the boxers met for the first time in the ring at the Miami Beach Convention Hall on 1 April 1961. After years immersed in this subject, there was a shiver of appreciation when picking up a fight programme to that first world title clash – when Griffith, the challenger, stopped Paret in the thirteenth round. I loved the fact I could hold Kaplan's ringside copy which included his scoring of the fight. Typically of Kaplan, there were two other pristine programmes in the collection.

Kaplan had also been a publicist for the 5th Street gym and he was especially close to Angelo Dundee. He was well-known to every major boxing figure from the early 1950s to the 21st century – and so his archive was studded with memorabilia and personal correspondence given to him by most of the boxing greats of the last sixty years.

Thomas Hauser and Angelo Dundee were, of course, illuminating on Ali – and Dundee and Kaplan were enthusiastic in their 5th Street gym memories of Miami and the training visits of Emile Griffith.

Dundee and Clancy remembered Clay v Banks at Madison Square Garden.

Ring of Fire was again useful. George Zeleny provided complete fight footage for Griffith v Paret I.

CHAPTER FIVE: Taunts & Beatings

Key interviews for this chapter were with Gil Clancy, Angelo Dundee, Jimmy Glenn, Thomas Hauser, Jerry Izenberg, Billy Johnson, Hank Kaplan, Luis Rodrigo, Ron Ross, Esther Taylor-Evans and George Zeleny.

Newspaper and magazine research included *Boxing News*, the *Daily Mirror*, the *New York Amsterdam News*, the *New York Herald Tribune*, the *New York Post*, the *New York Times*, the *Chicago Defender*, the *Los Angeles Times*, the *Miami Herald*, *The Ring* and the *Washington Post* – as well as the Hank Kaplan Archive.

Ron Ross, Gil Clancy and Luis Rodrigo shared much information about Matthew – and Emile's mood at the time. Clancy and Ross were also excellent on Emile's pre-fight rituals.

Clancy, Jimmy Glenn, Jerry Izenberg, Billy Johnson and Hank Kaplan relived the weigh-in and Emile's distress in vivid detail.

Ring of Fire documents this period – and Pete Hamill's comparison of Paret and a panel-beaten car comes from that documentary. George

Zeleny provided full fight footage of Griffith v Paret I and Paret v Fullmer.

CHAPTER SIX: Maricón

Key interviews for this chapter were with Gil Clancy, Angelo Dundee, Joe Frazier, Jimmy Glenn, Jerry Izenberg, Billy Johnson, Hank Kaplan, Luis Rodrigo, Ron Ross and Esther Taylor-Evans.

Newspaper and magazine research included *Boxing News*, the *New York Amsterdam News*, the *New York Herald Tribune*, the *New York Post*, the *New York Times*, the *Chicago Defender*, the *Los Angeles Times*, the *Miami Herald*, *The Ring*, *Sports Illustrated* and the *Washington Post* – as well as the Hank Kaplan Archive.

Esther Taylor-Evans described the context of the publicity shoots in which she and Emile engaged – after he had requested her help.

Jimmy Glenn, who looked after Emile's sparring partners, explained the mood of the camp up in the Catskills. He and Joe Frazier also helped describe the Concord hotel.

The mood of Benny Paret in his training camp emerged from various evocative newspaper features – and, especially, from Billy Johnson who visited Paret three times during preparations for the fight. He shared his notes with me from that period. He also followed the newspaper stories about Emile's sexuality and his two 'girlfriends' in Esther and Ce'Vara Livsey.

Johnson, Jerry Izenberg, Hank Kaplan, Gil Clancy and Ron Ross were riveting on the build-up and the weigh-in.

I re-read Dan Berry's *City Lights'* chapter on Benny and Lucy Paret – as well as Ross and Rondinone. I also read Norman Mailer's short essay on the death of Benny Paret.

Lucy Paret spoke about her emotions in *Ring of Fire* – and the documentary also contained Pete Hamill's powerful anecdote about Howard Tuckner and the *New York Times'* decision to use the meaningless word 'un-man' rather than 'homosexual' in his copy.

George Zeleny provided full fight footage of Griffith v Paret III.

CHAPTER SEVEN: The Letter

Key interviews for this chapter were with Gil Clancy, Jimmy Glenn, Jerry Izenberg, Billy Johnson, Hank Kaplan, Ron Ross and Alida Toweel.

Newspaper and magazine research included *Boxing News*, the *New York Amsterdam News*, the *New York Herald Tribune*, the *New York Post*, the *New York Times*, the *Chicago Defender*, the *Los Angeles Times*, *The Ring*, the *Rand Daily Mail*, *Sports Illustrated*, the *Star* and the *Washington Post* – as well as the Hank Kaplan Archive.

It was especially moving to read and discuss Willie Toweel's letter with his wife, Alida, and with Gil Clancy and Ron Ross.

Emile's Griffith's words, which are printed on the cover of this book, first appeared in the prologue to Ron Ross's *Nine...Ten...And Out!*

CHAPTER EIGHT: The Ghost of Benny Paret

Key interviews for this chapter were with Gil Clancy, Angelo Dundee, Joe Frazier, Jimmy Glenn, Jerry Izenberg, Billy Johnson, Hank Kaplan and Ron Ross.

Newspaper and magazine research included *Boxing News*, the *New York Herald Tribune*, the *New York Post*, the *New York Times*, the *Chicago Defender*, the *Los Angeles Times*, the *Miami Herald*, *The Ring*, *Sports Illustrated* and the *Washington Post* – as well as the Hank Kaplan Archive.

The haunting of Emile Griffith by Benny Paret was conveyed by Clancy, Frazier, Glenn, Kaplan and Ross – who included some of the nightmares in his book. Emile also described a few of his nightmares vividly to Gary Smith in a powerful interview in *Sports Illustrated* on 12 April 2005.

Billy Johnson shared all of his notes documenting his meetings with Emile Griffith for this chapter.

Interviewing Jerry Izenberg at his home in Las Vegas was extremely helpful when researching the Dupas fight in the same city. Angelo Dundee shared his gripping memories of that week when Ralph Dupas tried to change the narrative of his downtrodden life by beating Emile Griffith.

Izenberg, Hank Kaplan and Clancy captured Griffith's tentative mood around his first fight following the Paret tragedy.

George Zeleny provided full fight footage of Griffith v Dupas – and Jimmy Breslin features in *Ring of Fire*.

CHAPTER NINE: Cuban Missiles

Key interviews for this chapter were with Gil Clancy, Angelo Dundee, Jimmy Glenn, Jerry Izenberg, Billy Johnson, Hank Kaplan, Bobby Miles, Ron Ross and Freddie Wright.

Newspaper and magazine research included the relevant issues in *Boxing News*, the *New York Herald Tribune*, the *New York Post*, the *New York Times*, the *Chicago Defender*, the *Los Angeles Times*, *The Ring*, the *Saturday Evening Post* and the *Washington Post* – as well as the Hank Kaplan Archive.

George Zeleny provided full fight footage of Griffith v Don Fullmer – and Jimmy Breslin features in *Ring of Fire*.

CHAPTER TEN: Who Killed Davey Moore?

Key interviews for this chapter were with Gil Clancy, Angelo Dundee, Jerry Izenberg, Billy Johnson, Hank Kaplan, Bobby Miles and Ron Ross.

Newspaper and magazine research included the relevant issues in *Boxing News*, the *New York Amsterdam News*, the *New York Herald Tribune*, the *New York Post*, the *New York Times*, the *Chicago Defender*, the *Los Angeles Times*, *The Ring* and the *Washington Post* – as well as the Hank Kaplan Archive.

George Zeleny provided full fight footage of Griffith v Rodriguez II and Moore v Ramos.

Angelo Dundee, an incomparable witness, provided the definitive interview of this tragic night – and it shaped the entire chapter.

The Kaplan Archive also has detailed information on the fight and its deadly aftermath.

CHAPTER ELEVEN: A Man's Man

Key interviews for this chapter were with Jim Garcia, Jerry Izenberg, Luis Rodrigo, Nick Stone and Freddie Wright.

Newspaper and magazine research included *Boxing News*, the *New York Amsterdam News*, the *New York Herald Tribune*, the *New York Times*, the *Chicago Defender*, the *Los Angeles Times*, *The Ring*, *Sports Illustrated* and the *Washington Post* – as well as the Hank Kaplan Archive.

Jim Garcia and Nick Stone were both at the premiere of *Flaming Creatures* and described that night and the impact of Jack Smith, Mario Montez and Virginia Prince. Luis Rodrigo told me about Miss Coco.

Jerry Izenberg was brilliant in conveying his detailed memoires of the Griffith and Rodriguez fights – and he also told me about the surreal bath scene between Emile and his mother. Huston Horn also wrote about the night in *Sports Illustrated*.

George Zeleny provided full fight footage of Griffith v Rodriguez III and IV.

CHAPTER TWELVE: The Outsiders

Key interviews for this chapter were with Mickey Duff, Colin Hart, Alan Hubbard, Jim Garcia, Nick Stone, Esther Taylor-Evans, Freddie Wright and George Zeleny.

Newspaper and magazine research included *Boxing News*, the *Daily Mirror*, the *Guardian*, the *New York Herald Tribune*, the *New York Post*, the *New York Times*, the *Chicago Defender*, the *Los Angeles Times*, *The Ring*, *Sports Illustrated*, the *Sun*, the *Sunday Times* and the *Washington Post* – as well as the Hank Kaplan Archive.

In the mid-1990s, while interviewing Mickey Duff about Michael Watson, he produced a gripping fifteen-minute riff on the visit of Emile Griffith, Calvin Thomas, Frank and Nancy Sinatra to London. Duff, who seemed to know most of boxing's seamy secrets, suggested that the Kray Twins, who were gay, might also have met Emile at the Stork Club. I was not able to verify that claim. But Nick Stone confirmed the repeated visits of Emile and Calvin to La Duce in Soho.

Alan Hubbard and Colin Hart shared their memories of Emile in London – and of Brian Curvis. Alan wrote briefly about the moment he and the rest of the press pack walked in on Emile and Calvin kissing in the *Independent* in 2013. He discussed it with me in much more detail while he and Colin remembered their friend Reg Gutteridge and the state of boxing, repressed society and the press in Britain in the 1960s.

Jim Garcia and Nick Stone conveyed the depressing impact of *The Outsiders* when it was shown on network television. Charles Kaiser writes about the programme powerfully in *The Gay Metropolis* and he interviews some of the men featured in the documentary. I was able to watch *The Outsiders* on YouTube.

George Zeleny provided full fight footage of Griffith v Curvis, Griffith v Charnley and Griffith v Archer. He also spoke about his memories of all three fighters – and of Luis Rodriguez and Angelo Dundee's subsequent visits to London.

CHAPTER THIRTEEN: Stonewall

Key interviews for this chapter were with Gil Clancy, Joe Frazier, Jim Garcia, Nick Stone and Freddie Wright.

Newspaper and magazine research included the relevant issues in *Boxing News*, the *New York Amsterdam News*, the *New York Herald Tribune*, the *New York Times*, the *Chicago Defender*, the *Los Angeles Times*, *The Ring*, *Sports Illustrated* and the *Washington Post* – as well as the Hank Kaplan Archive.

I interviewed Joe Frazier in November 2008 for the *Guardian* – and that gave me the chance to record his memories of Emile Griffith. He was grittily detailed in recalling their training camps, their friendship and the night they shared a bill against Buster Mathis and Nino Benvenuti.

Freddie Wright gave me an extraordinary interview about Stonewall, and his involvement that night, and this was supplemented by the memories of Jim Garcia and Nick Stone.

David Carter's *Stonewall* and Charles Kaiser's *The Gay Metropolis* provided invaluable background and detail on the riots.

CHAPTER FOURTEEN: Wedding Fever

Key interviews for this chapter were with Joe Frazier, Jim Garcia, Alan Hubbard, Luis Rodrigo, Ron Ross, Nick Stone, Esther Taylor-Evans and Freddie Wright.

Newspaper and magazine research included the relevant issues in *Boxing News*, *Jet*, the *New York Herald Tribune*, the *New York Times*, the *New York Post*, the *Chicago Defender*, the *Los Angeles Times*, *The Ring*, *Sports Illustrated* and the *Washington Post* – as well as the Hank Kaplan Archive.

Mercedes Donastorg features in *Ring of Fire*. I also interviewed Ron Ross and Luis Rodrigo about her marriage to Emile. Esther Taylor-Evans described Emelda Griffith's reaction and thwarted ambitions to block the marriage in our interview. Joe Frazier recalled the marriage and his role as best man.

Ron Ross wrote about the Armando Muniz and Carlos Monzon fights – and gave me more background on the kindness Emile showed to Muniz.

George Zeleny provided full fight footage of Griffith v Monzon I.

Freddie Wright remembered his marriage to Dante in our final interview.

CHAPTER FIFTEEN: Soweto Blues

Key interviews for this chapter were with Bert Blewett, Stanley Christodoulou, Gil Clancy, Len Hunt, Jerry Izenberg, Ron Jackson, Billy Johnson, Hank Kaplan, Elijah 'Tap Tap' Makhathini, Ron Ross, Esther Taylor, Alan Toweel Jr, Alida Toweel and Natalie Toweel.

Newspaper and magazine research included the relevant issues in *Boxing News*, the *New York Herald Tribune*, the *New York Times*, *The Ring*, the *Rand Daily Mail*, the *Star* and the *Washington Post* – as well as the Hank Kaplan Archive.

Bert Blewett, Stanley Christodoulou, Gil Clancy, Len Hunt, Ron Jackson, Elijah 'Tap Tap' Makhathini and the Toweel family shaped this chapter with their memories of Emile and Willie Toweel in Johannesburg, the stand-off with the South African government and the fight in Soweto.

George Zeleny provided full fight footage of Griffith v Monzon II.

CHAPTER SIXTEEN: Hombre

Key interviews for this chapter were with Gil Clancy, Colin Hart, Alan Hubbard, Ron Katz, Juan LaPorte, Luis Rodrigo, Ron Ross, Esther Taylor-Evans and Freddie Wright.

Newspaper and magazine research included the *New York Herald Tribune*, the *New York Times*, the *New York Post*, *The Ring* and *Sports Illustrated* – as well as the Hank Kaplan Archive.

Luis Rodrigo detailed his meeting and relationship with Emile Griffith – supplemented by Ron Ross's account. He also described Emile's dejection after the Scypion fight and the terrible attack he suffered outside Hombre. Juan LaPorte, Gil Clancy and Ron Ross all added much more with their memories.

I read Michael Woods' excellent account of the Scypion-Classen tragedy. 'A Ten Count for Willie Classen' was written on 3 April 2012 and published on the boxing website The Sweet Science. It recounts the story of the fight from the perspective of Classen and his family. The Kaplan Archive has detailed information on the fight and its tragic outcome.

The meeting between Emile Griffith and Benny Paret Jr is captured on *Ring of Fire*. Ron Ross and Luis Rodrigo provided the full background.

George Zeleny provided full fight footage of Scypion v Classen.

EPILOGUE: Emile & Orlando

Key interviews for this chapter were with Orlando Cruz, Juan De León, Gil Clancy, Colin Hart, Alan Hubbard, Ron Katz, Juan LaPorte, Luis Rodrigo, Ron Ross, Esther Taylor-Evans and Freddie Wright.

Newspaper and magazine research included the *Boxing News*, the *Guardian*, the *Las Vegas Review-Journal*, the *New York Herald Tribune*, the *New York Times*, the *New York Post*, *The Ring* and *Sports Illustrated* – as well as the Hank Kaplan Archive

My first interview with Orlando Cruz was published by the *Guardian* on 18 October 2012. I also interveyed Cruz for *Boxing News* in October 2012. A year later, when visiting him at his training camp in Buffalo, a separate *Guardian* feature on Cruz was published on 11 October 2013.

I appreciated being able to end the book in the company of Luis Rodrigo, Freddie Wright and Esther Taylor-Evans.

ACKNOWLEDGEMENTS

This book could not have been written without the help and understanding of Luis Rodrigo, Emile's partner and adopted son, and Ron Ross, his biographer. They both offered generous support. It meant much to me to meet Emile Griffith, even in the depths of his dementia, and my visits to Hempstead were always unforgettable. Thank you, Luis.

Ron and his wife Susan welcomed me in Oceanside, Long Island, and Boca Raton, Florida, on repeated occasions and shared their memories and insights. It was also through Ron that I first heard about the opening of the Hank Kaplan Archive in Brooklyn – and one of the highlights of our time together was reading his brilliant *Bummy Davis vs Murder, Inc.*

Freddie Wright was always illuminating and entertaining whenever I interviewed him – and he offered gripping insights into Emile, Calvin Thomas, gay New York, Stonewall, Greenwich Village and Times Square.

I only interviewed Esther Taylor-Evans near the end of my research, but her memories were vivid and they added much to my understanding of Emile, his family and their lives in the 1960s.

I was also lucky enough to meet Hank Kaplan in London in the late 1980s and he helped me enormously in his reflections on both Emile Griffith and Willie Toweel. I also met Gil Clancy in 1999 in Las Vegas after he worked Oscar de la Hoya's corner against Felix Trinidad. That interview was another unexpected early start to this book.

My work in South Africa, and in writing about Willie Toweel, owes much to his wife Alida. I felt honoured to meet her and Willie Toweel. Thanks too to Alan Toweel Jr, Natalie Toweel, Ron Jackson, Len Hunt and Stanley and Mary Christodoulou – who looked after me so well in Durban on my way to meet 'Tap Tap' Makhathini.

Thank you to Orlando Cruz for talking so openly when we met.

Herminio Rodriguez became a good friend when we worked together with Orlando Cruz and Emile Griffith. Thanks to Herminio for the photographs, the translation, all the emails and the memorable assignments in San Juan, Hempstead and Buffalo.

It was of great benefit to interview the following people – and thank you to all of them:

Bert Blewett, Brin-Jonathan Butler, Stanley Christodoulou, Gil Clancy, Orlando Cruz, Juan De León, Mickey Duff, Angelo Dundee, Steve Farhood, Joe Frazier, Roberto Garcia, Colin Hart, Jimmy Glenn, Thomas Hauser, Alan Hubbard, Len Hunt, Jerry Izenberg, Ron Jackson, Hank Kaplan, Ron Katz, Juan LaPorte, Elijah 'Tap Tap' Makhathini, Bobby Miles, Luis Rodrigo, Ron Ross, Nick Stone, Esther Taylor-Evans, Alan Toweel Jr, Alida Toweel, Natalie Toweel, Mike Tyson, Freddie Wright and George Zeleny.

Thanks to George, too, for all the fight DVDs and memories at the Paper Mill and to Clinton van der Berg for all my South African contacts.

At the Hank Kaplan Archive in Brooklyn, I would especially like to thank Erin Alsop, Theresa Ferrara, Marianne LaBatto and Jahongir Usmanov.

Ian Prior and Steve McMillan at the *Guardian* were good enough to commission two interviews with Orlando Cruz.

Thanks, too, to Tris Dixon, Danny Flexen, Matt Christie and John Dennan at *Boxing News* – where I wrote about Orlando Cruz and the Hank Kaplan Archive. When Tris was still the editor, he kindly allowed me access to the massive Boxing News Archive which stretches over the last hundred years. He also helped me with many contact numbers and photographs. A special thank you to Tris.

Thanks too to Amrai Coen. We had fun in the crazy world of boxing in Buffalo and Las Vegas.

My agent Jonny Geller was typically brilliant in supporting me with this book. He believed in the subject from the outset and, as always, encouraged me to write the kind of book that meant most to me.

Ian Marshall has been an insightful and scrupulous editor and a great supporter of this book. I hope this is just the first of many colloborations between us. Thanks to Ian and everyone at my publishers Simon & Schuster who have shown great faith in my writing – as this is my fifth book at S&S.

I would like to thank Jonny Geller, Kirsten Foster and Tim Musgrave for reading the first draft and for all the help they gave me. A special note here to Kirsten for the memorable email she sent me, containing so many detailed comments and useful suggestions, even after she had moved into a different line of work.

As always, thanks to my parents Ian and Jess for all their support – and to Bella, Jack and Emma for being so used to their strange old dad and for helping me with my various computer and technical meltdowns.

Finally, one last thank you, most of all, to my wife Alison. For the eighth book in a row she kept me going and helped me reach the end. She shared every page and every chapter – from hearing blow-by-blow accounts during the research, to being my first and best reader, to being my incomparable corner-woman during the hardest and most difficult times of writing. This book also belongs to her.

INDEX